GEORGIA'S FOREIGN POLICY IN THE 21ST CENTURY

GEORGIA'S FOREIGN POLICY IN THE 21ST CENTURY

Challenges for a Small State

Edited by
Tracey German
Stephen F. Jones
Kornely Kakachia

BLOOMSBURY ACADEMIC
LONDON • NEW YORK • OXFORD • NEW DELHI • SYDNEY

BLOOMSBURY ACADEMIC
Bloomsbury Publishing Plc
50 Bedford Square, London, WC1B 3DP, UK
1385 Broadway, New York, NY 10018, USA
29 Earlsfort Terrace, Dublin 2, Ireland

BLOOMSBURY, BLOOMSBURY ACADEMIC and the Diana logo
are trademarks of Bloomsbury Publishing Plc

First published in Great Britain 2022
This paperback edition published by Bloomsbury Academic in 2023

Series design by Adriana Brioso
Cover image: Independence day parade in Tbilisi, Georgia, 2015. (© VANO
SHLAMOV/AFP/Getty Images)

A catalogue record for this book is available from the British Library.

Library of Congress Cataloging-in-Publication Data
Names: German, Tracey C., 1971-editor. | Jones, Stephen Francis,
1953-editor. | Kakachia, Kornely, editor.
Title: Georgia's foreign policy in the 21st century: challenges for a small state /
edited by Tracey German, Stephen F. Jones, Kornely Kakachia.
Other titles: Georgia's foreign policy in the twenty-first century
Description: London; New York: I.B. Tauris, 2022. |
Includes bibliographical references and index.
Identifiers: LCCN 2021025805 (print) | LCCN 2021025806 (ebook) |
ISBN 9781788313650 (hb) | ISBN 9780755645336 (epdf) |
ISBN 9780755645343 (ebook) | ISBN 9780755645350 (ebook other)
Subjects: LCSH: Georgia (Republic)–Foreign relations–21st century. |
National characteristics, Georgian.
Classification: LCC DK676.8.G468 2022 (print) | LCC DK676.8 (ebook) |
DDC 327.4758009/05–dc23
LC record available at https://lccn.loc.gov/2021025805
LC ebook record available at https://lccn.loc.gov/2021025806

ISBN: HB: 978-1-7883-1365-0
PB: 978-0-7556-4536-7
ePDF: 978-0-7556-4533-6
eBook: 978-0-7556-4534-3

Typeset by Integra Software Services Pvt. Ltd.

To find out more about our authors and books visit
www.bloomsbury.com and sign up for our newsletters.

CONTENTS

Part I
THE USES OF IDENTITY IN GEORGIAN FOREIGN POLICY

Part II
THE REGIONAL CONTEXT

Part III
GEORGIA AND THE 'WEST'

Part IV
GEORGIA AND THE GREAT POWERS

FIGURES

TABLES

CONTRIBUTORS

David Aprasidze is Professor of Political Science at Ilia State University and team leader of the EU-supported action aimed at promoting Civil Society Sustainability in Georgia. He received his PhD from Hamburg University, Germany. He was a Fulbright scholar at Duke University in the United States. At various times, he has worked for public agencies and international NGOs operating in Georgia. He has expertise in higher education management and reform. His research interest focuses on political transformation and democratization issues.

Michael Hikari Cecire is the Director of the Eurasia Democratic Security Network (EDSN), an international fellowship programme and research platform that examines linkages between democracy and security. Cecire is also an Associate at the Institute for Middle East, Central Asia, and Caucasus Studies at the University of St Andrews, where he is a doctoral researcher. He is also a member of the editorial board for the journal *Caucasus Survey,* and is a regular lecturer on Black Sea regional issues at the US State Department's Foreign Service Institute. Cecire has previously served as an international security fellow at New America, as a non-resident fellow at the Foreign Policy Research Institute, as a visiting scholar at Columbia University's Harriman Institute, and in a variety of policy advisory and political risk analysis roles. He is a co-founder of the Georgian Institute of Politics in Tbilisi and has published in a variety of international media and peer-reviewed publications on issues of international security, Black Sea regional affairs, and democracy.

Tracey German is a Professor of Conflict and Security in the Defence Studies Department at King's College, London. Her research focuses on Russia's use of force in the post-Soviet space, conflict and security in the Caucasus and Caspian regions, and the impact of NATO/EU enlargement on Russia's relations with its neighbours. Publications include *Regional Cooperation in the South Caucasus: Good Neighbours or Distant Relatives?* (Ashgate Publishing, 2012) and *Russia's Chechen War* (Routledge, 2003), as well as articles in journals such as *International Affairs, Journal of Southeast European and Black Sea Studies, European Security, Europe-Asia Studies, Central Asian Survey* and *Small Wars and Insurgencies.*

Stephen F. Jones received his PhD from the London School of Economics and Political Science in 1984. He has taught at the universities of California, London and Oxford. He was a Research Fellow at Harvard University and a Senior Associate Member at St Anthony's College, Oxford. Since 1989 he has taught at Mount Holyoke College (USA). His books include *Socialism in Georgian Colors: The European Road to Social Democracy, 1883–1917* (Harvard University Press,

2005), *War and Revolution in the Caucasus: Georgia Ablaze* (ed., Routledge, 2010), *Georgia: A Political History since Independence* (I.B. Tauris, 2013), and *The Birth of Modern Georgia: The First Georgian Republic and Its Successors, 1918–2010* (ed., Routledge, 2013). He was the English Language editor-in-chief of *kartlis tskhovreba* (The History of Georgia), (Georgian Academy of Sciences and Artanuji Publishers, 2014), and principal editor for a three-volume set in Georgian of Noe Jordania's speeches and writing. Professor Jones is a Foreign Member of the Georgian Academy of Sciences and received an honorary doctorate from Tbilisi State University in 2012, and Ilia State University in 2018.

Kornely Kakachia is Professor of Political Science at Ivane Javakhishvili Tbilisi State University, Georgia, and Director of the Tbilisi-based think tank, the Georgian Institute of Politics. His current research focuses on Europeanization of Georgia, foreign policy analysis, security issues of the wider Black Sea area and comparative party politics. He was a recipient of IREX and OSI fellowships and was a visiting fellow at Harvard University's Black Sea Security programme (2009–10), Harriman Institute, Columbia University (2011) and The Johns Hopkins University's School of Advanced International Studies.

Levan Kakhishvili is a Doctoral Fellow in Political Science at Bamberg Graduate School of Social Sciences (BAGSS) at the University of Bamberg, where he researches the nature of party competition in Georgia, Moldova and Ukraine. His expertise includes Georgian foreign policy, and democratization in the post-Soviet context.

Alexander Kupatadze is Assistant Professor at the School of Politics and Economics, King's College London. Prior to joining King's College, Dr Kupatadze taught at the School of International Relations, St Andrews University. He held postdoctoral positions at George Washington University (2010–11), Oxford University (2012–13) and Princeton University (2013–14). His research specialization is transnational crime, corruption, public sector reform, informal politics and the crime–terror nexus. His regional expertise is post-Soviet Eurasia. His work has appeared in the *Journal of Democracy, Theoretical Criminology, Non-proliferation Review, Central Asia Survey* and other leading journals. His research has been funded by the Russell Trust (St Andrews University), the British Association for Slavonic and East European Studies (BASEES) and the Harry Frank Guggenheim Foundation.

Bidzina Lebanidze is a Postdoctoral Fellow at the Institute of Slavic Studies and Caucasus Studies at the Friedrich Schiller University Jena, Associate Professor of International Relations at Ilia State University and a Senior Analyst at the Georgian Institute of Politics. He obtained his doctorate in Political Science from the Free University of Berlin, and his Master's degree in International Relations from Tbilisi State University. Previously, he also held various teaching and research positions at the University of Bremen, the University of Freiburg, the Berlin School for Economics and Law, the Free University of Berlin and Konrad-Adenauer-Stiftung.

Salome Minesashvili is an analyst at the Georgian Institute of Politics and a lecturer at Freie Universität Berlin, as well as at ESCP Europe. She holds a PhD in Political Science from Freie Universität Berlin, an MSc in International Political Theory from the University of Edinburgh, and an MSc in Transformation in the South Caucasus from Iv. Javakhishvili Tbilisi State University. She has worked in multiple research projects on the topics of foreign policy analysis, identity politics, soft power politics, EU–Eastern Neighbourhood relations, and transformation processes in the former Soviet Union.

Lincoln A. Mitchell is a long-time observer of Georgian politics. He is the author of *Uncertain Democracy: US Foreign Policy and Georgia's Rose Revolution* (Pennsylvania University Press, 2008), *The Color Revolutions* (Pennsylvania University Press, 2012), *The Democracy Promotion Paradox* (Brookings, 2016) and numerous academic and policy articles, briefings and columns regarding Georgia and the region. He is a scholar at the Arnold A Saltzman Institute of War and Peace Studies at Columbia University. Dr Mitchell also writes extensively on US politics, baseball and San Francisco history. He received his BA from the University of California, Santa Cruz and his PhD from Columbia University.

Ghia Nodia is a Professor of Politics at Ilia Chavchavadze State University in Tbilisi, Georgia. He is also the founder and chairman of the Caucasus Institute for Peace, Democracy and Development (CIPDD), an independent public policy think tank in Tbilisi, Georgia. In February–December 2008, he served as the Minister for Education and Science of Georgia. His most recent publications include *Democracy* (in Georgian, Ilia State University Publishing, 2019), and articles 'Democracy's Inevitable Elites', *Journal of Democracy*, January 2020, and 'The New Georgia: Politics, Economy and Society', in Galina M. Yemelianova and Laurence Broers (eds), *Routledge Handbook of the Caucasus* (Routledge, 2020).

Natalie Sabanadze is the former Head of the Georgian mission to the European Union and Ambassador Plenipotentiary to Belgium and Luxembourg. Currently, she is the Cyrus Vance Visiting Professor of International Relations at Mount Holyoke College. Previously, she served as Senior Adviser and Head of Section at the OSCE High Commission on National Minorities. She holds a PhD from Oxford University in International Relations as well as a Master's degree and BA from the London School of Economics and Mount Holyoke College respectively. She has lectured and published extensively on questions of globalization and nationalism, national minorities in inter-state relations, ethnic conflicts and models of accommodation, as well as on Georgia's relations with the European Union.

George Sanikidze is a Professor at Ilia State University and Director of the G. Tsereteli Institute of Oriental Studies, also at Ilia State University. His research focuses on the medieval and modern history of Islam, the history and politics of the Middle East (especially Iran) and of the Caucasus, and East–West relations. Professor Sanikidze was a visiting scholar at Paris-Sorbonne-III and Paris-Sorbonne-IV Universities, the

University of California at Berkeley, and the universities of Hokkaido and Osaka. Professor Sanikidze is the author of up to the eighty academic articles, chapters and monographs. His works are published in Georgia, the United Kingdom, France, Japan, the United States, Holland, Turkey, Iran, Armenia, Azerbaijan and Russia.

Renata Skardžiūtė-Kereselidze is Deputy Director at the Georgian Institute of Politics. She earned her MA at the Nationalism Studies Department at the Central European University (CEU) in 2009, and received her BA in Political Science at the Institute of International Relations and Political Science (IIRPS), Vilnius University (2008). Before joining GIP, Renata worked as a journalist covering foreign policy and European issues in Lithuania and was a recipient of the Heinrich Boell fellowship to research EU strategies in conflict resolution in Georgia. Her interests include collective identities, European integration and Eastern Partnership.

Mamuka Tsereteli is a Senior Fellow at the Central Asia-Caucasus Institute at the American Foreign Policy Council, based in Washington, DC. He has more than thirty years of experience in academia, diplomacy and business development. His expertise includes economic and energy security in Europe and Eurasia, political and economic risk analysis and mitigation strategies, and business development in the Black Sea-Caspian region. Dr Tsereteli serves as President of the America-Georgia Business Council. He is a member of the part-time faculty at SAIS, Johns Hopkins, and at the American University in Washington, DC.

ACKNOWLEDGEMENTS

The editors would like to acknowledge the help of all our colleagues and student assistants from Georgia who have helped us complete this project. Their support and research has been indispensable. We would like to extend our special thanks to Nino Samkharadze, Elene Panchulidze and Givi Silagadze, for their vital assistance and research support to authors in this volume. The editors would like to thank their respective institutions for support for our research endeavours during these very difficult times, and the external reviewers who helped us shape this book into a better-quality volume. Andrew Devine, our excellent copy editor, caught our errors, and the British-Georgian Society very generously paid for the indexing. We would like to thank the Georgian Institute of Politics for researching and drawing up our two introductory maps.

TRANSLITERATION

We use the simplest transliteration system for Georgian. We have removed all diacritic marks and we make no distinction between the Georgian letters ჟ and ჯ; ჶ and ც; ჳ and ძ; and ჴ and ჰ. The letters ღ and ყ, we have transliterated as *gh* and *q* respectively. In a few cases, we use the more familiar form rather than correctly transliterated spellings, such as Ossetia instead of Osetia, or Jordania instead of Zhordania. Georgians do not use capitals, a system we have followed, except for names and places. South Caucasia is a treacherous minefield of topographic names and orthography. We have kept to the Georgian version for the sake of consistency (Sokhumi, not Sukhum; Tskhinvali rather than Tskhinval; Achara, not Adjaria). We left it to the authors to use either Abkhazia and South Ossetia, as they are more familiar to English readers, or the Georgian forms – Abkhazeti and Tskhinvali District.

For Russian, we use the Library of Congress transliteration system (ALC-LC) but without the diacritic marks. In cases in which other forms are more common (such as Yeltsin, instead of El'tsin), the more familiar form is used.

ABBREVIATIONS

AA	Association Agreement
AIOC	Azerbaijan International Operating Company
AP	Action Plan
BRI	Belt and Road Initiative
BSEC	Black Sea Economic Cooperation project
BTC	Baku–Tbilisi–Ceyhan oil pipeline
BTE	Baku–Tbilisi–Erzurum gas pipeline
BTK	Baku–Tbilisi–Kars railway
CFE	Conventional Armed Forces in Europe treaty
CIS	Commonwealth of Independent States
CSDP	Common Security and Defence Policy
CSO	Civil society organization
CSTO	Collective Security Treaty Organization
CUG	Citizens' Union of Georgia
DCFTA	Deep and Comprehensive Free Trade Area
DFC	Development Finance Corporation
DRG	Democratic Republic of Georgia (1918–21)
EaP	Eastern Partnership
EC	European Commission
ENP	European Neighbourhood Policy
EPP	European People's Party
EU	European Union
FDI	Foreign direct investment
FMF	Foreign Military Financing
FSU	Former Soviet Union
GD	Georgian Dream
GOC	Georgian Orthodox Church
GTEP	Georgia Train and Equip programme
GUAM	Georgia, Ukraine, Azerbaijan and Moldova Organization for Democracy and Economic Development
IRI	International Republican Institute
ISAF	International Security Assistance Force

ISFED	International Society for Fair Elections and Democracy
MAP	Membership Action Plan
MFA	Ministry of Foreign Affairs
NATO	North Atlantic Treaty Organization
NDI	National Democratic Institute
NGO	Non-governmental organization
NRF	NATO Response Force
NMS	National Military Strategy
NSS	National Security Strategy
OIC	Organization of the Islamic Conference
OPIC	Overseas Private Investment Corporation
OSCE	Organization for Security and Cooperation in Europe
PfP	Partnership for Peace
ROC	Russian Orthodox Church
SREB	Silk Road Economic Belt
TANAP	Trans-Anatolian Natural Gas Pipeline
TRACECA	Transport Corridor Europe-Caucasus-Asia
UNM	United National Movement
UN	United Nations
USAID	US Agency for International Development

MAPS

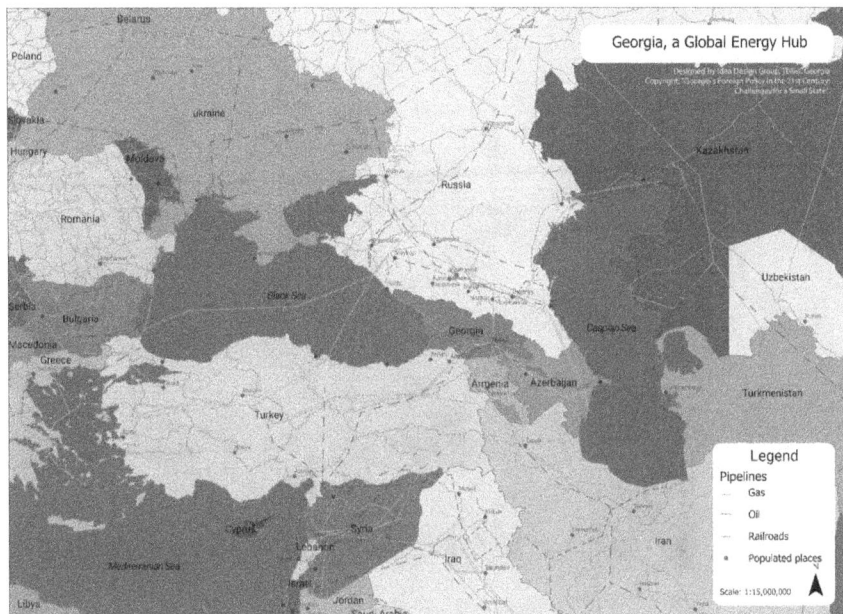

Map by Idea Design Group, Georgia

Georgia and Its Neighborhood

Map by Idea Design Group, Georgia

INTRODUCTION

Stephen F. Jones

Georgia's foreign policy has almost always been an instrument of defence and survival. From the early Middle Ages on, Georgia has been vulnerable to the ambitions of imperial neighbours and tribal marauders. The endurance of a small state like Georgia, which lacked the resources of its neighbours, depended on the art of diplomacy. Ilia Chavchavadze, the outstanding representative of Georgia's literary renaissance in the second half of the nineteenth century, recognized this when he had one of his characters (a wise peasant), declare 'where strength is not strong, then it requires some ploy'.[1] For Georgia before the twentieth century, state survival was not so much about independence, but dependence. That meant foreign patronage, alliances, adaptability and compliance, which were less risky than resistance. This did not exclude wars, which were often the only practical solution to intransigent neighbours. However, force was not a useful policy instrument in Georgian foreign policy. And Georgia's topography – its mountain fastnesses and narrow ravines – were overrated as a means of self-defence and survival. Mountains were helpful to the Georgian military, but never secured the state against multiple invasions. When Georgia experienced a brief period of independence (1918–21) a Georgian Military Commission evaluated Georgia's security. It concluded: 'Our small country can be attacked simultaneously from all sides, and the capital can be taken by a hostile army in one to two days.' From the Azerbaijani border to Tiflis was a 'one day cavalry ride', and from Armenia, a 'two-day march'.[2] The Georgian Military Highway, a traditional trade route across the Greater Caucasus range from the north, could be defended, but the coastal littorals along the Black and Caspian Seas were better alternatives for potential aggressors. From the south, Ottoman, Safavid and Byzantine armies could move through the river valleys of the Araxes, Mtkvari and Chorokhi to quickly reach Georgia's urban centres. Topography is crucial in planning Georgia's military defence – it has always been uppermost in the minds of Georgia's generals – but in the end, it is a secondary factor in Georgia's ability to control external threats.

Georgia's foreign policy magnets

If Georgia's geography, defined by its physical terrain, is overrated as a strategic variable, Tracey German and Kornely Kakachia point out in their opening contribution to this volume that geography has given Georgia foreign policy advantages. Georgia's difficult neighbourhood leads to multiple vulnerabilities, such as disputes over unsettled borders, the manipulation of internal conflicts and diasporas by contiguous powers, and the rise of organized crime around drug and people trafficking. But as German and Kakachia remind us, small states are not just victims of international systems and aggressive neighbours; they can present themselves as useful partners in a borderland region where empires (and modern states) have always sought strategic advantages. Georgia may be small and peripheral, but it is not without agency. German and Kakachia list three areas where Georgia can offer powerful states useful partnerships – as a military partner, a transit country or as a European proxy.

The Democratic Republic of Georgia (DRG, 1918–21), practically unknown in Western historiography, used all three of these measures to encourage Western patronage, and economic investment in the young state. The DRG was, successively, a partner for the Germans who sought trade and influence in the Middle East ('Ostpolitik'), and for the British, who, with 19,000 troops in Georgia between 1918 and 1920, anticipated the DRG would act as part of a Caucasian 'middle wall' against Bolshevik expansion into their colonial territories in the Middle East and South Asia.[3] Germany and Britain had plans to exploit Georgia's railways to transit oil and other goods across the South Caucasian isthmus to domestic markets. Winston Churchill, Secretary of State for War from 1919 to 1921, called the Transcaucasian railway '[one] of the greatest strategic lines in the world'.[4] The idea of a Caucasian trade corridor connecting China and Central Asia to Europe (German and Kakachia's second point) was promoted by prominent Georgian intellectuals and entrepreneurs like Niko Nikoladze (1843–1928), long before the EU came up with the Transport Corridor Europe-Caucasus-Asia (TRACECA) in 1993,[5] and the Chinese with the Belt and Road Initiative (BRI) in 2013.[5] The Georgian strategy for ensuring greater security through foreign partnerships and trade continued after 1991. There are multiple examples over the last quarter of a century of Georgia leveraging its resources to draw friendly Western states into economic and security alliances. Mamuka Tsereteli in his chapter on Georgian–US relations demonstrates how Georgia successfully promoted its geography to the United States in the 1990s. Georgia provided an opportunity for the United States to develop a Multiple Pipeline Strategy focused on developing diverse energy sources in Eurasia. US companies like Chevron and Exxon invested in Georgia's energy infrastructure which became, according to Tsereteli 'the primary focus and policy instrument of Western (and US) engagement with the South Caucasus' (p. 287). By the end of the 1990s, the energy partnership with the United States had evolved into a geopolitical one. There have been multiple treaties and agreements between Georgia and the United States on security, which serve the interests of the US as well as Georgia. Georgia played a pivotal role in the US-run Northern

Distribution Network to Afghanistan; it supplied troops to US and NATO operations in Iraq (Operation Iraqi Freedom and the UN Assistance Mission in Iraq), to Afghanistan (ISAF) and to the Central African Republic (EU Central African Republic Mission).

Georgian leaders have always used the idea of the country's 'European heritage' as an argument for integration into European political and security structures. In 1918–21, the DRG promoted itself as a European and Christian civilization in the East. In its campaign to secure international recognition, it submitted a memorandum to the Paris Peace Conference in April 1919, which declared Georgia 'was in close contact with the ancient civilizations of Greece … the seeds of Christianity sown there in the 4th century, found a terrain (in Georgia) already prepared for the growth of a secular culture'.[6] Ghia Nodia in his chapter on Russia, notes the weakness of this European connection historically, but the projection of Europeanness has always been useful to Georgian foreign policymakers. Levan Kakhishvili and Alexander Kupatadze in their contribution review six of the major strategic conceptual documents on Georgian foreign policy published since independence. They note that in every document, Georgia prioritizes its 'return to the European family' (p. 150). The stress on common European roots was strongly promoted by all of Georgia's presidents. Lincoln Mitchell, in his chapter, shows how the Saakashvili administration used public relations techniques to burnish Georgia's image as a progressive European state. Mitchell cites a speech Saakashvili made in 2004: 'It's not only geopolitics, transportation and economic projects or the issues of defence and security that are important for us', the new president declared, but 'the values that the advanced countries of the world have, and that I have been using as a guide during these years … The world's leading media covered the events in Georgia and today we have become an example to the whole world'.[7] A close look at the latest official Georgian Foreign Policy Strategy document (which covers the years 2019–2022), clearly demonstrates the country's cultural, historical and political self-image of Europeanness.[8]

But Georgia's connections to Europe are open to interpretation. The Georgian Orthodox Church (GOC), as Salome Minesashvili points out in her chapter, is far more ambivalent about the impacts of the 'West'. Before 1991, the church was on the whole an obedient instrument of Soviet foreign policy, useful in Soviet peace campaigns against US actions in Vietnam and elsewhere. Since independence in 1991, the church has become much more troublesome for the Georgian state and its pursuit of modernization and reform. For many in the church, Minesashvili argues, 'the West is associated with degraded values', which permit 'too much personal freedom' and support 'globalisation, cosmopolitanism and modernism' (p. 78). In 2014, the church opposed the government's anti-discrimination legislation, which aimed to bring Georgia closer to European Union (EU) standards. But, although the church significantly complicates the Georgian government's foreign policy goals toward Europe, it remains useful in Georgia's relations with Russia. The Georgian and Russian churches have close relations, which has provided important opportunities for back channel negotiations between the two states at times of crisis. The GOC has extraordinary influence and trust among the

Georgian population (although that has not always been the case). If foreign policy is an expression of identity and values, then any assessment of Georgia's relations to other states and the cultures they represent must include the role of the GOC. The church is an important source of Georgian identity and belonging, even if the church's understanding of 'Georgianness' is different from the government's. Minesashvili's contribution is an important reminder of the domestic context of foreign policymaking.

The search for Western patronage

In the early eighteenth century, Georgian king Vakhtang VI sent an emissary to Louis XIV and Pope Clement XI for support against the Iranian Shah Soltan Hosein. When Peter the Great began his Iranian campaign against the Safavids in 1722, Vakhtang VI joined with Russian forces in an attempt to secure Russian protection for Georgia. In the eighteenth century, Georgian leaders viewed Russia as a representative of European culture and Christian values. Georgian kings' search for a Russian protectorate persisted throughout the eighteenth century and culminated in the Russo-Georgian Georgievsk Treaty in 1783. Unfortunately for Georgia, Russian Tsars used the protectorate to assert military control. The treaty led to the absorption of the Eastern Georgian kingdom of Kartl'Kakheti into the Russian Empire in 1801. The other Georgian kingdoms quickly followed.[9] The Georgian attachment to Western ideas and models, exemplified by a group of Georgian intellectuals known as the *tergdaleulebi*, deepened in the nineteenth century.[10] The *tergdaleulebi* were among the first Georgians to highlight the cultural and political fissures between Russia and Europe. In the early twentieth century, Europe became associated with ideas of modernization and progress. Russia, on the other hand, was increasingly portrayed by Georgian intellectuals as part of the despotic 'East'.

The first Georgian republic in 1918–21, and all Georgian administrations after 1991 have focused on integration with the West, whether it was membership of the League of Nations in 1920, or the North Atlantic Treaty Organization (NATO) and the EU in the 2000s. Natalie Sabanadze and Michael Cecire, in their contributions, address Georgia's persistent European foreign policy focus. Michael Cecire looks at Georgian–NATO relations, and talks of Georgia's perceived 'civilisational affinities to the West' (p. 226). This association with Europe, combined with a need for protection against Russia, brought Georgia to the threshold of NATO and the EU. Both are external balances against Russia, but, as Cecire notes, there are limitations on Georgia's ability to integrate into NATO. In 2014, at NATO's summit in Wales, Georgia received a 'Substantial NATO-Georgian Package' of benefits, and permanent NATO bodies were established in the republic. But formal accession is stymied by the Russian threat and NATO's own internal differences. Sabanadze agrees – she sees Georgia's quest for European patronage as both geo-cultural, and a political project to ensure security. Both concur with German and Kakachia; they see Georgia as an active state (rather than a victim) exploiting its advantages. Georgia's goal today, as in 1918–21, is to institute in Western minds the idea of Georgia as a European state. Georgian citizens, as numerous opinion polls have demonstrated over the last twenty-five years, are overwhelmingly supportive of this idea.[11] Sabanadze writes that 'despite its geographic distance and interrupted historical ties, Georgia hopes with this narrative to shape boundaries in the minds of European decision makers, and to make Georgia's belonging to Europe uncontested' (p. 187).

There are multiple obstacles for Georgia in its attempt to secure Western patronage. Europeans are not convinced Georgia is European; distance across the Black Sea and its borders with Russia are discouraging factors for European policymakers, who must always consider Russia in the EU's relations with the South Caucasian states. Europeans – and NATO Member States – cannot agree on the principles of enlargement. They are internally divided. However much Georgia seeks succour from the EU and NATO, there is no guarantee it will be reciprocated. The EU, NATO and the United States have all extended vital support to Georgia – in part because of Georgia's identity as a devotee of Western market and democratic models – but this has not extended, as yet, to membership in any of the prestigious Western clubs. Both Cecire and Sabanadze remark that Georgia has attained almost every requirement for membership of either NATO or the EU. Sabanadze believes that the Deep and Comprehensive Free Trade Area (DCFTA) established between Georgia and the EU in 2014, represents a significant advance in Georgia's aspiration to join Western economic and political structures: it is 'contractual' rather than the 'soft' commitments embodied by the Eastern Partnership programme. But both Cecire and Sabanadze admit to the continuing 'reciprocity deficit' (Sabanadze, p. 177). As in 1918–21, the patronage of Georgia by Western states remains limited, characterized by internal divisions in the EU and NATO, and by the persistent shadow of Russia.

Regional security

Are there any alternatives to Georgia's focus on Western states for security? Some contributors to this volume suggest Georgia could benefit from the development of relations with regions outside Western Europe. Eastern Europe (Ukraine, Moldova and Belarus), Central Asia and the Baltics/Poland are all important clusters of states which play a significant role in Georgia's economic, security and political outlook. David Aprasidze's contribution, working closer to home, focuses on two alternate economic and security frameworks for Georgia: a union between the three South Caucasian states, the other a Black Sea connection with Ukraine and Moldova. The leaders of the first Georgian republic in 1918 attempted to create a Transcaucasian union. They argued that Transcaucasian cooperation improved security against common enemies, encouraged European support and enhanced prospects for economic growth. But the brief and tortured existence of the Transcaucasian Democratic Federative Republic in 1918, demonstrated why – at least in conditions of post-imperial collapse and civil war – such a union could not work. Conflicts over borders, the absence of a common enemy (the three South Caucasian states had different perceptions as to who their enemies were) and the search for different external alliances (Azerbaijan preferred Turkey, Armenia looked to the United States, and Georgia focused on Europe), quickly undid the union.

Attempts since 1991 under presidents Gamsakhurdia, Shevardnadze and Saakashvili to establish some form of Caucasian (or South Caucasian) cooperation, have failed for the same reasons. The conflictual patterns that plagued leaders at the beginning of the twentieth century remain in place. The hope that pipelines and a South Caucasian economic corridor would bring the three republics together was politically optimistic. Aprasidze argues that the 'Caucasus dimension has never played a serious role in the foreign policy of modern Georgia' (p. 103). He points out that in Georgia's latest *Foreign Policy Strategy* covering 2019–22 'there is no mention of the South Caucasus as a region' (p. 101). Rather, Georgia looks toward the Black Sea dimension, with a focus on Ukraine and Moldova, two countries that have followed the same European-oriented trajectory as Georgia (all three have signed Association Agreements with the EU). But the Black Sea dimension, embodied by the GUAM Organization for Democracy and Economic Development (GUAM is an acronym for the participants: Georgia, Ukraine, Azerbaijan and Moldova) and the Black Sea Economic Cooperation organization (BSEC) – which includes Russia and Turkey as Black Sea littoral states – have failed to challenge the pull of the EU and NATO. Regional coalitions like GUAM and BSEC as well as the informal grouping known as AGT (Azerbaijan, Georgia, Turkey) are useful instruments in Georgia's foreign policy, but limited in their resources and influence. Aprasidze concludes that the South Caucasus represents a 'regional complex' but he has little hope of a productive union of any kind. It seems odd, given the benefits all three states would accrue from cooperation, but geopolitical rivalries and geo-cultural stresses keep the three neighbours apart.

Bidzina Lebanidze and Renata Skardžiūtė-Kereselidze in their chapter point to the impact of other neighbourhoods on Georgia's regional security. Aprasidze, in his discussion of South Caucasian regional cooperation, reminds us that 'there are many *regions* and many different forms of *regionalisation*' (p. 91).[12] Lebanidze and Skardžiūtė-Kereselidze argue that Poland and the Baltic States are one of those more distant 'regions' relevant to Georgia's security. They admit that Poland and the Baltic countries have much more of a geographical connection with Ukraine. The latter, Lebanidze and Skardžiūtė-Kereselidze underline, is a contiguous country which directly impacts their security. Georgia does not qualify geographically or economically as a close partner, but it shares a broader historical and ideational 'region' with Poland and the Baltics, one which concretely impacts Georgia's foreign policy. The common history of Poland and the Baltic States with Georgia – all self-described victims of Soviet power – and their mutual aspirations to Europeanization have led to measurable effects on Georgia's foreign policy. Lebanidze and Skardžiūtė-Kereselidze argue that this was reflected by Poland's and the Baltic States' strong support for Georgian membership of NATO. They were, in addition, fierce supporters of Georgia during the Russo-Georgian War in 2008, and subsequently promoted the EU's Eastern Partnership programme in 2009, designed to bring former Soviet borderland states like Georgia closer to the EU. For Lebanidze and Skardžiūtė-Kereselidze, history and ideas, as well as common interests, can link countries together into 'regional' alliances. However, they point out that Poland and the Baltic States have their own interests in supporting Georgia against the Russian threat; they expect their actions in support of Georgia and the Eastern Partnership will raise their own profile within the EU. Whether the motives are pragmatic or ideational, Lebanidze and Skardžiūtė-Kereselidze show they can have real effects.

Georgia's economic and political security is not entirely bound up with Europe and the United States. Levan Kakhishvili and Alexander Kupatadze, in their analysis of Georgia's relations with countries from the former Soviet Union, using data on trade, international exchanges and treaty agreements, demonstrate the continuing importance of economic and political relationships with the former Soviet republics. Ukraine remains the most important strategic partner for Georgia; it is a fellow member of the Eastern Partnership, an important trading partner, and a democracy with the same political values as Georgia. But Central Asia has vital importance in Georgia's development of energy and transit policies toward Europe. Central Asia, as a provider of energy and transit links to the Far East, is a vital strand in Georgia's economic security as well as its geostrategic importance to Europe. The authors point to Georgia's participation in the China-Central Asia-West Asia Corridor, one of the six overland routes envisaged by China's BRI. Not all Central Asian countries have the same value for Georgia, and they cannot compare to the trade and investments provided by Russia or the EU, but they possess vital resources, supply Foreign Direct Investment (FDI) and tourists to Georgia, and a number of them are important trading partners. Establishing good relationships with Central Asian states helps Georgia balance Russia. None of the Central Asian states acceded to Russia's request to recognize the independence of Abkhazia and South Ossetia.

Georgia's 'others': Russia and the Muslim south

In his chapter on Georgian–Russian relations, Nodia writes that 'for Georgia, relations with Russia have been more than a foreign policy issue … Rather, they are related to the definition of its identity, and its survival as a state' (p. 250). The same could be said of Georgia's relations with the Ottomans and Iranians in earlier centuries. As much as foreign policy is about finding allies, it is also focused on identifying and deterring enemies. Nodia is right about the convergence of identity and survival for small states like Georgia, but Georgia's relationship toward its 'others', – those like Iran, Turkey and Russia, which at one time or another presented an existential threat to the state – has also been characterized by a large dose of pragmatism. Georgia's relationship with Russia, both in the nineteenth and twentieth centuries, was always ambivalent. Tsarist Russia was a Christian state, protecting Georgia from the Islamic empires to the south and the Muslim

Caucasian tribes to the north. It was a prestigious European power, a modernizing state, which brought industry, railways, urban life and trade to Georgia. At the same time, it was an imperial bulldozer. Its rule was bureaucratic and corrupt, and by the last third of the nineteenth century, the empire had shifted from progressive to backward, from multicultural to Russian, and from internationally prestigious to internationally incompetent.

President Shevardnadze's administration followed the traditional pragmatism of Georgian elites toward Russia, in part because many of Shevardnadze's colleagues were raised in the USSR. Russia was familiar, not alien. Opponents accused Shevardnadze of pro-Russian sentiments; his supporters defined it as realism. Shevardnadze's policy of Waltian threat balancing[13] (Shevardnadze initiated Georgia's application for NATO membership in 2002) had considerable support in Georgia, and still does. But the current Georgian Dream administration, led informally by billionaire Bidzina Ivanishvili, has taken a more conciliatory approach to Russia than the Saakashvili government. But, unfortunately for Georgia – as Nodia points out – Putin's Russia 'hardly considers Georgia as an independent political actor, but rather as an extension of Western influence in its neighbourhood' (p. 256). Contrary to the arguments of the authors in this book, Russia views Georgia as a country without agency. This, and Russia's ability to leverage national minorities against the Georgian state, has always made the Georgian–Russian relationship unique as well as a brutally asymmetric one.

Historically, Georgian leaders were focused on events in the Middle East. The Iranian, Byzantine and Turkish worlds were of far more significance for Georgia than northern or Western empires. The positive legacies of the Middle East remain in Georgia's literature, food and religions. In the eighteenth century, the Islamic empires of the Ottomans and the Persian (Iranian) dynasties of the Afsharids and Qajars (Nadir Shah and Agha Mohammed Khan were among the most destructive leaders of Persian armies in Georgia), threatened Georgian statehood. In the nineteenth century, Georgians in the Russian Imperial Army, saw Islamic threats as the most perilous menace to their heritage and to their cultural survival. The Ottomans overran Georgian territories during independence in 1918–21. The 'otherness' of the Turks (and Iranians), as George Sanikidze shows in his contribution, is still in place. Turkophobia is particularly extensive among Georgia's citizens.

Yet after the collapse of the USSR, Sanikidze argues that 'Turkey has become the most important neighbour and strategic partner of Georgia in the region' (p. 122). Turkey's NATO membership, its extensive military cooperation with Georgia, its transit and energy interests in the South Caucasus, and its position as Georgia's leading trade partner, have led to what the Georgian government defines as a 'strategic partnership'. It performs an important (though recently a less reliable) function as a balance against Russian pressure. Turkey has eliminated Georgia's economic dependence on Russia. Sanikidze – using data on trade and bilateral agreements – argues that Iran plays a less important role in Georgia's foreign policy. Its relations with Georgia are dependent on the context of Russian and US activities in the South Caucasus. But Iran, too, despite its pariah status in the West, is overcoming its historical otherness. Like Turkey, it refused to recognize Russian suzerainty in Abkhazia and South Ossetia and in 2017, its visa-free regime status with Georgia was restored (it had been temporarily suspended in 2013). Georgia has been able to use its geography (in particular its ports on the Black Sea), and its access to EU markets, as an attractive lure for Iranian investment and business. Georgia's relations with both Iran and Turkey are based on common interests, such as trade, investments, energy and tourism. The switch from being historical pariahs to friendly neighbours shows a contemporary Georgian foreign policy that is both pragmatic and flexible.

Conclusion

Georgia's policymakers are convinced Europeans, but there is little prospect for Georgia to join either the EU or NATO. There is, as Natalie Sabanadze puts it, 'a strong public consensus that the European Union is a cultural choice and a political destiny for Georgia' (p. 176), but the European commitment is soft. Georgia is a small and peripheral state in a region subject to geopolitical conflict, something the EU and NATO both want to avoid. The EU is perplexed over the future of the Eastern Partnership, and NATO lacks any clear policy conviction over its activities in the Black and Caspian Sea regions. Meanwhile, the upsurge in Chinese economic power in Central Asia and the Middle East is the latest challenge to Georgia's foreign policy calculations. Georgia's relationship with China and its potential role in the BRI is something we wished to cover in this book, but expertise on the relationship is hard to find.[14] Georgia's signing of a Free Trade Agreement with China in 2017, its participation in the BRI (specifically the China-Central Asia-Western Asia Corridor) and the rapid growth in trade (China is currently the second largest exporter to Georgia, surpassing Russia), suggest China will be a major factor in Georgia's economic and political future. The BRI gives Georgia usable advantages for attracting other trading countries to South Caucasia. China could also play a role in deterring Russian attempts at destabilization in Georgia.

The EU is facing a significant challenge in the region, the balance of power is shifting and the EU's vacillation may in the end lead to the strengthening of other foreign policy scenarios for Georgia. However, China's own authoritarianism is unlikely to influence Georgia's political course toward the West; in fact, as one report suggests, it may stimulate Europe and the United States to redouble their efforts to keep Georgia within the Western orbit.[15] Maintaining its attractiveness as a major transit corridor to all interested parties such as China, the EU, Iran and Turkey is one means Georgia has of improving its economy and protecting its sovereignty. But ultimately, it is the strength and capacity of the Georgian state which will sustain its independence. Today, Georgia has a well-trained cadre of younger diplomats, but without a firm base of popular legitimacy, well-integrated national minorities, trust in laws and a competent civil service, the government will not have the resources it needs at home to sustain difficult, and often controversial foreign policy decisions. The political crisis in Georgia after the 31 October 2020 elections – with the opposition boycotting parliament – is an unfortunate sign of Georgians' continuing propensity for division and drama over dialogue and cooperation. Borders have never been sufficient to protect Georgian democracy, but Georgian democracy – and with it agreement over the rules that govern democratic statehood – could, perhaps, protect its borders.

Notes

1 See Ilia Chvchavadze's conversation with Lelt Ghunia in part VII of his essay 'mgzavris tserilebi' (A Traveller's Letters) at Poetry.ge, https://poetry.ge/poets/ilia-chavchavadze/prose/9532.mgzavris-werilebi.htm

2 'Osnovi oboroni gosudarstva voobshche i v Gruzii v chastnosti', *The Georgian Archive* (Archives of the Delegation to the Conference of Peace and of the Government in Exile), Houghton Library, Harvard University, Box 10, Book 22, File 7.

3 For an assessment of the Democratic Republic of Georgia, see Stephen Jones, 'Georgian Social Democracy', in Zurab Karumidze et al. (eds), *Georgia's European Ways* (Tbilisi: 2015), pp.29–42.

4 R.A.S. Hennessey, *The Transcaucasian Railway and the Royal Engineers: With the Sappers to Baku* (Skipton, UK: Trackside Publications, 2004), p. 52.

5 Niko Nikoladze, a Georgian populist, journalist and entrepreneur, called his plan the BPP (Berlin, Poti, Peking), which he proposed to the German government in 1918. See Zourab Avalishvili, *The Independence of Georgia in International Politics, 1918–1921* (Westport, Hyperion Press, 1981), p. 71.

6 'La Delegation Géorgiènne à la Conference de la Paix', *sakartvelos sakhelmtsipo saistorio arkivi* (The Georgian State Historical Archive) Fond 1864/2/109, p. 1.

7 'Speech Delivered by President Mikheil Saakashvili at George Washington University', Mikheil Saakashvili Presidential Archives, 23 February 2004, www.saakashviliarchive.info/en/PressOffice/News?p=2778&i=1

8 sakartvelos sagareo sakmeta saministro (The Foreign Ministry of Georgia), *Georgia's Foreign Policy Strategy for 2019–2022*, https://mfa.gov.ge/MainNav/ForeignPolicy/ForeignPolicyStrategy.aspx

9 On the annexation, see R.G. Suny, *The Making of the Georgian Nation* (London: I.B. Tauris, 1989), Ch. 3.

10 Tergdaleuli (pl. tergdaleulebi), referred to a Georgian member of the intelligentsia who had studied in Russia or Europe. He or she had drunk from the river Terek (i.e. crossed the Terek river, the unofficial border between Georgia and Russia proper), and received a Russian/European education.

11 See, for example *Caucasus Barometer* in 2017 and 2019, for the latest data on Georgians' attitudes toward Europe, the EU and NATO, https://caucasusbarometer.org/en/datasets/. For public opinion polls on Georgian attitudes toward Europe going back to 2007, see International Republican Institute, www.iri.org/country/georgia?page=1

12 For a critical discussion of regional approaches to the South Caucasus see Tracey German, 'Good Neighbours or Distant Relatives?' Regional Identity and Cooperation in the South Caucasus', *Central Asian Survey*, 31:2 (2012), pp. 137–51.

13 I am referring here to Stephen Walt, who in his book *The Origins of Alliances* (1987) expounded the idea of a 'balance of threat' in contrast to a 'balance of power' as the primary calculation for state security and the formation of alliances.

14 For an excellent assessment of the burgeoning Chinese–Georgian relationship, see Joseph Larson, 'Georgia–China Relations: the Geopolitics of the Belt and Road', Tbilisi: Georgian Institute of Politics, 2017, http://gip.ge/georgia-china-relations-geopolitics-belt-road/

15 See the Foreign Policy Research Institute's and Black Sea Strategy Papers' report *On the Fault Line: Georgian Relations with China and the West*, (New York: Foreign Policy Research Institute, 2019), p. 12.

Part I

THE USES OF IDENTITY IN GEORGIAN FOREIGN POLICY

Chapter 1

ACHIEVING SECURITY AS A SMALL STATE

Tracey German and Kornely Kakachia

Small states face difficult decisions about the nature of their economic and political interaction with their neighbours and regional partners. This is more complex for the post-Soviet states such as Georgia, which, since independence, have had to establish a new global role for themselves. Small and weak in terms of size and capability, Georgia was not initially viewed by the international community as an important state, despite its presence in a strategically located region between Russia and the Middle East. This was compounded by its lack of any experience in international relations or its possession of the prerequisite instruments of policymaking. Georgia faced the complex task of determining the most appropriate geopolitical strategies vis-à-vis its immediate neighbourhood, as well as towards non-regional actors like the European Union (EU), the United States and NATO.

Since 1991, Georgia's approach to foreign policy has been shaped by its status as a small state. Its key foreign policy objective – with variable intensity and success – has been the preservation of sovereignty and territorial integrity within internationally recognized borders. Georgia has pursued a foreign policy that removes it from the Russian sphere of influence. It has sought to develop a democratic state in line with Western values and standards, under the protection of a Euro-Atlantic security umbrella. In spite of persistent diplomatic, economic and military pressure from Russia, there has been little substantive change in Georgia's foreign policy position for over two decades: even in the wake of the 2008 war with Russia, the pursuit of NATO membership and a closer relationship with the EU has remained a central pillar of Georgia's foreign policy, and Tbilisi has deliberately courted the West, particularly the United States, in an attempt to counterbalance Moscow's influence. China, along with Azerbaijan and Turkey, have also become increasingly important for Georgia in recent years, as Tbilisi seeks to diversify its trade partners and markets, as well as its diplomatic links.

Georgia is an interesting country for scholars of foreign policy and international politics. Since regaining independence in 1991, the Black Sea country has experienced multiple wars, conflicts and shifting alliance structures, against a backdrop of a rapidly changing international environment.[1] Georgia provides food for thought for each of the major disciplines of international relations and foreign policy analysis. Supporters of the power politics approach to international relations will be intrigued by Georgia's partly structure-deviant behaviour, i.e. not to bow to Russia's systemic pressure despite the absence of viable alternatives. To scholars of social constructivism,[2] Georgia offers interesting opportunities to explore how normative ideas shape foreign policy and whether they can trump rational behaviour based on a cost–benefit analysis. Finally, Georgia offers scholars who focus on domestic drivers of foreign policy a rich laboratory to explore various unit-level triggers of foreign policy, such as ideas, perceptions, public opinion and non-state actors.

This chapter explores the foreign policy behaviour of Georgia through the lens of the existing literature on small states. What are the diplomatic strategies Georgia uses to secure itself, advance its interests, and ensure its survival in an unstable neighbourhood? As a small state squeezed between powerful neighbours, does it have any freedom of action in its foreign policy? Traditional theories of the foreign policy behaviour of small states suggest that they tend to either 'bandwagon' with great powers or 'balance' against them. The example provided by Georgia demonstrates a far more nuanced set of foreign policy behaviours than these theories suggest. A number of scholars of Georgia's foreign policy prefer to use neoclassical realism as a framework for analysis. Neoclassical realism posits that, while the international system remains the most important driver of foreign policy for states both large and small, it is unit-level factors that shape the responsiveness of states and translate system-level variables into policy outcomes.[3] Studies exploring Georgian foreign policy through this lens focus on the impact of a variety of domestic issues including the significance of elite cohesion, elite identities, state capacity, political paternalism and religiosity, as well as ideologically informed elite perceptions.[4]

Despite a growing focus on the role of small states within the post-Cold War international system, there is a gap in the literature on the foreign policy behaviour of small states in the post-Soviet area. Much of the work on post-Soviet small states tends to focus on how they manage their relations with Moscow first and foremost, portraying them as vulnerable foreign policy 'recipients'; less attention has been directed towards the more positive aspects of their foreign policy behaviour. Small states are often located within the orbit of a larger power, and are defined by their relative lack of influence and capabilities. One way that they can secure themselves and get noticed in a world of growing great power competition and numerous small state rivals is to make themselves useful to bigger powers. They can demonstrate their strategic utility and reliability as 'trusted partners' in order to influence the perception of others about their standing within the international community.[5] This chapter contends that a significant focus of Georgia's diplomatic efforts has been to signal its status and reliability as a 'trusted partner' to the international community, and to reposition itself within both the global and regional hierarchy. The Black Sea state seeks to demonstrate its strategic utility to the broader international community in a variety of ways: firstly by using its military capabilities to contribute to international stabilization operations such as the NATO-led International Security Assistance Force (ISAF) in Afghanistan, in order to enhance its standing within the global community. This illustrates its standing as a 'good partner' for the West, despite facing a significant military threat to its territorial integrity; secondly, Georgia capitalizes on its geographic location, which is simultaneously a fundamental strength and critical vulnerability, to establish Georgia as a transit hub between Europe and Asia. Georgia might be a small country in terms of territory, but it is increasingly important as a strategic corridor and international partner. Finally, it has also been seeking to recast itself as a reforming 'European' state, explicitly differentiating itself from its Soviet past in order to be accepted as part of a broader Euro-Atlantic security bloc.

Defining small states

There is little scholarly consensus with regard to the definition of a small state. There is a range of terminology used to describe states that are not 'great' powers: small states, small powers and weak states are just some of the terms used, all of which have very different definitions that tend to focus on tangible and intangible aspects, including physical attributes such as size of territory or population, economic indicators and capabilities, as well as the capacity to influence, or a state's role in the international hierarchy.[6] Nevertheless, there is acknowledgement that the principal variable is a state's position in relation to others, as opposed to a material variable such as population size and territory. According to Archer et al., a small state is 'the weaker one in an asymmetric relationship, which is unable to change the nature or functioning of the relationship on its own.'[7] This emphasizes the relational aspect: 'a small state typically acts simultaneously in a number of different power configurations with different sets of actors, and therefore a state may be weak ("small") in one relation, but simultaneously powerful (a "great power") in another'.[8]

Thus, small states tend to be characterized in the scholarly literature as the weaker part of an asymmetrical relationship. A focus on material capabilities to conceptualize state size is useful up to a point, as it offers 'analytical certainty'. But when it comes to definitions, this becomes less useful as it does not explain the behaviour of one state toward another.[9] Are the diplomatic strategies employed by small states merely about ensuring security and survival, or are there other motivations that explain their foreign policy behaviour? To develop a comprehensive understanding, it is helpful to combine an objective, capabilities-based approach with an explanation of state behaviour, focusing on the drivers of international engagement and activism.

Based on material attributes such as population size and territorial area the states of the South Caucasus could be classified as 'small' states, as set out in Table 1.1 below. Their capacity to influence other states is limited. However, within the region there is a different set of power configurations. As an example, Azerbaijan is relatively 'small' in its relationship with Russia, the 'weaker part' of Archer et al.'s asymmetric relationship, but is simultaneously powerful in its relations with its two small state neighbours in the South Caucasus, Georgia and Armenia.

Table 1.1 Comparing the states of the South Caucasus

	Armenia	Georgia	Azerbaijan
Population	3m	4.9m (est. inc. separatist territories)	9.7m
Territory	29,743 km²	69,700 km²	86,600 km²
(comparable state)	(Belgium)	(Lithuania)	(Austria)
GDP (US$bn)	11.6	15.5	40.7
GDP per capita (US$)	3,813	4,194	4,184

Source: World Bank.[10]

Asymmetric power relationships are common across the post-Soviet space: Russia remains the dominant power in the region, in military, diplomatic and economic terms. For example, the economic relationship between Russia and the majority of the post-Soviet states tends to be asymmetrical, with Russian companies often the key investors, and Russian goods comprising a large percentage of imports for such states. In large part, this reflects the enduring legacy of Soviet economic links, what Libman has termed the 'inevitable inertia of Soviet economic ties'.[11]

While small states are vulnerable to external pressure, post-Soviet states are perhaps more so because of durable legacy ties such as economic and societal links, combined with the fact that they remain geographically adjacent to the successor state of the former imperial power. This is reflected in a lot of the literature on the foreign policy of post-Soviet states, which tends to focus on their relations with Moscow and the need to seek compromise as the weaker part of an asymmetrical relationship. Mouritzen proposes a strategy of 'Finlandisation'[12] or 'adaptive acquiescence' (making the best out of political and strategic dependence) for the smaller neighbours of strong regional powers with adjacent spheres of influence. He suggests that post-Soviet states on the Russian periphery are worse off and 'will need to come to terms with their larger neighbour (if, perhaps, after a short period of defiance)'.[13] The problem with this approach is the lack of agency assigned to small states. Small states do have choices in their foreign policy behaviour, they are not mere pawns of bigger states. If this were the case, Georgia would have acquiesced to Russian demands and changed its foreign policy stance after the persistent pressure from the Kremlin (particularly in the wake of the 2008 war), abandoning its overt ambitions to integrate more closely with the West, accede to NATO and 'return to Europe'. Instead of acquiescing and recognizing what scholars such as Mouritzen propose, Tbilisi has continued to state its NATO membership ambitions, and in 2014 signed an Association Agreement with the EU, setting up a bilateral Deep and Comprehensive Free Trade Area (DCFTA) – in direct defiance of what Moscow wanted. This lends credence to the approach of Cooper and Shaw, who emphasize the resilience and resourcefulness of small states rather than their vulnerability.[14] Thus, while existing work on small states in the post-Soviet space tends to focus on the vulnerability of these states and the need to accommodate Russia, this does not provide clear answers with regard to Georgia's foreign policy behaviour.

The literature on the status-seeking activity of small states is a useful tool for analysing Georgia's foreign policy behaviour. De Carvalho and Neumann assert that status is a key driver in the policies of small states, who 'suffer from status insecurity to an extent that established great powers do not'.[15] Status is defined as a state's standing or rank within a status community, which is related to the collective beliefs about a state's position within a global or regional community. It is less to do with a state's material capabilities than with its ability to influence the perceptions of others about its standing.[16] Wohlforth et al. identify two objectives of small state status-seeking behaviour: standing in one or more peer groups of similar states, as well as recognition by great powers:

> Being (by definition) not great, these states have difficulties in being seen. Great powerhood is about being a state to be reckoned with: smaller powers risk going unnoticed. As such, achieving status just below – not alongside – the great powers is for those states in lower ranks a guarantee of being noticed.[17]

Status-seeking behaviour therefore has an important signalling function, as a state seeks to indicate its position within the international system. This combines elements of both structure and agency: small states use their creative agency to signal their belief regarding the state's role and position within the international system, at the same time focusing on influencing the perception of other states about its utility, capability and authority. In spite of material constraints, such as a lack of economic and/or military capacity, small states may still seek to influence the international system and play a role in international politics, for example, by developing 'material niche capabilities' to make themselves useful or lending their support to the hegemon.[18] Thus, small states achieve status by making themselves useful to greater powers in order to be noticed and acknowledged as a 'good power'.

'Returning to Europe' as a foreign policy mantra?

Haugevik maintains that identity and identity formation play a key role in foreign policy, not just concerns about security.[19] If Georgia was seeking membership of the NATO alliance purely for security purposes, then it would be logical to expect it to have altered its position in the wake of the 2008 war with Russia, which demonstrated its vulnerability. This did not happen and Tbilisi has continued to pursue its accession ambitions in direct defiance of Moscow's wishes. Contrary to expectations, Georgia's successive regime changes have not overly influenced its foreign policy trajectory. Although there is no indication that Georgia will become a member of NATO or the EU in the near future, its strategic orientation towards the West remains. Moreover, most Georgians continue to support NATO and EU membership, which they perceive not only as a guarantee of security but as a symbol of their belonging to the West. According to an April 2020 survey commissioned by the US National Democratic Institute (NDI), support for

Georgia's integration into the EU and NATO remains strong at 82 per cent and 74 per cent, respectively.[20]

This lends credence to the thesis that concerns about identity and the desire to preserve a specific relational identity can eclipse security concerns.[21] For Tbilisi, being accepted as a European state and part of a broader Western security bloc, and moving away from being conceived of as a former/post-Soviet state is an important step. Since independence in 1991, and particularly since the Rose Revolution of 2003, Georgia has sought to construct a European identity for itself, explicitly differentiating itself from its Caucasian neighbourhood and the wider post-Soviet space. The notion of Georgia 'returning' to Europe and the West has become a common theme in Georgian political and popular discourse, part of the process of constructing a European identity.[22]

The European narrative in post-Soviet Georgian foreign policy emerged at the end of the twentieth century, most conspicuously when the late Prime Minister Zurab Zhvania declared 'I am Georgian and therefore I am European' during a speech to mark Georgia's accession to the Council of Europe in 1999.[23] There is generally no distinction made between Europe and the West. The two terms tend to be used interchangeably, emphasizing the sense of moving away from the past, which is connected with Russia and the post-Soviet space, towards a Western future. Georgia sees itself reclaiming its rightful place within the European family from which it has been estranged for centuries. Announcing the country's aspiration for NATO membership in 2002, Shevardnadze declared that Georgia had 'for centuries been cut off from western civilization although it always saw its rightful place there' and described the South Caucasus as 'an outpost of a civilization that regards freedom and humanism … as its central values'.[24] Geographically, Georgia is on the periphery of Europe, sitting at the crossroads between Europe and Asia. However, whilst the geographical dimension is important in attempts to define Europe and whether Georgia constitutes a 'European' country, it has been argued that Europe also has an important cultural component, that it is an 'idea', a civilization and a set of norms and values.[25]

In his presidential inauguration speech in 2004, Mikheil Saakashvili stated that 'not only are we old Europeans, but we are ancient Europeans', reinforcing the notion that Georgia had been driven from its 'natural' path of development and its rightful place in Europe.[26] This view was encouraged by many in Washington. Speaking in Tbilisi in 2007, US Assistant Secretary of State for European and Eurasian Affairs Daniel Fried declared that not only was Georgia 'in Europe' in geographical, cultural, political and historical terms, but that it was part of the Euro-Atlantic community: 'Georgians are a part of the transatlantic world, and therefore institutions of the transatlantic world should be open to Georgia as much as to any other European country'.[27]

The central role of self-identity in the development of the Georgian state was highlighted by former President Giorgi Margvelashvili in his first annual state of the nation address, when he stressed that 'Georgians with their individual self-identity are Europeans and part of Western civilisation'.[28] Ó Beacháin and Coene argue that Europe is seen as a symbol of hope, prosperity and quality, contrasting with the counter-concepts of Asia and Russia.[29] Georgia's efforts to recast itself as a democratic, European state can be viewed as part of its efforts to alter collective beliefs about its social standing, its status within the international system. The principal objective appears to be to challenge the collective view of Georgia as a 'post-Soviet' state: Georgia's determination to emphasize its 'Europeanness' and ensure a 'return to Europe' is an attempt to make a clear distinction between its past and its future, between the post-Soviet space and 'Europe'.

However, Georgia's European aspirations are not just about a desire to differentiate between the Soviet past and European future. Some scholars trace the roots of the country's embrace of its European identity back to the Democratic Republic of Georgia in 1918–21 and even earlier: Gia Tarkhan-Mouravi asserts that, while the question of Europeanness has been at the heart of discussions of Georgian identity since the nineteenth century, the connection to Europe is linked to the country's Christian tradition.[30] It is also important to highlight the fact that Georgia turned to the Russian Empire in the early nineteenth century seeking protection from the Persians, because it was perceived as 'European' (in contrast to the Ottomans and Persians) – thus, initially Russia was considered to offer security, a position that was reversed in the twentieth century.[31] This tension between Georgia's European aspirations and its security was evident in a speech given in 1917 by Noe Jordania, who went on to become the first head of state of the Democratic Republic of Georgia:

> This union [with Russia in 1801] was not the result of some kind of personal caprice or a matter of simple chance. It was a historic inevitability. At that time, Georgia stood before a dilemma: the East or the West. And our ancestors decided to turn away from the East and turn to the West. But the road to the West lay through Russia and consequently to go toward the West meant union with Russia.[32]

Thus, the narrative about Georgia choosing between East or West is not a new one. What has changed is the shift from the historic perception that the path to the West lay through Russia to the contemporary narrative, which emphasizes that a Western path constitutes a rejection of Russia.

Military partnership

Georgia has also been using its military capabilities to contribute to international security and stabilization operations such as ISAF in order to enhance its standing within the global community, by demonstrating its standing as a 'good partner' for the West. Despite the security challenges it faces at home, Georgia has provided troops for NATO- and US-led operations in the Balkans and Afghanistan. While all three South Caucasus states have contributed to international security efforts,[33] it is Georgia that has really sought to highlight its credentials as a reliable and trustworthy ally for the Euro-Atlantic community. The first Georgian peacekeeping platoon was deployed in the Balkans in 1999. Since then the level of troops participating in international peacekeeping and stabilization missions has increased dramatically. Georgia contributed to the NATO-led International Security Assistance Force (ISAF) in Afghanistan from 2004. Fifty soldiers (a platoon) were briefly deployed under German command as part of a security operation during the Afghan presidential elections in October 2004. In November 2009, it deployed 173 soldiers in Kabul under French command and the following year sent an infantry battalion to Helmand. Georgia became the largest non-NATO contributor to ISAF and the fifth largest contributor overall, following a substantial increase of its deployment in October 2012. It provided two infantry battalions serving with US forces in Helmand, an infantry platoon serving with the United States in Kabul at Camp Phoenix (primarily involved with the training of the ANA), medical personnel within the Lithuanian PRT, and a number of staff officers serving at various locations.

Georgian troops deployed with no national caveats, meaning that they were often sent to higher risk areas. This frontline led to the loss of 29 soldiers, as well as over 460 wounded, since 2010. Georgia continued to support the development of the Afghan security forces post-2014, providing over 800 troops for Operation 'Resolute Support', a much smaller operation aimed at training, advising and assisting the Afghan forces, and also pledged financial support for the future development of the Afghan National Security forces. Georgia also supports Operation Active Endeavour, NATO's counter-terrorist maritime surveillance operation in the Mediterranean and contributes troops to the NATO Response Force (NRF). A small number of Georgian troops (150) are participating in the EU-led mission in the Central African Republic, Georgia's first operational experience in Africa, as well as its first contribution to an EU mission.

The question arises as to why Georgia continues to focus on its contribution to international stabilization operations when it consistently stresses the threat to its territorial integrity posed by Russia. Its most recent strategic defence review, SDR2017–2020, identified Russia's 'aggressive foreign policy' as a major threat to national security and outlined a concept of Total Defence to ensure the defence of its entire territory. However, SDR2017 also states that the country will continue its active participation in NATO-led international missions and will continue to contribute troops to the NATO Response Force (NRF), with the intention of strengthening the capabilities of the Georgian Armed Forces, 'enhancing its interoperability with NATO' and demonstrating that 'Georgia is a reliable partner and an important contributor to international security'.[34] Georgia's contribution to the international security environment was an important element of Georgia's 2014 National Military Strategy (NMS), as well as a key objective of the Georgian Armed Forces (GAF). The NMS states that 'Georgia's national interests are intertwined with the strengthening of contemporary global security and stability' and makes it clear that increasing interoperability with NATO is a central part of the military transformation process.[35] Nevertheless, it is important to highlight the country's recognition that Georgia's contribution to missions such as ISAF is not a means of buying entry into NATO.

In contrast to its active participation in international stabilization efforts since 1999, Georgia has not participated in, or contributed to, any Russian-led operations in the post-Soviet space over the past decade. One possible explanation for this willingness to contribute to international operations, rather than more local ones, is the desire to demonstrate to the international community that it is a trustworthy ally for the West. Græger links the contributions that small states make to international operations to status seeking, asserting that the possession of adequate military capabilities and a willingness to deploy them can be important tools in 'seeking status and a place at the table in important forums'.[36] Participating in international stabilization efforts has helped Georgia to achieve a key strategic objective of contributing to the international security environment, whilst simultaneously boosting its visibility within the global system as a loyal ally willing to contribute troops to difficult operations, such as those in Iraq and Afghanistan. Of particular importance is the fact that Georgia contributed troops with no caveats on their deployment, in stark contrast to many other partners and member states, who placed strict caveats on where their troops could be deployed within Afghanistan. Following a suicide attack on a Georgian forward operating base in Helmand in June 2013, which left seven dead, former President Mikheil Saakashvili restated Georgia's determination to join NATO, describing the deaths as 'yet another sacrifice' the country has made 'on its difficult path to freedom, independence and joining the family of the world's civilised nations'.[37] Its actions have not gone unnoticed in Washington: the Georgian contribution to NATO operations in Afghanistan was praised by the acting US Ambassador to Georgia Elizabeth Rood, who stated in 2018 that the US 'knows about the bravery and reliability of Georgia's soldiers on the battlefield. Your valour, sacrifice, and honour protect peace around the world. We are in your debt … '[38]

Public opinion and political elites

Domestic factors play a key role in foreign policy behaviour and there is an important domestic dimension to Georgia's international contributions, as they signal to the Georgian population that the country is important to NATO (and the EU in terms of its contribution to CSDP missions in Africa), that it is perceived to be a valued and trusted partner. They also lend support to the country's efforts to recast itself as a democratic, European state and alter collective beliefs about its social standing, and its status, within the international system. By making a visible and valuable contribution to international security operations led by NATO or the EU, the country is emphasizing its constructed 'European' identity (as opposed to its legacy post-Soviet one) in an attempt to enhance its pursuit of closer integration with the Euro-Atlantic community.

Public opinion and civil society have a significant impact on Georgian foreign policy. During the late 1990s an active civil society and non-governmental sector started to develop in Georgia, which has become a guardian of the country's pro-Western orientation.[39] Other societal groups, such as student and youth grassroot organizations, also adopted a very pro-Western position. Finally, from the 2000s, public opinion among the Georgian population has consolidated around Western values and pro-Western foreign policy.[40] Regular surveys conducted across all EU Eastern Partnership countries since the mid-2000s reveal that support for NATO and EU membership is highest in Georgia. This has had significant ramifications for the country's foreign policy. Research by the Caucasus Research Resource Centre found that a majority of Georgians prefer some form of 'hedging', that is a pro-Western policy that maintains good relations with Russia, or a pro-Russian policy that maintains good relations with the West. The pro-Western hedge group was much larger than the pro-Russian hedge group, and the former was fairly evenly split – 54 per cent to 46 per cent – between those who perceive Russia as the main threat and those who do not.[41] Public opinion has limited the foreign policy choices of the ruling elites by making the country's pro-Western foreign policy the only option, and making détente with Russia at the political level nearly impossible. The 2019 political crisis and mass protests over the invitation of a Russian politician to the Georgian parliament was the latest indication of how civil society and public opinion both influence and limit the foreign policy choices of Georgian governments.[42]

As mentioned above, neoclassical realism, which attempts to synthesize domestic and systemic factors to explain foreign policy behaviour, has influenced a lot of the work on Georgian foreign policy. In their analysis of the linkages between state effectiveness and foreign policy assertiveness, Gvalia et al. maintain that a high degree of variation in assertiveness in Georgia's pro-Western policy before and after the 2003 Rose Revolution can be explained by the greater effectiveness of state institutions and stronger elite cohesion under Saakashvili's administration.[43] This empirical observation is in line with one of the major claims of neoclassical scholars that a government's extractive capacity and the effectiveness of state institutions are important determinants of a state's foreign policy:

> Foreign policy is made not by the nation as a whole, but by its government. Consequently, what matters is state power, not national power. State power is the portion of national power the government can extract for its purposes and reflects the ease with which central decision makers can achieve their ends.[44]

It is argued that Georgia's system-defiant foreign policy behaviour[45] of distancing from Russia, despite the absence of viable alternatives, is determined by domestic factors related to political elites. The dominance of pro-Western and liberal ideas in Mikheil Saakashvili's administration resulted in a hyperbolic pro-Western foreign policy, while a greater degree of elite cohesion made their foreign policy more effective and more assertive in comparison with the Shevardnadze era. Moreover, ideologically conditioned perceptions may even distort the realities on the ground and contribute to misperceptions and flawed expectations, in line with Neoclassical realist thinking:

> Neoclassical Realists regard the structure of the international system as providing states with information about the costs and benefits of particular courses of

action, but how that information is processed and weighed depends on the way states understand the world, their preferences, their ideas and their ethics.[46]

When addressing the domestic drivers of small state foreign policy, it is also important to mention the opposite direction of the foreign-domestic policy nexus; that is, how the external environment shapes and changes the domestic context of small states, what Peter Gourevitch calls the 'reversed second image perspective'.[47] From this point of view, the foreign policy choices of small states largely co-determine major domestic developments such as regime dynamics or the democratization process. Georgia's firm pro-Western orientation has often acted as a decisive external push for the country's democratization and significantly shaped regime dynamics. Over the last two decades, at every critical juncture of Georgia's democratic development, Western partners have empowered pro-democratic coalitions in Georgia and provided an external impetus for the country's democratic development. For instance, the EU and the United States supported the 2003 Rose Revolution in Georgia and discouraged Mikheil Saakashvili's government from rigging the ballot in the 2012 parliamentary elections. Hence, overall there is a tight interaction and interdependence between Georgia's external environment, its foreign policy choices and domestic dynamics.[48]

Conclusions: What drives Georgia's foreign policy?

While small states are considered to be vulnerable to pressure from external actors, post-Soviet states are perhaps more so because of the enduring diplomatic, economic and societal links with Russia, combined with the fact that they remain geographically adjacent. Thus, it is perhaps more important for post-Soviet states to seek external recognition of their sovereignty and statehood through status-seeking behaviour, as Russia has demonstrated an apparent disregard for these concepts vis-à-vis its neighbours. As a small state in relation to its larger neighbours, Georgia may lack structural power, but it is not a mere pawn or 'recipient' of foreign policy. This chapter has argued that a significant focus of Georgia's diplomatic efforts has been to signal its status and reliability as a 'trusted partner' to the international community and reposition itself within both the global and regional hierarchy. On the one hand, since independence in 1991, Georgia has been trying to recast itself as a European state committed to continued democratization, whilst simultaneously backing up this rhetoric with its highly visible military commitment to international stabilization operations such as ISAF. It may be small in terms of territory and young in terms of statehood, but Georgia has become increasingly important as a strategic corridor and military partner, and has sought to promote its objectives and achieve its goals through different, often unconventional, means, highlighting its creative agency in the face of structural deficiencies. Despite facing a continuing threat to the country's territorial integrity from Russia, the Georgian government has remained steadfast in its commitment to supporting international security and stabilization operations.

On a broader level, Georgia's foreign policy is dictated by two imperatives: distancing from Russia as the main source of threat and Euro-Atlantic integration, both as a rational and ideational choice. Georgia has been staunchly consistent in its pursuit of these two objectives. Georgia supplemented its Euro-Atlantic quest with hyperactive status-seeking behaviour through its active participation in Western military operations worldwide which boosted its profile as a regional leader of Europeanization and democratization. Moreover, in pursuing its goals, successive Georgian governments have withstood strong pressure from neighbouring Russia, in the shape of military invasion, occupied territories, endless hybrid warfare and full economic embargo. In doing so, the Georgian case has somewhat devalued claims by systemic power theorists that small states bow to pressure and bandwagon with the biggest source of power or the biggest source of threat when viable alternatives are absent. Part of this puzzle is explained by ideational approaches: the self-identification by Georgian political elites with Europe and with the West acts as an ideational driver of the country's foreign policy and often outperforms both systemic pressure and other rational incentives such as losing the Russian market during the 2005–12 Russian economic embargo. Domestic non-state actors, including civil society organizations, youth grassroot movements and non-governmental organizations, also act as an ideational driver, further limiting and streamlining the foreign policy choices of Georgian ruling elites.

Notes

1 For further details, see Svante Cornell, *Small Nations and Great Powers: A Study of Ethnopolitical Conflict in the Caucasus* (Abingdon: Routledge, 2005)

2 The social constructivist school focuses on the role of intersubjective ideas, beliefs and values. Its supporters maintain that (national) interests of [small] states are not given but socially constructed and can be changed over time. For more information, see Ted Hopf, 'The Promise of Constructivism in International Relations Theory', *International Security* 23:1 (1998), pp. 171–200; Peter J. Katzenstein (ed.), *The Culture of National Security: Norms and Identity in World Politics.* (New Directions in World Politics) (New York: Columbia University Press, 1996); Vendulka Kubálková, 'Foreign Policy, International Politics, and Constructivism', in *Foreign Policy in a Constructed World*, ed. Vendulka Kubálková (London: Routledge, 2001), pp. 15–37; Thomas Risse, *Social Constructivism and European Integration* (Oxford: Oxford University Press, 2004); Alexander Wendt, 'Anarchy Is What States Make of It: The Social Construction of Power Politics', *International Organization*, 46:2 (1992), pp. 391–425.

3 For further discussion of neoclassical realism, see Nicholas Kitchen, 'Systemic Pressures and Domestic Ideas: A Neoclassical Realist Model of Grand Strategy Formation', *Review of International Studies*, 36:1 (2010), pp. 117–43; Steven E. Lobell, Norrin M. Ripsman and Jeffrey W. Taliaferro (eds), *Neoclassical Realism, the State, and Foreign Policy* (Cambridge: Cambridge University Press, 2009); Brian Rathbun, 'A Rose by Any Other Name: Neoclassical Realism as the Logical and Necessary Extension of Structural Realism', *Security Studies*, 17:2 (2008), pp. 294–321; Norrin M. Ripsman, Jeffrey W. Taliaferro and Steven E. Lobell, *Neoclassical Realist Theory of International Politics* (Oxford: Oxford University Press, 2016).

4   See for example Giorgi Gvalia and Bidzina Lebanidze. 'Geopolitics and
     Modernization: Understanding Georgia's Pro-Western Assertiveness since the
     Rose Revolution', in *Modernization in Georgia*, ed. Giga Zedania (Bern: Peter Lang
     A.G., 2018), pp. 165–96; Kornely Kakachia, Bidzina Lebanidze and Volodymyr
     Dubovyk, 'Defying Marginality: Explaining Ukraine's and Georgia's Drive towards
     Europe', *Journal of Contemporary European Studies*, 27:4 (2019), pp. 451–62; Kevork
     Oskanian, 'The Balance Strikes Back: Power, Perceptions, and Ideology in Georgian
     Foreign Policy, 1992–2014', *Foreign Policy Analysis*, 12:4 (2016), pp. 628–52; Giorgi
     Gvalia, Bidzina Lebanidze and David Siroky, 'Neoclassical Realism and Small
     States: Systemic Constraints and Domestic Filters in Georgia's Foreign Policy', *East
     European Politics*, 35:1 (2019); Giorgi Gvalia, David Siroky, Bidzina Lebanidze
     and Zurab Iashvili, 'Thinking outside the Bloc: Explaining the Foreign Policies
     of Small States', *Security Studies*, 22:1 (2013), pp. 98–131; David S. Siroky, Alan
     James Simmons and Giorgi Gvalia, 'Vodka or Bourbon? Foreign Policy Preferences
     toward Russia and the United States in Georgia', *Foreign Policy Analysis*, 13:2 (2017),
     pp. 500–518.
5   Deborah Welch Larson and Alexei Shevchenko, 'Status Seekers: Chinese and Russian
     Responses to US Primacy', *International Security*, 34:4 (2010), pp. 63–95.
6   For further information on definitions see Clive Archer and Neill Nugent,
     'Introduction: Small States and the European Union', in *Current Politics and
     Economics of Europe*, 11:1 (2002), pp. 1–10; Baldur Thorhallsson and Anders Wivel,
     'Small States in the European Union: What Do We Know and What Would We Like
     to Know?', *Cambridge Review of International Affairs*, 19:4 (2006), pp. 651–668.
     See also R.P. Barston (ed.), *The Other Powers: Studies in the Foreign Policy of Small
     States* (London: George Allen & Unwin, 1973); Michael Handel, *Weak States in the
     International System* (London: Frank Cass, 1990); David Vital, *The Inequality of States:
     A Study of the Small Power in the International System* (Oxford: Oxford University
     Press, 1967); Burton Benedict (ed.), *Problems of Small Territories* (London: Athlone
     Press, 1967); The World Bank in Small States, www.worldbank.org/en/country/
     smallstates
7   Clive Archer, Alyson J.K. Bailes and Anders Wivel (eds), *Small States and
     International Security: Europe and Beyond* (Abingdon: Routledge, 2014), pp. 8–9.
8   Archer *et al*, pp. 8–9.
9   Moch Faisal Karim, 'Middle Power, Status-seeking and Role Conceptions: The Cases
     of Indonesia and South Korea', *Australian Journal of International Affairs*, 72:4 (2018),
     pp. 343–363.
10   The World Bank defines small states as 'characterised by a small population, limited
     human capital, and a confined land area'. See *The World Bank in Small States*, www.
     worldbank.org/en/country/smallstates
11   Alexander Libman, 'Regionalisation and Regionalism in the Post-Soviet Space:
     Current Status and Implications for Institutional Development', *Europe-Asia Studies*,
     59:3 (2007), p. 415.
12   Mouritzen's concept of 'Finlandisation' derives from Finland's foreign policy from
     1944 to 1991, when it adapted to the defensive security interests of USSR in northern
     Europe, while maintaining a version of neutrality as well as shielding a flourishing
     Western democracy. Hans Mouritzen, 'Small States and Finlandisation in the Age of
     Trump', *Survival*, 59:2 (2017), pp. 67–84.
13   Mouritzen, pp. 67–8.

14   Andrew F. Cooper and Timothy M. Shaw (eds), *The Diplomacies of Small States: Between Vulnerability and Resilience* (Basingstoke: Palgrave Macmillan, 2013).

15   Benjamin de Carvalho and Iver B. Neumann (eds), *Small State Status Seeking: Norway's Quest for International Standing* (Abingdon: Routledge, 2015), p. 1.

16   DW Larson & A Shevchenko, 'Status seekers: Chinese and Russian responses to U.S. primacy', International Security 34:4 (2010), pp. 63–95.

17   William C. Wohlforth, Benjamin de Carvalho, Halvard Leira and Iver B. Neumann, 'Moral Authority and Status in International Relations: Good States and the Social Dimension of Status Seeking', *Review of International Studies*, 44:3 (2018), p. 530.

18   Ibid., p. 534.

19   Kristin M. Haugevik, 'Status, Small States, and Significant Others: Re-reading Norway's Attraction to Britain in the Twentieth Century', in Benjamin de Carvalho and Iver B. Neumann (eds), *Small State Status Seeking: Norway's Quest for International Standing* (Abingdon: Routledge, 2015), pp. 42–55.

20   https://civil.ge/archives/334775

21   Haugevik, p. 44.

22   For more detail see Ghia Nodia, 'The Georgian Perception of the West', in *Commonwealth and Independence in Post-Soviet Eurasia*, ed. Bruno Coppieters, Alexei Zverev and Dmitri Trenin (London: Frank Cass, 1998), pp. 12–43; Tracey German, 'Heading West? Georgia's Euro-Atlantic Path', *International Affairs*, 91:3 (2015), pp. 601–14, https://doi.org/10.1111/1468-2346.12286.

23   See www.youtube.com/watch?v=P4KX1IVvrHg (accessed 22 January 2015).

24   'Statement by President of Georgia Eduard Shevardnadze at the EAPC Summit'.

25   See for example Richard Swedberg, 'The Idea of "Europe" and the Origins of the European Union – A Sociological Approach', *Zeitschrift für Soziologie*, 23: (Oktober 1994), pp. 378–87.

26   Sabine Freizer, 'The Pillars of Georgia's Political Transition', *Open Democracy*, (2004), www.opendemocracy.net/democracy-caucasus/article_1732.jsp.

27   *Developing Europe's East,* Daniel Fried, Assistant Secretary for European and Eurasian Affairs, Remarks at Conference, Tbilisi, 1 November 2007, www.state.gov/p/eur/rls/rm/94553.htm. Fried went on to clarify his view that, whilst Georgia may be in Europe, it was the 'rougher end of Europe'.

28   President Giorgi Margvelashvili, 'The State of the Nation Address', 21 February 2014, *The Administration of the President of Georgia,* www.president.gov.ge/en/PressOffice/Documents/AnnualReports?p=8674&i=1

There is generally no distinction made between Europe and the West: the two terms tend to be used interchangeably, emphasising the sense of moving away from the past, which is connected with Russia and the post-Soviet space, towards a Western future and modernity. Despite the consistency in both the foreign policy discourse and popular support, there is some debate within Georgia regarding the motivations behind the country's Western/European orientation. Several Georgian scholars argue that Georgia's European choice is linked to its efforts to modernize the state, which elites believe is only possible by integrating with both the West and Euro-Atlantic structures. Nodia argues that Georgia's choice of a Western liberal democratic model of governance is largely identity-driven (as opposed to being value-driven) and that what it is actually seeking is access to 'Western modernisation'. In his view, Georgia's experience with 'Westernness' is minimal: 'Never in its history has Georgia been in close contact with the West' (Nodia 2005, 69). Gvalia et al. support the notion of Georgia's European self-identification being directly linked to modernization of the state, asserting that for the country's political elite, 'foreign policy is the means to a domestic end: a modern state and society'.

(Gvalia et al., 2013, p. 113)

29 Donnacha Ó Beacháin and Frederik Coene, 'Go West: Georgia's European Identity and its Role in Domestic Politics and Foreign Policy Objectives', *Nationalities Papers*, 42:6 (2014), pp. 923–41.

30 Gia Tarkhan-Mouravi, 'Georgia's European Aspirations and the Eastern Partnership', in *The Making of Modern Georgia, 1918–2012: The First Georgian Republic and its Successors*, ed. Stephen F. Jones (Abingdon: Routledge, 2014), p. 49.

31 One of Russia's first concerns was to halt the lucrative trade in slaves common in the region, driven largely by the Ottomans. For more details, see Bruce Grant, *The Captive and the Gift: Cultural Histories of Sovereignty in Russia and the Caucasus* (London: Cornell University Press, 2009), pp. 22–5.

32 Quoted in Thomas de Waal, *The Caucasus: An Introduction* (Oxford: Oxford University Press, 2010), p. 61.

33 Both Armenia and Azerbaijan have been keen to contribute openly to international security efforts and have played a role in international stabilization operations in countries such as Kosovo, Iraq and Afghanistan. However, their contributions have been smaller and often come with caveats, and neither are seeking membership of NATO or the EU.

34 Ministry of Defence of Georgia, *Strategic Defence Review 2017–2020 (SDR2017)*, https://mod.gov.ge/uploads/2018/pdf/SDR-ENG.pdf, p. 55.

35 Ministry of Defence of Georgia, *National Military Strategy*, 2014, https://mod.gov.ge/uploads/2018/pdf/NMS-ENG.pdf, p. 10.

36 Nina Græger, 'From "forces for good" to "forces for status"? Small State Military Status Seeking', in Benjamin de Carvalho and Iver B. Neumann (eds), *Small State Status Seeking: Norway's Quest for International Standing* (Abingdon: Routledge, 2015), p. 93.

37 *Civil Georgia*, 'Seven Georgian Soldiers Die in Afghan Truck Bomb Attack', 6 June 2013, http://civil.ge/eng/_print.php?id=26154

38 Embassy of the Republic of Georgia to the United States of America, 'Georgian soldiers leave for Afghanistan equipped with Made in Georgia', Press Release, 28 April 2018' http://georgiaembassyusa.org/2018/04/28/georgian-soldiers-leave-for-afghanistan-equipped-with-made-in-georgia/

39 Marina Muskhelishvili and Gia Jorjoliani. 'Georgia's Ongoing Struggle for a Better Future Continued: Democracy Promotion through Civil Society Development', *Democratization*, 16:4 (2009), pp. 682–708, https://doi.org/10.1080/13510340903083000; Kornely Kakachia and Bidzina Lebanidze, 'Georgia's Protracted Transition: Civil Society, Party Politics and Challenges to Democratic Transformation', in *25 Years of Independent Georgia: Achievements and Unfinished Projects*, ed. Ghia Nodia (Tbilisi: Ilia State University, 2016), pp. 130–62.

40 Comprehensive databases of public opinion surveys in Georgia include The Caucasus Research Resource Centre, 'Caucasus Barometer', www.crrccenters.org/caucasusbarometer; International Republican Institute, 'Georgia' www.iri.org/country/georgia, National Democratic Institute, 'Library of NDI Georgia Public Opinion Research' www.ndi.org/georgia-polls.

41 Caucasus Research Centre, 'Georgia's Foreign Policy Trilemma: Balance, Bandwagon or Hedge, Part 2', 13 January 2020, https://crrc-caucasus.blogspot.com/2020/01/georgias-foreign-policy-trilemma_5.html.

42 For further information see Kornely Kakachia and Bidzina Lebanidze, 'Georgian Dream Meets Georgia's Nightmare the Party Tried to Improve Ties with Russia. Then the Public Intervened', *Foreign* Policy, 25 June 2019, https://foreignpolicy.com/2019/06/25/georgian-dream-meets-georgias-nightmare/; Amy Mackinnon, 'In Georgia's Parliament, One Russian Too Many', *Foreign Policy*, 21 June 2019, https://foreignpolicy.com/2019/06/21/georgia-tbilisi-protests-political-russia-west/.

43 Giorgi Gvalia, Bidzina Lebanidze and David Siroky, 'Neoclassical Realism and Small States: Systemic Constraints and Domestic Filters in Georgia's Foreign Policy', *East European Politics*, 35:1 (2019).

44 Fareed Zakaria, *From Wealth to Power: The Unusual Origins of America's World Role* (Princeton, NJ: Princeton University Press, 1999), p. 99.

45 This point needs further elaboration. From the point of view of the 'balance of power' theorists such as Mearsheimer and Waltz, Georgia's pro-Western foreign policy, intended to balance Russia, is certainly deviating from systemic logic. Stephen Walt's 'balance of threat' theory could better explain Georgia's stubborn refusal to accept Russia as a hegemonic power. For Walt, for a smaller state to bandwagon a more powerful state (which represents the source of threat), the latter should be amenable. In the case of Georgia, it is unclear to what extent Russia is an amenable power: Russia has made its occupation of Georgian territories irreversible and shows no interest in restoring political ties with the Georgian government. These circumstances make bandwagoning Russia for Georgian ruling elites a very daunting task. From a different point of view, Georgia's pro-Western foreign policy could also be viewed not as balancing against Russia, but bandwagoning with the West. Schweller posits that states do not only bandwagon to accommodate the source of danger, but very often their primary interest is gaining profit from making alliances with stronger sides in the conflict. From this point of view, Georgia's attempt to align with the West may be explained not only as an attempt to balance Russia but primarily to gain economic and political profit from the West. A counterargument to Georgia's bandwagoning for profit behaviour would be the huge economic and political costs that have resulted from Georgia's attempts to balance Russia. For instance, as a result of tit-for-tat escalation in 2005–07, Georgia simultaneously lost the Russian market (its main export market), was deprived of a principal source of energy and saw its migrant workers deported from Russia. More importantly, distancing from the Kremlin cost Tbilisi two occupied territories, one full-scale military conflict with Russia, as well as continuous hybrid war that further destabilizes Georgia's security and undermines its statehood. Hence, overall it is hard to say that Georgia has benefited politically or economically from its balancing behaviour against Russia. For more detail see John J. Mearsheimer, *The Tragedy of Great Power Politics* (London: W. W. Norton, 2001); Kenneth N. Waltz, *Man, the State, and War: A Theoretical Analysis* (New York: Columbia University Press, 2001); Stephen M. Walt, 'Testing Theories of Alliance Formation: The Case of Southwest Asia', *International Organization*, 42:2 (1988), pp. 275–316; Stephen M. Walt, *The Origins of Alliances* (Ithaca, NY: Cornell University Press, 1990); Randall L. Schweller, 'Bandwagoning for Profit: Bringing the Revisionist State Back', in *International Security*, 19:1 (1994), pp. 72–107.

46 Kitchen, p. 143.

47   Peter Gourevitch, 'The Second Image Reversed: The International Sources of
     Domestic Politics', *International Organization*, 32:4 (1978), pp. 881–912. An extensive
     body of work on Europeanization, including the neighbourhood Europeanization,
     draws on the same logic to explain domestic changes in the EU's neighbourhood
     states. For a few examples, see Tanja Börzel, 'The Transformative Power of Europe
     Reloaded: The Limits of External Europeanization', *KFG Working Paper Series*. KFG
     Working Paper Series 11, 2010; Tanja Börzel and Yasemin Pamuk, 'Europeanization
     Subverted? The European Union's Promotion of Good Governance and the
     Fight Against Corruption in the Southern Caucasus', Working Paper 26, 2008;
     Andrea Gawrich, Inna Melnykovska and Rainer Schweickert, 'Neighbourhood
     Europeanization through ENP: The Case of Ukraine', *JCMS: Journal of Common
     Market Studies*, 48:5 (2010), pp. 1209–35; Heather Grabbe, *The EU's Transformative
     Power: Europeanization through Conditionality in Central and Eastern Europe* (New
     York: Palgrave Macmillan, 2006).

48   Some scholars use two-level game theoretical models to explain various modes of
     interactions between domestic and foreign fields and predict their outcomes. For
     more information, see Jeffrey W. Knopf, 'Beyond Two-Level Games: Domestic–
     international Interaction in the Intermediate-Range Nuclear Forces Negotiations',
     International Organization 47:4 (1993), pp. 599–628; Andrew Moravcsik, 'Taking
     Preferences Seriously: A Liberal Theory of International Politics', *International
     Organization*, 51:4 (1997), pp. 513–53; Robert D. Putnam, 'Diplomacy and Domestic
     Politics: The Logic of Two-Level Games', *International Organization*, 42:3 (1988),
     pp. 427–60.

Chapter 2

PUBLIC RELATIONS, INTERNATIONAL POLITICS AND GEORGIAN DEMOCRACY

Lincoln A. Mitchell

During Georgia's thirty years of independence, efforts to make Georgia more democratic have been a preoccupation of the West, but for Georgia's own political leaders, it has been a more sporadic goal. Additionally, the international context in which these democratic efforts have occurred has changed dramatically over the last three decades. Events like the terrorist attacks on the United States on 11 September 2001, the long US-led wars in Iraq and Afghanistan, the Arab Spring and Donald Trump's presidency, have all changed the global political environment and diminished the triumphant liberalism of the 1990s. But despite such changes, Georgia's democratic progress has continued, periodically renewed by dramatic political changes at home such as those in 1992, 2003 and 2012.[1] This is clearer now from the perspective of three decades of independence. The tension between these changing international dynamics and the slow-moving and frequently steady state of Georgian democracy is an interesting puzzle. Dramatic events internationally and domestically have not led to any durable changes in the overall momentum of Georgian democracy. But overcoming the persistent and enduring obstacles to democratic growth in Georgia has proven difficult for Western governments to understand. They often face a dilemma when strategizing over how aid for democracy building in Georgia should work.[2]

Georgia's political journey is easy to (mis)understand when we filter it through major breakthroughs such as the Rose Revolution in 2003–4 and the unexpected election victory of the Georgian Dream (GD) in 2012, or in the context of crises such as the war with Russia in 2008 and the violent crackdown on anti-government protesters in Tbilisi on 7 November 2007. In 2005 Zurab Karumidze and James Wertsch argued that the Rose Revolution was a turning point for Georgian democracy.[3] In 2010, Ronald Asmus accurately anticipated growing tensions between the United States and Russia, but overstated the extent to which the 2008 war changed the trajectory of Georgia and the region.[4] Georgia, despite political turmoil over the last three decades, has maintained a relatively constant focus on democracy and pluralism. But the international dimension has both facilitated and obstructed Georgian democratic development, and understanding its multiple impacts is essential to understanding Georgian politics since independence.

Measuring Georgia's democracy

Throughout the post-Soviet independence period, Western powers, particularly the United States, but frequently European countries as well, have sought to make Georgian democracy stronger by helping the country build fairer elections and institutions. They have sought to do this through bilateral discussions, working groups, foreign assistance programmes and direct support both to the Georgian government and to local non-governmental organizations (NGOs). Table 2.1 below illustrates the amount of direct aid for democracy building that Georgia has received from Western states in recent years.

USAID's assistance alone on democracy-related programmes has totalled more than US$1.5 billion to date.[5] All Georgian governments have professed a commitment to democratic goals, but the importance of democracy, and the government's commitment to it, have varied over the years. Understanding how Georgian governments have sought to present Georgia to the rest of the world is an important part of understanding Georgia's political development and the success of its democracy-related reforms. Many of the democratic reforms in Georgia have been driven by how Georgians view themselves, and how they want the world to see them. On the eve of the 2012 election, Damien McGuinness described how the Georgian government had sought to portray the country to the West: 'The version pushed by the Georgian government rests on a common perception of the country: a small, plucky state, keen to shake off its Soviet past and join NATO, bullied by Russia, and invaded in 2008 … Georgia's charismatic US-educated president, Mikheil Saakashvili, has pushed it relentlessly.'[6]

Table 2.1 Gratuitous financial support for Georgia (1995–15)

Top 10 countries	Amount (in million US dollars)
USA	912.1
Germany	118.1
Netherlands	65.9
Japan	40.9
China	38.0
Ukraine	12.6
United Kingdom	7.6
Sweden	4.0
Switzerland	2.6
France	1.6

Source: Institute for Development of Freedom of Information (IDFI), https://idfi.ge/en/total-grants-disbursement-by-donors-1995-2015.

In the mid to late 1990s, just a few years after Eduard Shevardnadze's return to power in Tbilisi in 1992, Georgia had a reputation for being more democratic than most other countries in the Caucasus region. However, this was only in a 'tallest building in Topeka' kind of way. Rampant corruption, an extremely weak state, the inability of the central government to exercise sovereignty over significant swathes of Georgian territory, widespread election fraud and more than occasional political intimidation, all made Georgia an inconsistent democratic state during this period. Yet the image abroad was a positive one. In 2000, former US Secretary of State James A. Baker III recalled how in the early 1990s '[i]f there was one special place in that region, one country above all that we knew we needed to help, it was Georgia'.[7] Georgia, for example, was the fourth country in the Commonwealth of Independent States to be admitted to the Council of Europe in April 1999, Europe's human rights and democracy body.[8]

However, elements of Georgian political and civic life, including the ability of opposition political forces to contest elections, the evolution of the parliament as a place for debate and disagreement and the development of civil society organizations (CSOs) which were independent of the government, suggested Georgian governments would not be able to sustain an authoritarian regime, even if they wished to. Although fraud and other abuses of power by the ruling party, such as intimidating voters at the polls or manipulating voter lists, precluded elections from being totally free and fair, elections were always contested. Opposition parties were able to run and win seats in parliament and local councils. In the 1990s, parliament remained dominated by Shevardnadze's party, the Citizens Union of Georgia (CUG), but there was also pluralism and debate on the floor of the chamber. Frequently, debates were just between different CUG factions, but they were real nevertheless.

Civil society in Georgia during these years was also stronger than in most neighbouring countries in the South Caucasus and Central Asia such as Azerbaijan, Armenia, or Kazakhstan, where there was much less political freedom throughout this period (see Table 2.2). By the end of the 1990s, foreign donors had helped nurture a relatively active civil society that served as a watchdog and occasional check on government abuses. These Western-funded NGOs and CSOs included the Liberty Institute, the Georgia Young Lawyers Association and the International Society for Fair Elections and Democracy (ISFED). The media was more or less free, as there was no formal government censorship or insurmountable obstacles to publishing or broadcasting. Newspapers printed stories that were often critical of Shevardnadze's government, while television stations broadcast rancorous political programmes where speakers argued over the issues of the day. However, while there was no official government censor during this period, widespread poverty functioned as an unofficial one. For many Georgians the money needed to buy a newspaper was better spent on a loaf of bread or other essential items. Frequent power outages, particularly outside Tbilisi, meant that over half of the population had little ability to watch television as a source of news and alternative perspectives. Table 2.2 shows Freedom House's assessment of Georgia's democratic status in the last five years of the Shevardnadze era, compared to neighbouring states.

Table 2.2 Political rights – Freedom House

	1998	1999	2001	2002	2003
Armenia	4	4	4	4	4
Azerbaijan	6	6	6	6	6
Georgia	3	4	4	4	4
Kazakhstan	6	6	6	6	6

Note: Countries are graded between 1 (most free) and 7 (least free).
Source: https://freedomhouse.org/regions/eurasia

The impact of Georgian Public Relations

In the 1990s, the Georgian government successfully promoted itself in the West as a place where democracy was stronger than in neighbouring post-Soviet states. For example, a June 1998 article on Georgia in the *New York Times* referred to 'several dozen bright and energetic young people who are playing important roles in building a new post-Communist order'. The article went on to describe how Zurab Zhvania, then an MP and ally of Shevardnadze 'had been sent by President Shevardnadze (to New York) to recruit talented young Georgians to enter politics. The desired qualifications were intelligence, energy, idealism and no connection to the old Communist elite'.[9] Georgia's ability to present itself as pro-Western was bolstered by the presence of Eduard Shevardnadze. Shevardnadze could draw on substantial reservoirs of goodwill among Western governments, dating from his work as Soviet Foreign Minister during the waning days of the Cold War. No other post-Soviet leader from the Caucasus or Central Asia enjoyed Shevardnadze's reputation among Western leaders, which had its origins in the late 1980s. Shevardnadze made a point of promoting young politicians, like Mikheil Saakashvili, who became Chair of the Tbilisi City Council and Justice Minister during the Shevardnadze period, and who could speak the language of democracy in English. Shevardnadze may have been frequently feuding with some of these young politicians at home, but he used them overseas to promote the image of a democratic Georgia.

As the 1990s wound down and Western states became increasingly aware of the failure of their democracy-building programmes in Georgia, corruption and the political manipulation of elections became increasingly difficult for Shevardnadze to ignore. The government and opposition consistently clashed over the issue of accountability and political corruption, as exemplified by fraudulent elections or biased courts and partisan judges. Each Georgian government since then, in varying degrees, has overstated the strength of Georgia's democracy, while opposition forces have raised alarms about its imminent collapse. Following the Rose Revolution in 2003, the Georgian government began to aggressively promote itself as the democratic miracle of the post-Soviet world. At a speech at George Washington University in Washington DC, shortly after becoming Georgia's president in 2004, Saakashvili alluded both to shared values between Georgia and the democratic West, and to Georgia being a model for other countries seeking to become democratic:

> I understood that it's not only geopolitics, transportation and economic projects or the issues of defence and security that are important for us, but the values that the advanced countries of the world have, and that I have been using as a guide during these years, are of central importance … What happened in Georgia was a real miracle. The Georgian nation has proved that strength is in unity. The world's leading media covered the events in Georgia and today we have become an example to the whole world.[10]

Other English-speaking Rose Revolutionaries, comfortable in the vernacular of NGOs, democracy, and democracy promotion, fanned out abroad to trumpet the democratic accomplishments of the new regime in Georgia. These forces received a boost when President George W. Bush, on a visit to Tbilisi, referred to Georgia as a 'beacon of liberty' in 2005.[11] Foreign and domestic cheerleaders for Georgian democracy, following Bush's lead, did not let the more complex reality of post-Rose Revolutionary democracy in Georgia dampen their enthusiasm.

The years immediately following the Rose Revolution were the height of Georgia's 'democratic glory'. But following the violent crackdown in 2007, when police destroyed the headquarters of Georgia's most influential independent television station, the plausibility of Georgian democratic progress was weakened. The Georgian government would never again be able to be as effective in persuading Western powers of its democratic credentials. The Rose Revolutionaries and their party, the United National Movement (UNM) continued to have strong support in the West, but as Human Rights Watch remarked:

> (S)ince the peaceful Rose Revolution in 2003, Western governments have hailed Georgia as an example of a successful transition to democracy and a human rights champion in the former Soviet Union. The November 7 violence exposed the government's shaky commitment to human rights and the rule of law.[12]

Georgia continued to present itself as democratic and pro-Western after 2007, but the Georgian government's emphasis shifted to presenting Georgia as the leading anti-Putin force in the region. This shift was made evident by how frequently the UNM leadership spoke of their hatred for Russia's political system. Emphasizing Georgia's own democratic development seemed to take second place. For example, at a dinner on 22 July 2009 welcoming US Vice President Joseph Biden to Georgia, President Saakashvili mentioned democracy only very briefly, and only to stress that he did not see it as incompatible with national security. However, his statements about Russia in the speech were much harder hitting: 'It is important for the world to understand that we will never surrender, that we will continue, with the help of our natural friends, to resist peacefully the imperialists who aim at destroying our territorial integrity, cancelling our independence and reversing our history.'[13] This example is illustrative: it captures the tone of the Georgian government during the post-2008 period. Moreover, regardless of whether they said it publicly or not, all but the most ardent loyalists in Washington and elsewhere recognized that, by 2010, Georgia was no longer on the democratic path they had hoped for.

The GD government, which came to power in 2012, also sought to present Georgia as a democratic success story. GD leaders described their victory as a democratic breakthrough. The GD's pre-election programme in 2012 pointed out that 'since 2004, the principle of checks and balances between different branches of government is non-existent. This resulted in an authoritarian regime led by the president.'[14] However, the GD has made its case to the West less deftly. Conversely, after losing power in 2012 the UNM successfully presented Georgia under the leadership of the GD as insufficiently democratic. In its years in power, the UNM had cultivated relationships between Western politicians and Georgian leaders like Giga Bokeria, Kaha Lomaia, Salome Samadashvili and Saakashvili himself, who were all fluent in English and understood the political culture of Europe and the United States. The UNM was also able to bring much more expertise and experience to the issue of 'democratic reform'. In the months immediately following the 2012 election, in Western journals as well as in briefings, former UNM leaders highlighted the arrests of former comrades, which the GD contended was due to criminal activities, but which the UNM presented to Western governments as purely political.[15] UNM leaders had the support of neo-conservative circles in Washington and right-wing political movements like the European People's Party (EPP) in the European Parliament. A 2015 statement by EPP leader Joseph Daul captured the EPP view of the GD and its own support for the UNM:

> The EPP strongly condemns such politically motivated cases and is shocked at the continuous interference of the government in the work of the judiciary. Ivanishvili's group must understand that the justice system is not a playground without rules. Blackmailing judges, cherry picking laws to incarcerate the opposition and abusing power are not characteristic of a Georgia that Europe wants as a partner.[16]

The EPP was silent about problems concerning the rule of law during the Saakashvili era in Georgia.

For Georgia over the last thirty years, democratic development has occurred alongside Georgian leaders' efforts to sell their story to Western governments in a language they would understand. It is not easy to disaggregate these two things. There is an indirect causal relationship between the two. During the UNM period, the democratic spin was widely accepted, particularly in the early years, and particularly in Washington DC. This helped insulate Saakashvili from criticism, but also from pressure to reverse his more authoritarian policies. This dynamic, in turn, accelerated the democratic backsliding. After 2012, the failure of the GD government to spin its successes in the West led to more criticism which, in turn, has made the GD feel more embattled and defensive. Either way, Western politicians and governments are explicitly involved in the 'official' success or failure of Georgian democracy. By shaping the narrative they impact the chances of a genuine liberal democracy taking root in Georgia.

The Russian factor

After 1991, the Russian Federation replaced the USSR as the dominant presence in the Caucasus region. Concerns about Russia have never been far from the minds of Georgia's leaders. Russia's role in supporting Abkhazian and South Ossetian separatist movements in the 1990s and 2000s, are a reminder. Russia, too, has always been a key factor in the development of Georgian democracy because of the enduring threat it has represented to Georgia as well as the complex and multi-vectored influence it has had on Georgian domestic political life. In the 1990s, the Russian model of a super-presidency and a managed legislature were enduring influences on the Georgian political elites when they began designing their new constitution in 1995. Russia has also been a consistent threat to Georgia's national security and has at times supported non-democratic elements in Georgian society, such as Aslan Abashidze, the pro-Russian leader in Achara in the early 2000s and various illiberal parties in more recent years. Upon coming to power, the government of Mikheil Saakashvili sought to address Russia's belligerence towards Georgia and its efforts to undermine Georgian sovereignty and territorial integrity. Initially this took the form of Tbilisi reincorporating Achara into the Georgian political system, and ousting Aslan Abashidze, the Russian-backed warlord who had run Achara like a personal fiefdom. That was an important initial success, but similar efforts to reassert Georgian control over Abkhazia and South Ossetia were ultimately unsuccessful. Only four and a half years after the Rose Revolution that brought Saakashvili to power, in 2008 Georgia and Russia fought a short war which pushed the two conflict regions out of Tbilisi's orbit.

During the run-up to the 2008 war and immediately following the conflict, Western powers began to value Georgia less as a democratic success and more as a bulwark against Russian aggression in what Moscow referred to as its 'Near Abroad'. Western pressure for democratic reform waned as initial hopes around Georgia's democratic progress, represented by the Rose Revolution, gave way to the reality that Saakashvili was building a new form of hybrid democracy. The UNM government used the tension with Russia as a rationale for its continuing emphasis on security, rather than furthering democratizing reforms. Western powers acknowledged, at least rhetorically, that an anti-Moscow government in Tbilisi was extremely important. For example, in his 2009 trip to Georgia US Vice President Joseph Biden, in a speech that barely mentioned democracy despite clear evidence that it was imperilled in Georgia, stated:

> I know that some are concerned, and I understand it, that our efforts to reset relations with Russia will come at the expense of Georgia. Let me be clear: They have not, they will not, and they cannot … we stand by the principle that sovereign democracies have the right to make their own decisions, and choose

their own partnerships and their own alliances ... And we call upon Russia to honour its international commitments clearly specified in the ... ceasefire agreement, including withdrawal of all forces to their pre-conflict positions, and ultimately out of Georgia.[17]

Saakashvili eloquently and compellingly emphasized Georgia's role in standing up to Russian aggression. He wrote in *The Washington Post*:

Russia's invasion of Georgia strikes at the heart of Western values and our 21st-century system of security. If the international community allows Russia to crush our democratic, independent state, it will be giving carte blanche to authoritarian governments everywhere. Russia intends to destroy not just a country but an idea.[18]

While these words were sincere, they appealed directly to a US foreign policy elite that was growing visibly more hawkish towards Russian and Vladimir Putin, while still unable to turn such hawkishness into concrete policy. Even after the 2012 election in Georgia, when the UNM was defeated, Georgia's relationship with the West emphasized a common position against Russia, rather than putting the commitment to democracy at its centre.

Georgian democracy: View from the West

Despite the drama of reform and revolution, Georgia's democracy has been an incremental process that has not been derailed by the dramatic events over the last thirty years, such as civil war, 'revolution' and foreign invasion. Figure 2.1 below lists the Freedom House score for every year of Georgia's independence. Freedom House uses a scale ranging from one to seven; lower numbers indicate freer societies. A country with a 1/1 score would be a democratic ideal, while the most authoritarian regime would score a 7/7. The two areas we are looking at – political freedom which emphasizes institutions, and civil freedom which focuses on individual and group rights – show quite a consistent pattern in Georgia over the last three decades. Freedom House's methodology raises some questions, but it is an adequate method for establishing general patterns, particularly when looking at any country over a period of many years.[19] Other sources of democracy related data, such as the *Economist's* Democracy Index, provide similar findings and trends.[20]

The data here shows a gradual upward trend toward improved democratic practices. In 1991, the last year of Soviet Georgia, Georgia was described as unfree. In each of the following four years, Georgia scored a combined nine or ten, suggesting that the country was more free than it had been during the Soviet years, but was still struggling with the establishment of democratic norms and rules. This

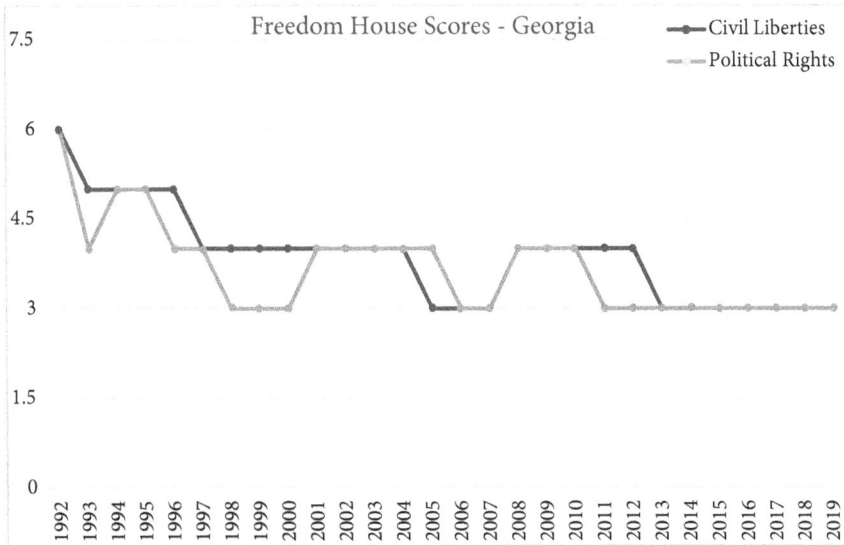

Figure 2.1 Freedom House scores for Georgia: 1992–2019[21]

Source: https://freedomhouse.org/country/georgia/freedom-world/2020
Note: Scores range from 1 (most free) to 7 (least free).

is consistent with the broadly accepted narrative about democracy in Georgia, as typified by Ghia Nodia's assessment in 2005. He wrote:

> Over the past 10–15 years, the civil society sector in Georgia has developed in many important respects. There is a pool of qualified and experienced personnel in the sector … Traditions and a culture of cooperation and collaboration have been established … CSOs operating in Georgia, which have proved to be consistent advocates of democratic values and human rights, have accumulated a degree of moral capital … A network of CSOs active throughout Georgia has become a platform for the dissemination and protection of liberal values ….[22]

The shift in 1997, from a 4/5 to a 4/4 (based on data collected in 1996), reflects an improvement after Eduard Shevardnadze consolidated his power. However, the data from 1997 to 2020, which covers a period of twenty-four years, shows very little fluctuation. During this period, the score for both political and civil freedoms, a total of forty-eight different scores, was either a 3 or a 4. The composite scores range from 6 (attained ten times), 7 (six times) or 8 (eight times). The evaluation of Georgian democracy has to be based on more than these post-Soviet numbers, but, compared to its neighbours, as Figure 2.2 shows below, Georgia's scores have been remarkably steady and quite positive. From 1995 through 2020, Armenia's Freedom House scores range from 8 to 10. Azerbaijan has had greater fluctuation than Georgia and showed consistently less democracy. Its scores have

Armenia

Azerbaijan

Georgia

Russia

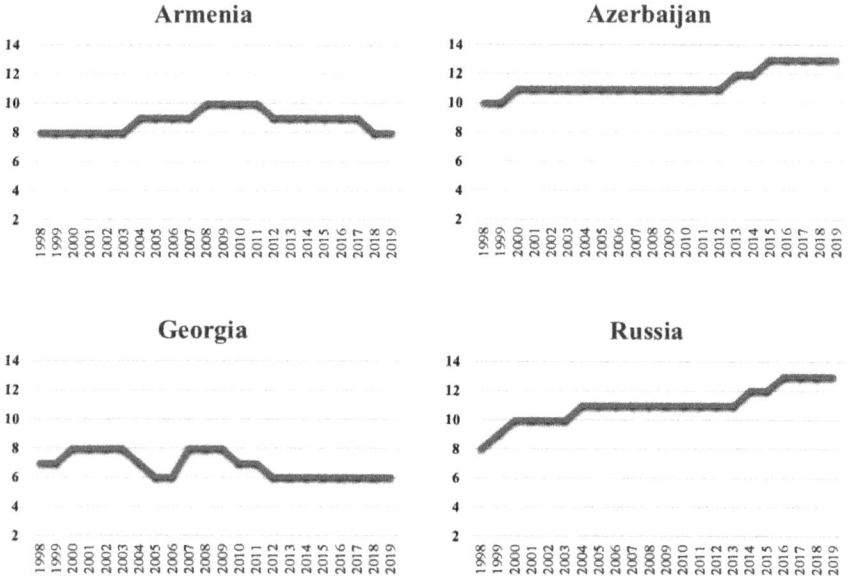

Figure 2.2 Freedom House scores for Azerbaijan, Armenia, Georgia and Russia (1998–2019)

Source: https://freedomhouse.org/sites/default/files/2020-02/2020_Country_and_Territory_Ratings_and_Statuses_FIW1973-2020.xlsx
Note: Political Rights (range 1–7) and Civil Liberties (range 1–7) combined. The lowest possible score is 2 (most free) and the maximum possible score is 14 (least free).

ranged from 10 to 13 since becoming an independent country. Most dramatically, since 1997, Russia's Freedom House scores have ranged from 7 to 13, a much more volatile pattern. Unfortunately, the curve has been in the wrong direction for Russia, as it has become steadily less democratic since the mid-1990s.

Modern Georgian history has been punctuated by democratic breakthroughs and serious setbacks. There was the Rose Revolution in 2003–4 and the GD electoral victory in 2012; the late Shevardnadze years leading up to 2003 represented a democratic rollback, as did the last few years of UNM rule between 2008 and 2012. However, the data reminds us that there has been much less change in the state of Georgian democracy over these years than we might suppose if we just looked at the peaks and troughs. Focusing on democratic breakthroughs overlooks the less interesting, at first glance, possibility that dramatic changes at the top, though exciting, did not have a dramatic impact on the underlying and overall progress of Georgia's democracy.

The story of democracy and its relation to foreign policy in Georgia cannot be complete without examining the extent to which governments, particularly the United States, but also those of less influential states like Poland and the Baltics, continued to believe that the UNM was a democratizing force in Georgia long after that notion had lost its credibility among the Georgian citizenry. The story of the Rose Revolution, complete with the young English-speaking hero Mikheil Saakashvili, and a youthful government deeply familiar with the buzzwords and jargon of democracy, was too powerful for Western politicians to resist. The initial successes of the Saakashvili administration in areas such as corruption and judicial reform were genuine and compelling, but the continuing positive responses of Western leaders when liberalism was clearly under threat in Georgia, reflected a tendency to accept the official story over the one of local experience.

The accomplishments of the Saakashvili government came with an intensive public relations attempt to promote the new Georgian government abroad as the face of post-Soviet democracy and reform. The Georgian government sent legions of young English-speaking representatives to Washington, Brussels and other Western capitals to boast of the great strides Georgia was making and of Georgia's efforts to become a free and democratic state. Western powers were impressed by these representatives in no small part because of their age and linguistic skills, and rarely questioned their assertions about Georgia.[23] The early years of the Rose Revolution are often perceived as the most democratic, but according to Freedom House, Georgia made relatively modest advances in this period, from a combined score of 8 in the late Shevardnadze period to a peak of 6, but usually a 7 or an 8. During these alleged halcyon years of democratic progress, Georgia's overall score went from 8 to 6. This is impressive, but hardly the stuff of a major democratic breakthrough. Moreover, within a few short years, that Freedom House composite number had risen again to 8 and remained there throughout the rest of the period of UNM governance. Foreign policymakers, most notably in the United States, either refused to recognize Georgia's limited progress or could not see it. Instead of framing Georgian democracy as frail, or under pressure, Western politicians continued to trumpet the Georgian democratic success story after 2007 and through 2012, by which time the democratic promise of the Rose Revolution had become little more than a memory.

Following a meeting between President Bush and President Saakashvili late in the latter's presidency, George W. Bush remarked: 'I admire the President. I admire what Georgia has gone through and what Georgia is doing. We talked about Georgia's contribution to democracy movements – not only her own, but to democracy and freedom movements in places like Iraq.'[24]

Support for Saakashvili was not a partisan issue for Washington. In 2010, Secretary of State Hillary Clinton commented about Georgia: 'The potential of this country to serve as a beacon and model for democracy and progress is extraordinary, and for me, it is in large measure rooted in day-to-day changes that have occurred here in Georgia.'[25] A year and a half later, reporting on a meeting between the presidents of the two countries, the White House press office described how 'President Obama congratulated President Saakashvili for what he and the people of Georgia have built during this period – an independent, sovereign, and democratic nation. Georgia has made impressive progress in strengthening democratic institutions, fighting corruption, and advancing its ties with Euro-Atlantic institutions.'[26]

The GD's defeat of the UNM in 2012 was, in many respects a democratic breakthrough following the declining years of the Saakashvili administration.

However, policymakers, particularly in Washington, refused to recognize it as such. For the first year after the 2012 election, the GD victory was perceived by many in Washington as something between a fluke and a coup. A December 2012 letter from five US Senators, Democrats and Republicans, warned the new Georgian government that:

> We are deeply troubled by reports of detentions, investigations, imprisonment and allege persecution of political figures associated with the opposition party in Georgia … We write today to express our growing concerns about the possibility that these moves are politically motivated and designed to settle political scores in the aftermath of the recent election.[27]

This reflected the view from Washington that the new government was somehow a threat to the democracy the UNM had created. The GD administration did not make the situation any easier for itself. Shortly after the election, it substantially reduced the amount of resources devoted to the government's public relations in the West. It stopped promoting Georgia's democratic and pro-Western story and assumed a much lower profile. This contrast in approach contributed to the shortcomings of Western understanding of Georgian politics, and revealed the power of public relations and strategic communication. But it also has policy implications for both Georgia and its Western allies. During the Saakashvili era, assistance continued along with democracy programmes based on the view that the government was a supporter of democratic reform. There was little external pressure on Georgia to prove its democratic credentials during these years.

Democracy regressed in Georgia from 2008–12. The United States and other Western powers failed to prevent this democratic rollback, blinded in part by the slick lobbying of the Saakashvili administration. Moreover, following the 2008 war, legitimate concerns about Georgia's security in the West pushed democracy-related issues into the background. As the GD arrested or indicted several high-ranking members of the former UNM government, including former Prime Minister Vano Merabashvili and former President Mikheil Saakashvili, the perception of a narrowing of democracy persisted. But the decision to arrest or indict former government officials is always a complex one, and there was a legal case to be made against a number of former ministers.[28] There are legitimate reasons why the new Georgian government should or should not have taken action against former government members, but Western leaders saw it as prima facie evidence of the nefarious and non-democratic intentions of the GD. Fewer than three months into the GD's tenure, a bipartisan group of US Senators including Republicans John McCain, Lindsay Graham and James Risch, along with Democrat Jeanne Shaheen and independent Joe Lieberman, signed a letter to the new Georgian government which scolded the Georgian leadership while ignoring the nature of the UNM regime:

> We are deeply troubled by reports of detentions, investigations, imprisonment and allege persecution of political figures associated with the opposition party in Georgia. We write today to express our growing concerns about the

possibility that these moves are politically motivated and designed to settle political scores in the aftermath of the recent election. We urge you to ensure that your administration does everything necessary to avoid even the perception of selective justice against member of the previous government.[29]

Georgia's efforts to establish a democratic regime in the years following the Cold War occurred in a world where the word democracy bestowed unique legitimacy on any regime, and several distinctly non-democratic regimes sought to present themselves as liberal democracies despite obvious authoritarian features. One important example of this is Russia where long-time President Vladimir Putin sought to persuade the world that his transparently non-democratic regime represented a new type of polity called a 'sovereign democracy'.[30] Western policymakers have struggled to determine what a democracy is. For many it has become shorthand for a country that is pro-Western, more or less market-oriented and led by somebody under fifty who speaks English. George Bush, Vice President Biden and others overlooked the problems of democracy in Georgia while praising Saakashvili and his allies who all had these attributes. This reflects a wilful naivety on the part of American and European leaders. The UNM leaders understood that if they checked the three boxes – market-oriented, pro-Western and young English-speaking – nobody would look too closely at their record, which included harassing political opponents, limiting freedoms of speech and assembly, and high-level corruption.

Western ideas on democracy-making in Georgia

Democracy promotion in Georgia must be understood within the context of democracy promotion in the post-Cold War era more generally. While democracy promotion has been a significant part of Georgia's political development, it has also been, for several decades, the default setting of the American presence in most of the world's less affluent and less powerful countries.[31] It is a standard part of both American foreign assistance and American bilateral relations with many countries. Georgia has received more than its share of democracy assistance from Western states. According to the Congressional Research Service, in the 2000s 'Georgia became the largest per capita recipient of US aid in Europe and Eurasia.'[32] This is partially because Georgia has consistently been more receptive than most other countries in the region to political and economic reform. The hope was that Georgia, with assistance, would consolidate those gains and move firmly and irreversibly towards democracy. This view has long shaped the perceptions of donor countries. Money spent on democracy promotion in Georgia has, for this reason, been understood to be a better investment than similar programmes in, for example, Russia or Azerbaijan.

Georgia has been the recipient of significant democracy support because the country has, for decades, demonstratively aligned itself with the West. Democracy promotion in Georgia has taken many forms including programmes by major American democracy organizations like the National Democratic Institute (NDI) and the International Republican Institute (IRI). They have given support to Georgian NGOs for domestic election monitoring efforts and a range of programmes, often implemented by American contractors, aimed at strengthening legislatures, supporting civil society, helping local governments and bringing women into politics.[33] But the impact of these programmes has been mixed and has evolved over the years. It is not easy to determine what democracy promotion can accomplish or whether these programmes matter at all. The data that is available, including the level of democracy expenditures from various US government agencies, or changes in scores and rankings by organizations like Freedom House, have, in the end, only limited value. They prove correlation, but there are many possible causal factors which have not been properly examined. In broad terms, in the pre-Rose Revolution years from 1995–2002, the activities of Western democracy promotion played a positive but limited role in Georgia. During these years, Eduard Shevardnadze charted a course for Georgia that was semi-democratic. The country was more free than democratic. There was more freedom for the media, for speech and assembly than elsewhere in the South Caucasus, but democratic institutions such as elections were frail, the state was weak and corruption was rampant.

Among the most important Western democracy promotion activities during the Shevardnadze era was the establishment of strong financial, technical and political support to Georgian NGOs. NGOs including watchdog groups, media outlets, election monitors and similar groups, were instrumental in Georgia's emergence in the 1990s as one of the South Caucasus's most pluralistic states. Without Western support these NGOs would not have had sufficient resources and would have had very limited access to information and expertise. The Rose Revolution reflected the apex of democracy promotion in Georgia. Democracy promotion did not play a central role in the Rose Revolution as suggested by Russian propaganda, but it was still very important.[34] The parallel vote tabulation (PVT) that was so instrumental in persuading the Georgian people, and ultimately foreign governments, of just how widespread election fraud was, was the product of Western democracy promotion, as was ISFED – which executed the PVT. A number of other civil society organizations which drew attention to the corruption and democratic shortcomings of the late Shevardnadze government, like GYLA, were funded by Western foundations and governments. NDI played a critical role in advising the major political actors in the months and days preceding the Rose Revolution.

The Rose Revolution occurred almost twenty ago. We are now further removed from the events of 2003–4, than those events were from the collapse of the Soviet Union, yet the Rose Revolution remains the highest profile accomplishment of the democracy promotion project in Georgia. Since that time democracy promotion efforts in Georgia have struggled to have a meaningful impact. Since 2003, there have been some positive contributions in the field of Western democracy promotion, in particular ongoing support for election monitoring. However, in other ways, the record has been quite mixed.

Crafting meaningful democracy promotion policies in the last decade has proven difficult. The UNM and, to a much lesser extent, the GD were adept at feigning action on democracy while frequently doing very little. Foreign powers have not recognized and confronted this issue adequately. By contrast, in the early years of the post-Soviet era in Georgia, it was relatively easy to craft and fund programmes that provided information on democracy building as well as basic skills.

Over time, the appetite for these basic kinds of democracy-building programmes began to wane. Georgia became increasingly saturated with Western NGOs and their activities. More and more citizens became exposed to the democracy and community-building ideas through training initiatives, workshops and other projects. This was particularly true among the political and civic elites. By 2006–10, the roadblocks to democracy in Georgia were political in nature, but the programmes aimed at breaking down those roadblocks remained too technical in character and did not wrestle with the real obstacles in the political realm. Some of the problems Western organizations encountered in crafting meaningful democracy programmes in Georgia after 2012 reflected broader, global conditions. In the years following the Rose Revolution, Western states' democracy strategies in Georgia recognized the significance of the democratic breakthrough and sought to work closely with the new government to accelerate democratic reform in Georgia. This made sense at first, but as the initial democratic promise of the Rose Revolution waned, this proved less effective. Overemphasizing the democratic aspects of the post-Rose Revolution Georgia made it more difficult to recognize the problems. Many were stuck in the tautology, thinking that the West cooperated with the Georgian government because the government was committed to democracy, and that the proof that government was committed to democracy was the extent to which Western powers worked with it. The result was that Western governments in the end did little to combat the democratic rollback of the late UNM years and failed to stop Georgia's evolution into a semi-authoritarian regime during the period 2009–12. The US government in particular was not prepared for the anger that the UNM fuelled among ordinary Georgians, which led to the GD's decisive election victory in 2012. This contributed to the US view of the GD as neither a strong political force, nor as an engine of democracy in Georgia. Neither did the new Georgian government have a lot of confidence in the Western project of democracy promotion.

Tensions within Georgian democracy

The Western role in Georgia's democratic development since 1991 has been encumbered by the tension between the West's preferred paradigms for framing Georgia's political development and the reality of that development. Western governments have long viewed Georgia through metaphor, characterized by phrases such as 'the country is going in the right direction', or it is 'on the wrong path', or it is 'veering off the democratic track', 'experiencing a setback' and so on. It all suggests that Georgia is a progressive and dynamic country, but that every step backward requires an immediate response, and that every step forward represents momentum upon which further gains can be built. From a funding perspective, every step backwards demonstrates the need for more programmes and funding to stop further backsliding while every step forward is an opportunity for more funding that will build on the momentum. There is a logic to this, but it is a bureaucratic, rather than a political, logic.

This framework is myopic, unhelpful and not supported by reality. It is myopic because it places greater emphasis on trends over periods of a few months and occasionally a few years, rather than longer more enduring patterns. This suggests a much more dynamic political experience for Georgia than the broader perspective, which in the context of the last thirty years indicates slower, steadier progress toward democracy. In almost any given year, events in Georgia might suggest democratic progress or democratic regression. This indicates to the outside observer that Georgia's path towards democracy is characterized by vacillation, rather than stability or relatively slow change. This way of thinking has made it harder to craft programmes based on longer term trends. Instead of thinking in terms of an interrupted journey toward democratic consolidation, Western leaders would be better served looking at Georgian democracy as the politics of cycles and continuity.

Seeing Georgia's democratic development as cyclical would lead to different policy approaches toward democracy building in Georgia. Since independence, Georgia has seen the consolidation of one-party governance which has had a distinctively negative impact, often followed by regime collapse and the emergence of a new political force, as in 1992, 2003 and 2012. These sudden changes of power have often been perceived as a democratic breakthroughs, but it should be interpreted rather as part of a political cycle. This pattern has always been evident in Georgia, first the rise, consolidation and collapse of Zviad Gamsakhurdia's Round Table, second the rise and fall of Shevardnadze's Citizen's Union of Georgia, and then the same with Saakashvili's UNM. It is not yet clear whether GD's time in power is following a similar pattern.

Thus, for most of the last thirty years, Georgia has not moved closer to or further away from democracy. It has wavered between semi-democratic and semi-authoritarian periods. For most of the first decade of independence, Georgia was semi-democratic. There was freedom of speech and assembly, but corruption was rampant, elections were undemocratic and the state was weak. The Rose Revolution ended that situation, but not, as was thought at the time, by moving the country closer to democracy, but by shifting over time to a semi-authoritarian regime. As early as 2006, Georgia under the UNM was showing signs of becoming less free, but also less corrupt.

There is yet another interpretation of Georgian political development. When we step back from our reading of presidential statements, watching disputes in parliament, crackdowns on civil liberties or the most recent elections in October/November 2020, a different picture of Georgia emerges. This picture is one of continuity. In this picture, the main players change, but the general character of

Georgian political life changes much more slowly. While it is hard to dispute the notion that Georgia is a more affluent, stable and democratic country than it was fifteen or twenty-five years ago, that change has been gradual and may be better understood as regime consolidation, rather than regime change.

The consolidation and collapse of one-party governments and the vacillation between more or fewer freedoms, are differences of degree, not of kind. The lives of ordinary Georgians have by some measures steadily improved over the last decade. For example, according to the World Bank, in constant dollars, per capita income increased by 52 per cent between 2008 and 2018.[35] However, this in and of itself is insufficient evidence of democratic development. Yet, central to understanding Georgian politics is the need to look at the bigger picture and to avoid the methodological rabbit hole of overanalysing the events of last week, last month or last year.

Conclusion

There are at least five dimensions that have framed the international context of Georgia's democratic aspirations: first, the role and importance of democracy in Georgia's foreign policy; second, Georgia's varying commitment to democracy; third, Russia's impact on Georgian democracy and foreign relations in the region; fourth, foreign assessments of the state of democracy in Georgia and the ways in which the international context impacts relations between Russia and the West; and fifth, the degree and nature of interventions in Georgia, and the ability of external actors to understand and address Georgia's democratic deficits. All of these dimensions have changed over the last thirty years, creating new and sometimes unforeseen obstacles, challenges and opportunities.

The role of foreign powers in Georgia's political development has been complex. Some powers, like the United States, have sought to make Georgia more democratic, while others, notably Russia, have sought to undermine Georgia and Georgian democracy. Georgia has been the recipient of tens of millions of dollars in direct democracy assistance and of billions more in overall assistance from the West. It has also been among the most frequent target of Moscow's belligerence in the form of military intervention, and other efforts by Russia to manipulate Georgia's domestic politics. Through all this, Georgia's democratic development has occurred in a relatively small bandwidth, with only relatively minor changes in the state of its overall democracy.

Major events, notably the Rose Revolution in 2003–4 and the upset victory by the Georgian Dream in 2012, have contributed to the notion that democratic development in Georgia during these years has been dynamic and fast paced. However, a wider lens suggests that continuity and cycles are a better way to understand political development in Georgia, particularly since the mid-1970s. The paradox of Georgian democracy is that while there have been ample Western resources dedicated to supporting its democratic efforts though critical elections, a 'revolution', and war, upon closer inspection, not all that much has changed in Georgia.

Notes

1   1992 was the first full year of Georgian independence following the collapse of the USSR. It was also the year that Eduard Shevardnadze became Georgia's leader; 2003 was the year that the Rose Revolution ousted Shevardnadze from power; 2012 was the year that Bidzina Ivanishvili's Georgian Dream coalition defeated Saakashvili's United National Movement in a parliamentary election, effectively bringing an end to the Saakashvili era.

2   https://carnegieendowment.org/2011/11/29/foreign-assistance-to-what-degree-has-western-aid-helped-armenia-azerbaijan-and-georgia-pub-46179; https://carnegieendowment.org/2012/12/18/supporting-democracy-in-georgia-and-ukraine-time-for-rethink-event-3904

3   'After more than a decade of turmoil and decline, Georgia has emerged as one of the world's most dynamic laboratories of democracy. The major event in this new chapter of its history is the Rose Revolution. A three-week period of political intrigue and public demonstrations in November 2003 led to Eduard Shevardnadze's resignation, and the result was that a demoralised and lethargic society suddenly seemed to turn into an energetic experiment in democracy.' Zurab Karumidze and James Wertsch, *Enough! The Rose Revolution in the Republic of Georgia 2003* (New York: Nova Science Publishers, 2005), p. vii.

4   Ronald Asmus, *A Little War that Shook the World: Georgia, Russia, and the Future of the West* (London: St. Martin's Press, 2010).

5   'About Georgia', USAID, www.usaid.gov/georgia

6   Damien McGuinness, 'Georgia's Elections: Furious PR Battle for Western Minds', BBC News, 20 September 2012, www.bbc.com/news/world-europe-19638775

7   Michael Specter, 'Rainy Days in Georgia', *The New Yorker,* 18 December 2000, pp. 54–63.

8   See www.coe.int/en/web/tbilisi/the-coe/objectives-and-missions

9   Stephen Kinzer, 'Tbilisi Journal: The "Man of the Year" Just 29 and via Manhattan', *New York Times,* 4 June 1998. The primary subject of the article was Saakashvili himself who had left his job at a Manhattan law firm to go back to Georgia.

10   'Speech Delivered by President Mikheil Saakashvili at George Washington University', Mikheil Saakashvili Presidential Archives, 23 February 2004, www.saakashviliarchive.info/en/PressOffice/News?p=2778&i=1

11   'Bush: Georgia "Beacon of Liberty"', CNN.com, 10 May 2005, www.cnn.com/2005/WORLD/europe/05/10/bush.tuesday/

12   'Georgia: Government Used Excessive Force on Protesters', Human Rights Watch, 17 December 2007.

13   'The toasts made by the President of Georgia and Vice President of the United States at the official dinner', Saakashvili Presidential Archive, 22 July 2009.

14   For the full 2012 electoral programme, see www.ivote.ge/images/doc/pdfs/ocnebis%20saarchevno%20programa.pdf, p. 4.

15   See, for example, Giga Bokeria, 'First Ukraine, Now Georgia', *Foreign Policy,* 8 February 2014; 'No Change for the Better', *The Economist,* 12 October 2013; 'Will Political Crisis Derail Georgia's Future', Wilfried Martens Centre, 13 November 2014, www.martenscentre.eu/sites/default/files/event_report_georgia_eod.pdf

16   'EPP outraged at re-arrest and political suppression of Georgian Opposition Leader Ugulava' EPP Press Release, 15 September 2015, www.epp.eu/press-releases/1015/

17 'Remarks by The Vice President to The Georgian Parliament', The White House, 23 July 2009, https://obamawhitehouse.archives.gov/the-press-office/remarks-vice-president-georgian-parliament

18 Mikheil Saakashvili, 'Russia's War is the West's Challenge', *The Washington Post*, 14 August 2007.

19 https://freedomhouse.org/reports/freedom-world/freedom-world-research-methodology. Freedom House reports conditions in the year before the report is issued, so the 1992 report describes Georgia in 1991, the 1993 report covers Georgia in 1992, etc. Freedom House relies upon consultants and experts to write these reports and assign scores, so it is open to a degree of subjectivity as well as, in some cases, political pressure. For more on this, see Diego Giannone, 'Political and Ideological Aspects in the Measurement of Democracy: The Freedom House Case', *Democratization*, 17:1 (2010), pp. 68–97.

20 See www.eiu.com/topic/democracy-index; https://infographics.economist.com/2019/DemocracyIndex/

21 Prior to the 2020 edition, Freedom in the World assigned a country or territory two ratings – one for political rights and one for civil liberties – based on its total scores for the political rights and civil liberties questions. Each rating of 1 to 7, with 1 representing the greatest degree of freedom and 7 the smallest degree of freedom, corresponded to a specific range of total scores. The average of the ratings determined the status of Free, Partly Free, or Not Free. While the underlying formula for converting scores into status remains identical, starting in the 2020 edition Freedom in the World no longer presented the 1–7 ratings as a separate element of its findings. The ratings are still included in the raw data available for download.

22 Ghia Nodia, 'Civil Society Development in Georgia: Achievements and Challenges', Caucasus Institute for Peace, 2005, Democracy and Development Citizens Advocate! Program.

23 For more on this see Thomas de Waal, 'So Long, Saakashvili', *Foreign Affairs,* 29 October 2013.

24 'President Bush Meets with President Saakashvili of Georgia', The White House, 19 March 2008. https://georgewbush-whitehouse.archives.gov/news/releases/2008/03/20080319-4.html. Hilary Clinton had something similar to say in 2010: 'The potential of this country to serve as a beacon and model for democracy and progress is extraordinary, and for me, it is in large measure is rooted in day-to-day changes that have occurred here in Georgia.' Hillary Clinton, 2010, www.rferl.org/a/Clinton_Heads_To_Georgia/2091014.html

25 'Clinton Pledges US Support for Georgia', *RFE/RL*, 5 July 2010, www.rferl.org/a/Clinton_Heads_To_Georgia/2091014.html

26 'President Obama Meets with Georgian President Mikheil Saakashvili', The White House, 3 February 2012, https://obamawhitehouse.archives.gov/blog/2012/02/03/president-obama-meets-georgian-president-mikheil-saakashvili

27 Josh Rogin, 'Senators Call on Georgian Prime Minister to Avoid Political Retribution', *Foreign Policy*, 11 December 2012. The Senators were Jeanne Shaheen (D-NH) Joseph Lieberman (I-CT), Lindsay Graham (R-SC), John McCain (R-AZ) and James Risch (R-ID).

28 For more on this, see Kenneth S. Yalowitz, William Courtney and Dennis Courtney, 'Rough and Tumble of Building Democracy in Georgia', Wilson Center, www.wilsoncenter.org/publication/rough-and-tumble-building-democracy-georgia

29 Josh Rogin, 'Senators Call on Georgian Prime Minister to Avoid Political Retribution', *Foreign Policy*, 11 December 2012.

30 See Maria Lipman, 'Putin's "Sovereign Democracy"', *The Washington Post*, 15 July 2006.

31 For more on this see Lincoln A. Mitchell, *The Democracy Promotion Paradox* (Washington: Brookings, 2016).

32 'Georgia: Background and US Policy', Congressional Research Service, 17 October 2009, p. 17.

33 'In Georgia, NDI worked with 14 political parties to sign the Win with Women Global Action Plan', which recommends internal reforms to boost women's participation. See www.ndi.org/democracy-without-women-is-impossible

34 For more on this see Lincoln A. Mitchell, *Uncertain Democracy: US Foreign Policy and Georgia's Rose Revolution* (Philadelphia: Pennsylvania University Press, 2008).

35 GDP Per Capita: Georgia, The World Bank, https://data.worldbank.org/indicator/NY.GDP.PCAP.KD?locations=GE

Chapter 3

THE GEORGIAN ORTHODOX CHURCH AS A FOREIGN POLICY ACTOR

Salome Minesashvili

As Tracey German and Kornely Kakachia note in their introductory contribution, since 1991, closer relations with the West have remained a central pillar of Georgia's foreign policy. However, the value and identity aspects of this direction are contentious in the domestic arena, particularly among leading circles in the Georgian Orthodox Church (GOC). Theoretically, the church deals with the spiritual and moral dimension of society, whereas the state focuses on policy formation and implementation, on national security, and on foreign policy. However, rarely is the distinction so clear, and the church and state often intersect, especially in a highly religious country like Georgia. According to the 2014 general population census, the majority (84 per cent) considers itself Orthodox Christian; other groups include Muslims (10 per cent), Armenian Apostolic (3 per cent) and Catholics (0.5 per cent).[1] Measured by Georgians' own assessment of their religiosity, Georgia is one of the most religious countries in the world. In 2015, 94 per cent of the Georgian population believed religion played an important role in their lives.[2] The GOC is the most trusted and most favoured institution among Georgians.[3] Given its unchallenged popularity, the GOC has the capability to influence Georgia's foreign policy. This chapter will highlight the intersection between foreign policy and the Georgian Orthodox Church and examine the ways in which the GOC impacts foreign policy. Throughout its history, the Georgian Orthodox Church has aspired to influence Georgia's relations with other states. Christianity is an integral part of Georgian identity, formed by a long history of struggle against Muslim invaders. In that sense, the GOC has always been part of Georgia's foreign relations.

The level of the GOC involvement in political life has been diverse over the centuries, dependent on state policies, engagement with foreign powers, and on personal relations between the Patriarch and royal leaders. During the Middle Ages, the GOC complemented the state – it blessed the army and its kings, and helped organize resistance against foreign enemies. In the nineteenth century under Russian rule, it remained a symbol of Georgian identity despite its absorption into the Russian Orthodox Church and a general decline in its integrity, especially at the village level. In the Soviet period, the Georgian church continued to complement state foreign policy but under the tight control of an imperial atheistic state. After Georgian independence in 1991, the church gradually developed into the most powerful and most trusted institution in Georgian society. Its involvement with domestic and foreign policy reached a new high in the 2000s.

Georgia's foreign policy over the last two decades has drawn religious actors into its orbit. Since the Rose Revolution in 2003, there has been an intensification of Georgia's pro-Western foreign policy. Georgia's belonging to the West is interpreted as 'civilizational'. The country belongs, it is claimed 'to the European cultural and value system'.[4] Georgia's striving for a European identity contrasts to the Eurasian, Russian and Asian identities linked by Georgian media and politicians with backwardness and conservatism. Russia is seen as the major 'other', which challenges progressive and European Georgia. Orthodox Christianity occupies a large role in the notion of Georgianness, and religion and church naturally become part of the battle over identity.

Yet Georgian state policy is often in tension with the church's version of identity. While Georgia's politicians embrace Western values, the Georgian Orthodox Church is hostile to Western ideas, considering them inimical to traditional Christian values.[5] Georgia's pro-Western foreign policy excludes Orthodox Russia. This raises discontent among some groups in the GOC who consider religion an important marker for selecting allies. They argue that Eastern Orthodoxy is under threat and in need of protection. Such a view drives the GOC closer to the Russian Orthodox Church (ROC) and into involvement with foreign policy aimed at protecting Georgia from 'Western values'.

The GOC has been connected to Georgian foreign policy in two ways. First, it is concerned with foreign policy issues that connect with morality and values. The GOC was actively opposed to Georgian anti-discrimination legislation in the spring of 2014, which was part of the package of reforms promised as a result of Georgia's 2014 Association Agreement with the EU. GOC members participated in the discussion at the parliamentary and presidential levels and lobbied hard against the bill. The bill condemns all types of discrimination including those based on language, gender, religion and sexual orientation, and was a precondition for visa facilitation with the European Union. The GOC opposed the law, arguing that it was against Georgian traditions and a deadly sin since it included the words 'sexual orientation' and 'gender identity'.[6] However, despite ideological resistance to the West, the GOC as an institution has not shown open opposition to the West as a political ally. On the contrary, the Patriarch makes favourable statements on the virtue of Georgia's European path. The GOC is not a homogenous institution and the positions of different groups often contradict one another.

The second way in which the GOC engages with foreign policy is as an independent foreign policy player. The GOC, for example, maintains good relations with Russia and the ROC, even following the Russo-Georgian War in August 2008, after which diplomatic relations between the two states ended. Between 2008 and 2016, the Patriarch visited Russia five times on religious missions. He has met with Russian politicians and proposed a mediating role for the GOC in Georgian–Russian conflicts. The Patriarch's visit to Moscow in December 2008, where he attended the funeral of the Patriarch of Russia, included a meeting with President Dimitri Medvedev. This visit, according to former President Mikheil Saakashvili, was discussed beforehand and welcomed by the Georgian government.[7] However, some later visits were not agreed upon with the government.[8] The church, as an independent foreign policy player, often takes its own initiative. It has been accused of carrying out a pro-Russian foreign policy but the GOC's interests and motivations are complex. The Georgian Orthodox Church's foreign policy varies according to its interests, and interests can change according to shifting conditions.

This chapter hopes to explain the extent to which the Georgian Orthodox Church influences Georgia's foreign policy by direct or indirect involvement; to what extent must Georgia's foreign policy decision makers take the church's position into account. To answer such questions, this chapter will evaluate GOC behaviour and attitudes as reflected in its statements on foreign policy. It will try and determine the degree to which GOC views impact government policy. The first section will provide a historical overview of the GOC's foreign policy involvement. It will briefly cover the long period from early church history until 2003. The second section will deal with the period from the Rose Revolution onwards, when the GOC's role in Georgian political life in the twenty-first century becomes more public and more powerful. The conclusion will sum up the main patterns of church behaviour in Georgia's foreign policy since independence.

History of the Georgian Orthodox Church in Georgian foreign relations

The GOC before the Soviet Union

The notion of Georgianness has always been tightly intertwined with religion, not only for Georgians themselves, but also in the eyes of Georgia's neighbours. The church was always central to political life and especially to Georgian relations with neighbouring powers, such as the Byzantine, Persian and Ottoman Empires. During the Persian, Arab, Mongol and Turkish invasions of Georgia throughout the medieval period, the Georgian church was one of the main targets of foreign powers. There was little relief under the Russian Empire in the nineteenth century, as the ROC adopted a hostile attitude to Georgian religious autonomy. The GOC suffered as an institution, and the Georgian clergy were systematically persecuted.

Georgia converted to Orthodox Christianity in the fourth century. It was founded as a state church, which became largely self-governing in the fifth century and fully self-governing in the seventh century. In the eleventh century, the Georgian Orthodox Church achieved full autocephaly. After the inauguration of the first Patriarch Melkisedek I (1010–33), according to historian Zaza Abashidze 'the Church was fully independent in its domestic and foreign relations'.[9] In the eleventh century, after Melkisedek visited Constantinople, the Georgian patriarchate received official recognition as an independent church.[10]

The Georgian Orthodox Church has long been a symbol of Georgian values expressed through religious customs, traditions, festivals, music, literature and visual arts. The church became the focus of Georgian cultural identity, and a mechanism for self-preservation during periods of oppression by external forces.[11] On many occasions, the church actively participated in the struggle against foreign enemies. For example, during the war between Georgia and Byzantium in the first half of the eleventh century, the church organized military units in Georgian regions.[12] The hierarch Giorgi Mtasmindeli, head of the Iveron Monastery on Mount Athos in Greece, was an important part of the delegation during the negotiations and meetings of Georgian King Bagrat IV in Constantinople in 1054–57.[13] Georgian church representatives directly participated in governing the country. David IV Aghmashenebeli (1073–1125) created a new position called *mtsignobartukhutses-chkondideli*, which united the ecclesiastical position of Bishop of Chkondidi and the secular position of chancellor. This position was occupied by the second most powerful actor in the kingdom and was highly influential in foreign policy.

Eastern Georgia entered the Russian Empire willingly in the early nineteenth century in its search for an Orthodox Christian patron, though the removal of the Georgian monarchy along with rights of self-government was unexpected and deeply resented by Georgian elites. It was a challenging relationship for the GOC. The GOC lost its formal independent status in 1811 and remained under constant pressure from the Russian Orthodox Church. Its reduced power weakened its role in political life, but individual members resisted Russian policies. In 1801 Tsarist troops entered Tbilisi, led by the cross of St Nino, a symbol of protection and God's mercy.[14] The church members welcomed Russian representatives who, it was thought, would protect Georgia from its Islamic enemies. Archbishop Ambrosi of Nekresi, addressed his flock with the following statement:

> Our enemies will be crushed by his majesty`s power and we shall be forever saved from the Muslim yoke. Georgia shall be delivered from the bonds of hell. Weep not and grieve not, for Georgia is saved and our enemies, the Persians, have fallen![15]

But such optimism was not justified. The East Georgian kingdom of Kartl'Kakheti was abolished against the terms of the Russian–Georgian Georgievsk Treaty (24 July 1783), and in 1811, the Russian Empire removed the autocephaly of the Georgian Orthodox Church. Within ten years, the Georgian church became subordinate to the Holy Synod of Russia. A Russian Exarch replaced the Patriarch.[16] The Russian Empire interfered in all the affairs of the Georgian church and introduced centralizing 'reforms'. The church's property was nationalized and the Georgian language was almost entirely eradicated from church services.[17]

After the abolition of autocephaly in 1811, the Georgian clergy fought for its restoration. Resistance included raising the matter in St Petersburg, not only before the Russian Church but also by appeals to the secular authorities.[18] But resistance by the GOC was poorly organized and the church was weak. Effective institutional resistance was out of the question. It was primarily individual members of the church who took action. In 1819, discontent with the closure of Georgian churches, the eviction of clergymen and a new tax, caused protests and armed rebellion in Western Georgia. Church representatives took part in the uprising. Two hierarchs, Metropolitan Dositheos of Kutaisi and Metropolitan Euphemios of Gelati, were accused of leading the rebellion.[19] There were numerous instances of resistance to Russification. Churchmen Gabriel Kikodze and Alexander Okropiridze, for example, strongly criticized the Exarch for dismissing Georgian teachers from theological schools.[20]

At the end of the nineteenth century, the issue of church autocephaly became a central part of the Georgian national movement, headed by Ilia Chavchavadze. The national movement included clergymen like Bishops Kirion Sadzaglishvili and Leonide Okropiridze, Archimandrite Ambrosi Khelaia and Archpriest Kalistrate Tsintsadze.[21] The Russian government feared restoration of autocephaly would be followed by demands for political independence, and strongly resisted Georgian petitions and prolonged investigative commissions.[22] The restoration of autocephaly came just before the renewed political independence of Georgia (26 May 1918). In March 1917, the autocephaly of the GOC was declared in Svetitskhoveli cathedral after coordination between the clergy and Georgian political leaders, including Noe Jordania, a Social Democrat, and future leader of the Democratic Republic of Georgia (1918–21). The Russian Orthodox Church refused to restore the Eucharistic communion with the Orthodox Church of Georgia. The restoration of autocephaly was followed by political independence. The GOC assumed its active role in the country's political life.[23] However, its influence was constrained by the policies of the new socialist government under Noe Jordania, who believed in separation of church and state. The government declared the GOC would not enjoy any privilege above other religious bodies and banned religious teaching in schools.[24]

The short period of independence was followed by the Soviet annexation of Georgia in 1921, after which the GOC once again became an object of brutal oppression. The GOC continued to resist and in 1922, Patriarch Ambrosi Khelaia appealed to the International Peace Conference in Genoa, which was discussing reparation claims arising from the First World War, with an open letter. The Patriarch urged the twenty-eight nations present not to abandon his country to Soviet Russia:

> The occupiers seek to convince everybody at home and abroad that they have brought freedom to the Georgians and have made them happy. But I, as the spiritual father of the nation and as a priest, am aware of the secret threads coming from the heart of this nation and, hearing its moaning and lamentations, I know better than others just how 'happy' the Georgian nation is.[25]

Soviet Russia's Commissar of Foreign Affairs was put in an embarrassing situation. The Patriarch was arrested with other church leaders, and the church repressed for the rest of the decade.

The GOC in the Soviet Union

During the Soviet period, the Georgian Orthodox Church was unable to maintain any autonomy from the state. The Soviet government, however, saw the GOC as a useful instrument in its foreign policy. After 1921, religious policy in Georgia was directed from Moscow. In the first two decades of the Soviet Union, Soviet laws dramatically weakened the GOC both economically and legally. The GOC tried to maintain external religious ties but without much result. In the 1920s, GOC leaders wrote letters to the Ecumenical Patriarchate of Constantinople, which remained unanswered due to consideration of the position of the Russian Orthodox Church. The latter refused to acknowledge Georgian autocephaly. However, some support came from the United Kingdom, where the Archbishop of Canterbury and primate of England expressed solidarity with the Georgian Orthodox Church.[26]

The GOC tried to use patriotic sentiment during the Second World War to improve its status, and strongly supported the Soviet state's foreign policy. When Germany attacked the Soviet Union in 1941, Patriarch Kalistrate wrote to the Soviet government, and declared the church's commitment to the patriotic cause. The church organized a collection in support of the Red Army, and its legal status as an autocephalic church was restored by Stalin's order in 1943.[27] After the Second World War, existing restrictions on the GOC were relaxed. But the church remained weak and its membership significantly decreased. During the 1950s and 1960s, the USSR under Nikita Khrushchev in particular undertook an active and aggressive anti-religious campaign.[28] During the Khrushchev period (1956–64), the state interfered in church affairs through the Soviet supervisory body known as the Council for Religious Affairs. At the same time, the GOC became more active in the Orthodox world by becoming a member of the World Council of Churches (WCC). However, it had very limited influence on the international affairs of the Soviet Union or Georgia. The GOC was a useful tool for Soviet influence in the World Council of Churches.[29] Georgian Patriarch Epremi in 1965, in typical fashion, praised the programme of the Communist Party and suggested that church representatives were its firm supporters.[30]

In the 1970s, Eduard Shevardnadze as the new Georgian party boss, launched an anti-religious campaign, and established new Soviet organizations and festivals to try and displace religious traditions. The anti-religious campaign drove Georgian religious followers underground. Religiosity among youth started to increase. In the 1970s the church suffered from internal problems, such as corruption and controversies over the election of the Patriarch. The KGB infiltrated the GOC and was able to influence the elections. The situation changed in the late 1970s, when Ilia Shiolashvili was elected as Patriarch Ilia II. The church improved its position vis-à-vis the Georgian communist leadership. A foreign relations department was established in the Patriarchate. In previous years, the GOC's participation in the Ecumenical movement had remained minimal due to restrictions, but in the 1970s international relations increased with multiple trips of the Georgian clergy to Europe and the United States. In 1979, Patriarch Ilia II became one of the six presidents of the World Council of Churches, which enhanced the image of the church abroad as well as domestically. Ilia II strengthened ties with Anglican and other Protestant churches including Switzerland and Germany and in the 1980s re-established relations with the Roman Catholic Church. In 1980, Ilia II visited the Vatican to meet Pope John-Paul II. However, the church still had to stay in line with official policy, including foreign policy. Thus, the church condemned right-wing militias in Lebanon, the Chinese invasion of Vietnam, the neutron bomb and praised the peace programme of the Soviet Union. Domestically it celebrated the 1783 Treaty of Georgievsk with the Russian Empire. However, in one case the Patriarch went against state policy and in 1980 signed a statement of the World Council of Churches condemning the invasion of Afghanistan.[31]

During the Gorbachev era, the conditions for the church eased tremendously as bureaucratic and legal obstacles were removed. Former church members were released from prison and labour camps and returned to the church. But state control remained in place along with allegations about links between the church and the KGB. In the late 1980s, Georgian nationalist movements intensified and the church took an increasingly patriotic stand. Some members took a critical position against the Soviet government, accusing it of an anti-national policy.[32] After independence was declared in 1991, the church once again became a powerful symbol of national unity. The GOC's influence grew dramatically among ordinary Georgians within a few years.

The GOC after independence: 1991–2003

After independence, the GOC re-emerged as a powerful institution that managed to fill the ideological vacuum left by the collapse of the Soviet Union and by weak state institutions, corruption and an economic and social crisis. The GOC became the only institution with consistently high public trust. Its foreign policy involvement was still tentative at this time.[33] President Gamsakhurdia (1991–92) blamed the West for failing to provide support for independent Georgia and adopted a strong nationalistic foreign policy which isolated Georgia from international politics. Until his removal from power in 1992, Gamsakhurdia pursued the idea of a common 'Caucasian Home' which was associated with defending native Caucasian cultures against Western influence.[34] Gamsakhurdia opposed the Georgian Patriarchate as former agents of the Soviet security services, but his religious-messianic rhetoric was in line with the church's own message.[35] State policy aligned with the church's narrative, but the state itself lacked a well-defined foreign policy. It had complicated relations with Russia in which the church remained relatively neutral. During the 9 April 1989 events, when Georgians demonstrated for independence and were slaughtered by Soviet troops (twenty-one were killed in front of the Georgian parliament building), the Patriarch urged the demonstrators to avoid conflict.

After 1992, when Shevardnadze came to power, the church's authority gave it significant leverage. Despite popular support for President Eduard Shevardnadze (elected President in 1995), in the second half of the 1990s state and church foreign policy diverged. State policy became pro-Western and Georgia applied for

NATO membership in 2002. The GOC, on the other hand, rejected the cultural and ideological offerings of the West. The Patriarch voiced the idea of foreign policy neutrality.[36] Increased nationalism and the emergence of fundamentalist groups both within and outside the church, encouraged the GOC to cut its relations with European Christian churches and organizations. In 1997 a group of hierarchs from Shio-Mghvime Monastery, Betania Monastery, the Lavra of David Gareji, the Zarzma Monastery and the Shemokmedi diocese demanded Georgia's withdrawal from ecumenical platforms on the grounds that it was not acceptable for Orthodox Christians to pray next to Protestants and Catholics. This threatened a schism. In May 1997, the Georgian Church withdrew from the WCC and from the Conference of European Churches, though it also suspended the rebellious clergymen from their positions.[37] Thereafter, the Georgian Orthodox Church essentially ceased its relations with Western churches, and took a strong line against the West in ideological terms.

Foreign policy of the GOC since 2003

After the Rose Revolution in 2003, state policy shifted dramatically: it became starkly pro-Western and anti-Russian. Unlike the government, the Georgian Orthodox Church abstained from clear-cut positions on foreign policy, at least on the official level. It rejected an exclusively one-sided attitude and tried to avoid the dichotomy between Russia and the West. When the Patriarch stated his support for Georgia's EU membership in 2014, he added that joining the European structure did not put limitations on relations with other organizations (such as the Russian dominated Eurasian Economic Union).[38] The GOC expressed a contradictory attitude towards the West by voicing both pro- and anti-Western sentiments, and tried to fill in the space that the Georgian government created in its relations with Russia. The GOC has acquired a relatively more active role in its foreign relations with Russia since 2003, but its involvement with Western foreign policy is generally expressed at the domestic level, with attacks on Western values.

Relations with the West

After the Rose Revolution, differences widened between the GOC and the state on foreign policy issues. Official state policy was based on civic nationalism or as Giga Zedania calls it, 'revolutionary nationalism' with inclusive citizenship, but also with heightened distinctions between 'friend' and 'enemy'.[39] State modernization under President Saakashvili became closely linked with foreign policy, with an emphasis on globalization linked to Western economic and political values. The GOC proposed an alternative identity based on ethnic nationalism with biological terminology grounded in theological propositions. The kernel of this narrative is about Orthodoxy saving 'Georgian blood', 'Georgian genes and Georgian identity ... '.[40] Ideologically, the GOC is opposed to the underlying values of Western foreign policy. The GOC insists on defining such values as 'false liberalism'. Opposing such liberal values is not new for Eastern Orthodoxy (nor Catholicism for that matter), but what is different in the case of the GOC is an attempt to relate damaging liberal values to Europe and the United States. Western countries are portrayed as lacking a sense of tradition and proper morality by allowing too much personal freedom and by supporting globalization, cosmopolitanism and modernism.[41] Particular emphasis is on the Western 'perversion' of homosexuality. Homosexuality is contrasted with family values in Georgia that are considered as the basis for society and state strength. Family is also a primary part of Georgianness according to the church, therefore Western values directly pose a threat to Georgian traditions. In his speech in November 2011, the Patriarch said that the 'Georgian nation should take care of its history, past, and traditions; what flows from the West is often unacceptable for Orthodoxy'.[42] This ideological resistance and the myth of the morally depraved West are very strong. When the EU Commissioner Stefan Füle met the Georgian Patriarch in 2014, he had to assure him that EU membership did not mean undermining Georgian traditions.[43]

The GOC, however, has refrained from directly opposing state policy. In several cases it has expressed support. The Patriarch has made statements that are in favour of Georgia's foreign policy priority of integrating with the European Union. During his meeting with Stephen Füle in March 2014, the Patriarch told the European Commissioner that the church would do everything 'to help Georgia become an EU member'.[44] The Patriarch further emphasized his support during a meeting with Austrian President Heinz Fischer. He stated that Georgia's choice of a European path was firm, very much in line with state policy.[45] Such statements of support increased as Georgia–EU relations became closer, including the lifting of visa requirements for Georgians travelling to the EU, and the signing of the EU Association Agreement. The Patriarch again expressed his support. In 2015, during a visit to the Patriarchate by Prime Minister Irakli Gharibashvili and the EU ambassador to Georgia, the Patriarch called Georgian–EU relations a huge achievement. But at the same time, he urged the protection of Georgian culture, underlining the narrative of cultural resistance.[46]

Whereas the church as an institution remains ambivalent towards the West and expresses controversial opinions, this cannot be applied to all of its members. The GOC is a heterogeneous organization. It contains a large group who consider Russia as less of a threat to Georgian values and traditions than the 'West,' because of a common religion. The West is considered to be fighting the Orthodox world. Spiritual apostasy is seen as worse than territorial conflict and Russia, Ukraine and Serbia, as fellow Orthodox countries, are natural allies.[47] The eparchial journal *kvakutkhedi* (The Cornerstone) called the 2008 war between Georgia and Russia 'heavenly pincers which blocked Georgia's drive towards the West. It is God's blessing to submit to the patronage of Russia.'[48] Supporters of such ideas are pro-Russian, but there is also a group in the GOC who see no link between immorality and the West. They assert Georgia is European, and praise certain qualities of the West. They understand there are negative Western values, but suggest they can be avoided.[49]

Today, the GOC pursues a policy of indirect involvement in state policy. The church frequently interferes in legislative debates when they concern the church's interests. In 2014, in response to the anti-discrimination law that was proposed as part of closer integration with the West, the church expressed stark opposition to equal rights for sexual minorities. Church representatives participated in the discussion of the bill and attended plenary meetings in parliament. Eventually the bill was adopted, but with some revisions that took the church's position into consideration. The revised text removed the establishment of an inspector who would have worked against discrimination. The new bill stated that discrimination is only punishable if it does not conflict with public morality, or the Constitutional Agreement with the Orthodox Church.[50] The church joins resistance movements to the rights of sexual minorities in other ways. In May 2013, about fifty pro-LGBT activists at a rally on the International Day Against Homophobia and Transphobia were attacked by a mob. The mob was led by several members of the church, who claimed to be protecting the Georgian nation from negative influences. The Patriarch named the date of the International Day Against Homophobia and Transphobia to be the day of family strength and respect for parents.[51]

Family values are used as the main counter to homosexuality. In 2015 a campaign was launched that proposed a constitutional amendment asserting marriage as the union of a man and woman. Signatures were collected demanding a referendum. The initiators of the proposal were closely connected to the church. Eventually the President vetoed the proposal, but the constitutional committee continued its discussion and parliament finally passed it.[52]

The GOC tries to resist the ideology of the West, but it functions in a complex political reality and has to manoeuvre. State foreign policy remains strongly pro-Western and according to the International Republican Institute (IRI) public opinion polls (2016), about 85 per cent of Georgia's population support EU membership and 80 per cent, NATO membership.[53] This political environment constrains the GOC's political choices; constantly clashing with the government risks its status in society. However, the GOC still maintains a virtual monopoly over the country's moral agenda and resistance to the West remains its central perspective. But it cannot dictate modification of plans for Western integration. The church has to be flexible and consider public opinion and state policy.

Relations with Russia

In relations with Russia, the Georgian Orthodox Church should be considered an independent foreign policy player. The GOC has good relations with the Russian Orthodox Church (ROC), but its relations go beyond friendly contacts between religious actors. The ROC is subordinate to the Russian state. It is one of the main supporters of the *Russkii Mir* (Russian World) project, which aims to integrate post-Soviet Eastern Orthodox peoples into a single political or cultural category.[54] The close relations between the ROC and the Russian state link the GOC to Russian politics. After the August War in 2008, the GOC was far more visible following the cessation of diplomatic relations with Russia, but the church continued to maintain its relations with the ROC.

The two churches support each other when it comes to religious authority in breakaway territories. The Russian state recognized the independence of Georgian breakaway territories, Abkhazia and South Ossetia, in August 2008, yet the ROC supports the canonical integrity of the Georgian Orthodox Church and recognizes its rights to rule over the Abkhazian and South Ossetian churches. However, the ROC's position does not oppose Russian state policy. It is in the Kremlin's interests to maintain the mediating role of the ROC in the Caucasus. The ROC, by supporting the GOC's jurisdiction, maintains its legitimacy in the Orthodox world and avoids pushing the GOC into the camp of the Ecumenical Patriarch.[55] In exchange, the GOC supports the canonical rights of the ROC in Estonia, Moldova and Ukraine. In 2014, when the Russian-Ukrainian military conflict started in Ukraine, the GOC refused to express any position.

The two churches cooperate in the international arena. Their close relations have turned them into political players in the foreign policies of Georgia and Russia. During the 2008 August War, the two churches were the only communication channel between the two countries. Both of them supported their states and expressed nationalist arguments. However, both condemned violence. By maintaining good relations with the ROC, the GOC sees its opportunity to keep the channel for communication open with Russia. The Georgian Patriarch told his Russian counterpart during one of his visits in Moscow: 'Although we are not politicians and cannot take serious steps in this sphere, it is possible to influence the processes.'[56] In November 2016, Patriarch Ilia II visited Russia to celebrate the seventieth birthday of the Russian Patriarch Kirill I. Ilia II declared that the 'regulation of relations between Russia and Georgia is very important for both countries. We need each other.'[57]

On the other hand, ideological closeness between the two churches does not necessarily mean ideal relations. In fact, the GOC still holds keeps its distance from the ROC and has expressed scepticism about the relationship when its interests are at stake. Despite the ROC's position on the Georgian church's jurisdiction in Abkhazia and South Ossetia, it maintains relations with breakaway churches in both regions. This leads to scepticism within the GOC about the ROC's intentions. In 2013, the GOC condemned the ROC for sanctifying new churches in Abkhazia. In 2015 the Georgian Patriarchate asked UNESCO to provide monitoring of the monasteries and churches beyond the control of the Georgian government.[58]

The GOC is not simply choosing allies based on a common ideology, it is a political player which reacts to external events. Thus, the GOC is flexible in its position towards the West but also towards the ROC; the church can change positions according to its own practical reasoning. The GOC also has direct relations with the Russian state. The GOC considers the Georgian government incapable of reconciling with Russia and aims to facilitate this process. The church wants to act as a mediator, using religion as a tool for mutual understanding. The Patriarch and church representatives have met several times with Russian politicians to discuss this goal.

In 2016, the Georgian Patriarch visited Moscow for the fifth time since the August War. He met with both Dimitri Medvedev and Vladimir Putin. In 2013 the Patriarch received an award from Moscow for his work on the unity of Orthodox Christian churches. Ilia II declared:

> Russia and Georgia have always been friends and brothers, but apparently someone envies us and deliberately creates hostility between us. I believe Vladimir Putin, a wise leader of state, can change the situation so that Georgia can become united again … The role of Russia is to protect spirituality … Russia and Georgia both have huge spiritual value and we should take care of our Orthodox/true faith. Orthodoxy helped us and helped Russia.[59]

The Russian government expresses a positive attitude toward the GOC and its activity. Back in 2013, President Putin congratulated Ilia II on his eightieth birthday with the following well-crafted statement:

> We highly appreciate your warm attitude towards Russia, and the Russian Orthodox Church. Your personal efforts, your calls for peace, for love … harmony and unity, contribute to our many centuries of friendship and understanding at difficult stages of our history. I am convinced that fruitful spiritual, cultural, and humanitarian dialogue will become a reliable basis for further development of relations between Russia and Georgia.[60]

Impact of the GOC on foreign policy

To what extent can the GOC influence foreign policy once it decides to intervene? Domestically the GOC has great influence on public opinion, but also among politicians for whom the GOC provides legitimacy and authority. As noted in Chapter 1 in this volume, public opinion remains a significant domestic factor for Georgian foreign policy, and EU and NATO membership have high support among Georgians. At the same time, the narrative supported by the GOC about the threat from the West resonates with the Georgian public. According to Caucasus Research Resource Centre (CRRC) polls, in 2017 between 40 and 45 per cent of Georgians thought the EU threatened Georgian traditions.[61] This gives the church leverage to contest value-related aspects of the Georgian government's pro-Western policy, including changes in legislation. Regarding legislation, direct influence is a mixed bag. Thus the law on the registration of religious minorities (which granted them greater equality with the GOC) was adopted despite opposition from the church. On the other hand, the final text of the anti-discrimination law, adopted in 2014, was the result of significant changes due to church lobbying. This caused criticism from Georgian civil society organizations.[62] There is also indirect influence: Georgian politicians must take the church's position into account if they want to survive politically. However, this type of influence is harder to document.

In the international arena, the church is more limited. Even though it has achieved a mediating position with Russia, outcomes are less predictable. On returning from Moscow in 2008, the Patriarch delivered Putin's statement on some intended concessions and urged Georgia to start a dialogue with Russia.[63] However, no changes have taken place in any of the state's policies on Russia. In a complex situation where many factors play a role, the church's power remains limited in complex foreign policy decisions. On the other hand, the church remains the only channel of communication that is acceptable to both sides of the Russo-Georgian conflict. For example, in 2008 it was only upon the Georgian church's request that the Russians opened a corridor to let Georgian soldiers move corpses out of Russian controlled villages. EU representatives frequently visit the Patriarch to convey messages directly, as they are aware of the church's powerful role in Georgian society.

Conclusion

Over time, the GOC has played a significant role in foreign policy. The extent of involvement and influence, however, has varied considerably. Much depends on the extent to which the state's foreign policy interests coincide with the church's position. These circumstances have varied along with the GOC's engagement in foreign policy. The intersection of the church's position with state foreign policy usually falls along the value and identity dimension. The historical overview suggests that when religion is seen as an inherent part of Georgian identity, and survival is at stake, then the church's role takes on greater foreign policy significance. But the church has no policy expertise in foreign policy and its influence works on the individual or personal level.

The last two decades mark the most powerful period in GOC influence, but it is also a time of heightened awareness of identity and values. As a result, we observed frequent cases of church involvement in foreign policy debates. The cases looked at indicate two types of involvement: domestic resistance, or lobbying to modify foreign policy. The case of European integration illustrated the former, and relations with Russia, the latter. The GOC has been most successful in lobbying changes in legislation and in shaping public opinion.

Notes

1 'General Population Census', *National Statistics Office of Georgia*, 2014 http://census. ge/files/results/Census_release_ENG.pdf

2 'Knowledge of and Attitudes toward the EU in Georgia', *Caucasus Research Resource Centres*, 2017, http://caucasusbarometer.org/en/eu2017ge/codebook/

3 'Survey of Public Opinion in Georgia', *International Republican Institute*, 2017, www. iri.org/sites/default/files/iri_poll_presentation_georgia_2017.03-general.pdf

4 'Foreign Policy Strategy', *Ministry of Foreign Affairs of Georgia*, https://mfa.gov. ge/#str_m_03

5   Salome Minesashvili, 'Orthodoxy as Soft Power in Russia–Georgia Relations', in *Religion and Soft Power in the South Caucasus*, ed. Ansgar Joedicke (London: Routledge, 2018), p. 42.

6   'Georgia's Orthodox Church Opposes Anti-discrimination Bill', *Radio Free Europe*, 29 April 2014, www.rferl.org/a/georgias-orthodox-church-opposes-antidiscrimination-bill/25366250.html

7   Tamara Grdzelidze, 'The Orthodox Church of Georgia: Challenges under Democracy and Freedom (1990–2009)', *International Journal for the Study of the Christian Church*, 10:2 (2010), pp. 160–75.

8   'Georgian Foreign Ministry Cannot Evaluate the Visit of Catholicos-Patriarch in Moscow', *Interpressnews*, 28 November 2011, http://bit.ly/2pFJhUW

9   Zaza Abashidze, 'Abolition of Autocephaly and Formation of the Exarchate, 1801–1840s', in *Witness through Troubled Times: A History of the Orthodox Church of Georgia, 1811 to the Present*, ed. Tamara Grdzelidze, Martin George and Lukas Vischer (London: Bennet & Bloom, 2006).

10 Anania Japaridze, 'sakartvelos eklesiis mokle istoria' [Short History of Georgian Church], *Meufe Anania*, https://bit.ly/2WpfDEf

11 Grdzelidze, p. 162.

12 Japaridze, p. 26.

13 Ibid., p. 27.

14 Abashidze, p. 113.

15 Quoted in Grdzelidze, p. 171.

16 Abashidze, p. 120.

17 Ibid., p. 127.

18 Ibid., p.111.

19 Ibid., p.129.

20 Eldar Bubulashvili, 'The Georgian Exarchate, 1850–1900', in *Witness through Troubled Times: A History of the Orthodox Church of Georgia, 1811 to the Present*, ed. Tamara Grdzelidze, Martin George and Lukas Vischer (London: Bennet & Bloom, 2006).

21 Gocha Saitidze, 'Between the Two Revolutions, 1901–1917' in *Witness through Troubled Times: A History of the Orthodox Church of Georgia, 1811 to the Present*, ed. Tamara Grdzelidze, Martin George and Lukas Vischer (London: Bennet & Bloom, 2006).

22 Ibid., p. 183.

23 Sergo Vardosanidze, 'Restoration of Autocephaly and Times of Trial, 1917–1952', in *Witness through Troubled Times: A History of the Orthodox Church of Georgia, 1811 to the Present*, ed. Tamara Grdzelidze, Martin George and Lukas Vischer (London: Bennet & Bloom, 2006).

24 Ibid., p. 201.

25 Quoted in Vardosanidze, p. 204.

26 Ibid., p. 210.

27 Ibid., p. 220.

28 Stephen F. Jones, 'Soviet Religious Policy and the Georgian Orthodox Church: From Krushchev to Gorbachev', *Religion, State and Society: the Keston Journal*, 17:4 (1989), pp. 292–312.

29 Ibid., p. 297.

30 Ibid., p. 298.

31 Ibid., p. 306.

32 Ibid., p. 309.

33 Stephen F. Jones, 'The Role of Cultural Paradigms in Georgian Foreign Policy', in *Ideology and National Identity in Post-Communist Foreign Policies*, ed. Rick Fawn (London: Frank Cass, 2004).

34 Rick Fawn, 'Ideology and National Identity in Post-Communist Foreign Policies', *Journal of Communist Studies and Transition Politics*, 19:3 (2003), pp. 1–41.

35 Eka Chitanava, 'The Georgian Orthodox Church: National Identity and Political Influence', in *Traditional Religion and Political Power*, ed. Adam Hug (London: The Foreign Policy Centre, 2015).

36 Ibid., p. 43.

37 'Meeting Record of Georgian Orthodox Church Synod', 20 May 1997. In author's possession.

38 'Patriarch: Church Will Do Everything to Make Georgia EU Member', *Civil Georgia*, 4 March 2014.

39 Giga Zedania, 'The Rise of Religious Nationalism in Georgia', *Identity Studies in the Caucasus and the Black Sea Region,* 3 (2011).

40 Ibid., p. 125.

41 'sakartvelos katolikos-patriarkis sashobao epistole' [Christmas Epistle of Georgia's Catholicos-Patriarch], *Orthodox Theology*, 7 January 2014, www.orthodoxtheology.ge/shoba2014/

42 'sakartvelos katolikos-patriarki ruis-urbnisis eparqias stumrobs' [Catholicos-Patriarch of Georgia Visits Ruis-Urbnisi Eparchy], *Interpressnews*, 10 November 2011, www.interpressnews.ge/ge/sazogadoeba/184026-saqarthvelos-katholikos-patriarki-ruis-urbnisis-eparqias-stumrobs.html?ar=A

43 'EU Commissioner Fule Visits Georgia', *Civil Georgia*, 4 March 2014, www.civil.ge/eng/article.php?id=27006

44 'Patriarch: Church Will Do Everything to Make Georgia EU Member', *Civil Georgia*, 4 March 2014, www.civil.ge/eng/article.php?id=27008

45 'Head of Georgian Church: Our European Choice is Very Firm', *Civil Georgia*, 19 May 2015, http://civil.ge/eng/article.php?id=28283

46 'Ilia II: imedia evropa ara marto bevr siketes mogvitans, aramed daitsavs chvens kulturas' [Ilia II: I Hope that Europe Will not Only Bring Much Goodness to Us, But Will Also Protect Our Culture], *Netgazeti.ge*, 20 December 2015, http://netgazeti.ge/news/86231/

47 'Interview with Father Eprem Gamrekelidze', in *ara ars daparuli [There is Nothing Hidden]*, Georgia and the World (Tbilisi: Istoriuli Memkvidreoba, 2012).

48 Salome Asatiani, 'kulturuli kavshirebis labirintshi' [In the Labyrinth of Cultural Ties], *Radio Free Europe,* 6 March 2013, www.radiotavisupleba.ge/content/blog-salome-asatiani-cultural-contacts/24930756.html

49 Minesashvili, p. 49.

50 'Georgia Passes Antidiscrimination Law', *Human Rights House*, 6 May 2014, https://humanrightshouse.org/articles/georgia-passes-antidiscrimination-law/

51 "Family Day", Rally against Gay "Propaganda" Planned for May 17', *Civil Georgia*, 16 May 2014, www.civil.ge/eng/article.php?id=27237

52 'Definition of Marriage', *Jumpstart Georgia*, 2017, https://marriage.jumpstart.ge/ka#!61

53 'Public Opinion Survey: Residents of Georgia', *International Republican Institute*, 2016, www.iri.org/sites/default/files/wysiwyg/georgia_2016.pdf

54 Alicja Curanovic, 'The Guardians of Traditional Values: Russia and the Russian Orthodox Church in the Quest for Status', in *Faith, Freedom and Foreign Policy: Challenges for the Transatlantic Community*, ed. Michael Barnett, Clifford Bob,

Nora F. Onar, Anne Jenichen, Michael Leigh and Lucian Leustean (Washington DC: Transatlantic Academy, 2015).

55 Kristina M. Conroy, 'Semi-recognised States and Ambiguous Churches: The Orthodox Church in South Ossetia and Abkhazia', *Journal of State and Church*, 57:4 (2015), pp. 621–39.

56 'Georgian Foreign Ministry Cannot Evaluate the Visit of Catholicos-Patriarch in Moscow', *Interpressnews*, 28 November 2011, http://civil.ge/eng/article.php?id=29640

57 Ibid.

58 Andrey Makarychev, 'The Limits to Russian Soft Power in Georgia', *PONARS Eurasia Policy Memo*, 412. (2016).

59 'Rech Ilii vtorogo na vstreche s Gruzinskoi diasporoi Rossii' [Speech by Ilia II at the Meeting with Georgian Diaspora in Russia], *Грузия Online*, 23 January 2013, www.apsny.ge/2013/soc/1359267799.php

60 'Katolikosu-patriarkhu vseia Gruzii Ilii II' [to Catholicos-Patriarch of Georgia Ilia II], *Kremlin.ru*, 11 January 2013, http://kremlin.ru/events/president/letters/17319

61 'Knowledge of and Attitudes toward the EU in Georgia', *Caucasus Research Resource Centres*, 2017, http://caucasusbarometer.org/en/eu2017ge/codebook/

62 'Georgia Passes Antidiscrimination Law', *Human Rights House*, 6 May 2014, http://humanrightshouse.org/Articles/20133.html

63 Grdzelidze, p. 168.

Part II

THE REGIONAL CONTEXT

Chapter 4

IN THE CAUCASUS BUT TOWARD THE BLACK SEA: GEORGIA'S REGIONAL IDENTITY IN FLUX

David Aprasidze

The Caucasus has long had a regional identity, but in recent years Georgia has increasingly sought to distance itself from this region and invent a new Black Sea regional identity. It tries to connect to countries such as Moldova and Ukraine, located outside the South Caucasus and deals with its immediate neighbours Armenia and Azerbaijan on a bilateral basis. Georgia has strong links to its Caucasian neighbours – evident in its culture, language and cuisine. The national anthem imagines the country in its geographic region: 'The Morning Star will rise above us, and lighten up the land between the two [Black and Caspian] seas.'[1] These words of the anthem symbolize Georgia's geographical connection to the South Caucasus. Yet, why is Georgia rejecting this geographical bond?

In this chapter we will examine the Georgian understanding of regional identity. We assume that the behaviour of Georgia is rational, and is conditioned by a lack of modern 'regional identity' in the South Caucasus itself. In Kurban Said's novel *Ali and Nino*, which depicts the short period of independence of Armenia, Azerbaijan and Georgia in 1918–21, a schoolteacher asks his pupils to define the eastern border of Europe. According to the teacher, it is the way of life, not the physical location, which determines the answer.[2] The novel imagines the Caucasus as one region, but the behaviour of the novel's protagonists tells us the opposite: their actions reveal deeply conflicting foreign policy perceptions of three nations. Almost a century later not much has changed. It is widely recognized that regional cooperation would have a positive impact on overcoming the political and economic challenges all three countries in the South Caucasus face. A number of proposals from Caucasian leaders regarding regional cooperation are evidence of that. However, none of these proposals has ever been seriously attempted. They remain intellectual exercises. This chapter will address the questions: What undermines the regional identity of the South Caucasus today? Are current dividing lines new phenomena or, are they deeply rooted in history? This chapter has the following structure: it starts by reviewing the historical and modern foundations of the region in the South Caucasus, followed by the pro- and anti-regional impulses of Georgia, and ends with the Georgian perception of Armenia and Azerbaijan.

The South Caucasus – Why is there no modern regional identity?

The South Caucasus is a geographic unit circumscribed by the Caucasus Mountains (Greater Caucasus in the North and the Lesser Caucasus in the South), and the Black and Caspian Seas in the West and the East. However, is the geography sufficient to qualify the South Caucasus as a region in political, economic and security terms? Can we observe since the collapse of the USSR a process of regionalization or increasing 'regionness' in the Caucasus?[3]

Geographic proximity helps explain why regions emerge. It is difficult to regard territorially distant and detached areas as one distinct region. However, this is not impossible as Canada and the United States are members of the Organization for Security and Cooperation in Europe (OSCE), and Armenia is part of the Eurasian Economic Union, even though it has no land border with other members. Yet, physical proximity facilitates interactions in political, economic and in societal fields. However, geography is a necessary but not a sufficient factor for establishing a distinct region.[4] There is no clear scholarly definition of a region against which one can measure the degree of regionalization. While some authors may prefer cultural boundaries (language, religion and other common characteristics) others rely more on the degree of interdependence in economic and political terms. Perceptions about commonalities and interdependence probably matter more than objective realities. There are many *regions* and many different forms of *regionalization.*[5]

In our understanding, a region first of all is a social phenomenon and therefore a conceptual construct. Secondly, the determining factors may change over time and contribute to a rethinking of regional identities.[6] In this section, we will compare the evolution of broader, historical–cultural ties between the three major nations in the South Caucasus and investigate relatively specific and measurable economic and political dimensions in the present.

Based on that idea, the South Caucasus faces at least two significant sets of problems as a region. The *first* relates to historically conditioned diversity – all three societies are built on different cultural foundations and they have contradictory perceptions about the evolution of the region. Armenian is defined as an Indo-European language; Azerbaijani belongs to the Turkish language group, while scholars are inclined to regard Georgian as a part of a distinctive group of Kartvelian languages.[7] Armenians and Georgians have their own alphabets, and Azerbaijanis use Latin (in Soviet times they used Cyrillic, and before that, Arabic). The three titular nations of the South Caucasus have different religious backgrounds: about 96 per cent of Azerbaijanis are Shia Muslims, the Armenian Apostolic Church is an independent Christian denomination followed by 92 per cent of the population, and the majority of Georgians (83 per cent) are Orthodox Christians.[8]

Azerbaijanis historically regarded the region as a part of the broader Middle East, seeking to retain their political and cultural ties with their former political patrons, especially with Turkey but also Iran, where a considerable part of the population (around 18 per cent) are Azerbaijani or Turkic speaking.[9] In Armenian understanding, while the Caucasus was a crossroads for many civilizations and empires, it was in the interest of small nations to seek a balance between big neighbours. However, when the prospect of a balance was exhausted (due to Russian conquest and especially after the 1915 genocide), the Armenians gave priority to survival and security and regarded Russia as the least of the evils among its many antagonistic neighbours. The Georgian perspective changed over time as well. In the eighteenth century, the kings of Eastern Georgia sought protection from the Russian Empire, and Georgians helped the Russians to conquer other peoples in the Caucasus, particularly in the north. However, Georgian elites since the beginning of the twentieth century were more interested in connecting with Europe directly.[10]

These contradictions between the three nations were critical to the failure of the short-lived Transcaucasian Democratic Federative Republic – a union of Armenia, Azerbaijan and Georgia, which emerged in April 1918 as a result of the disintegration of the Russian Empire. The republic lasted only one month and broke up into three independent states, largely because of different foreign policy orientations among the elites of the three nations. Armenia, Azerbaijan and Georgia continued to quarrel over territorial issues, and Yerevan fought some short wars with Tbilisi and Baku. The three countries never managed to achieve common goals, and one by one fell to the Bolsheviks between 1920 and 1921.[11]

Societies in the three states have shared a common history, often with the same imperial rulers. The Persians and Ottomans left a visible impact behind in terms of language, religion and broader culture in all three societies. Various Persian dynasties directly or indirectly controlled the eastern parts of the South Caucasus, corresponding to contemporary Armenia, Azerbaijan and Eastern Georgia. The Ottoman Empire conquered ancient Armenian lands and dominated in West Georgia. The Persian–Ottoman struggle over the Caucasus was exemplified by the Peace of Amasya signed in 1555, when the two empires defined their borders and divided Armenia and Georgia equally, with the western parts of both going to the Ottomans and the eastern parts as well as Azerbaijan to Persia.[12]

The Russian conquest in the nineteenth century unified the three emerging nations under single rule and established a united institutional framework under a Viceroy which covered both the South and North Caucasus. The Soviet Union, based on its ideological preference for larger units, created a unified Transcaucasian Socialist Federative Soviet Republic in 1922, which was dissolved fourteen years later in 1936.[13] Soviet nationality policy played an important role in shaping the contemporary South Caucasus. On the one hand, it succeeded in producing more or less similar Soviet elites across all the republics, and left behind specific, post-Soviet behavioural patterns, such as corruption and patrimonialism. On the other hand, the USSR boosted national identities and contributed to the invention of nationalistic narratives.[14] The homogenizing Soviet legacy created many commonalities and today the three states may look quite similar to external observers. But such similarities based on the Soviet legacy cannot overcome their deep-rooted ethnic, religious and cultural disagreements.

The *second* and possibly more decisive set of political problems revolve around the lack of acknowledgement among local elites of the need for regional cooperation. There are different and conflicting ontological understandings about present-day challenges in the Caucasus among all three states. There might be cultural or even economic potential for regionness, but there is no political will for regionalization.[15] These divergent views among all three elites have their roots in history, but since the 1990s, they are increasingly linked to different models of statehood.

Azerbaijan is a consolidated autocracy with rich hydrocarbon resources, which makes the regime self-sufficient. Baku views both Russia and the West as potential challengers to regime survival, although the underlying factors differ. Russia is a close ally of Armenia and assisted Armenians in the hot phase of the Nagorno-Karabagh conflict in the early 1990s. Russia has attempted to isolate Azerbaijan from global energy markets and views Baku as small, but still a competitor, especially in terms of gas supply to the European market. At the same time, Russia is an authoritarian regime. It promotes 'authoritarian'[16] agendas in neighbouring countries and is suspicious of any attempts at democratization, especially if embodied by peaceful coloured revolutions like the Armenian 'Velvet Revolution' in 2018. The West, on the other hand, recognizes the priority of energy cooperation over democratization in the case of Azerbaijan but always highlights the democratic and human rights agenda, thus endangering the stability of the Azerbaijani regime. Therefore, limiting cooperation with the West and using the Russian experience to handle political instability – this is how the Azerbaijani ruling elite perceives the current balance between the West and Russia.[17] Baku has demonstrated very limited interest in the European Neighbourhood Policy, and the legal framework between the EU and Azerbaijan is still based on the old Partnership Agreements, in force since 1999.[18] While close to the West, Azerbaijan is imitating the current foreign policy stance of its principal ally – Turkey – which despite strategic links to the West, is prepared to ally itself with Russia on specific matters.

Armenia is a semi-democratic country with some prospects for democratizing its political system. The 2018 street protests led to a peaceful revolution and the sudden deconstruction of the prior, relatively stable-looking pro-Russian regime. These events have confirmed that although political contestation is limited in hybrid regimes, it can still yield results. The country has had a stable and consolidated ruling elite over the past fifteen–twenty years. However, opposition and civil society could exercise partial checks on the government and this, together with a growing political opposition, ultimately achieved a breakthrough. But Russia is still omnipresent in Armenia. It has military bases on the ground and controls significant assets of the Armenian economy.[19] Nevertheless, Armenia has been attempting to balance Russia by increasing its ties to the West, foremost with the European Union. It was regarded as one of the exemplary partners in the process of elaboration of the Association Agreement with the EU.[20] In 2013 Russia prevented Armenia from signing the Association Agreement and soon after, Yerevan was persuaded to enter the Moscow dominated Eurasian Economic

Table 4.1 Political regimes in the South Caucasus and the Black Sea region (EU Eastern Partnership – EaP)

	Political rights	Civil liberties	Freedom rating	Aggregated score* (1–100)	Status**
Armenia	4	4	4	51	Partly free
Azerbaijan	7	6	6.5	11	Not free
Georgia	3	3	3	63	Partly free
Ukraine	3	4	3.5	60	Partly free
Moldova	3	4	3.5	58	Partly free
Belarus	7	6	6.5	19	Not free

Source: Freedom House, Freedom in the World 2019. https://freedomhouse.org/report/freedom-world/freedom-world-2019
* Most Free (100), Least Free (1).
** Free (1.0 to 2.5), Partly Free (3.0 to 5.0), Not Free (5.5 to 7.0).

Union. This decision was a strategic U-turn,[21] and was received negatively at home despite an understanding of the limitations imposed by surrounding geopolitical realities, such as conflict with Azerbaijan and security dependence on Russia. Nevertheless, Armenia – the only member of the Eurasian Economic Union in the South Caucasus, signed the Comprehensive and Enhanced Partnership Agreement with the EU in 2017. Armenia's dependence on Russia is apparent, even though the local elite recognize the need to reduce such dependence. The question is whether this is feasible, especially after the November 2020 defeat in the last Karabagh war of 2020, which has increased Armenia's dependence on its northern neighbour.

Georgia is the only country in the South Caucasus which signed the Association Agreement and the DCFTA (Deep and Comprehensive Free Trade Area) with the EU. Since 2017, Georgian citizens have been able to travel visa-free to the Schengen Area. Georgia is seen as a regional champion in democratizing and modernizing its political and economic institutions. The political system of the country suffers from political polarization and limited political competition as ruling parties have traditionally dominated the political landscape since independence.[22] The West has enormous political and financial leverage over Georgia, while Russian–Georgian political relations are almost non-existent following the Russo-Georgian War of 2008. Russia subsequently recognized the independence of Abkhazia and South Ossetia, the two breakaway regions within Georgia.

The political differences among the three states are magnified by dividing lines in the economic sector. As we will see in the next section, there are bilateral economic relations but not regional ones. Even during Soviet times, these three republics had limited economic interactions. They had intensive industrial and trade ties with Russia, but almost no significant links with one another.[23] Russia remains the major economic actor in the region, although its presence differs from country to country and across sectors. Currently, Armenia has the most economic ties with Russia, and Azerbaijan – the least (see Table 4.2). The unresolved conflict between Armenia and Azerbaijan eliminates any possibility for economic cooperation among those two countries, and therefore the establishment of a region-wide framework.[24] Azerbaijan and Georgia have a relatively more intense economic collaboration, based on the transit of Caspian oil and gas. Similar to Azerbaijan, Georgia is a strategically important transit route for Armenia. However, Georgia and Armenia belong to two competing economic unions, which may create some tensions in the future. The states are not major trading partners and they have more active trade relations with other states outside the region.

Table 4.2 Caucasus economic links to Russia

	Gas/ energy	Imports from Russia	Exports to Russia	Remittances from Russia	FDI from Russia	FDI in Russia	Bank claims in Russia	Assets of Russian banks subsidiaries and branches
Armenia	>50%	>50%	20–50%	>50%	>50%	<10%	<10%	>50%
Azerbaijan	<5%	20–50%	10–20%	10–20%	<10%	<10%	<10%	N/A
Georgia	<5%	20–50%	10–20%	20–50%	20–50%	<10%	<10%	20–50%

Source: Selected from IMF (2015), Spill-over Effects from Russia's Slowdown on Neighbouring Countries. www.imf.org/external/pubs/ft/dp/2015/eur1501mcd.pdf
Note: Gas/energy scaled by country's energy consumption; other variables are scaled by GDP.

Table 4.3 Trade among South Caucasian countries (as % of total exporting/importing country) 2015

Importer Exporter	Armenia	Azerbaijan	Georgia
Armenia	—	0.22/na	7.69/1.86
Azerbaijan	na/0.01	—	3.97/2.93
Georgia	7.12/2.05	10.93/0.74	—

Source: 2015 Data generated from World Bank https://wits.worldbank.org/Default.aspx?lang=en

Table 4.4 Five major trade partners for South Caucasian countries (%) 2015

	Export to	Import from
Armenia	Russian Federation (15.23), China (11.24), Germany (9.78), Iraq (8.81), Georgia (7.69)	Russian Federation (30.43), China (9.69), Iran (6.09), Germany (5.59), Italy (4.54)
Azerbaijan	Italy (21.3), Germany (10.8), Spain (9.58), Indonesia (9.41), Greece (6.84)	Russian Federation (15.6), Turkey (12.73), United States (9.19), Germany (7.48), Italy (6.38)
Georgia	Azerbaijan (10.93), Bulgaria (9.72), Turkey (7.64), Russian Federation (7.23), Armenia (7.12)	Turkey (17.17), China (7.6), Russian Federation (6.67), Ireland (5.9), Ukraine (5.89)

Source: 2015 Data generated from World Bank https://wits.worldbank.org/Default.aspx?lang=en

The foundation of the South Caucasus as a political (and economic) region is fragile. There is no shared understanding of the past and the future of the region by the elites of the three countries. Wherever there are commonalities and interdependence, they are either based on the shared memory of being subjugated and dominated by external powers, or by being drawn into opposing geopolitical axes.[25] In some respects, the region or region-like complexes could be constructed in negative terms, where countries are interconnected based on a sense of 'enmity', when primary security concerns are linked together so closely that their national safety cannot realistically be considered apart.[26] However, a region requires some shared perception on how to address those security challenges and how to overturn a negative present into a positive future. That does not exist in the South Caucasus.

Georgia in the South Caucasus

In the next two sections, we will look in more detail at how Georgia perceives its role in the South Caucasus and the extent to which it regards itself as being connected to the region. We will examine the evolution of the regional dimension in Georgian foreign policy and try to understand why and how the South Caucasus as a region has faded for Georgian leaders.

The regional conception of the South Caucasus has some limited foundations in modern Georgia. The first president of independent Georgia in the early 1990s, Zviad Gamsakhurdia, cultivated the idea of Caucasian solidarity and developed a pan-Caucasian vision with his idea of a common 'Caucasian Home'. The Caucasian union he envisaged included not only the southern part of the region but also the ethnically heterogeneous area of the Northern Caucasus. Georgians, he believed, bore a historical responsibility to unify the Caucasus. But it was the same Gamsakhurdia who contributed to the escalation of the conflict in South Ossetia inspired by ultra-nationalistic radicalism. Gamsakhurdia never formalized his ideas about Caucasian unity beyond vague statements, and no effort was undertaken to implement the concept after the brief period of Gamsakhurdia's rule (November 1990–January 1992). Georgia had barely any foreign policy under Gamsakhurdia.[27]

The next President, Eduard Shevardnadze (1995–2003), elaborated a concept of the 'Peaceful Caucasus'. Shevardnadze did not claim Georgia to be the pivot of regional unity. He did not pursue the political unification of the region. His understanding was that regional cooperation would deal with ethnic conflicts and promote economic cooperation. Shevardnadze elaborated six points: (1) the preservation of territorial integrity; (2) the protection of human rights; (3) the development of transport and communications, and the rejection of blockades; (4) protection of the environment; (5) ethnic and religious tolerance and the containment of nationalism; (6) the promotion of international investments into the region.[28] These points were vital to the Georgian perspective of regional development, and suggest some continuity in Georgian foreign policy with Shevardnadze's successors. In 1996–7 the Georgian parliament was relatively active in promoting the concept of regional cooperation and produced several analytical papers dealing with challenges and prospects for integration. However, the reality in the region – such as the conflict between Armenia and Azerbaijan – led the Georgian leadership to a realization of the limits of its regional aspirations. At the same time, international projects around the Caspian oil sector showed a strategic priority in linking up with Azerbaijan. Georgia and Azerbaijan had much in common; both lost territories in conflicts, they were eager to minimize dependence on Russia and regarded energy and transport projects as ways to attract Western attention and thus balance Moscow's omnipresence. Azerbaijani-Georgian cooperation, with the active support of Turkey, revealed once again the lack of perspective for all-inclusive regional cooperation in the South Caucasus.

A final attempt to revitalize the Caucasian dimension in Georgian foreign policy came unexpectedly from President Mikheil Saakashvili after the five-day war with Russia in 2008. In his speech to the UN General Assembly in 2010, Saakashvili spoke about the Caucasus as a place where unity, freedom and prosperity should replace artificial division, oppression and exploitation.[29] However, Saakashvili's interest (similar to that of Gamsakhurdia) was directed more toward the northern part of the Caucasus, and constituted potential leverage in the Georgian–Russian quarrel. The government in Tbilisi sought to improve people-to-people relations with North Caucasian nationalities, thereby creating greater unity against Russia. Georgia went on to remove visa requirements for residents of the North Caucasus, launched a Russian-speaking TV station, allocated funds for students and scholars from the region to study and research in Georgia, and parliament officially recognized the genocide of the Circassian people, committed by the Russian Empire in the nineteenth century.[30] These gestures had nothing to do with South Caucasian unity and it was rather quickly abandoned by the new Georgian government of Bidzina Ivanishvili, which came to power in 2012 and tried to ease tensions with Russia.

Georgia's impulses against regionalism

In the Foreign Policy Strategy of Georgia for 2019–22 (similar to the previous 2015–19 strategy), there is no mention of the South Caucasus as a region. Instead, the current strategy refers to *the Black Sea* as its preferred regional dimension, where Georgia is looking for multilateral cooperation with EaP countries which have signed association agreements with the EU (i.e. Ukraine and Moldova).[31] Two organizations outlined by Georgia's current government as significant in the region, are GUAM (known as the Organization for Democracy and Economic Development, it includes Georgia, Azerbaijan and Moldova) and BSEC (Black Sea Economic Cooperation). These are the only regional organizations Georgia is currently a member of in the immediate neighbourhood since it left the CIS (Commonwealth of Independent States) in 2009.[32]

The primary driver behind Georgian separation from its neighbours is Europe and the Euro-Atlantic aspirations of Georgia. Current and previous Georgian governments declare membership of the EU and NATO to be in their national interests, and a strategic priority. Regional memberships can sometimes facilitate integration into the EU, but the prospects for a new wave of expansion for the EU or NATO are slim. Ukraine and Moldova – countries which also signed Association Agreements with the EU – seem a more 'promising' pair in comparison to Armenia and Azerbaijan. In Georgian understanding, it is more pragmatic to position itself in the Black Sea region, and in particular as a Ukraine-Moldova-Georgia trio ('DCFTA-Trio'), rather than as a member of the unstable South Caucasus. Indeed, in December 2019, these three countries addressed the EU with a proposal to set a new cooperation format of EU+3.[33]

Georgia is the only country in the South Caucasus with explicit ambitions to join the EU and NATO. Azerbaijan has very narrow and focused interests regarding cooperation with the EU and NATO. Armenia looks very eagerly at approximation with the EU, especially since the 2018 revolution (see Table 4.5); however, its membership in the Eurasian Union sets clear limits in this regard. The strategic U-turn of Armenia in 2013 confirmed for Georgia the unreliable prospects for greater unity in the South Caucasus. For westward-looking Georgia, being 'part of the Caucasus' is not an asset but a burden.

The most intense Georgian attempt to escape the South Caucasus is associated with the government of Mikheil Saakashvili and his ambitious plans to rebuild national state institutions and reinvent the identity of the country. In 2004, the new government as one of its first steps, introduced a new five-cross flag (and a new anthem) symbolizing Georgia as an indispensable part of *Pax Europaea*. Saakashvili's new Georgian government justified the foreign policy orientation of Georgia towards the EU and NATO as a natural and legitimate desire to return to its European family.[34] The first steps toward Europe were made earlier under President Shevardnadze, when he succeeded in obtaining Georgia's accession to the Council of Europe (CoE) in 1999. In the second half of the 1990s, Georgia was still a fragile state with two recent secessionist wars in Abkhazia and South Ossetia. Torn apart and devastated economically, Georgia was forced to join the Russian-led Commonwealth of Independent States to accommodate Russian

Table 4.5 Eastern Partnership Index 2017 (0–100 max)

	Armenia	**Azerbaijan**	**Georgia**
Approximation	*0.66*	*0.56*	*0.64*
Democracy and human rights	0.60	0.32	0.70
EU integration and governance	0.65	0.57	0.65
Sustainable development	0.72	0.79	0.57
Linkage	*0.50*	*0.47*	*0.71*
Int. security, pol. dialogue and cooperation	0.46	0.38	0.75
Sectoral cooperation and trade flows	0.36	0.46	0.56
Citizens in Europe	0.68	0.55	0.81

Source: Based on Eastern Partnership Index 2017, https://eap-csf.eu/wp-content/uploads/EaP-Index-2017.pdf

interests. Georgian accession to the CoE was a personal foreign policy triumph of Shevardnadze, as it located Georgia on the political map of Europe.

We might conclude that the Caucasus dimension has never played a serious role in the foreign policy of modern Georgia. Even the concept of 'Peaceful Caucasus' from the mid-1990s was linked to the personal ambition of Shevardnadze, as a former Soviet Foreign Minister, who wanted to attract the attention of the international community and to stabilize the weak Georgian state. The concept was abandoned as soon as Georgia found its place on the energy and transport map connecting the Caspian Sea basin with the Turkey and further to Europe. It was forgotten with the accession of Georgia to the CoE and subsequent integration towards the West.

Georgian perceptions of Armenia and Azerbaijan

Georgians do not know much about the domestic political and economic developments, or the social and cultural problems, of neighbouring Azerbaijan and Armenia. National media rarely pay attention to the events across the border unless something exceptional – political turmoil, an outbreak of conflict, or natural catastrophe – occurs. Even regular elections are not noticed by the Georgian media if they are not causing fundamental change. The westward orientation of the country is somehow reflected in its relative neglect of what is going on the eastern and southern side of its borders. According to *Caucasus Barometer 2019*, only 7 per cent of Georgians see Azerbaijan as a friendly country (none see it as an enemy) and even less – 2 per cent – view Armenia as such (the same number regard Armenia as an enemy). In contrast, 21 per cent of Georgians regard the United States as a friend and 49 per cent regard Russia as an enemy.[35]

This chapter does not intend to provide a detailed account of Georgia's foreign policy towards its neighbours. Instead, it provides some general perceptions (and, of course, misperceptions or even stereotypes) which set certain domestic limits on regional cooperation. The remaining part of this chapter presents the Georgian perception of Armenia and Azerbaijan and their current roles in the region.

Armenia

The Georgian view of Armenia is rooted in history, and relations between the two nations represent an excellent example of what Freud calls the 'narcissism of minor differences'.[36] But the differences between Armenians and Georgians are not always minor. The two nations have had a common destiny of subjugation, internal division and external rule.[37] Both are among the oldest Christian nations in the world, but with significant differences in their religious foundations. The two churches separated in the seventh–eighth centuries and an ecclesiastic ban was introduced on trade and marriage among the two communities.[38] With time, this historical antagonism became less important, but mixed families are still unwelcome. According to Caucasus Barometer 2019, only 36 per cent of

Georgians approve of a Georgian woman marrying an Armenian (33 per cent of Armenians think the same way about Georgians).[39] Later, especially in the eighteenth–nineteenth centuries, large Armenian communities emerged in Tbilisi and other parts of Georgia. These communities were involved in trade and small manufacturing. They accrued considerable wealth and were viewed by ethnic Georgians with envy and suspicion.[40] The small differences became politically salient during the short-lived independence period of 1918–20/1. Besides foreign policy differences, Georgia and Armenia had territorial disputes and fought a short border war in December 1918, causing several hundred casualties on both sides. The military confrontation stopped after the involvement of British representatives.[41]

Separate foreign orientations intensified after the collapse of the Soviet Union. Newly established Georgia became engulfed by ethnic conflicts in its two regions – Abkhazia and South Ossetia. The central government practically lost control over areas populated by Armenian and Azerbaijani ethnic minorities in the southern parts of the country. In parallel, Armenia along with Karabagh Armenians, engaged in fighting with Azerbaijanis. Georgia accused Russia of supporting separatists in Abkhazia and South Ossetia, even though Georgian ultra-nationalism of the early 1990s was also in many ways to blame. Russian involvement in the Nagorno-Karabagh conflict was not straightforward. However, with time Moscow focused its support on Armenia, and this contributed significantly to the success of the Armenian armed forces. For Georgians, the Nagorno-Karabagh war illustrated Russia's support for separatists: Russia supported Armenian separatism in Azerbaijan, and Abkhazian and South Ossetian separatism in Georgia. The separatist conflicts fuelled Georgian–Armenian suspicions of one another. From the Georgian perspective, Armenia had become a Russian ally.[42] This perception was diminished over time by a mutual pragmatism between the two governments, but Georgia and Armenia still remain in opposite camps – the former joining the EU-led Free Trade Area and integrating with NATO, while the latter allied with the Moscow dominated security and economic organizations such as the Collective Security Treaty Organization and the Eurasian Economic Union. From Georgia's perspective, Tbilisi lost its two territories but managed to escape the Russian orbit. Moscow gave up its leverage over Georgia after the recognition of Abkhazia and South Ossetia as independent entities in 2008. On the other hand, Armenia kept control over Nagorno-Karabagh and adjoining parts of Azerbaijan, but paid a very high price by accepting Russian domination. Complementarity as a foundation for Armenian foreign policy, transformed into dependence on Russia: the strategic U-turn of 2013 was confirmation for this when Armenia abandoned the EU for the Eurasian Economic Union. Georgia perceives Russian military bases in Armenia as a potential threat since they are only 50 kilometres away from the Armenian-Georgian border. There is no guarantee that the Armenian authorities will be able (even if they were willing) to stop a Russian military advance against Georgia.[43]

The political changes in Armenia in 2018 – the peaceful Velvet Revolution – have been received in Georgia mostly with distrust. From the Georgian perspective, the democratic breakthrough in Armenia will change nothing, as the foreign and security orientation of Armenia remains the same. In Georgian understanding, Russia will not allow Armenia to democratize further and will apply all means to control the new ruling elite of the country. The new Armenian government has pledged its loyalty to Russia, although it tries to loosen such dependence.[44] Georgians regard the outcome of the Karabagh war in 2020 as further proof of Armenia's indissoluble links with Russia.

The relations between Armenia and Georgia are formally cordial thanks to pragmatism on both sides. Both governments acknowledge the leverage each possesses. In the Armenian case, there is a sizeable community of ethnic Armenians living in different parts of Georgia, but especially in the southern Javakheti region. Georgia, on the other hand, is the only route connecting Armenia with Russia and the rest of the world, since the Azerbaijani and Turkish directions remain blocked.[45] It is important to underline that this interdependence between the two countries is conditioned by negative factors (the potential to manipulate ethnic kin on the one hand, or to disrupt communication on the other) and not by positive dynamics, such as economic interdependence and mutual trade.

Azerbaijan

Georgia's relations with Azerbaijan are not as historically complex as the Armenian case. There are comparatively fewer 'narcissistic differences' between the two nations. In the 1990s, the two countries demonstrated more similarities than differences. Azerbaijan and Georgia fought to preserve their territorial integrity, and both were defeated. Both blamed Russian intervention. The Azerbaijani community in Georgia reacted with fear and suspicion to the radical nationalism of the first years of independent Georgia; many left the country for good. However, Azerbaijani-populated areas in Georgia, especially in the Kvemo Kartli region, have transformed into electoral strongholds for the national government of Georgia and have played a significant role in garnering votes for Georgia's ruling parties.[46]

Azerbaijan and Georgia established close contacts based on mutual interests to develop energy and transport routes to connect the Caspian with the Black Sea, and further on to Turkey. Azerbaijan was keen for strategic reasons on bypassing Russia for transporting its oil and gas resources, while Georgia wanted to minimize its energy dependence on Russia. Georgia was able, as a transit country, to attract attention, investment and resources from the West by establishing a regional niche for itself. By 2019, most of these regional transit projects have materialized – the Baku–Supsa, Baku–Tbilisi–Ceyhan and South Caucasus (Baku–Tbilisi–Erzurum) pipelines as well as the Baku–Tbilisi–Kars railway, which is in the final phase of its construction.[47]

Georgia was a hybrid, semi-free regime under Shevardnadze. Azerbaijan's Heydar Aliev, on the other hand, succeeded in consolidating his authoritarian rule in the early 1990s. Nevertheless, the shared perceptions regarding the external source of conflicts, the desire to escape from Russian domination and to increase their strategic value for the West, helped both Azerbaijan and Georgia to overcome the differences between their domestic political systems. Good personal relations between Shevardnadze and Heydar Aliev, and subsequently between Saakashvili and the younger Ilham Aliev, contributed to the positive political relationship. Saakashvili's swift elevation to political power after the Rose Revolution and his early statements about the need to replace kleptocratic elites across former Soviet states raised concerns in Azerbaijan, but personal relations quickly readjusted between Saakashvili and Ilham Aliev.[48]

The difference in regime types still creates tensions between the two countries. In recent years, since the Azerbaijani Government tightened control over civil society at home, a few activists have moved to Tbilisi.[49] Also some international donors who are not allowed to operate in Azerbaijan try to reach the country from Georgia. They conduct events in Georgia which target Azerbaijani citizens and provide funding to Azerbaijani civil society or media activists. This creates a certain mistrust in Baku. In 2017, an Azerbaijani journalist Afgan Mukhtarli, who was critical of the Azerbaijani authorities, was abducted from Tbilisi and later jailed at home. Questions were raised as to whether the Georgian government assisted its Azerbaijani colleagues in conducting this covert operation.[50] Since 2019, tensions have increased over a border dispute between the two countries straddled by the David Gareji Monastery, a complex treasured by the Georgian population as a symbol of its Christian history. Despite the domestic political implications of the dispute in both countries, especially in Georgia, both governments are attempting to contain it and ensure it will not overshadow the bilateral strategic relationship.[51] More disconcerting for Georgia is the outcome of the 2020 Karabagh war. Georgia and Azerbaijan share a similar vision about the nature of post-Soviet conflicts. They both support a solution of ethnic conflict based on the principle of territorial integrity. Tbilisi may welcome the success of Azerbaijan in recapturing territories lost in the 1990s, but it is also concerned with increased Russian military presence in the region. Georgia remains explicitly neutral toward the conflict in Nagorno-Karabagh, but Russia's mediation in the conflict carries multiple risks for Georgia. There is always the risk of a potential spill-over of ethnic tensions into the Armenian and Azerbaijani communities living in Georgia.[52]

Conclusion

Georgia is part of the South Caucasus in a physical sense. Although geography is hard to escape, perceptions may change. Since the 2000s, Georgia has been looking toward the Black Sea as its strategic priority and wants to connect with countries like Moldova and Ukraine. This is conditioned in part by the foreign policy goal of approximation with the European Union and NATO, since Ukraine and Moldova are geographically parts of Europe. The EU is beginning to cluster Georgia together with Moldova and Ukraine due to their participation in the Association Agreement and the Deep and Comprehensive Free Trade Area.[53]

This does not imply that Georgia is free from the historical and cultural threads to its South Caucasian neighbours. However, these links are today more bilateral than they are trilateral. Georgia has forged a strategic alliance with Azerbaijan and pragmatic relations with Armenia. Nevertheless, these links do not create the foundation for a regional identity, and certainly not its institutionalization. The South Caucasus is a region of states, but the states are new and weak, drawn into the orbits of more powerful neighbours. All three states have divergent visions about the past; their historical narratives clash, which contributes to the disputes over territory. They have a different understanding about the current challenges and opportunities and connect to different external actors in pursuing their own interests.

These cultural, historical and political ruptures shape the current landscape of the South Caucasus. The three states of Armenia, Azerbaijan and Georgia have been unable to find intra-regional solutions since the 1990s. We might term the South Caucasus as a 'regional complex' or 'primitive region', where the actors remain 'selfish' states, with no sense of common security interests. They 'look towards the larger external system rather than the region'.[54] There is little reason to believe that the three states will evolve into a functioning region any time soon. The greatest stimulus for political unity would come from the outside, from an external actor. Georgia would welcome this kind of development, but only under the umbrella of Europeanization. This remains highly unlikely given Azerbaijan's development toward authoritarianism and Armenia's dependence on Russia.

Notes

1 Government of Georgia, The Georgian State Anthem, www.gov.ge/index.php?lang_id=ENG&sec_id=58 (accessed 8 February 2019).
2 Said Kurban and Jenia Graman, *Ali & Nino* (New York: The Overlook Press, 2016).
3 Björn Hettne and Fredrik Söderbaum, 'Theorising the Rise of Regionness', *New Political Economy*, 5:3 (2000), pp. 457–72. The authors try to combine 'macro' and 'micro' regions. The new regionalism regards regions not only as 'aggregations of states' (macro) but also 'regions' (territories) penetrating individual states and combining different domestic regions (micro) with all types of cross-border cooperation and non-state actor interactions. In the South Caucasus, we do not have cases of cross-border regionalism and therefore consider the South Caucasus as a macro, state-based region.
4 Ibid.
5 For a detailed account of specific concepts relevant to the South Caucasus, see Tracey German, 'Good Neighbours or Distant Relatives? Regional Identity and Cooperation in the South Caucasus', *Central Asian Survey*, 31:2 (2012), pp. 137–51.
6 Economic ties and political links may change more easily than cultural identities; however, perceptions about 'friends and foes' can also shift, as we see when looking at Georgian–Turkish relations since the 1990s.
7 Kevin Tuite, 'The Rise and Fall and Revival of the Ibero-Caucasian Hypothesis', *Historiographia Linguistica. International Journal for the History of the Language Sciences Historiographia Linguistica*, 35: 1–2 (2008), pp. 23–82.
8 Central Intelligence Agency (CSI), The World Factbook, www.cia.gov/library/publications/the-world-factbook/ (accessed 8 February 2019).

9   Ibid.

10 Svante E. Cornell, *Small Nations and Great Powers: A Study of Ethnopolitical Conflict in the Caucasus* (London: Routledge Curzon, 2005).

11 Firuz Kazemzadeh, *The Struggle for Transcaucasia (1917–1921)* (London: Anglo Caspian Press, 2008). On the short-lived Transcaucasian Federation, see Thomas De Waal, 'A Broken Region: The Persistent Failure of Integration Projects in the South Caucasus', *Europe-Asia Studies*, 64:9 (2012), pp. 1709–23.

12 Alexander Mikaberidze, *Conflict and Conquest in the Islamic World: A Historical Encyclopedia* (Santa Barbara, CA: ABC-CLIO, 2011), p. 95.

13 De Waal, 'A Broken Region', pp. 1714–20.

14 Rogers Brubaker, 'Nationhood and the National Question in the Soviet Union and Post-Soviet Eurasia: An Institutionalist Account', *Theory and Society*, 23:1 (1994), pp. 47–78.

15 De Waal, 'A Broken Region', pp. 1721–22.

16 Thomas Ambrosio, *Authoritarian Backlash: Russian Resistance to the Democratization in the Former Soviet Union* (Burlington, VT: Ashgate, 2009).

17 Kamran Ismayilov and Konrad Zasztowt, 'Azerbaijan's Risky Game between Russia and the West', *Polish Institute of International Affairs*, Policy Paper 32/134 (2015), www.pism.pl/files/?id_plik=20615 (accessed 8 February 2019).

18 For Azerbaijan–EU relations see Anar Valiyev, 'Azerbaijan's Policy Towards EU Integration: Unrecognised Strategic Partner', in *Geopolitics and Security: A New Strategy for the South Caucasus*, ed, Kornely Kakachia (Tbilisi: Konrad Adenauer Stiftung, 2018), pp. 128–52.

19 On the Russian military presence in the South Caucasus see Jakob Hedenskog et al., '*Security in the Caucasus: Russian Policy and Military Posture*', Swedish Defence Research Agency, 10 April 2018, www.foi.se/en/foi/news-and-pressroom/news/2018-04-10-russia-sees-caucasus-as-its-sphere-of-interest.html (accessed 10 February 2019).

20 Laure Delcour and Kataryna Wolczuk, 'The EU's Unexpected "Ideal Neighbour"? The Perplexing Case of Armenia's Europeanisation', *Journal of European Integration*, 37:4 (2015), pp. 491–507.

21 Richard Giragosian, 'Armenia's Strategic U-Turn', *European Council on Foreign Relations* (2014), www.ecfr.eu/page/-/ECFR99_ARMENIA_MEMO_AW.pdf (accessed 8 February 2019).

22 David Aprasidze, 'Consolidation in Georgia: Democracy or Power?', in *OSCE Yearbook 2015*, ed. IFSH (Nomos Verlagsgesellschaft mbH & Co. KG, 2016), pp. 108–15.

23 Tracey German, 'Good Neighbours or Distant Relatives?'.

24 The Russian-mediated ceasefire agreement between Armenia and Azerbaijan proposes joint economic activities, including the opening of transportation lines. However, it is too early to assess the feasibility of these ideas. Crisis Group, '*Improving Prospects for Peace after the Nagorno-Karabagh War*', Europe and Central Asia, Briefing 91, 22 December 2020, www.crisisgroup.org/europe-central-asia/caucasus/nagorno-karabagh-conflict/b91-improving-prospects-peace-after-nagorno-karabagh-war (accessed 21 February, 2021).

25 Richard Giragosian, 'Promise and Peril: The Armenia-Russia-Iran Axis', and Svante Cornell, 'The Impact of the Ukraine and Syria Conflict on the Geopolitics of the South Caucasus', both articles in *Geopolitics and Security. A New Strategy for the South Caucasus*, pp. 177–206 and pp. 231–65 (Tbilisi: Konrad Adenauer Stiftung, 2018).

26 Barry Buzan, *People, States and Fear: An Agenda for International Security Studies in the Post-Cold War Era* (Colchester: ECPR Press, 2016), 190. In a later modification, Buzan involves state and non-state actors ('set of units') and issues of 'securitization' and 'desecuritization'. See Barry Buzan, 'Regional Security Complex Theory in the Post-Cold War World', in *Theories of New Regionalism*, ed. Fredrik Söderbaum and Timothy M. Shaw (London: Palgrave Macmillan, 2003).

27 Stephen Jones, 'The Role of Cultural Paradigms in Georgian Foreign Policy', *Journal of Communist Studies and Transition Politics*, 19:3 (2003), pp. 83–110, especially 93–4.

28 Parallel to Shevardnadze, President of Azerbaijan Heydar Aliev suggested the establishment of a Security and Cooperation Pact for South Caucasus, and Armenian President Robert Kocharian also supported ideas of regional cooperation in order to overcome conflicts. Eleni Fotiou, 'Caucasus Stability and Cooperation Platform: What is at Stake for Regional Cooperation?' *International Center for Black Sea Studies (ICBSS)*, Policy Brief 16 (2009), p. 3, www.files.ethz.ch/isn/104737/PB (accessed 8 February 2019).

29 United Nations, Remarks of H.E. Mikheil Saakashvili, President of Georgia on the 65th Session of the United Nations General Assembly on 23 September 2010, www.un.org/en/ga/65/meetings/generaldebate/Portals/1/statements/634209147655000000GE_en.pdf, (accessed 10 February 2019).

30 George Khelashvili, 'Georgian Perceptions of the North Caucasus and of US–Russian Relations', *PONARS Eurasia Policy Memo*, May/148 (2011), http://css.ge/files/Papers/George_Khelashvili,_Ponars,_May_2011.pdf (accessed 10 February 2019).

31 Ministry of Foreign Affairs of Georgia, Foreign Policy Strategy 2019–22 (in Georgian), http://mfa.gov.ge/MainNav/ForeignPolicy/ForeignPolicyStrategy.aspx, (accessed 10 February 2019).

32 Foreign Policy Strategy 2019–22.

33 'Georgia-Ukraine-Moldova deal, requesting EU+3 format for sectoral integration, new benefits', *Agenda.ge*, 5 December 2020, https://agenda.ge/en/news/2019/3317 (accessed 7 February 2020).

34 On the role of identity in Georgian foreign policy, see Kornely Kakachia and Salome Minesashvili, 'Identity Politics: Exploring Georgian Foreign Policy Behaviour', *Journal of Eurasian Studies*, 6:2 (2015), pp. 171–80.

35 The 2019 Georgia Barometer does not show significant changes if compared to previous studies in 2017 or 2015. The only difference is that in 2017 and 2015, Armenia is not named as an enemy. The 2019 data from Armenia show that 57 per cent of Armenians regard Russia as a friend (only 4 per cent said the same thing about Georgia); 75 per cent believe that Azerbaijan is an enemy and 16 per cent say the same about Turkey. Georgia is not mentioned as an enemy. Latest Data available for Azerbaijan are from 2013. See Caucasus Research Resource Centre (CRRC), Caucasus Barometer, https://caucasusbarometer.org/en/datasets (accessed 10 February 2019).

36 The term was coined by Sigmund Freud. See Sigmund Freud and James Strachey, *Civilization and Its Discontents: Sigmund Freud* (New York: W. W. Norton & Company Inc., 1961).

37 George Tarkhan-Mouravi, 'Armenia and Georgia: Resilient Relationship', *Heinrich Böll Stiftung, South Caucasus*, 15 December 2017, https://ge.boell.org/en/2017/12/15/armenia-georgia-resilient-relationship (accessed 10 February 2019); Robert Nalbandov, 'Uncertain Old Friends: Georgian–Armenian Relations', in *Georgian Foreign Policy: The Quest for Sustainable Security*, ed. Kornely Kakachia and Michael Cecire (Tbilisi: Konrad Adenauer Stiftung, 2013), pp. 175–89.

38 Stephen H. Rapp Jr., 'Georgian Christianity', in *The Blackwell Companion to Eastern Christianity*, ed. Ken Parry (Malden, MA: Wiley-Blackwell, 2010), pp. 137–55; V.A.Arutionova-Fidanian, 'K voprosu o sushchestovavanii khalkidonitskoi tserkvi v armenii' (On the Question of the Existence of the Chalcedonian Church in Armenia), *Вестник ПСТГУ III: Филология*, 4:22 (2010), pp. 7–22.

39 See Caucasus Research Resource Centre (CRRC), Caucasus Barometer 2019 https://caucasusbarometer.org/en/datasets/ (accessed 10 February 2019).

40 Timothy K. Blauvelt and Christofer Berglund, 'Armenians in the Making of Modern Georgia', Manuscript (2016), http://eprints.iliauni.edu.ge/4587/1/22.05.final.Berglund.pdf (accessed 10 February 2019).

41 Ibid., p. 6.

42 Sergey Minasyan, 'New Challenges and Opportunities for Armenia and Georgia in the Context of Regional Security', Caucasus Institute and Republican Institute, *Armenia and Georgia in the Context of Current Political Developments: New Challenges and Opportunities in the Realm of Regional Security* (Yerevan-Tbilisi, 2016), pp. 4–10.

43 Liberal Academy, Tbilisi 'Threats of Russian Hard and Soft Power in Georgia' (Tbilisi, 2016), 81–4, www.ei-lat.ge/images/doc/threats%20of%20russian%20soft%20and%20hard%20power.pdf (accessed 10 February 2019).

44 Shota Gelovani, '3 Reasons Why the Armenian Revolution Means Nothing for the Foreign Policy of the Country and 3 Reasons Why We Thought it Would', *Georgian Institute of Politics (GIP)*, 25 May 2018, http://gip.ge/3-reasons-why-the-armenian-revolution-means-nothing-for-the-foreign-policy-of-the-country-and-three-reasons-why-we-thought-it-would/ (accessed 10 February 2019); Ghia Nodia, 'What Georgians Think about the Armenian Revolution', *Caucasus Analytical Digest*, August 2018, www.css.ethz.ch/content/dam/ethz/special-interest/gess/cis/center-for-securities-studies/pdfs/CAD104.pdf (accessed 10 February 2019).

45 Tarkhan-Mouravi, 'Armenia and Georgia'.

46 Zaur Shiriyev and Kornely Kakachia, 'Azerbaijani-Georgian Relations: The Foundations and Challenges of the Strategic Alliance', *Center for Strategic Studies (SAR)*, 7–8 (2013).

47 For Azerbaijani-Georgian relations see Zaur Shiriyev, 'An Alliance Built on Understanding: The Geopolitics of Georgian-Azerbaijani Relations', in *Georgian Foreign Policy: The Quest for Sustainable Security*, pp. 149–73; Mamuka Tsereteli, 'Azerbaijan and Georgia: Strategic Partnership for Stability in a Volatile Region', *Central Asia-Caucasus Institute & Silk Road Studies Program*, September 2013, www.files.ethz.ch/isn/173440/2013-Tsereteli-Azerbaijan-and-Georgia1.pdf (accessed 10 February, 2019). For the geopolitical implications of energy and transportation in the South Caucasus see Samuel Lussac, 'The Baku-Tbilisi-Kars Railroad and Its Geopolitical Implications for the South Caucasus', *Caucasus Review of International Affairs*, 2:4 (2018), pp. 34–46.

48 Shiriyev and Kakachia, 'Azerbaijani-Georgian Relations', p. 20.

49 'Repression Beyond Borders: Exiled Azerbaijanis in Georgia', *Human Rights Education and Monitoring Centre (EMC)*, 21 November 2017, https://emc.org.ge/en/products/represia-sazghvrebs-mighma-azerbaijanidan-devnili-mokalakeebi-sakartveloshi (accessed 10 February 2019).

50 Civil Georgia, 'State Security Service Denies Involvement in Afgan Mukhtarli's Case', 11 June 2017, www.civil.ge/eng/article.php/test/article.php?id=30179&search=mukhtarli, (accessed 10 February 2019).

51 Giorgi Lomsadze, 'Azerbaijan-Georgia Relations Newly Strained by Monastery Tensions', *Eurasianet*, 17 July 2019, https://eurasianet.org/azerbaijan-georgia-relations-newly-strained-by-monastery-tensions (accessed 28 February 2021).

52 Tarkhan-Mouravi, 'Armenia and Georgia'. Indeed, during the 2020 war in Karabagh, Georgia was accused of supporting the conflicting sides in both Armenian and Azerbaijani media, even though the Georgian government issued a statement of neutrality. See Natia Seskuria, 'The Nagorno-Karabagh Conflict and the Challenge for Georgia', 29 October 2020, www.rusi.org. https://rusi.org/commentary/nagorno-Karabagh-conflict-and-challenge-georgia (accessed 28 February 2021).

53 Although DCFTAs are implemented bilaterally as parts of respective Association Agreements with Georgia, Moldova and Ukraine, this creates certain regional dimensions, since only three countries in the Eastern Partnership signed the agreement. For details see European Parliament, 'Association Agreements between the EU and Moldova, Georgia and Ukraine', www.europarl.europa.eu/RegData/etudes/STUD/2018/621833/EPRS_STU(2018)621833_EN.pdf (accessed 10 February 2019).

54 Hettne and Söderbaum, 'Theorising the Rise of Regionness', p. 464.

Chapter 5

GEORGIA'S RELATIONS WITH TURKEY AND IRAN

George Sanikidze

Throughout its history the South Caucasus has been an arena for fierce rivalry and expansion among competing regional powers, including Iran and the Ottoman Empire, which have exerted influence over most of the region for centuries. Iran and Turkey's ties with the region diminished considerably after the incorporation of South Caucasia into the Russian Empire in the nineteenth century, although intellectual and revolutionary contacts with Iranian and Turkish reformists and revolutionaries continued, especially in the early twentieth century during the successful Iranian and Ottoman constitutional revolutions in 1906 and 1908–9 respectively. The Ottoman Empire was a powerful shaper of South Caucasian politics during the Russian revolution and civil war between 1918 and 1920. Such contacts practically ceased under the USSR, but after the collapse of the Soviet Union new possibilities emerged for Iran and Turkey. The unique geopolitical and geo-economic location of the region, along with its resources, spurred Turkey and Iran to renew their activity in the region. For the newly independent states in the South Caucasus, diplomatic relations with Turkey and Iran acquired new significance as it provided them with the opportunity to balance relations with an assertive Russia.

After gaining independence in April 1991, Georgia renewed its relations with Middle Eastern countries, focused mainly on extending friendly contacts with Turkey and Iran. In the past, especially in the nineteenth and twentieth centuries, relations had been hostile, underlined by popular cultural mistrust of Islam. The goal after 1991 was to shore up commercial and diplomatic relations after such a long hiatus. But these two southern neighbours required different strategies. Turkey, a NATO member and an EU supplicant, was a 'bridge', linking Georgia to the West; Iran served as a counterbalance to Russia, and as an important trading partner (especially potential revenues from Iranian tourism and energy linkups). Georgia could serve as a transport link for Iran to the outside world.

Georgia also developed significant economic and political relations with the Arab countries of the Middle East at this time, excluding Syria (Georgia severed diplomatic relations with Syria in 2018 after the Assad regime recognized Abkhazia and South Ossetia as independent states). Relations with Arab countries

160000
140000
120000
100000
80000
60000
40000
20000
0
-20000

UAE   Qatar   Egypt

■ 2015   2016 ■ 2017 ■ 2018

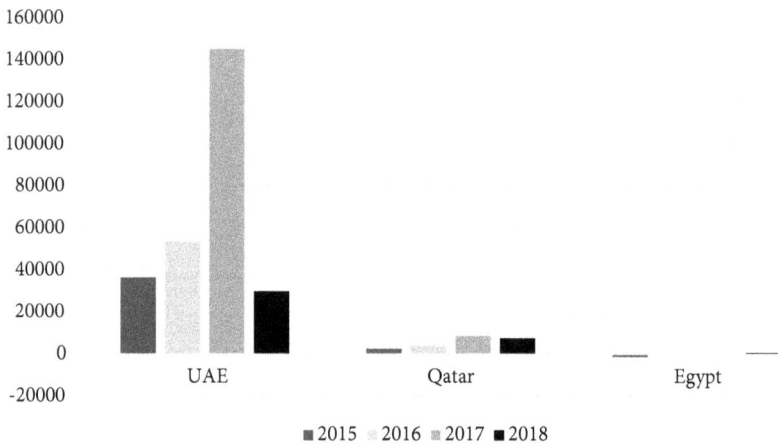

Figure 5.1 Foreign direct investment in Georgia by Arab countries (2015–18).

Source: Geostat: www.geostat.ge/en/modules/categories/191/foreign-direct-investments

like the UAE, Qatar, Jordan and others, are primarily economic – Georgia is seeking to attract investment from the rich countries of the region and has gained some success: levels of foreign direct investment (FDI) from the UAE and Qatar increased between 2015 and 2018 (see Figure 5.1). There has been considerable growth in tourist numbers in Georgia from Arab countries, facilitated by newly established direct flights from Doha, Dubai, Amman and from three cities in Saudi Arabia.

This chapter focuses on key aspects of the evolution of Georgia's foreign policy towards the Middle East, but specifically Turkey and Iran, Georgia's closest and most powerful southern neighbours. I examine the interests of both countries in Georgia and the extent to which these interests converge with Georgia's own; what is the role of the Turkish and Iranian communities in Georgia, and how do both the Georgian government and the Georgian public assess the Turkish and Iranian 'factor' in Georgian foreign policy.

Turkey: From economic interaction to strategic partnership

The border between Georgia and Turkey reopened in 1989. With Georgia's economic collapse in the 1990s, goods delivered from Turkey to Georgia – whether legally or illegally – were of vital importance (particularly in the first few years of independence) to the economic survival of many Georgians, especially in the Western part of the country. The political significance of Turkey for Georgia grew with the rise of an increasingly aggressive Russia. Turkey became a key factor in weakening Russia's military and political influence, and as a facilitator of Georgia's Western orientation. Turkey, too, was searching for a new identity and a new role in the Middle East, the Caucasus and Black Sea region. Ian Lesser and Stephen Larrabee note that 'the instability of these zones and Turkey's geographical location ... put Turkey in an important position and paved the way for Turkey to emerge as a potential dynamic player'.[1] In this context, the South Caucasus took on its old significance for Turkey as a vital geopolitical region transiting energy, and serving as a bridge to potential political and trading alliances in Central Asia. The South Caucasus was also important for any multilateral ambitions Turkey had in the Black Sea region.

For Turkey, Georgia has always played a role as a primary link to Azerbaijan and to the Turkish-speaking world of Central Asia. In the nineteenth and twentieth centuries this evolved into a Pan-Turanian movement in Turkey, a policy pursued by the Young Turks after 1908, which aimed to extend Turkey's influence eastwards into Central Asia, based on common cultural, linguistic and religious features.[2] Forced to avoid the rival powers of Russia and Iran, there was only one physical route between Turkey and Central Asia, which traversed Georgia, Azerbaijan and the Caspian Sea.[3] Today, the Sarpi checkpoint on the Georgian–Turkish border[4] has become a commercial hub linking not only these two countries, but also connecting Turkey to Azerbaijan and Central Asia. There was major traffic the other way, especially in the 1990s as Georgian citizens sought employment in Turkey and beyond. According to William Hale, 'in 1992 alone, 800 thousand ex-Soviet citizens visited Turkey for commercial purposes, and half of these were from Georgia'.[5] Emigration of Georgians to Turkey was helped by the introduction of a visa-free regime for Georgians, followed by a passport-free regime in 2011. By the beginning of 2020, Turkey had become the top partner country for Georgia in terms of imports and the fifth largest regarding exports (see Figures 5.2, 5.3).

Share of the top trading partners in total Imports in January 2020*

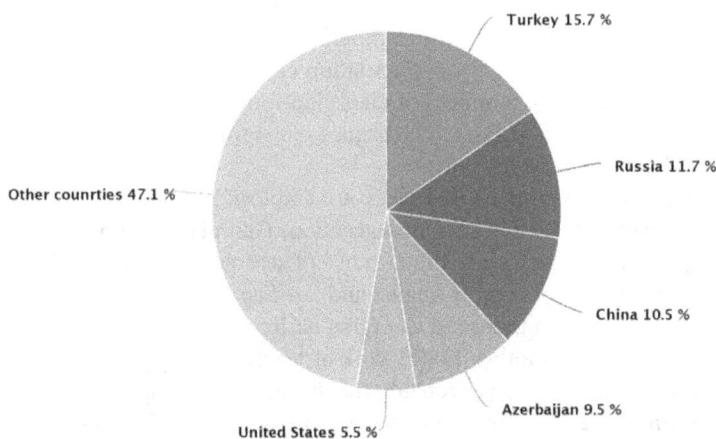

Figure 5.2 Share of the top trading partners in total imports, January 2020.

Source: Geostat: www.geostat.ge/en/modules/categories/638/import

Share of the top trading partners in total exports in January 2020*

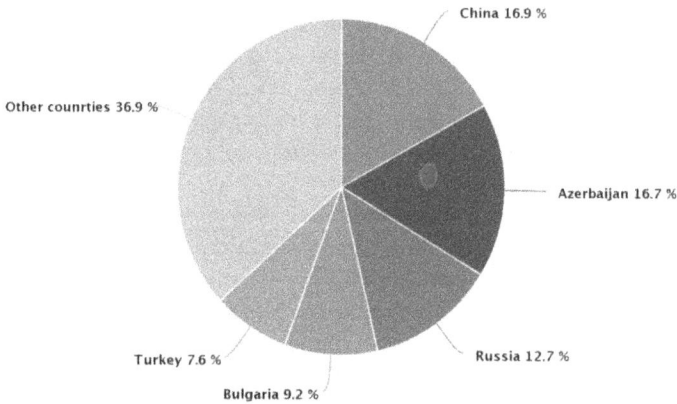

China 16.9 %

Other counrties 36.9 %

Azerbaijan 16.7 %

Russia 12.7 %

Bulgaria 9.2 %

Turkey 7.6 %

Figure 5.3 Share of the top trading partners in total exports, January 2020.

Source: Geostat: www.geostat.ge/en/modules/categories/637/export

Opening the border with Georgia was important for the economic development of Turkey's own eastern Anatolian regions such as Kars, Ardahan and Trebizond, which were among the poorest parts of the country. The new transit role helped revive local economies.[6] Dire economic conditions in Georgia in the 1990s forced a large number of Georgian citizens to seek work in Eastern Turkey (Trebizond), as well as Istanbul.[7] There are no accurate statistics on the number of Georgian job seekers who crossed into Turkey (both long-term and short-term) because the purpose of the visit was not recorded at border crossings in the 1990s. Their numbers were highest in the first decade after independence, but have declined since 2010 due to Turkey's tightening of restrictions on foreign job seekers. Since 2000, the number of Georgian emigrants has remained stable. According to the Georgian population census data of 2014, Turkey is the third largest country by numbers of Georgian immigrants[8] and the amount of remittance inflow from Turkey to Georgia grew significantly between 2012 and 2017 (see Figures 5.4, 5.5).

The majority of Georgians in Turkey are employed in the agricultural sector as seasonal workers. Under current legislation, Georgian nationals can stay in Turkey up to 90 days per year. The number of seasonal job seekers rises during the tea and hazelnut harvests in August and late September. According to official data in 2018, at least ten thousand Georgian nationals were employed on Turkish tea plantations, while another 1,000[9] work at tea processing plants. The number of illegal seasonal workers is probably much higher. On Turkey's initiative, the Organization of the Black Sea Economic Cooperation (BSEC) was established in Istanbul in 1992. Georgia and Turkey were joined by Bulgaria, Romania, Ukraine, Russia, Moldova, Azerbaijan, Armenia, Albania and Greece.[10] An important aspect of this organization's proposed activity, apart from environmental and

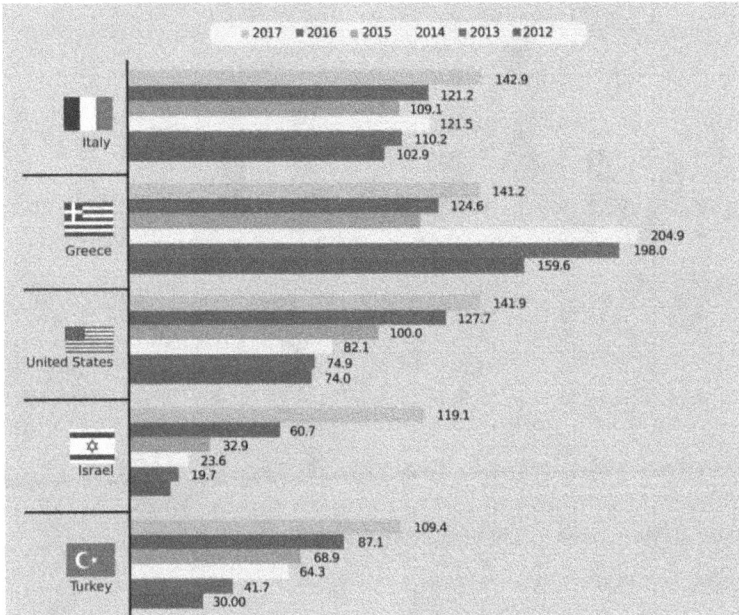

Figure 5.4 Remittances in Georgia: 2012–17 (in millions of US Dollars).

Source: https://idfi.ge/en/remittances_in_georgia

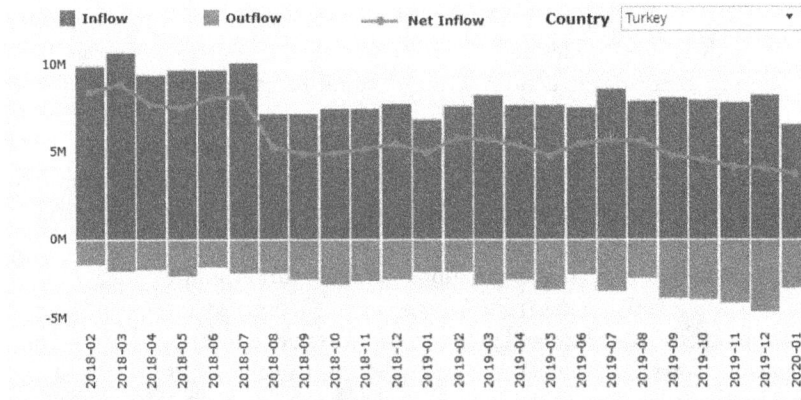

Figure 5.5 Remittances from Turkey: 2018–20 (in millions of US Dollars).

Source: National Bank of Georgia https://nbg.gov.ge/en/page/money-transfers

economic cooperation, is the facilitation of small and medium-sized businesses and the deepening of trade relations (see Figure 5.6).

Turkey hoped to use BSEC, which was part of the EU's 'Greater Black Sea Area', as an economic leader in the region, which would help establish Turkey's

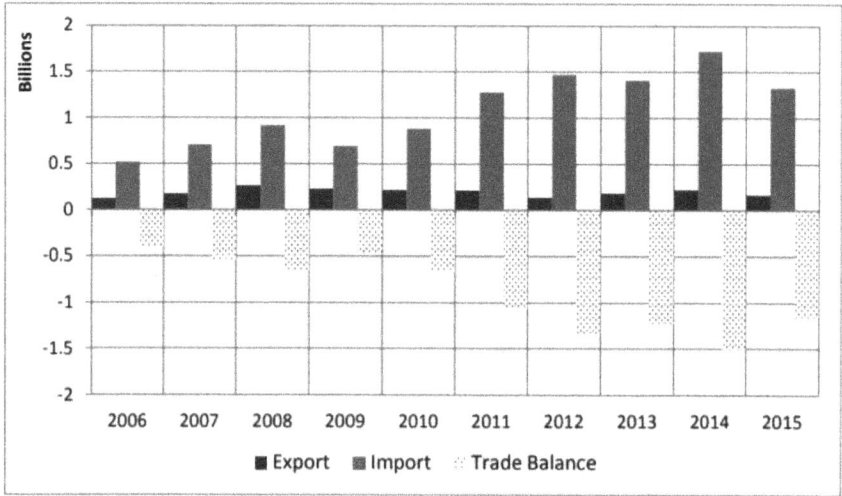

Figure 5.6 Exports, imports and trade balance with Turkey (USD).

Source: www.research.pmcg-i.com/policypapers_file/b4485c8fbd91e238c.pdf

regional influence in the Black Sea. It is almost impossible for Turkey to match Russia's power in the Black Sea, but multilateral organizations like the BSEC are useful, especially after Russia's expansion into Crimea and Ukraine. The official purpose of BSEC includes stabilization and the preservation of peace and stability in the region.[11] Turkey's accession negotiations to the EU (Turkey's prospects were brighter in the 1990s) underlined Turkey's pivotal role in connecting the Black Sea region to European structures. Georgia stood to gain by developing strong economic and political relationships with Turkey and the BSEC; it helped to create a balance with Russia and the Commonwealth of Independent States (CIS). Turkey's current alliance with Russia – in the energy field, in Syria, in their anti-Western attitudes – is shallow and could quickly be disrupted. Turkey, for example, has taken on the defence of Crimea's Tatars.

The most important factor in relations between Turkey and Georgia was the transit of Caspian oil and gas from Azerbaijan via Georgia to Turkey and thence to world markets. After Iran and Armenia were excluded from projected oil and gas pipeline routes for political reasons (Iran's poor relations with the West and the Armenian–Azerbaijani conflict were the two major factors), Turkey assigned this transit role to Georgia. The government of Georgia, headed by Eduard Shevardnadze at the time (1992–2003), considered the project vital for Georgia's national security. It would be a source of revenue outside Russian territory and Russian control. Western investment in the pipelines would also increase Georgia's geopolitical significance as an invaluable lever in resistance to Russia's hegemonic claims in South Caucasia. The Baku–Tbilisi–Ceyhan (BTC) pipeline project was authorized by the Ankara declaration in 1998; it was signed by the presidents of Turkey, Georgia, Azerbaijan, Kazakhstan and Uzbekistan. Between 2006 and

2018, the BCT pipeline carried about 3.12 billion barrels (around 417 million tons) of crude oil, which were loaded onto 4,085 tankers in Ceyhan in the Eastern Mediterranean and sent to world markets.[12] Construction of the Baku–Tbilisi–Erzurum gas pipeline, which largely followed the oil pipeline route, was completed in 2018. The extension of this pipeline will be the Trans-Anatolian gas pipeline (TANAP), which will supply Azerbaijan's natural gas to Europe. Turkey remains, however, Russia's largest non-EU natural gas export market. Russia attempted a number of projects to ensure the direct delivery of gas to Turkey. After the failure of the first South Stream plan in 2014 (it was planned to carry gas by pipeline under the Black Sea), Russia and Turkey agreed on a new pipeline named Turk Stream, which began delivering gas to Turkey in January 2020.[13]

The transit of energy resources is pivotal to the political and economic relationship between Azerbaijan, Georgia and Turkey. Construction of the Baku–Tbilisi–Ceyhan oil pipeline was a sign of Russia's diminished influence in the South Caucasus. Russia suffered a further setback, as the pipeline bypassed Armenia – Russia's only ally in the region. The inclusion of Russia's on-and-off partner, Iran, in South Caucasian energy projects was ruled out. Much of Georgia's economic growth and FDI in the 1990s depended on the construction of energy pipelines. The pipelines are not just about economic interests. The energy routes also connect Turkey with the Turkish-speaking world, and Georgia with Europe.

Georgia, Turkey and NATO

Turkey has become the most important neighbour and strategic partner of Georgia in the region, and as a long-time member of NATO, Turkey has taken a favourable view of Georgia's own NATO aspirations. At the World Economic Forum's fiftieth annual meeting in Davos in January 2020, the Foreign Minister of Turkey, Mevlüt Çavuşoğlu, stated that 'Georgia needs us, and we need an ally like Georgia, Georgia should also become a NATO member'.[14] Georgia, as an 'aspirant country', has participated in several NATO-led missions, such as the International Security Assistance Force (Afghanistan, 2004–14), and its successor, the Resolute Support Mission (Afghanistan, 2015–21). Georgia sends many of its officers to NATO-supported military schools and academies in Turkey.[15] An agreement on cooperation in military education led to the establishment of a Joint Military College, which functions in Georgia. Georgian officers can also sign up for four years of schooling in Turkish military academies. In Georgia, at the Vaziani and Kojori Special Forces' bases, Georgian troops are trained by Turkish army instructors. Together with the United States, the Turkish and Georgian militaries have formed a Caucasus Working Group seeking to improve cooperation and provide training for the Georgian military.[16] In 2010, Azerbaijan and Georgia formed a joint defence industry working group, which has received substantial aid from Turkey. A number of agreements have been signed between Georgia and Turkey on military cooperation. An example is the agreement between the governments of Georgia and Turkey on military training, technologies and science. (1996). Turkey has also modernized the military airfield in Marneuli (east

Georgia), and supplies Georgia with military equipment, training and finance to help Georgia's army become interoperable with NATO.

Despite political differences, common security challenges have cemented Georgia, Azerbaijan and Turkey into a strategic partnership.[17] Turkey and Georgia signed a free trade agreement in 2008, which led to intensified trade relationships between the two countries. However, the balance of trade is massively in Turkey's favour. In 2013–16 the annual average turnover of Turkish goods in Georgia amounted to almost 1.5 billion USD; Georgia's average turnover was just under 200 million USD in Turkey. In 2018, Georgia and Turkey agreed on the expansion of the existing free trade agreement. According to the Georgian Minister of Economy and Sustainable Development, Dimitri Kumsishvili, 'based on the outcome of negotiations, Georgian business will be able to increase its exports to the Republic of Turkey by 20 percent'.[18]

Georgia has more international agreements with Turkey than almost any other country. Two examples are the 'Treaty between Georgia and the Republic of Turkey on mutual legal assistance in civil, trade and criminal matters' and the 'Agreement between the Government of the Republic of Georgia and the Government of the Republic of Turkey on cooperation in the field of security', signed in 1998 and 2012 respectively.[19] In cooperation with Turkey, Georgia is participating in the trilateral field with a series of military exercises under the name 'Caucasian Eagle'. It is aimed at ensuring the security of the Caucasus region, particularly in relation to pipelines.[20] The rapprochement between Turkey and Russia, represented by multiple gas transit agreements and cooperation over Syria and the Middle East, has not had any significant impact on Georgian–Turkish relations. Turkey has refused to recognize the independence of either Abkhazia or South Ossetia and continues to invest heavily in Georgia. Turkey is Georgia's primary strategic partner. Former President Mikheil Saakashvili, during his visit to Turkey in 2004, summed up Georgia's position: 'Turkey is Georgia's "friend" and "window to Europe".'[21]

A trilateral axis?

Trilateral cooperation between Turkey, Azerbaijan and Georgia has increased significantly since the construction of the oil and gas pipelines. Trilateralism between the three countries is a major factor in the economic development of the South Caucasus, and represents a challenge to Russia, which still views the region as its sphere of influence. Any strengthening of cooperation between the three countries conflicts with Russia's own goals in the region; the three partners continue to exclude Armenia, Russia's ally, from a role in South Caucasian economic affairs. In addition to the existing oil and gas pipelines, the Baku–Tbilisi–Kars railway (BTK), which opened in 2018, connects Azerbaijan and Turkey via Georgia, and further cements trade and cultural contact between the three countries. Justyna Szalanska notes that the line not only opens 'a new route for bilateral trade', but transforms 'Georgia into Turkey's window to the greater market of Eurasia'.[22] Given the trade barriers introduced by Russia for European goods (2014), the railway line, which bypasses Russia, could acquire special significance for South Caucasia's trade with Europe. As of now, the BTK railway has a capacity of one million passengers and five million tons of cargo per year – the latter is slated to increase to 15 million tons when a parallel track is constructed some time in the near future.[23] After the 2020 war in Nagorno-Karabagh, opportunities for alternative railway corridors across the South Caucasus have opened up. The Azerbaijani government, for example, is promoting a railway project linking Azerbaijan to Nakhichevan, which will link up with Turkey's rail network. This will cross Armenian territory and will be expensive, but it is a viable competitor to the BTK, and could diminish Georgia's importance as a railway transit country. However, as yet there are significant political and economic obstacles to the construction of this railway.

The Russia factor in the region is perceived differently by all three states. They all share considerable scepticism about their northern neighbour. Turkish leaders have sought to rapidly restore ties with Russia after the 2016 July coup attempt against the Turkish government, but retain lingering suspicions of Russia's intentions and regional designs which sit just below the surface.[24] Improvement in relations between Russia and Georgia is not likely in the short term. Turkey has overtaken Russia as Georgia's main economic partner. From 2006 to 2018 Turkey took the top place in Georgian imports, increasing from a 14.13 per cent share of total imports to 16.12 per cent, while Russia' proportion declined from 15.18 per cent to 10.23 per cent.[25] Since 2004 the flow of investment from Turkey into Georgia has increased, especially under President Saakashvili (2003–12). Turkish firms were actively involved in Georgia's privatization programmes in the 1990s and 2000s. The Georgian government continues to urge Turkish companies to invest more in Georgia. It will help reduce economic dependence on the Russian Federation and compete with the expansion of Russian firms in the country.[26] Turkey's investments in Georgia are primarily in construction, transport, telecommunications, banking, energy projects, the food industry, tourism, and agriculture.[27]

Tbilisi's offers of favourable investment opportunities for Turkish businesses has fuelled an intensification of economic ties between Turkey and Georgia. Turkish businesses are most active in Achara, in south-west Georgia. The autonomous republic of Achara is adjacent to Turkey. For many centuries (until the Treaty of Berlin in 1878), Achara was part of the Ottoman Empire. A significant part of the Georgian population of Achara, particularly in the rural areas of Upper Achara, is Muslim. According to the 2014 census, 132,850 Muslims are living in Achara, which is approximately 40 per cent of the region's population.[28] The number of Turkish tourists along with Turkish business activity has increased every year. In 2017 there were 1.24 million visitors to Georgia from Turkey.[29] Turkish tourists remain among the most numerous in Georgia, which has led to some tensions with local Georgian residents.

Despite the prosperity Turkish business brings, historical animosities remain. Turkish companies are invested in large construction and hydropower projects in Georgia[30] and hold the management rights for the Tbilisi and Batumi airports

(TAV).[31] The Batumi airport operates local Turkish flights, and residents of Artvin province in northeastern Turkey use Batumi airport because of its proximity. The activity of TAV Airports Holding in Georgia is controversial.[32] Many experts believe that freedom of action for both local and international air carriers has been limited by TAV.

The Russo-Georgian War of 2008

During the August War of 2008, Turkey proposed a regional security project called the 'Caucasus Stability and Security Platform'. Turkish Prime Minister Recep Erdoğan first announced this initiative on 11 August 2008 at a meeting with President Medvedev in Moscow. The primary goal of this initiative was to ensure conflict resolution among countries of the region, particularly those concerning Russia and Turkey. Five states – Russia, Turkey, Georgia, Armenia and Azerbaijan – were to be organized under a three (the South Caucasian states) plus two (Russia and Turkey) arrangement. The UN would be included in any negotiations conducted by the five states.[33] However, these efforts only revealed Turkey's weak position in relation to Russia and its role in the South Caucasus.[34] The proposed pact was unpopular in Georgia due to its practical exclusion of any Western partners. Any talk of compromise with Russia was not acceptable to Georgia. The platform quickly lost its meaning with Russia's recognition of Abkhazia and South Ossetia as independent states on 26 August 2008. Moscow's official position is that there were five countries in the region (including South Ossetia and Abkhazia). Russia, officially, has 'diplomatic relations with four of them, while relations are temporarily suspended with Georgia'.[35] The Turkish initiative received a lukewarm reception in Washington. Matthew Bryza, then Deputy Assistant Secretary of State, claimed the Americans had not even been informed about the initiative.[36]

A constraint on Turkey's intervention in the South Caucasus at the expense of Russia is Turkey's trading relationship with Russia. It is far more significant for Turkey than trade with the small South Caucasian states. Turkey is compelled to balance Georgia and the United States on the one hand with Russia on the other.[37] The pro-Russia business lobby in Turkey is a powerful pressure group, and Turkish construction companies have made significant investments in Russia. Turkey has to be cautious in its relations with Georgia, given the damage it could do to its close relationship with Russia.[38] Georgia is uncomfortably squeezed between Russia and Turkey, though given its importance as a transit route and its close relationship with the United States, it has leverage.[39] But since the Russo-Georgian War of 2008, it has become increasingly clear that Turkey has shifted strategically toward Russia.

Turkophobia

A serious problem for Georgia is managing powerful negative attitudes toward Turkey in Georgian society. Compared to commercial and strategic engagement between Turkey and Georgia, citizen links, especially through the mutual engagement of civil society organizations, have been minimal. There is no significant analysis in Turkey regarding its Georgian neighbour, and Turkish soft power has largely been restricted to its educational and religious influence in Georgia. This is the result of at least three factors: first, the fear of Turkey's economic dominance (this applies above all to Achara, despite the fact that Turkish business activity greatly contributes to economic development of the autonomous republic); second, Turkey has invested significant amounts in Georgia's educational sector including religious schools; third, Turkey has always been seen as the 'other' for Georgians, historically perceived as religiously alien. In Achara, formerly a part of the Ottoman Empire where a significant part of the population is Muslim, the Turkish influence often creates resentment.

Turkophobia is a sensitive issue in Georgian–Turkish relations. It concerns both local Muslims (ethnically Georgian Acharians and resident Azerbaijanis), as well as the growing Turkish community in Georgia. Georgian Muslims in Achara and elsewhere are often referred to as 'Tatars'; orthodox Christianity is perceived to be the source of Georgian identity. The widespread term 'Tatar' in reference to Muslims is related to religion more than ethnic affiliation. The word 'Tatar', when used to refer to all Muslims, bears negative connotations and causes much frustration among Muslims. Georgian Muslims do not use this term to refer to themselves, but the term 'Tatar' has long been rooted in the Georgian mind as synonymous with 'Muslim', carrying connotations of violence and aggression.[40]

According to Eto Buziashvili 'the spread of narratives regarding the threat of "Turkish expansionism" have intensified, as a number of pro-Kremlin actors, including media outlets and Facebook trolls, have increasingly characterised Turkey as an existential threat for Georgia'.[41] Pro-Russian journalists and politicians claim the Treaty of Kars between the Soviet Union and Turkey (1921) will expire soon, and it will lead to Turkey's annexation of Achara as a result. But the 100-year agreement has no expiration date, and Turkish officials no longer express any such irredentist claims. Other websites promote anti-Turkish stories. On the site *tvalsazrisi.ge*, the title of one article is 'Georgian Muslims are Ready to Obtain Independence with Arms'.[42] On YouTube, a new Russian news channel called Russian Arms (RA), promoted a story entitled 'The Islamisation of Georgia is Fast Approaching'.[43]

The Georgian–Turkish relationship is sensitive to mutual sleights. There was controversy in the village of Chela over a building which local Christians regard as the ruins of an old Christian church, but which is now a mosque. There is a widespread belief, even among Georgia's academic and political circles (although it must be noted that the majority of scholars do not share this view) that Turkey is using local Georgian Muslims as a fifth column for increasing its influence in Georgia.[44] Turkey's expansion of religious opportunities for young Georgian Muslim men adds to this fear. A considerable number of Acharan students receive religious education in Turkey. Many of them are financed by the Turkish 'Marmara Foundation for Education' (Marmara Egitim Vakfi).[45] The education of these young Acharans is often financed by their relatives, Turkish citizens of Georgian origin.[46]

The official religious administration of Turkey, known as Diyanet, along with Turkish 'non-governmental' religious organizations such as Süleymancı (supporters of the Turko-Muslim thinker Hilmi Tunahan (1888–1959), and Fehtullahçı – the network created by Fethullah Gülen – are all active in Georgia. The presence of such religious groups in Georgia has caused considerable unease among the orthodox clergy in Georgia. Turkish proselytizing is seen as a threat to Georgian identity.

Georgia, as a small neighbouring state, is often under pressure to comply with Turkey's demands. Two examples are illustrative. On 23 March 2017 the parliament of Georgia in a first reading, passed a bill to make the Battle of Didgori, on 12 August, a 'great victory day' and a public holiday. The Battle of Didgori took place in 1118 near Tibilisi. The Georgian army defeated the combined forces of the neighbouring Islamic powers. In the collective memory of Georgians, this battle holds a special place. As a result of the victory, Georgia established its dominance in the South Caucasus and adjoining territories. The so-called 'Golden Age' of Georgia began. However, the draft legislation was put on hold. The sponsor of the bill, Nukri Kantaria, explained this was for two reasons: first there was a need for further consultation with historians; but second, delay was requested by the Turkish embassy. The Turkish embassy argued, according to Kantaria, that 'Didgori is a day of defeat for Turkey and such a move by the parliament might cause certain discomfort in (Georgian–Turkish) relations. It was a friendly request.'[47]

The other example is the controversy surrounding the Chaglar educational network in Georgia. This is associated with the Gülen movement, which is antagonistic to the current Turkish administration under Recep Erdoğan. The Gülen movement began its activity in Georgia in the 1990s. The establishment of Gülen's educational network in Georgia was facilitated by Turkey's economic progress in the 1980s and by favourable conditions for educational activities created in Central Asia and the Caucasus following the collapse of the Soviet Union. Although the central tenets of the movement are based on Islamic ideas, the network is focused more on Turkish nationalism and Turkish values. The schools opened by the movement in Georgia were secular. Turkish educational institutions in Georgia include Demirel College and the International Black Sea University, both in Tbilisi, and the Shahin Friendship Lyceum and the Demirel primary school in Batumi. There is a Turkish Language Centre in Kutaisi. They functioned under the auspices of Chaglar Ltd. In 2016 the Turkish parliament established the Maarif Foundation, its goal was to replace the philanthropic activities of the Gülen movement.

Turkey's consul in Batumi remarked that parents should not send their children to educational institutions like the Shahin School, which are 'raising generations serving not the state, but a terrorist group'. These schools had no contact with terrorists or radicals – they were ordinary secondary schools, but were connected with the Gülen movement. As a result of Turkish actions, the Demirel College manager, Mustafa Emre Çabuk, was dismissed and subsequently spent nine months in a Georgian prison, accused of having links to what the Turks classified as a 'terrorist organization'. He was denied a request for asylum in Georgia. Georgian civil society organizations protested and emphasized that Çabuk would be subject to political persecution if he was returned, and issued a joint statement calling on President Giorgi Margvelashvili to grant Georgian citizenship to Çabuk and his family members.[48] Amnesty International called for urgent action, appealing to the Georgian authorities 'to comply with their obligations under international human rights law not to deport, extradite or otherwise return Mustafa Çabuk to a country where he would be at risk of torture, other ill-treatment or other serious human rights violations'.[49]

Bilateral relations between the two states have been exacerbated by the issue of Abkhazia. The Abkhazian minority of Turkey is a well-organized community, lobbying Turkish political and business circles for recognition of the self-proclaimed republic. The Abkhazian minority wants to reinstate the ferry service between Trabzon and Sokhumi which was ended by Turkey in 1996 at Georgia's request. The Abkhazian minority of Turkey maintains commercial connections with Abkhazia.[50] Ankara publicly supports Georgia's territorial integrity, but it turns a blind eye to Turkish businessmen trading with Abkhazia. Unofficially, Turkey is the second largest trading partner with Abkhazia, after Russia. Turkish private companies are actively involved in Abkhazia. The attempts by the Abkhazian community in exile to deepen ties between Turkey and Abkhazia have caused disagreements between the Georgian and Turkish governments. On several occasions Georgia has detained Turkish ships (1998, 2004, 2009, 2013, etc.) en route to Abkhazia.

Turkey, Russia and Georgia

Georgia's foreign policy strategy document (2015–18) emphasizes Turkey is Georgia's strategic partner and that Georgia seeks to deepen existing political dialogue and relations with the republic of Turkey in areas of trade, economy, transport, energy and culture.[51] A strategic cooperation council between the two states has been set up. But Turkey's foreign policy, as expressed by Ahmet Davutoğlu, Turkey's former prime minister between 2014 and 2016, has raised Georgian concerns. Davutoğlu in his speech in 2011 spoke about the reintegration of major towns of the former provinces of the Ottoman Empire into the Turkish state.[52] Among the towns Davutoğlu mentioned was Batumi, Georgia's vital seaport.[53] Particularly after the failed coup d'état in Turkey in July 2016, Georgia is in a delicate position in its relations with Turkey. Former Georgian Prime Minister, Giorgi Kvirikashvili, was the first foreign official to arrive in Ankara following the failed coup, and Georgia's officials have not expressed any negative attitudes regarding purges and human rights violations in Turkey, only neutral statements about the importance of Turkey for Georgia and encouragement of its democratic development. Kvirikashvili stressed that 'Turkey is our strategic partner and stability in Turkey is very important for us'.[54] The oppositional United National Movement (UNM) also underlined that 'peace, stability, and functioning democratic institutions in our neighbouring state and strategic partner are of vital importance for Georgia'.[55] The Georgian delegation voted against the resolution of the Council of Europe adopted in April 2017 which called on Turkey to lift its state of emergency as soon as possible, to release detained journalists and politicians, and to restore freedom of expression and rights of the media.

Political stability in Turkey is in the security interest of Georgia. Turkish membership of the EU would benefit Georgia's own aspirations for deeper integration, though at present, Turkish–EU relations are frosty. Before the coup attempt in 2016, Erdoğan used the Syrian refugee crisis to try to obtain visa-free travel for Turkish citizens in the EU and refused to change the country's controversial anti-terror laws which it employs against its Kurdish minority. Thus, under present circumstances, Georgia cannot make any predictions regarding Turkey's relations with the EU and the West more generally. On a visit to Ankara in January 2018, NATO Deputy Secretary General Rose Gottemoeller emphasized that the NATO alliance would stand by Turkey.[56] For Georgia, any improvement of Turkey's relations with Europe is important. The escalating Syrian crisis, in which Turkey has become embroiled, and its increasingly difficult relations with Russia, may work to Georgia's advantage. Turkey's foreign policy direction may, at some stage, return to its alliance with the West as Russia's power in the Middle East grows.

Iran

After the dissolution of the Soviet Empire and the creation of independent states in the Caucasus, Iran tried to be as active as possible in the South Caucasus. But it was unable to compete with major foreign actors like Russia, Turkey and the United States.[57] But for the independent states of the South Caucasus, the establishment of close economic contacts with Iran was important in a practical sense and provided some leverage against other powerful neighbours. Thomas de Waal has noted, 'Much of the Western world treats Iran as a pariah state. But countries surrounding Iran cannot afford to take an aggressive stance towards a big and powerful neighbour with whom they have so much everyday business'.[58] Iran is in the peculiar position of having land and sea borders with fifteen different states. Georgia has no direct border with Iran but historically and geopolitically Georgia and Iran could be considered neighbours. 'South Caucasus-Iranian relations are influenced and shaped not only by the regional context but also by Russian-Iranian, US-Iranian and European-Iranian relations'.[59] Iran has taken a pragmatic attitude toward its South Caucasian neighbours. Mesbahi and Homayounvash point out that 'a predominantly secular posture toward the South Caucasus has made it all but imperative for Tehran to keep its Transcaucasia policy as distinct as practicable from its Middle East policy'.[60] There are, however, some complications in the Georgian–Iranian relationship, generated by three factors: tense relations between Russia and Georgia (Russia is an important partner of Iran especially in the Middle East); a close Turkish–Georgian relationship; and Georgia's pro-Western aspirations and ties with NATO.

The context

In the autumn of 1991, prior to the collapse of the Soviet Union, Iranian diplomats arrived in Georgia to meet President Gamsakhurdia. They wanted information from the highest-ranking Georgian official regarding political changes in the country. The visit was unofficial.[61] After the proclamation of Georgia's independence in April 1991, the first official visit of the head of the sovereign state of Georgia was to the Islamic Republic of Iran. Iran was one of the first states to recognize Georgia's independence and to open an embassy in Tbilisi in 1993. The first official agreement on the establishment of diplomatic relations after the collapse of the Soviet Union was signed with Iran.

The former President of Iran, Hassan Rouhani (who was replaced as president by Ebrahim Raisi on 5 August 2021), visited Georgia twice, first as the First Deputy Speaker of the Islamic Consultative Assembly-Iranian Parliament (1995), and subsequently as the Secretary of the Supreme National Security Council (2001). During the presidencies of Mohammad Khatami, Mahmoud Ahmadinejad and Hassan Rouhani, high-level visits between the two countries were rare. President Saakashvili visited Iran in 2004. In 2017, an official visit of the Georgian Prime Minister Giorgi Kvirikashvili to Iran suggested a warming of relations was taking place. In the framework of the visit, a number of memoranda of understanding between Georgian and Iranian ministries and government departments were signed. Economic relations between the two countries have gradually increased since Georgian independence. According to the National Statistics Office of Georgia, since 1995, the two countries show a steady increase in trade and FDI, most notably from Iran to Georgia (see Figure 5.7).

Import, Export, FDI (Thsd USD)

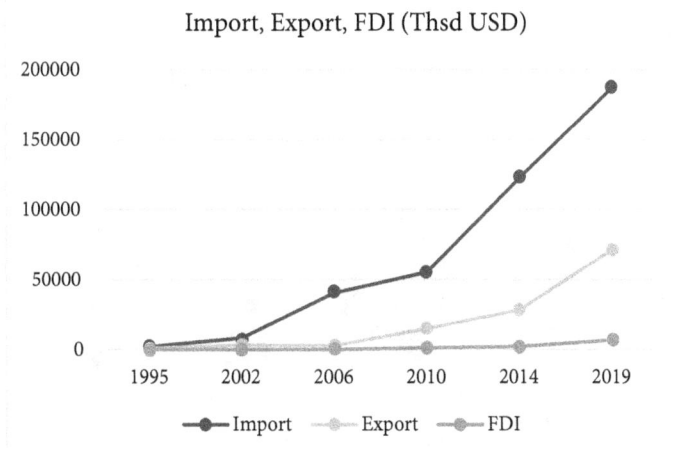

Figure 5.7 Import, export and FDI with Iran: 1995–2019.

Source: Geostat: www.geostat.ge/en/modules/categories/35/external-trade

The leading five products imported by Georgia from Iran are: (1) mineral fuels, oils, distillation products; (2) iron and steel; (3) ceramic products; (4) plastics; and (5) edible fruits, nuts, peel of citrus fruit, melons.[62] The top exported products from Georgia to Iran are: (1) meat; (2) lumber and articles made from wood; (3) man-made filaments; (4) iron and steel; and (5) pharmaceutical products.[63] Energy resources like gas and oil are important factors in economic relations between Georgia and Iran. Since 2016 up to 14 million cubic metres of natural gas per day are supplied to Georgia for use in its thermal power plants and for other private companies. In 2016, Iran and Georgia concluded an agreement on crude oil to be supplied from two Iranian oil fields – Ahvaz and Dezful.[64] As a result of sanctions against Iran, between 2013 and 2016, exports as well as imports and FDI have decreased between the two countries (see Figure 5.8).

Georgia, Iran and Russia

The 2008 Russo-Georgian War demonstrated the importance of Iran to the Georgian leadership. Without loudly condemning the Russian invasion, Iran officially declared its support for Georgia's sovereignty and territorial integrity and emphasized its fidelity to international standards and agreements. Iran refused to recognize the independence of Abkhazia and South Ossetia after the 2008 war, despite Russia's request.[65] At the same time Iran did not express a well-defined position concerning the conflict. Then Iranian President Mahmud Ahmadinejad declared in the UN General Assembly on 23 September 2008 that 'the lives, properties and rights of the people of Georgia, South Ossetia and Abkhazia are victims of policies and provocations of NATO and certain Western powers, and the underhand actions of the Zionists'.[66] However, Georgia, South Ossetia and Abkhazia were all placed on the same level in the president's statement, which was taken badly by the Georgian government. In general, Tehran's message on

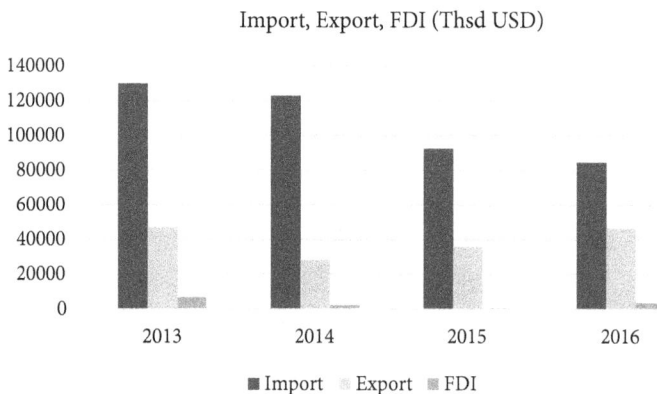

Import, Export, FDI (Thsd USD)

Figure 5.8 Import, export and FDI with Iran: 2013–16.

Source: www.geostat.ge/en/modules/categories/35/external-trade

the August War was that Georgia was wrong to take US promises for granted and that it paid a price for its naivety. Ahmadinejad argued it would be better for the regional states to establish closer mutual links with Iran in the security sphere, rather than seeking security from an unpredictable United States.

Concerning the resolution of regional conflicts, Iran argues that only regional actors (Russia, Turkey, Iran, Azerbaijan, Georgia and Armenia) should be involved. In 2001, during an official visit to Georgia, then Secretary of the National Security Council of Iran, Hasan Rouhani declared: 'Regional cooperation is strategically important for stabilization of the world and security in the Caucasian region. Continuous political consultations with Iran will help Georgia to solve regional problems effectively, without resorting to the help of foreigners.'[67] Tehran portrays itself as a 'protector' of nearby small states, while promoting anti-hegemonic (anti-US) policies in the region.[68] At the same time Tehran is aware that Georgia can be used as a strategically important base for the West in case of any military action against Iran. This question became relevant in 2011–12 when there was some discussion of a possible Western or Israeli military strike against Iran. Tehran was concerned about Georgia's close relations with Israel (the temporary cancellation of the visa-free regime with Iran in July 2013 coincided with the establishment of a Georgian–Israeli visa-free agreement). In the Iranian press at the time, it was stressed that 'Israel uses these countries for collecting espionage information on Iran.'[69]

Russia has lost its credibility and political influence in Georgia. But Iran must consider Russia in any of its relations with Georgia. Iran's rapprochement with Georgia does not correspond with Russian interests. Russian officials point out to Iranians that Georgia is an ally of the United States and will be used by Americans in any military action against Iran. At the same time, Iran, despite its partnership with Russia, does not fully trust Moscow. Iran is concerned that Russia might disregard Iran's interests when faced with international pressure, or when it can gain some advantage by taking sides with the EU or the United States.[70] Glen Howard, President of the Jamestown Foundation, has noted that Russia will do its best to prevent Georgian–Iranian rapprochement, as it did with Armenia. Russia prevented Armenia from constructing a gas pipeline and railway connection with Iran; and, in 2005, most likely under Russian pressure, the Armenian government rejected a proposal to consider the transit of natural gas from Iran to Europe via Georgia and Ukraine. Prime Minister Andranik Margaryan declared that the government could not neglect Russia's interests.[71] Armenia has also been trying to build an Iran–Armenian railway to connect Iran and the Russian-led Eurasian Economic Union. The railway initiative was launched in 2012 but Russia did not show any interest in financing the project.[72] Iran will continue to promote the idea of the south–north transport corridor but the promotion of such an idea is not in Russia's interests – it would give Armenia greater economic independence – and would require major investment.[73]

Relations between Georgia and Iran hit a low in 2008 when Georgia extradited an Iranian citizen to the United States to face charges related to breaking the arms embargo against Iran – which Tehran saw as an anti-Iranian act. Relations

Tourists from Iran

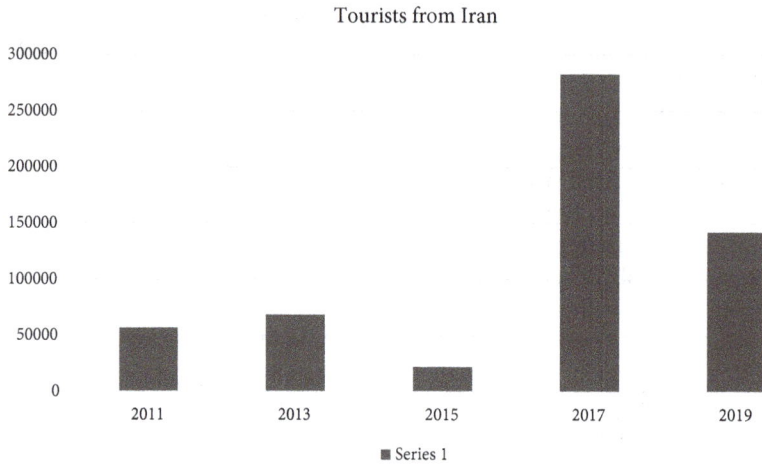

Figure 5.9 International travel from Iran to Georgia: 2011–19.

Source: https://gnta.ge/statistics/

between the two countries were essentially frozen until Iran and Georgia reached an agreement on a visa-free regime on 26 January 2011. Georgia became one of the forty countries of the world where Iranians could travel without visas and quickly became one of the most popular destinations for Iranian tourists (see Figure 5.9).

Iranian tourism led to increased economic exchange. Since 2011, Georgia has become a stable partner with Tehran, along with Turkey, Armenia and Azerbaijan.[74] But Georgia's position as a particularly close partner of the United States attracts intense attention in Iran's policymaking circles. According to former Ambassador of the United States to Georgia, John Bass (in a WikiLeaks release): 'Georgia tries to build relations with Iran. Georgia agreed with many of our arguments about the policy of Iran and was ready to put these questions directly to the Iranians. Georgia still faces lingering anger from Tehran for extraditing an Iranian arms smuggler to the United States several years ago.' At the same time, Bass continued, Georgia is reluctant to 'alienate an influential regional neighbour and chief trading partner'.[75]

Georgian–Iranian relations are determined by a number of contradictory factors. We might sum it up as follows: Iran, as a large state, has no territorial pretensions towards its neighbours, including Georgia; it resists US and NATO influence in the Caucasus, and generally supports Russian interests in the region; the Baku–Tbilisi–Ceyhan pipeline does not correspond to Iranian economic interests and diminishes the importance of Iran as a transit route for Caspian oil and natural gas. Iran is interested in Georgian transit routes to the Black Sea and Europe and shows public concern for the Muslim minorities of Georgia. Yet despite a declared good-neighbourly relationship, Georgia has no vitally important ties with Iran. The Western orientation of Georgia and its complicated relations with

Russia do not help its rapprochement with Iran. A new factor is President Biden's new administration, and its policy towards Iran. A return to the 2015 nuclear deal would, overall, be in Georgia's interests and make both political and economic relations with Iran easier.

The Iranian presence in Georgia

Iran wishes to establish closer economic links with Georgia, but there is a significant gap between potential and actual economic relations between the two countries. In the early 1990s, the first trade and industrial exhibitions were held in Tbilisi with Iranian participation. Agreements were made at the inter-regional level. A 'friendship and cooperation' agreement between the Imereti region of western Georgia and Gilan Province in Iran was signed. A permanent Gilan trade centre was established first in Kutaisi (Imereti's regional centre) and later in Tbilisi. In February 2001, Iranian businessmen living in Georgia established 'The Union of Iranian Businessmen in Georgia'.

After the 'Rose Revolution' in 2003 and the liberalization of the economy, the number of Iranian businesses in Georgia increased, attracted by a more open business climate, easier migration and increased foreign investment opportunities. Georgia's adherence to a free economy and Western values was attractive for Iranian businessmen, but Georgia was also a country which had been historically, culturally and geographically close to Iran. Since the 1970s, Iranian citizens of Georgian descent have been able to obtain residence in Georgia, and even citizenship after 1992. Most of them are from the isolated Fereydan region of the Isfahan Province in the centre of Iran, where native Georgians were forcibly taken to in the seventeenth century by Shah Abbas I.[76]

For Iranian businessmen, there was a faint prospect that Georgia would gain EU membership. Georgia could once again become a corridor connecting Iranians with Europe. There was, as a result, a boom in Georgian residence permits for Iranians (see Figure 5.10). Intermediary agencies were set up to ensure the registration of Iranian companies in Georgia; Iranian companies opened bank accounts and obtained temporary residence permits for their employees. The possibility of open immigration of Iranians to Georgia, and the increased number of Iranian companies aroused concern among Georgia's Western partners who conjectured that the Islamic Republic of Iran was avoiding Western economic and banking sanctions, and was engaged in money-laundering activities via its companies registered in Georgia. Joint Iranian–Georgian companies based in Georgia were accused of laundering the money of Iranian state-sponsored organizations (such as the Corps of the Islamic Revolutionary Guards). The *Wall Street Journal* reported in June 2013, that 'Iranian businessmen are flocking to Georgia, a long-time US ally in the Caucasus region, to pursue profits evaporating in much of the world'.[77] As a result, several Iranian companies had their accounts in Georgian banks frozen by the Georgian government.

In July 2013, Georgia unilaterally cancelled the visa-free regime for Iranian citizens (it was reinstated in 2017). According to Georgian officials, this measure

Immigration from Iran

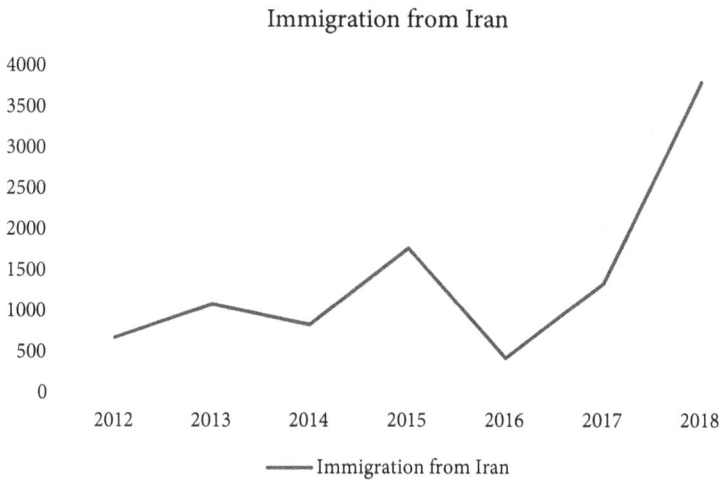

Figure 5.10 Immigration from Iran to Georgia: 2012–18.

Source: www.geostat.ge/en/modules/categories/322/migration

had a temporary character. Georgian authorities denied any connection between this decision and pressure from European and American partners. The unilateral decision of Georgian authorities to re-introduce a visa regime for Iranian citizens was naturally assessed negatively in Iran. Mark Mullen, former chairman of Transparency International in Georgia, challenged the view that the Iranian presence in Georgia was dangerous for Georgian security. In a post entitled 'Georgia and Iran, Georgians and Iranians' he wrote

> ninety nine per cent (of Iranian visitors to Georgia) were quite educated, Western looking, wealthy people who just wanted to have an option near but out of Iran. But only 1 per cent were money launderers or worse. In any case, the system worked and there were many Iranians who began to rebuild ties … Most of the Iranians weren't so worried about working, they just wanted to buy an apartment and get their kids in schools; they had plenty of money that they hoped to invest.[78]

Iran and Georgia have limited economic relations today. Iranian businessmen invest mostly in machinery, construction and tourism, but there is no official data about the total amount of Iranian investments. While closer ties with Iran have bolstered imports and encouraged investment, Iran's overall impact on the Georgian economy is minimal.[79] When the visa-free regime was in place, there was a sharp rise in level of trade and tourism between two countries. Iranian imports increased between 2011 and 2013 by 1,590 per cent and were valued at over 100 million USD. But they started from a very low level (by comparison Georgia's trade with Turkey in 2012 amounted to more than 1.34 billion USD).[80] Yet the increase in the flow of Iranian tourists to Georgia was undeniable; it reached over 80,000 people in 2012, and after the reintroduction of the visa-free regime, in 2017, the number of Iranian tourists reached 300,000.[81] According to 2017 data, bilateral trade reached 181 million USD, an increase of 38 per cent over the previous year. Georgian exports to Iran reached 64 million USD (a 64 per cent increase). Between 2015 and 2019, 42 per cent of the real estate sold in Georgia was bought by Iranian citizens.[82] However, despite such progress, one of the major obstacles facing trade between the two countries is the difficulties of bank transfers. Another is the tightening of rules of entry into Georgia for Iranian citizens (despite the visa-free regime). In the first half of 2019, 13,165 people were denied entry into Georgia and 5,656 (42 per cent) of them were Iranian citizens.

An important aspect of Iran–Georgian relations is Iranian 'soft power' in Georgia. Since the 1990s, the Iranian embassy in Georgia has funded Iranian studies (Persian language and literature, the history of Iran) in Georgian universities. 'Iranian Centres' have been opened throughout the country. In 2001 a branch of the Great Ayatollah Sistani Institute 'Al ul-Beit' was opened in Tbilisi. There are, in addition, Shi'a madrassas and mosques, funded by Iranian foundations, in the towns and villages of Eastern Georgia where Muslim Azerbaijanis are in a majority. After the reintroduction of the visa-free regime, air travel between the two countries has intensified and there are now regular flights – four to six flights a week on average – from Tehran to Tbilisi. The overwhelming majority of passengers are Iranian.

The Georgian authorities have shown considerable tolerance of Iranian political and cultural expansion in Georgia, but the Georgian government is aware of its obligations towards its Western partners. The Iranian side understands that Georgia is not fully independent in making decisions, like the ending of Iranian visa-free travel. Georgian–Iranian relations are not simply determined by bilateral decisions, but exist in the context of Iran's and Georgia's relationship with the West. Should Iran return to the international arena, political and economic relations between Georgia and Iran could develop in at least three directions: an increase in tourism and cultural exchange, intensification of business contacts, and greater investments in Georgia's transit system. Considering Georgia's favourable geographical position, and Iran's rich energy resources and commercial potential, if sanctions on Iran were removed, Georgia would become a vital and cost-saving bridge to Europe. Iran has already announced an expansion of its role in the South Caucasus energy sphere with negotiations over an Iranian–Armenia gas pipeline. Iranian officials visiting Georgia have noted the potential of the Georgian ports of Batumi and Poti, but any steps toward greater Iranian involvement have met with scepticism from Georgia's Western partners, and in particular the United States. In 2014, during a meeting with the new ambassador of Georgia in Iran, President Rouhani stressed Iran's interest in developing commercial relations with Georgia. 'We appreciate our contacts with Georgia. Your country represents for Iran an entry into the Black Sea ports, especially to Batumi that has for us paramount value. In this regard it is difficult to overestimate the importance of laying a railway line from Iran to Georgia.'[83] The signing of the 'Deep and Comprehensive Free Trade Agreement' (DCFTA) by Georgia with the EU in 2014, creates further opportunities for the Iranian business community which could establish and distribute joint Iranian–Georgian products to the EU market.[84] But in 2020, given the general instability in the Middle East, especially in Syria and Iraq, and Iran's tense relations with the United States and EU, we can hardly be optimistic about the future of Iranian–Georgian relations.

Conclusion

Georgia's perception of Turkey as a major regional partner and strategic ally has not been affected by recent changes in Turkish policy. Turkey has been a reliable partner for Georgia since the 1990s. The current Georgian government's positive image of Turkey persists regardless of changes to ruling political forces in Georgia. Both the authorities and pro-Western opposition groups support deepening the relationship with Turkey, which has a crucial role for Georgia in the process of interoperability with NATO. Pro-Russian and anti-Western political parties and groups have a negative attitude towards the intensification of Georgia's relations with Turkey, but these organizations are supported by only a small minority of Georgia's population. The necessity of preserving and deepening relations with Turkey means that the Georgian authorities (including the pro-Western opposition) rarely criticize Turkish policy, including human rights abuses. Ankara's neutral position on the issue of Abkhazia and economic projects with Russia are not in Georgia's interest (although the recent differences between Turkey and Russia over Syria suggest the Russian–Turkish relationship is not a solid one). Trilateral cooperation between Turkey, Georgia and Azerbaijan is of vital importance for all the parties. Turkey's presence in Georgia is also crucial in balancing Russia. However, the 2020 Nagorno-Karabagh war has created a new geopolitical situation in the region which is not particularly favourable to Georgia. Russia has increased its military presence in the region, and Turkey's attention is now focused on economic and political support for Azerbaijan. Turkish and Russian military cooperation (though tenuous) in the South Caucasus is not in Georgia's interests.[85] It is a reminder of the damaging effect Soviet Russian and Turkish cooperation brought to Georgia in 1921, when the two powers agreed among themselves on the division of influence in the region.

Georgia's Western orientation and its complicated relations with Russia will not facilitate a warming of relations with Iran. Economic relations between Iran and Georgia cannot be compared with the scale of Georgian–Turkish interactions. Georgia cannot compete with its neighbours Armenia and Azerbaijan, which have deeper ties with Iran. Iran is interested in Georgia's transit potential for exporting its goods to the West, but there is currently little chance of Tehran exploiting this advantage. In recent years Georgia has become one of the most popular destinations for Iranian tourists and it is not uncommon for Iranian citizens to seek permanent residence permits in Georgia. Many Iranians of Georgian origin try to acquire Georgian citizenship or the so-called 'compatriot status' and settle in Georgia. But overall, in the light of the West's anti-Iranian policy and general instability in the wider Middle East, there is unlikely to be any significant change in Georgian–Iranian economic and political relations in the short term, even after the Nagorno-Karabagh war and Turkish President Erdohan's proposal for a new regional platform that would include Russia, Turkey, Azerbaijan, Georgia, Iran and Armenia. Georgia is unlikely to look favourably upon such a proposal, which would give Turkey and Russia a dominant position in the region.[86]

Notes

1   F.S. Larrabee and I.O. Lesser, *Turkish Foreign Policy in an Age of Uncertainty* (Santa Monica, CA: RAND, 2003).

2   G.G. Arnakis, 'Turanism: An Aspect of Turkish Nationalism', *Balkan Studies*, 1 (1960), pp. 19–32.

3   David Batashvili, 'How Turkey Exercises its New Grand Strategy: An Outline', Georgian Foundation for Strategic and International Studies, *Expert Opinion*, 85, 2017.

4   Based on the 1921 treaty of Kars the village of Sarpi on the Black Sea coast was divided in two. The Sarpi checkpoint was opened in 1989. Today Sarpi is the main border checkpoint on the Georgia–Turkey border.

5   William Hale, 'Turkey and Transcaucasia', in David Menashri (ed.), *Central Asia Meets the Middle East* (London: Frank Cass, 1998), p. 165.

6   See for example: Revaz Gachechiladze. sakartvelo msoplios kontekstshi. XX da XXI saukuneebis politikuri tskhovrebis dziritadi momentebi (Georgia in the World Context: Highlights of Political Life in XX and XXI Centuries) (Tbilisi: Sulakauri Publishing, 2017), p. 605.

7   A substantial number of citizens of Georgia have settled in Turkey and found employment as cheap labour. 'Among illegal labour migrants in Turkey, citizens of Georgia are currently in the lead', www.sabah.com.tr/Ekonomi/2013/04/28/hepsinin-umudu-turkiye. This draws certain historical parallels with the nineteenth century when the Achara region was part of the Ottoman Empire and a large portion of the local population would go to other Turkish provinces in search of seasonal jobs. After the incorporation of Achara into the Russian Empire and border restrictions, such opportunities were eliminated. This triggered the migration of a large part of Achara's population to the Ottoman territory (the so-called 'Muhajirs', i.e. the emigrants). Thus, the migration of 'Muhajirs' which is often explained by the religious factor (Acharian expatriates were Muslim) was also driven by economic reasons.

8   State Commission of Migrant Issues (2017). *Migration Profile of Georgia*, http://migration.commission.ge/files/migration_profile_2017_eng__final_.pdf

9   www.info9.ge/sazogadoeba/195980-thurqethis-6-regionshi-chais-sezonze-saqarthvelos-10-000-moqalaqe-mushaobs.html?lang=ka-GE

10 See www.bsec-Organisation.org/main.aspx?ID=About_BSEC

11 Ibid.

12 www.bp.com/en_az/caspian/operationsprojects/pipelines/BTC.html

13 S.E. Garding, M. Ratner, C. Welt and J. Zanotti, *TurkStream: Russia's Newest Gas Pipeline to Europe*, Congressional Research Service (CRS), 2020.

14 Civil.ge, 'Turkish FM Çavuşoğlu: Georgia Should Become NATO Member', 23 January 2020, https://civil.ge/archives/335679 (accessed 9 March 2020).

15 Radiotavisupleba.ge, (The Reality and Perspective for Georgian-Turkish Military Collaboration), 3 May 2007, www.radiotavisupleba.ge/a/1552356.html (accessed 9 March 2020).

16 Zeyno Baran, 'Turkey and the Caucasus', in Bal İdris (ed.), *Turkish Foreign Policy in Post-Cold War Era* (Irvine, CA: BrownWalker Press, 2004), pp. 279–80.

17 Alexandre Rondeli, 'Security Threats in the Caucasus: Georgia's View', *Perceptions*, 3:2, (1998), pp. 43–53.

18 http://netgazeti.ge/news/254520/ (accessed 9 February 2018).

19 Ministry of Internal Affairs of Georgia, 'International Agreements', https://police.ge/en/ministry/structure-and-offices/international-relations-department/international-legal-cooperation/saertashoriso-khelshekrulebebi

20 Ministry of Defence of Georgia, The Trilateral Field Exercise 'Caucasian Eagle 2017', https://mod.gov.ge/en/news/read/5831/scavleba-kavkasiis-arcivi-2017 (accessed 9 March 2020).

21 See https://civil.ge/archives/111648, 20 December 2006 (accessed 30 July 2021).

22 Justyna Szalanska, 'Turkey and Georgia: Strategic Connections', www.bilgesam.org/en/incele/452/-turkey-and-georgia–strategic-connections/#.WoHcbiWuyM823 March 2012 (accessed 9 October 2017).

23 Wade Shepard, 'How Azerbaijan, Georgia, and Turkey Subverted Russia and Isolated Armenia with New Railway', 30 October 2017, www.forbes.com/sites/wadeshepard/2017/10/30/new-silk-road-azerbaijan-georgia-and-turkey-unite-over-new-rail-line-armenia-further-isolated/#338c53903aff (accessed 7 January 2018).

24 Michael Hikari Cecire, 'Georgia-Turkey-Azerbaijan Cooperation: Pragmatism Proves Durable Formula', *Eurasianet.org*, 1 June 2017, https://eurasianet.org/s/georgia-turkey-azerbaijan-cooperation-pragmatism-proves-durable-formula

25 World Bank, 'World Integrated Trade Solution database: Georgia Exports, Imports and Trade Balance by Country and Region', https://wits.worldbank.org/CountryProfile/en/Country/GEO/Year/2018/TradeFlow/EXPIMP

26 V. Modebadze, F.M. Sayın and R. Yılmaz, 'Georgian–Turkish Relations since the Breakdown of Soviet Union', Çankırı Karatekin Üniversitesi İktisadi ve İdari Bilimler Fakültesi Dergisi, 4:1 (2014), p. 365.

27 M.P. Arunova, 'Turtsiia-Gryziia: sotrudnichestvo i problemyi' [Turkey–Georgia: cooperation and problems], www.iimes.ru/?p=7629#more-7629

28 2014 General Population Census in Georgia, https://georgia.unfpa.org/en/publications/2014-general-population-census-georgia

29 www.tabula.ge/ge/story/128300-10-qvekana-saidanac-sakartveloshi-2017-tsels-kvelaze-meti-ucxoeli-vizitori-shemovida

30 Khelvachauri Hydro Power station 1 launched in 2017, Kirnati Hydro Power Station launched in 2018. S. Guthrie, 'Turkish Investments in Adjara Shrinks', *Georgia Today*, 20 August 2018, http://georgiatoday.ge/news/11913/Turkish-Investment-in-Adjara-Shrinks (accessed 23 April 2020).

31 Diba Nigar Göksel, 'Turkey and Georgia: Zero-Problems?' *On Wider Europe*, Black Sea Trust for Regional Cooperation, The German Marshal Fund of the United States, June 2013, www.gmfus.org/file/3054/download

32 Revaz Gachechiladze. *sakartvelo msoplios kontekstshi. XX da XXI saukuneebis politikuri tskhovrebis dziritadi momentebi* [Georgia in the World Context: Highlights of Political Life in XX and XXI Centuries] (Tbilisi: Sulakauri Publishing, 2017), p. 605.

33 Iran, one of the regional players, was excluded from the 'Five'. This naturally ruffled feathers in Iran. During a visit to Iran at the beginning of November 2009, Turkish Prime Minister Erdoğan underscored the significance of Iran's inclusion in the 'Pact for Caucasus Stability', but by that time 'the platform' had already sunk into oblivion.

34 Bayram Balci, 'Strengths and Constraints of Turkish Policy in the South Caucasus', *Insight Turkey*, 16:2 (Spring 2014), pp. 43–52.

35 Rossiia ne zhelaet vmeshatel'stva tret'ikh stran v protsessy na kavkaze. Mnenie. (Russia does not want the intervention of third countries in the processes in the Caucasus. Opinion) www.regnum.ru/news/24.10.2008 (last retrieved 15/05/2018).

36 https://hetq.am/eng/news/40364/peace-and-stability-in-the-caucasus-according-to-recep-tayyip-Erdoğan.html/

37 Bülent Aras and Pinar Akpinar, 'The Relations between Turkey and the Caucasus in the 2000s', *Perceptions*, 16:3 (Autumn 2011), pp. 53–68.

38 Ibid.

39 Revaz Gachechiladze. *sakartvelo msoplios kontekstshi*, p. 604.

40 *Political Aspects of Islam in Georgia*, ed. Irakli Menagharishvili, Giorgi Lobjanidze, Natela Sakhokia and Giorgi Gvimradze (Tibilisi: Strategic Research Institute, supported by the Friedrich-Ebert-Stiftung, 2013), p. 63.

41 https://medium.com/dfrlab/pro-kremlin-actors-fuel-anti-turkish-sentiment-in-georgia-4ee24aa17ceb

42 https://tvalsazrisi.ge/kartveli muslimebi mzad arian.

43 www.youtube.com/channel/UCQIHwaN7EMlx9cn1dO8pTvA?reload=9. The Battle of Didgori was fought between the armies of the Kingdom of Georgia and the Great Seljuq Empire in 1121 and in Georgia it is considered as the most important victory over the Turks which inaugurated the medieval Georgian Golden Age.

44 See, for example, Tamuna Uchidze, 'Turkophobia – istoriuli mekhsiereba tu realuri saprtkhe turketidan' [Turkophobia – Historical Memory or Real Danger from Turkey] 11 June 2014, http://sknews.ge/index.php?newsid=2753#.UoEHE3AwoV8 (accessed 15 February 2018).

45 Elizabeth Sieca-Kozlovski and Alexandre Toumarkine, *Geopolitique de la mer Noire: Turquie et pays de l'ex-URSS* (Paris: Karthala, 2000), p. 92.

46 Ekatherina Meiering-Mikadze, 'L'islam en Adjarie: Trajectoires historiques et implications contemporaines', *Cahiers d'études sur la Méditerranée orientale et le monde turco-iranien*, 27 (1999), p. 41.

47 http://netgazeti.ge/news/207421/ 14.07.2017

48 'Appeals Court Denies Refugee Status to Turkish Citizen Civil Georgia', *Civil Georgia*, 26 January 2018, http://civil.ge/eng/article.php?id=30826

49 'Amnesty: Turkish Teacher Detained by Georgia "at Imminent Risk" of Extradition', *Civil Georgia*, 29 May 2017, http://civil.ge/eng/article.php?id=30132&search=emre

50 Balci, 2014.

51 Ministry of Foreign Affairs of Georgia, *Foreign Policy Strategy 2019–2022*, https://mfa.gov.ge/MainNav/ForeignPolicy/ForeignPolicyStrategy.aspx?lang=ka-GE (accessed 09 March 2020).

52 Speech delivered by H.E. Ahmet Davutoğlu, Minister of Foreign Affairs of the Republic of Turkey, 'Vision 2023: Turkey's Foreign Policy Objectives' at the Turkey Investor Conference: The Road to 2023, London, 22 November 2011, www.mfa.gov.tr/speech-entitled-_vision-2023_-turkey_s-foreign-policy-objectives__-delivered-by-h_e_-ahmet-davutoglu_-minister-of-foreign-af.en.mfa

53 Ahmet Davutoğlu, 'Turkish Vision of Regional and Global Order: Theoretical Background and Practical Implementation', Keynote Lecture at the Conference on

Turkey's Foreign Policy in a Changing World at the University of Oxford, 1 May 2010, transcribed and published by *Political Reflection* 1:2 (2010), pp. 42–3. Erdoğan's statement regarding the 'inseparability of Rize and Batumi' caused irritation in Georgian society. 'Erdoğan: Eğer Misak-ı Milli diye bir derdimiz varsa … ', www. aljazeera.com.tr/haber/Erdoğan-eger-misak-i-milli-diye-bir-derdimiz-varsa (accessed 3 February 2018). It should be noted that some Georgian media outlets have reported that Erdoğan had allegedly spoken of holding a referendum in Batumi on unification with Turkey, but that is not true.

54　www.cacianalyst.org/publications/analytical-articles/item/13388-real-friends?-georgia-turkey-relations-in-the-wake-of-the-july-15-coup-attempt.html

55　Ibid.

56　NATO Deputy Stresses Alliance's Dedication to Turkey, https://search.proquest.com/docview/1991139460/FCC79941DA7540F3PQ/17?accountid=143042

57　A.H. Cordesman, B. Gold, R. Shelala and M. Gibbs, *US and Iranian Strategic Competition: Turkey and South Caucasus.* Centre for Strategic and International Studies, 2013, https://csis-prod.s3.amazonaws.com/s3fs-public/legacy_files/files/publication/130206_turk_casp_chap9.pdf (accessed 10 March 2020).

58　Thomas de Waal, 'Iran's Relieved Neighbors in the Caucasus', Carnegie Moscow Centre, http://carnegie.ru/eurasiaoutlook?fa=52215 (26 June 2013).

59　Alexandre Rondeli, 'Iran and Georgia – Relations Could be Closer', *Expert Opinion*, 18. Georgian Foundation for Strategic and International Studies, 2014, p. 5.

60　Mohaiddin Mesbahi and Mohammad Homayounvash, 'Iran and the Changing Geopolitics of the South Caucasus', Shireen T. Hunter (ed.), pp. 195–222, 203.

61　Levan Asatiani, 'A Brief Overview of Iranian–Georgian Diplomatic Relations', *Expert Opinion*, 55. Tbilisi: Georgian Foundation for Strategic and International Studies, 2016, p. 4.

62　Tradingeconomics.com, *Georgia Imports from Iran*, 2018, https://tradingeconomics.com/georgia/imports/iran. (accessed 10 March 2020).

63　Tradingeconomics.com, *Georgia Imports from Iran*, 2018, https://tradingeconomics.com/georgia/imports/iran. (accessed 10 March 2020).

64　Civil Council on Defense and Security, *Report on Georgia–Iran Economic Relations*, 2018, http://civilcouncil.org/media/com_form2content/documents/c3/a68/f30/180501_Policy per cent20Pper_Georgia-Iran-Eng.pdf. (accessed 10 March 2020).

65　See, for example: G. Sanikidze, 'Turkey, Iran and the South Caucasus: Challenges for Regional Policy after the 2008 August War', *Electronic Journal of Political Science Studies*, 2:1 (2011), pp. 78–89, www.esbadergisi.com/index.php?lang=en

66　'Iran's President Blames West for Georgia War', *Civil Georgia*, 24 September 2008, http://civil.ge/eng/article.php?id=19585&search=

67　Vladimir Mesamed, *Iran i nemusulmanskie strany Yuzhnogo Kavkaza (Armeniia i Gruziia)* [Iran and the non-Muslim countries of the South Caucasus (Armenia and Georgia) (Moscow: Near East Institute, 2015), p. 132.

68　Kornely K. Kakachia, 'Iran and Georgia: Genuine Partnership or Marriage of Convenience?', *PONARS Eurasia Policy Memo*, No. 186, September 2011, p. 2.

69　Quoted in Mesamed, p. 145.

70　Bülent Aras, 'Turkey's Policy toward the South Caucasus', p. 188.

71　A. Grigoryan, *Armenia and the Iran Deal*, 2015, https://cacianalyst.org/publications/analytical-articles/item/13263-armenia-and-the-iran-deal.html (accessed 10 March 2020).

72   Beltandroad.news, 'Armenia fails to realise railway project with Iran', 18 September
     2019, www.beltandroad.news/2019/09/18/armenia-fails-to-realise-railway-project-
     with-iran/. (accessed 10 March 2020).

73   www.amerikiskhma.com/a/georgia-iran-relationship/3011846.html

74   Ghia Nodia, 'Georgia Walks a Line between Washington and Tehran', *RFERL*,
     19 November 2010, www.rferl.org/content/Georgia_Walks_A_Line_Between_
     Washington_And_Tehran/2224653.html

75   https://matiane.wordpress.com/2010/12/14/wikileaks-ambassador-john-bass-on-
     situation-in-georgia/

76   B. Rezvani, 'The Islamization and Ethnogenesis of the Fereydani Georgians',
     Nationalities Papers, 2008, pp. 593–623.

77   B. Faucon, 'As Sanctions Bite, Iranians Invest Big in Georgia', *The Wall Street Journal*,
     20 June 2013, www.wsj.com/articles/SB10001424127887323864304578320754133982
     778

78   www.georgianjournal.ge/blog/27882-georgia-and-iran-georgians-and-iranians.html

79   Molly Corso, 'Georgia: Is Tehran Trying to Use Tbilisi to Evade Sanctions?'
     Eurasianet, 15 July 2013, www.eurasianet.org/ 67253 8/16/2013

80   National Statistics Office of Georgia, Tbilisi, 2013.

81   https://1tv.ge/news/iranis-elchi-iraneli-turistebis-raodenoba-sakartveloshi-
     qoveltsliurad-izrdeba/ (accessed 7 March 2018).

82   www.tabula.ge/ge/story/154238-iranidan-motkhovnis-shemtsirebis-gamo-
     sakartvelos-ekonomika-80-milion-dolars-dakargavs

83   http://isna.ir/fa/news/93020201446 (22/04/2013)

84   L. Asatiani, p. 7.

85   In Azerbaijan (in Agdam, near the conflict zone) a joint military center has been
     opened.

86   'Erdogan says Caucasus platform can turn new page in Turkey-Armenia ties -NTV',
     Reuters, 11 December 2020, www.reuters.com/article/armenia-azerbaijan-turkey/
     erdogan-says-caucasus-platform-can-turn-new-page-in-turkey-armenia-ties-ntv-
     idUSKBN28L21G

Chapter 6

END OF THE POST-SOVIET ERA IN GEORGIA'S FOREIGN POLICY?: GEORGIA'S RELATIONS WITH FORMER SOVIET REPUBLICS

Levan Kakhishvili and Alexander Kupatadze

Most of the scholarly literature on Georgia's foreign policy over the last thirty years has focused on Tbilisi's relations with Western states, international institutions and with Russia. This is understandable – geography and history has placed Georgia in the shatter zone where imperial competition between the Ottomans, Russia and Western powers has taken place. Georgia's search for Western patronage has persisted over a number of centuries. In the nineteenth century, Russia was seen as a European patron.[1] Today, there is continuing competition between Russia and the West (and now China) over what Russia since 1991 has called its 'near abroad'. This competition has shaped Georgian foreign policy choices in the twentieth and twenty-first centuries. Since independence, Georgia has attempted to distance itself from Russia, while integrating into Euro-Atlantic structures.[2]

But Georgia's policy towards other countries and regions has been largely overlooked, not only by Western and Georgian scholars, but also by Georgian policymakers. The Georgian political elite is focused on Georgia's Europeanization, on its integration into NATO and on the complicated relations with Russia. There is little foreign policy discourse involving regions such as Latin America, Africa, the Middle East, Asia or the post-Soviet countries. The absence of attention on post-Soviet countries is particularly odd, especially given Georgia's long history of association with them during the Soviet period. This chapter tries to remedy this omission. It examines the evolution of Georgia's political and economic relations with other states in the post-Soviet space over the last decade. It aims to uncover patterns in Georgia's bilateral interactions with the Central Asian states, Belarus, Moldova and Ukraine.[3] In our chapter, Georgia's relations with Ukraine will take centre stage, as the two countries see themselves as 'natural' partners. They share colonial legacies, a range of cultural and political links going back to the nineteenth century, hostility to Moscow post-1991, and both have experienced common political challenges – such as corruption, economic collapse and revolution, almost simultaneously in 2003 and 2004. Today they share foreign policy orientations toward the EU and NATO.

A recent study by Bidzina Lebanidze and Mariam Grigalashvili examines Georgia's economic as well as political and security dependency on external actors: the latter was measured by indicators including political and diplomatic assistance, political integration, civil–military ties and ideological affinity of the ruling elite, while economic dependency was measured by indicators of export, import, remittances, vulnerable sectors and FDI.[4] The study finds that in 2017, Georgia was most 'dependent' on the European Union (EU), followed by Russia, Turkey, the United States, Azerbaijan and China. Ukraine and the Commonwealth of Independent States (CIS) were slightly above China in the study. However, before 2012 the situation was different and Georgia's economic and political dependency on the CIS and Ukraine was significantly higher. But Georgia's focus on Western powers is combined with an increasing dependency on China and to some extent (in terms of trade and remittances) on Russia. It is apparent that Georgia's foreign policy cannot be discussed simply in terms of dichotomies.[5]

Our chapter is divided into three sections. The first analyses the Georgian government's own strategic analysis of target countries (located in the former USSR), and how the dynamic has been changing. This is followed in the second section by our own analysis of political relations between Georgia and other post-Soviet countries, exploring political linkages such as official visits, bilateral agreements,[6] the impact of internal developments such as coloured revolutions in Kyrgyzstan and Ukraine, the role of energy (its import and transit) and the effects of the Eastern Partnership Initiative. The third section explores economic interactions between Georgia and the FSU countries looking at trade, foreign direct investment (FDI) and tourism.

Post-Soviet countries in Georgia's strategic documents

Since 1991, Georgia has adopted six major strategic conceptual documents that were designed to articulate the key goals of Georgia's foreign and security policy. The first ever document of any sort was elaborated under Eduard Shevardnadze's presidency in late 2000 entitled 'Georgia and the World: A Vision and Strategy for the Future'. This was a mixture of both foreign policy strategy and national security; it contained a long preamble on Georgia's history and cultural heritage. Since this document, Tbilisi has adopted two more national security concepts – both of them under the government of Mikheil Saakashvili's United National Movement's (UNM) – the first in 2005 and the second at the beginning of 2012. In addition to these, there have been three foreign policy strategies. The first was elaborated by the Saakashvili government and covered the years 2006–2009. The second was formulated by the Georgian Dream (GD) government and covered the period 2015–18. The third was published in 2019, again under GD rule, and covers the years 2019–22. In every document, Georgia prioritizes its 'return to the European family', and barely focuses on its immediate neighbourhood, or the post-Soviet region. The 2000 Shevardnadze document, for example, declares: 'Georgia actively seeks to broaden and strengthen its ties with those nations that share its values of democracy, respect for human rights, the market economy, and the free flow of ideas … Georgia's goal is to integrate in all of the major institutions of the European and Euro-Atlantic communities.' Later documents conform to this practice, but there is some evolution on strategies toward the post-Soviet region.[7] Later Georgian security assessments have shown increasing attention to FSU states, and in particular to Ukraine. In the latest security and foreign policy strategies, Ukraine is considered as one of three strategic partners of Georgia and is listed as second in importance after the United States (Turkey is in third place). Central Asian countries are designated as members of an identifiable region. Belarus, Moldova and Ukraine, on the other hand, are not. All the documents mention Central Asian countries, while the 2000 document, as well as the Georgian foreign policy strategy published in 2006, do not mention Belarus and Moldova at all. The 2005 national security concept only refers to Moldova in the context of Georgia's strengthening relations with the GUAM,[8] now known as the Organization for Democracy and Economic Development.

Ukraine is seen as the most important partner for Georgia. However, in 2000, in the conceptual document concerning foreign policy, there is little focus on Ukraine.[9] It is mentioned in two different contexts, neither of which is directly related to bilateral relations between Tbilisi and Kyiv. The first mention occurs in reference to Georgia's territorial integrity, noting that Ukraine, along with a range of other countries, is involved in the United Nations-led Georgian-Abkhaz negotiations within the framework of the Geneva process.[10] The second mention refers to the military exercises in which units from Georgia, Azerbaijan and Ukraine are trained for the purpose of ensuring the security of the oil pipeline transiting Georgia.[11] The creation of the Transcaucasian energy corridor, or Transport Corridor Europe-Caucasus-Asia (TRACECA), and the Baku–Tbilisi–Ceyhan (BTC) oil pipeline, were strategic achievements for Georgia. These energy projects stimulated Georgia's turn to the West. When both Ukraine and Georgia were weak states, the transportation of energy resources and other commodities was the primary bond between the two countries, along with a common Soviet past. Belarus and Moldova are not Black Sea littoral states and were not thought of as part of these infrastructure projects.

For reasons of trade, Central Asia takes considerable space in the 2000 document and is mentioned in three different sections: in a description of the international environment in which Georgia operates; in the section on foreign policy objectives and bilateral relations; and as part of Georgia's international economic strategy. The focus on Central Asian countries was determined by the large oil and gas reserves these countries hold. Georgia portrayed itself as an important transit corridor focusing on the revival of the 'Silk Road' through three projects: the Transport Corridor Europe-Caucasus-Asia (TRACECA), a Transcaucasian strategic energy corridor and a Transcaucasian telecommunication network. The focus on energy, transportation and economic security is consistent in all the documents we reviewed. However, Ukraine is upgraded to a strategic partner in the 2005 national security concept, and subsequent texts focus on military cooperation between Tbilisi and Kyiv in bilateral and multilateral formats such as the United Nations, the Organization for Security and Cooperation in Europe (OSCE), the Council of Europe, Black Sea Economic Cooperation (BSEC), GUAM, the Black Sea Naval Cooperation Task Group (BLACKSEAFOR) and others. There is little focus on Belarus and Moldova, but they are mentioned in the 2012 Concept in the context of the Eastern Partnership initiative.

In the various documents we reviewed, Belarus, Moldova and Ukraine change places both regarding their strategic importance, and in terms of how they fit in with the Georgian perspective on Europe. In the 2006 strategy, Belarus and Moldova are not mentioned, and Ukraine is placed in the section on 'Relations with European countries' alongside Romania and Bulgaria. The latter are described as 'advancing democracy and peace in the Black Sea area. 'They are', the document continues, important to the development of 'European and Euro-Atlantic integration'. Ukraine is included as a strategic partner. By contrast, in the 2015 strategy, Ukraine and Moldova are included, along with Georgia, as countries 'from the region', while European countries now have a separate section. The 'region' in which Georgia now finds itself includes Azerbaijan, Turkey (in the context of the Southern Corridor, the Baku–Tbilisi–Kars railway, and security cooperation in a trilateral format with Azerbaijan), Armenia, Bulgaria and Romania, Ukraine and Moldova, Russia, Iran and, finally, Belarus. On the other hand, this understanding of 'region' and what countries are included in 'regional policy' changes in 2019 and covers only the immediate neighbourhood of Armenia, Azerbaijan, Russia and Turkey. Such fluctuations in the perceptions of the configuration of the environment in which Georgia has to operate, indicates a lack of "institutionalization" in Georgia's strategic foreign policymaking. The way Georgia's immediate environment is presented in these documents largely depends on the worldviews of the civil servants employed in the Ministry of Foreign Affairs at that particular moment. Alternatively, or rather complimentarily, it may also indicate that Georgian governments are still searching for Georgia's place on the world political map. But this uncertainty can lead to misidentification of policy problems in the security domain – i.e. the failure of Georgia's policymakers to accurately assess facts and their significance.[12]

In the 2015 document, there is no longer mention of a strategic partnership with Ukraine. Instead, it refers to 'friendly, mutually beneficial and close' relations. However, the strategic partnership with Ukraine re-emerges again in the 2019 document. The Georgian government's reluctance to reiterate its strategic partnership with Ukraine in 2015 could be because Georgian–Ukrainian relations deteriorated after the migration of Georgian politicians and bureaucrats, including the former President Mikheil Saakashvili, to Ukraine and their employment in Ukrainian government agencies. Georgia repeatedly requested the extradition of Mikheil Saakashvili from Ukraine for abuse of power.[13] The Ukrainian authorities rejected these requests and deported Saakashvili to Poland a few months after the Prosecutor's Office of Georgia re-submitted a request for extradition.[14] On the other hand, Saakashvili was stripped of his Ukrainian citizenship on 26 July

2017,[15] which came almost a week after Georgia and Ukraine, in the framework of President Petro Poroshenko's visit to Tbilisi, signed a declaration on strategic partnership.[16] Thus, it could be argued that Georgian politicians and bureaucrats working in Ukrainian government agencies had an impact on how Georgian–Ukrainian relations were framed in Georgian strategic documents, and once this issue was eliminated, the two countries returned to the usual state of affairs.

Georgia's relationship with Central Asian countries is consistent. Every strategic document recognizes their importance for Georgia's economic and energy security, especially regarding the functioning of the transportation corridor in the South Caucasus. Kazakhstan and Turkmenistan are the two countries most frequently mentioned in the strategic documents due to their resources and their openness to exporting gas and oil to Europe through the South Caucasus. The presence of Central Asia is stronger in the national security concept of 2012, compared to 2005. In 2005 Central Asia is described as a region, which significantly influences Georgia's security environment, its policy on inter-regional cooperation, and energy security. The 2012 document expands on this and adds that Central Asia impacts the prospects of cooperation in the South Caucasus. It underlines that economic security, which connects Georgia to Central Asia, is a central pillar of Georgia's national security. Tbilisi is focusing on Central Asia as a potential source of energy and economic security for Georgia. The relationships with Central Asia are expected to gain more traction in the context of China's Belt and Road Initiative (BRI). Georgia is part of the China–Central Asia–West Asia Corridor, which is one of the six overland corridors making up the Silk Road Economic Belt (SREB) aimed at increasing the amount of transported goods and hydrocarbons between China and Europe at large.[17] This will contribute to strengthening Georgia's relations with Central Asian countries.

A few patterns can be identified in Georgia's strategic documents in terms of Tbilisi's relations with the former Soviet countries. First, Georgian governments, barring the 2015 document, have consistently identified Ukraine as the country's strategic partner. Second, Belarus and Moldova do not always feature in Georgia's strategic arena and even when they do, they are not among the main partners of the country. Third, Central Asian countries are always recognized for their importance in terms of trade and economic relations as well as for successfully transporting oil, gas and other goods through Georgia. Georgian views of the immediate international environment shift from time to time. Sometimes it was the South Caucasus that was prioritized, at other times it was the Black Sea region. As noted above, such shifts can be attributed to the lack of institutionalization in strategic thinking, as well as transient political conditions.

Political ties and bilateral relations with the FSU

The range of countries this chapter covers can be divided into two regions: the Eastern European region, which includes Belarus, Moldova and Ukraine, and the Central Asian region which includes Kazakhstan, Kyrgyzstan, Tajikistan,

Turkmenistan and Uzbekistan. Georgia is closely connected with the Eastern European region institutionally through the Eastern Partnership, the Organization of the Black Sea Economic Cooperation (BSEC) and GUAM. Consequently, one would expect the political ties with Belarus, Moldova and Ukraine to be more intensive than with Central Asia. However, Georgia's political ties with the two regions uncover interesting and sometimes unexpected trends.

The number of high-level official visits to and from each of the countries (see Figure 6.1) between 2007 and 2017, shows that the overwhelming majority of the visits from Georgia (74 per cent) and to Georgia (80 per cent) involved one of the three Eastern European countries. Judging from the ratio of visits to a target country compared to the visits from a target country, Georgia invests significant effort in maintaining ties with Turkmenistan, Kazakhstan, Ukraine and Belarus. These are countries to which Georgia sends more delegations than it receives. Especially interesting are Turkmenistan and Kazakhstan to which Georgia sends 3.3 and 2.3 times more delegations than it receives from these countries (the figures for Ukraine and Belarus are 2.1 and 1.3 times respectively). This can be explained in large part by Turkmenistan's and Kazakhstan's possession of mineral and energy resources. They are open to exporting their resources through the prospective trans-Caspian pipeline as well as by trade across the Caspian Sea. It is not surprising, by contrast, that there have been no high-level visits to and from Tajikistan, which is a small country with no significant energy resources. There is no apparent motive for building political ties. On the other hand, visits to

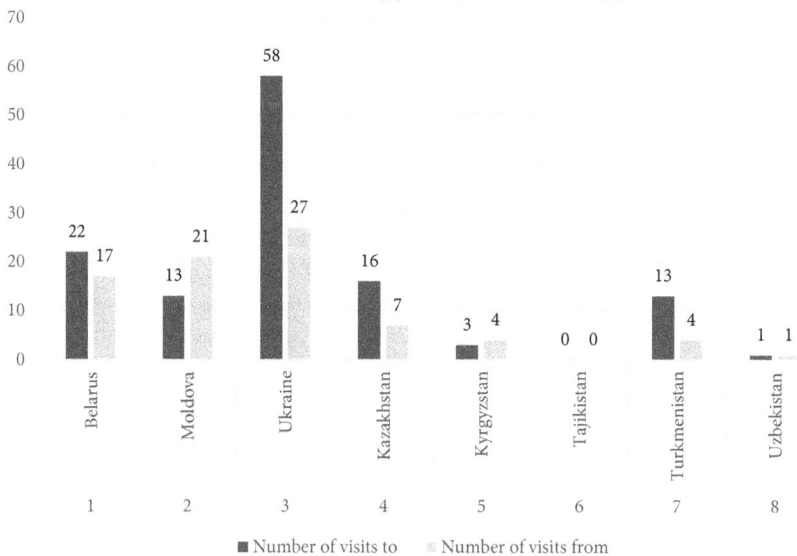

Figure 6.1 Number of visits to and from all target countries: 2007–17.

Source: Ministry of Foreign Affairs of Georgia. Emailing 01/314 [letter] (Personal communication, 4 January 2018).

and from similarly resource-poor Kyrgyzstan, although low in frequency, can be explained by the fact that both Georgia and Kyrgyzstan were part of the wave of coloured revolutions. In the late 2000s there was a debate in Kyrgyzstani political circles about wanting to share Georgia's reform model. According to Marat, the attempts to imitate Georgia's reforms have been unsuccessful due to dissimilarities in local conditions.[18] However, sharing reform experiences has remained an important issue between Georgia and Kyrgyzstan, even in the 2010s, in the field of tax reforms[19] as well as the police[20] and security services.[21]

A somewhat different story is apparent in the number of bilateral agreements between Georgia and FSU countries in the period 1991–2017. Ukraine is still the leader in terms of the intensity of political ties with Georgia (39 per cent of all bilateral agreements have been signed with Ukraine since independence). However, as figure 6.2 shows, two interesting patterns emerge. In terms of the total number of bilateral agreements signed during 1991–2017, Belarus and Moldova fall behind Uzbekistan, Kazakhstan and Turkmenistan. On the other hand, if we look at the last ten years, there has been an intensification of political ties with Belarus and Moldova and less so with Central Asian countries. During 2007–17 only two bilateral agreements with Central Asian countries (both of them with Kazakhstan) were signed and/or entered into force. All the rest of the documents date back to the period before 2007. However, 90 per cent of agreements with Belarus and 59 per cent of agreements with Moldova were concluded during the last ten years (the figure for Ukraine is 18 per cent). This suggests that Georgia is much more motivated to keep close connections with Belarus, Moldova and

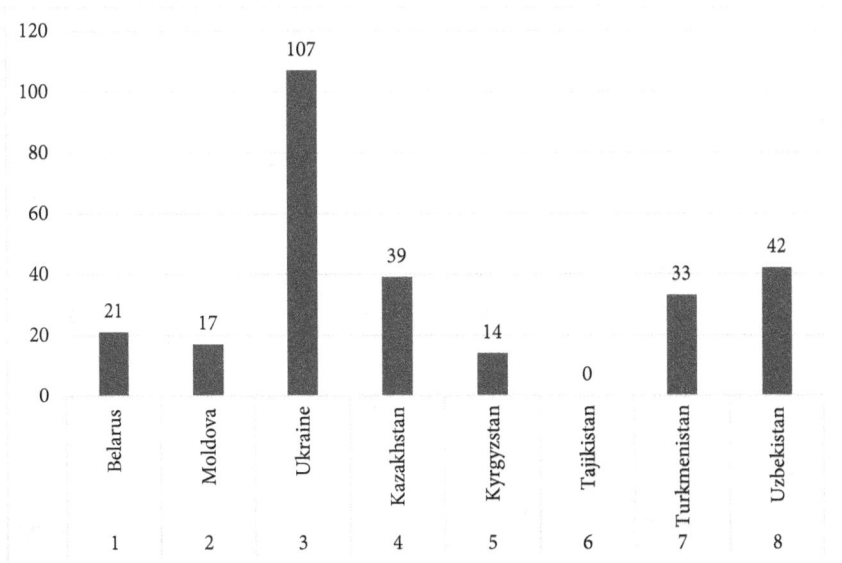

Figure 6.2 Bilateral agreements signed between Georgia and FSU countries: 1991–2017.

Source: Ministry of Foreign Affairs of Georgia. Emailing 01/314 [letter] (Personal communication, 4 January 2018).

Ukraine than with countries from Central Asia. For example, Georgia has virtually no political ties with Tajikistan, and no agreement has been concluded with its government during the independence period.

In October 2012, the Georgian Dream (GD) coalition replaced the United National Movement (UNM). The rise of Bidzina Ivanishvili, a billionaire who had made his fortune in Russia and was the founder and leader of the GD, led some analysts to warn of Georgia's return to the post-Soviet region under Russian influence.[22] However, Georgia did not change its foreign policy orientation after the 2012 elections, although it changed its emphasis. Tbilisi has become more active in terms of institutionalizing bilateral relations with the former FSU countries such as Belarus and Moldova (see Figure 6.3). Georgia's overwhelming focus remains on Eastern Europe, rather than Central Asia. President Alexander Lukashenko of Belarus made his first official visit to Georgia only in 2015[23] under Georgian Dream's rule. This was an important expansion in relations with a country seen as pro-Russian, but which also borders the EU.

At the same time, overall, the frequency of bilateral agreements (see Figure 6.4) has decreased during the GD's rule compared to the UNM – with the exception of Belarus. Thus, the number of initiated bilateral agreements decreased dramatically with Ukraine and increased almost four-fold with Belarus. However, this has an explanation. Georgia has over one hundred agreements with Ukraine, many initiated long before the UNM came to power in 2003. Only 18 per cent of bilateral agreements were concluded during 2007–17. In other words, Georgian–Ukrainian relations were well institutionalized as a result of former Georgian governments' efforts to build close ties with Kyiv, and there was no need for a multiplication of

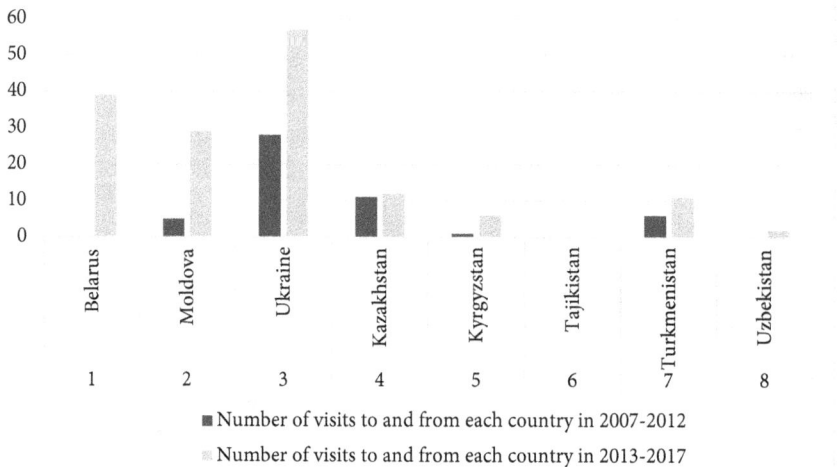

■ Number of visits to and from each country in 2007-2012

▨ Number of visits to and from each country in 2013-2017

Figure 6.3 Aggregated number of visits to and from each country during rule of the UNM (2007–12) and GD (2013–17).

Source: Ministry of Foreign Affairs of Georgia. Emailing 01/314 [letter] (Personal communication, 4 January 2018).

treaties when the GD came to power. The institutional framework of Georgian–Belarus agreements, on the other hand, was almost non-existent with only two agreements in force and four more signed and/or entering into force during 2009–2010. These agreements were triggered by Lukashenko's decision in 2008 (after the August War and Russia's recognition of the independence of Abkhazia and South Ossetia) to put the issue of recognition of the two breakaway regions of Abkhazia and South Ossetia on the agenda of the Belarussian parliament.[24] Soon after this decision Tbilisi and Minsk concluded agreements aimed at intensifying economic cooperation, maintaining a free trade area, agreeing on economic and scientific-technical cooperation in the field of agricultural industry, and creating an inter-governmental agency for economic cooperation. These agreements provided a foundation, on which the GD could build cooperation between the two states. One explanation for the poor relations before 2009 could be Lukashenko's fears of Saakashvili's Georgia exporting its colour revolution to Belarus.[25]

Given these patterns, we argue that there are a few important and distinct drivers of Georgian foreign policy towards FSU countries. First and foremost, is the extent to which the declared foreign policy goals of a given country align with those of Georgia. Ukraine is a good illustration of the country with which Georgia has the closest political relations. Ukraine together with Moldova, is part of the EU's Eastern Partnership Initiative, which also ties the three countries together due to shared interests in deepening European integration. Though Belarus is part of the Eastern Partnership, Minsk does not have the same foreign policy goals

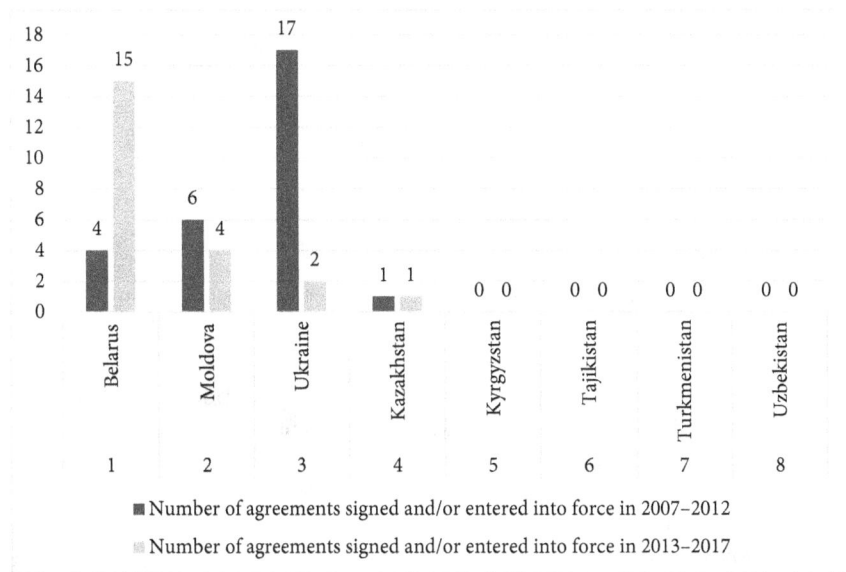

■ Number of agreements signed and/or entered into force in 2007–2012
▩ Number of agreements signed and/or entered into force in 2013–2017

Figure 6.4 Number of bilateral agreements concluded with FSU countries under UNM (2007–12) and GD (2013–17).

Source: Ministry of Foreign Affairs of Georgia, Emailing 01/314 [letter] (Personal communication, 4 January 2018).

as Georgia, Moldova and Ukraine. Consequently, Belarus together with Armenia and Azerbaijan – two other Eastern partnership countries – does not show much desire to build closer ties with other Eastern Partnership member states. For them, Russia is always an alternative partner.[26]

Ukraine not only has a similar foreign policy orientation as Georgia but also a similar relationship with democracy. Ukraine, like Georgia, was part of the same transnational phenomenon of coloured revolutions, which were directed against corruption and greater government accountability to citizens. This is the second most important factor influencing Georgian foreign policy toward Ukraine. To understand the effects of this phenomenon on bilateral political linkages, we can look at Georgia's relations with Kyrgyzstan and Tajikistan. The two Central Asian countries are both small and poor in terms of energy resources. Georgia has not concluded any agreement with Tajikistan, an authoritarian state closely tied with Russia; nor has it sent or received any high-level official delegation from the Central Asian state. On the other hand, Kyrgyzstan, which experienced its own coloured revolution in 2005, known as the Tulip Revolution, has fourteen bilateral agreements with Georgia. Georgia and Kyrgyzstan exchanged seven official visits with each other during 2007–17. Georgia and Tajikistan have expressed little interest in establishing better bilateral relations.

The third factor which has most influenced Georgia's decision to seek bilateral ties with countries in the FSU is economic trade and resources, particularly energy resources. If a country is open to the idea of exporting its oil and gas through the Caspian Sea region bypassing Russia, or to using the Caspian Sea link as an alternative trade route for other goods, this is a positive attraction for Georgia. Georgia has significantly more intensive links with oil- and gas-rich countries like Kazakhstan and Turkmenistan than with fellow democratic aspirant, Kyrgyzstan. Uzbekistan has been lukewarm to the idea of exporting hydrocarbons through the Southern Gas Corridor but has signed three times more agreements with Georgia than Kyrgyzstan. The latter offers no potential gas or oilfields as a source of energy diversification for Georgia. Consequently, Tbilisi's approach to energy-rich countries in Central Asia is more active in comparison to Kyrgyzstan (or indeed with Tajikistan). Kyrgyzstan, which like Georgia, has been described as the most democratic country in its neighbourhood,[27] does not feature in Georgia's political preferences as much as Turkmenistan, the most authoritarian country in the region, which is often compared to North Korea.[28] One other factor that has influenced Georgian foreign policy behaviour in its relations with other FSU countries is the August War of 2008 and its consequences. Particularly damaging for Georgia is any country that recognizes the independence of Abkhazia and South Ossetia. When such a possibility arose in Minsk, Tbilisi became more proactive in managing the issue and intensifying relations with Belarus.

Georgian foreign policy choices in the FSU are pragmatic. The dynamics of official visits and bilateral agreements show that Georgia under the GD's rule has become more active in the FSU than under the UNM. The UNM was preoccupied with Georgia's relations with Western countries and institutions, especially the United States and NATO, while the FSU, excluding Ukraine, was a secondary focus. The consequences of the August War, and the postponement of Georgia's membership prospects in NATO, led the GD leadership to increase relations with countries in the post-Soviet space. Georgia's main foreign policy goal since regaining independence was 'to disassociate itself from its Soviet past and escape from Russia's historic, geographic, and civilizational space'.[29] President Giorgi Margvelashvili summed this up during his inauguration ceremony in 2013: 'the post-Soviet period has ended [in Georgia] and the age of building contemporary democracy has started … we have laid the ground for the new European-type political culture'.[30] However, despite such rhetoric, Georgia's economic and strategic interests, particularly after 2008, have forced Georgian foreign policymakers to readjust. The GD has not completely refocused Georgian foreign policy on the FSU – it has largely maintained the foreign policy line of the UNM – but it has added a new 'normalization' policy with Russia and focused more attention on other FSU countries which can offer investment, energy and trade.

Business as usual?

Looking at trade relations, FDI flow and tourism between Georgia and our eight FSU countries listed in our comparative tables below, the data suggests that Ukraine is the single most important economic partner for Georgia. At the same time, Georgia has close economic ties with Kazakhstan and Turkmenistan in comparison to any other country from Central Asia. Our data from 1995 until 2017, shows there is a downward trend for the share of exports and imports to and from Central Asian countries in Georgia's total trade, while the trend is upward in case of the Eastern European countries. Yet FDI flow indicates that Kazakhstan has been the most important investor in Georgia among the eight FSU countries. However, the data also suggests that in terms of investments, the FSU countries are far behind the EU Member States and Georgia's four neighbours: Armenia, Azerbaijan, Russia and Turkey. When it comes to tourism, the only FSU country, which features in the data of the National Statistics Office of Georgia (GeoStat), is Ukraine.

GeoStat data shows that exports from Georgia to the FSU countries (see Figure 6.5) has experienced peaks and troughs over the past two decades. The first peak was in 2004 when exports to Turkmenistan more than doubled in comparison to the previous year, reaching ten times the amount registered in the late 1990s. However, this peak quickly withered and by 2008 returned to levels similar to those of the 1990s. The second peak was in 2008 when exports to Ukraine grew substantially following the August War. The third peak was with Kazakhstan in 2011 and the fourth with Ukraine again in 2013. There was a significant surge in exports between 2013 and 2015 with Uzbekistan. These four countries have been the top destinations for Georgian exports. However, Ukraine leads, and over 41 per cent of all the goods Georgia sells in the eight FSU countries find their way to Ukraine. Ukraine has the largest population of the eight countries we are investigating (over 44 million people), but the size of the market does not

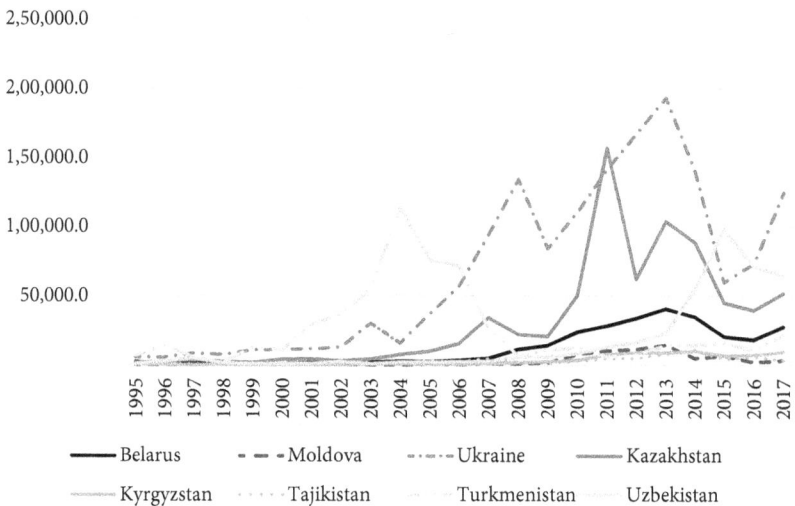

Figure 6.5 Georgia's annual exports to each target country (in 1,000 USD).

Source: 'Georgian Exports by Countries: Export 1995–2018', *GeoStat*, www.geostat.ge/cms/site_images/_files/english/
bop/2018/Export%20Country_1995-2018_eng.xlsx (accessed 19 August 2018).

determine the amount of exported goods. Turkmenistan, which is in third place in terms of Georgian exports, has consumed about 50 per cent more Georgian goods than Uzbekistan, which has over five times the population size. There must be some other mechanism leading to these results.

But overall a downward trend in the share of exports to Central Asian countries in the total exports of Georgia and the gradual but steady increase for the three Eastern European countries, suggests a shift in economic ties between Georgia and the two regions (see Figure 6.6). However, these trends apply generally to the period 1995–2017. If we focus on the period since 2012, when the GD came to power, the trends switch. The share of the three Eastern European countries gradually decreases while the share of Central Asian countries does not, and even increases slightly.

When it comes to imports from FSU countries, Georgia imports almost three times more goods from the eight FSU countries than it exports. Yet the pattern largely holds. Ukraine remains the most important partner: 72 per cent of all goods Georgia imported from the eight FSU countries since 1995, came from Ukraine. Following Ukraine, come Turkmenistan and Kazakhstan with much less share overall, but still significantly more than Kyrgyzstan, Moldova, Tajikistan or Uzbekistan (see Figure 6.7).

Overall, in the past two decades, the share of imports from East European countries in Georgia has been steadily increasing, while the opposite is true for Central Asian countries (see Figure 6.8). But if we limit the time frame to the last five years under GD leadership, the trend switches again. In terms of political and

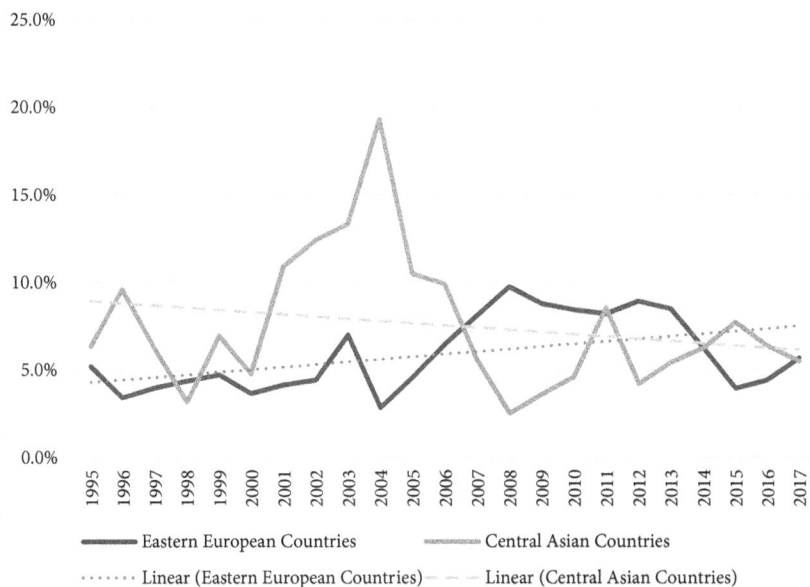

Figure 6.6 Georgia's annual exports to Belarus, Moldova and Ukraine (Eastern European countries) and Kazakhstan, Kyrgyzstan, Tajikistan, Turkmenistan and Uzbekistan (Central Asian countries) as a percentage share of total exports.

Source: 'Georgian Exports by Countries: Export 1995–2018', *GeoStat*, www.geostat.ge/cms/site_images/_files/english/ bop/2018/Export%20Country_1995-2018_eng.xlsx (accessed 19 August 2018).

trade ties, Georgia has been intensifying its relations with Central Asian countries since 2012.

When it comes to foreign direct investments (FDI), it becomes clear that Georgia has much stronger ties with its immediate neighbours and EU member countries. On average the balance of FDI flow with each of the eight FSU countries was a little less than 3.5 million USD annually between 2005 and 2017. By comparison, FDI from each of Georgia's four neighbours: Armenia, Azerbaijan, Russia and Turkey – was almost 25 times higher at over 86.5 million USD, while the figure for each of the EU 27 Member States is almost six times higher at over 20 million USD annually. The only significant contributor to net positive FDI balance with Georgia was Kazakhstan but even in this case the phenomenon was short-lived. Kazakhstan was an important investor in Georgia only during 2006–08 (see Figure 6.9). In 2006 Kazakhstan's share of the total FDI balance in Georgia was over 13.8 per cent. However, in any other year during the 2005–17 period, the share of each of the eight countries in Georgia's FDI balance ranged between −5 to 5 per cent. Ukraine, which is the second largest contributor out of the eight countries to investments in Georgia, has been investing on average a little over 3 million USD in Georgia per annum, a paltry amount. Countries from the FSU consistently lag behind the top ten investors in Georgia. For example, in 2017, those countries that

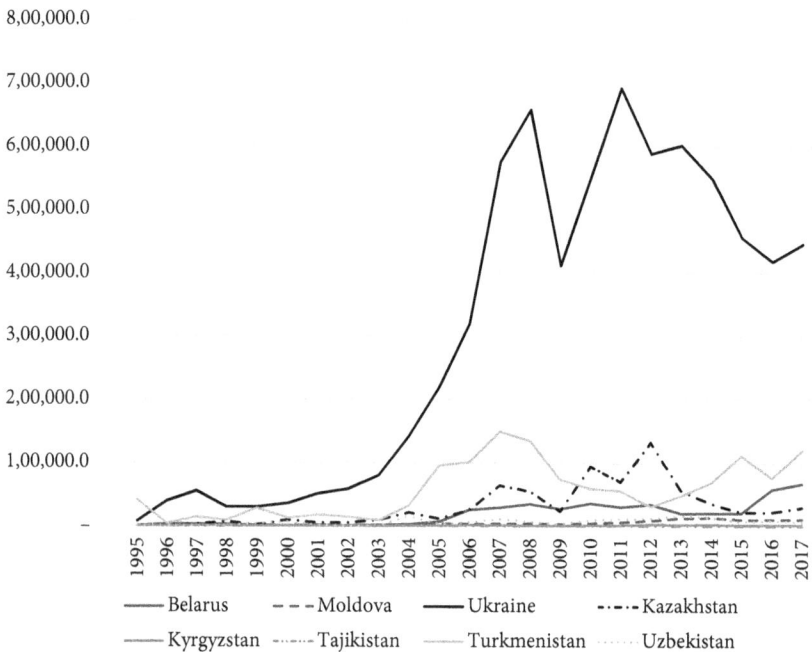

Figure 6.7 Georgia's annual imports from each FSU country (in 1,000 USD).

Source: 'Georgian Imports by Countries: Import 1995–2018', *GeoStat,* www.geostat.ge/cms/site_images/_files/
english/bop/2018/Import%20Country%201995-2018_eng.xlsx (accessed 19 August 2018).

did not make it to the top ten investors, combined amounted to only 4.8 per cent of total investments. This figure was unusually low in 2017, but as a rule the top three investors account for more than half of incoming investments in Georgia.

One final data point is the flow of tourists. How do the FSU countries fare in this regard? GeoStat has only published data for 2015–17.[31] The data is limited, as it includes only the top eight countries as well as a cumulative figure for the EU. Data from all other countries is aggregated into a single figure. Out of the FSU countries under consideration, only Ukraine is included in the list of top countries sending foreign tourists to Georgia. However, the figures are not as significant as in the case of the four neighbouring countries of Armenia, Azerbaijan, Russia and Turkey. These four are much higher than Ukraine each year in the three-year period. Even though the number of visitors from Ukraine has increased from 111,000 in 2015 to over 150,000 in 2017, these figures are five to eight times lower than each of the four neighbouring states. Moreover, although the absolute number of visitors from Ukraine has increased by 35 per cent over the three-year period, the share of Ukrainian tourists among all foreign tourists has remained largely unchanged at 2.8, 3.2 and 2.9 per cent respectively each year.

The analysis of trade relations between Georgia and the eight FSU countries, which includes FDI, tourists, trade and bilateral exchanges, demonstrate some

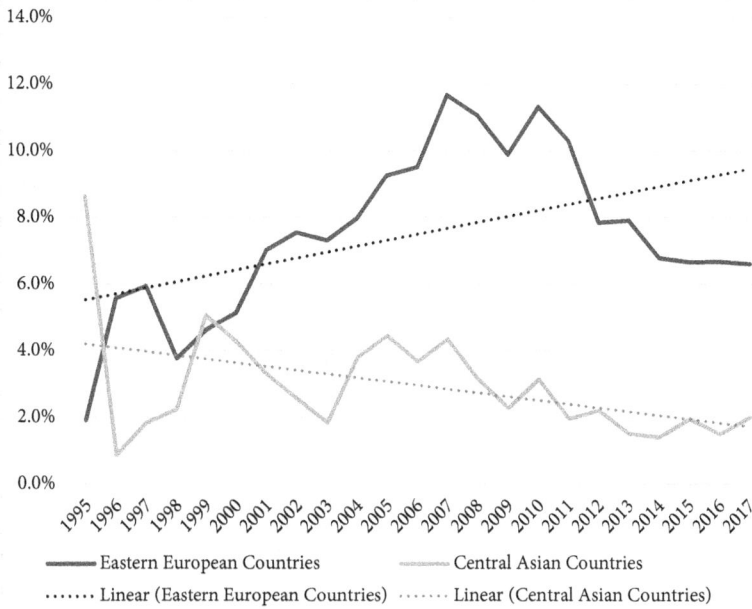

Figure 6.8 Georgia's annual imports from Belarus, Moldova and Ukraine (Eastern European countries) and Kazakhstan, Kyrgyzstan, Tajikistan, Turkmenistan and Uzbekistan (Central Asian countries) as a percentage share of total imports.

Source: 'Georgian Imports by Countries: Import 1995–2018', *GeoStat*, www.geostat.ge/cms/site_images/_files/english/bop/2018/Import%20Country%201995-2018_eng.xlsx (accessed 19 August 2018).

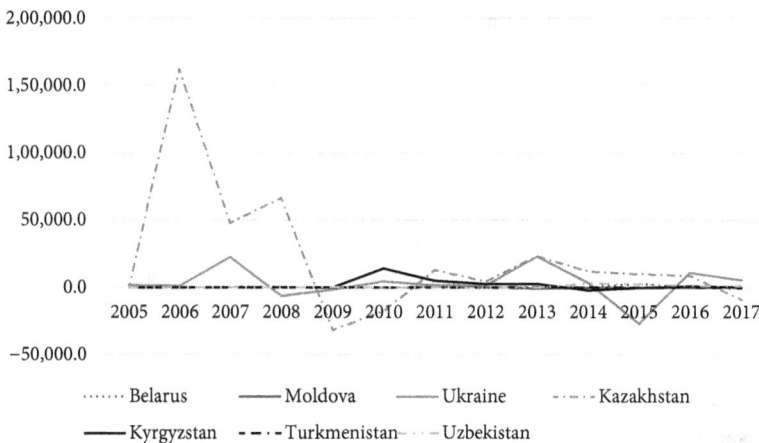

Figure 6.9 FDI flow with the eight FSU countries.

Source: 'Foreign Direct Investments by Countries: FDI by Countries', *GeoStat*, www.geostat.ge/cms/site_images/_files/english/bop/FDI_Eng-countries.xlsx (accessed 14 August 2018).

important patterns. First, in terms of the trade, Ukraine is by far the most important country for Georgia. This underlines the solidity of the partnership between Tbilisi and Kyiv. They are natural trade partners. In contrast, the amount of trade with Central Asian countries has been decreasing over the last two and a half decades, although that trend has reversed since 2012. Second, Georgia does not receive any significant amount of FDI from the eight FSU countries we are considering. With the exception of Kazakhstan in 2006, the share of FDI from any FSU country has never exceeded 5 per cent of total FDI in Georgia. Finally, the only FSU country to provide a considerable number of tourists among the eight we have data for, is Ukraine. The figures for Ukraine are still relatively low in comparison to Georgia's four neighbours, Armenia, Azerbaijan, Russia and Turkey. All things considered, Ukraine is the country with which Georgia has the most complex economic relations.

Conclusion

This chapter has analysed three important features of Georgia's relations with former FSU states. Based on content analysis, Georgia's foreign policy and strategic documents adopted over the last two decades, show that among the FSU countries, Ukraine is perceived as the most important to Georgia's security. It is referred to as a strategic partner. Ukraine's two neighbours, Belarus and Moldova, do not receive nearly as much attention from the Georgian government in these documents, despite the fact that both are part of the EU's Eastern Partnership initiative together with Georgia, Armenia and Azerbaijan. Simply being an EaP country does not lead to strategic attention from Georgia. There are other factors, which will make a former FSU state strategically important to Georgia. On the other hand, the region of Central Asia receives far greater attention than Belarus or Moldova. Kazakhstan and Turkmenistan are considered to be especially important sources for Georgia's energy supply and the network of pipelines that transport oil and gas to the EU across Georgia through the southern energy corridor. We can see the pragmatic interest of Tbilisi, and why it prioritizes relations with the Central Asian region as a whole.

Secondly, we analysed political ties by evaluating the number of bilateral agreements signed by Georgia with each of the eight FSU countries for which we had data, along with the number of high-level official visits between Georgia and post-Soviet countries over the past ten years. What these data reveal is that when a country considers recognition of Abkhazia and South Ossetia, as in the case of Belarus, there is increased intensity of political ties, reflected by signed bilateral agreements and official visits. Overall, the frequency of official visits significantly increased among all FSU countries during the period of the GD government (after 2012) in comparison with the period of the UNM government (2003–12). This finding contradicts the research by Lebanidze and Grigalashvili, who argue that Georgia's integration with CIS countries has been gradually decreasing over the past ten to fifteen years.[32] The mere frequency of visits does not suggest that

Georgia is reorienting itself toward post-Soviet countries, but it is a trend that must be considered in evaluating Georgia's foreign policy. Factors that might help explain the upward trend in relations with FSU countries are the alignment of foreign policy goals between Georgia, Moldova and Ukraine, shared historical dynamics such as the coloured revolutions, an aspiration to Western type democracy, and dependence on mutual energy networks. The different worldviews of two ideologically opposed governments over the past fifteen years undoubtedly contribute to the shifting trends in political ties, most notably with Russia, but also – according to our data – with FSU states.

The chapter also analysed the intensity of economic ties between Georgia and eight FSU states. Our variables included trade relations, FDI and the tourist trade. According to these indicators, Ukraine is the most important partner for Georgia. Of all the FSU states we studied, it is consistently the largest trade partner with Georgia from the second half of the 1990s. It accounts for 41 per cent of all Georgian products exported to the eight listed FSU states. Seventy-two per cent of these countries' imports to Georgia also came from Ukraine. Trade relations between Georgia and Ukraine are more intense than any other FSU republic. We noted a gradual increase in the share of the three East European countries – Moldova, Ukraine and Belarus – in Georgia's trade – largely due to Ukraine – and a gradual decrease in the share of the five Central Asian countries in Georgia's total exports and imports. However, when the last five years are considered, the trends are reversed. This may indicate a slight shift in priorities under the GD leadership. In terms of investments, Kazakhstan appears to have invested most in Georgia during the period 2005–17, followed by Ukraine. However, Kazakhstan's lead can largely be explained by energy and real estate. In 2006, investments from Kazakhstan accounted for 13 per cent of all FDI coming to Georgia. However, at any other point since then, the FDI from the eight FSU countries we considered, were relatively insignificant compared to countries from Georgia's immediate neighbourhood, or the EU Member States. Finally, Georgia does not enjoy any significant number of tourists from Central Asia, Belarus or Moldova. The only largish number of tourists comes from Ukraine, and even then they account for only 3 per cent of all visitors to Georgia annually. Of course, these patterns have already been impacted by the COVID-19 pandemic in 2020 and it is not yet clear how the resulting disruption of international travel and trade will affect Georgia's relations with FSU countries. The pandemic and associated measures, such as lockdowns, have also affected tourists' ability to travel to Georgia. What the new picture will look like after the re-opening of borders and what role the FSU countries will play in tourism in Georgia remains to be seen.

Yet we can conclude that overall, Ukraine is the closest state to Georgia, both politically and economically, most certainly in comparison with other countries in the former Soviet space. For the foreseeable future, the alignment of their foreign policy interests and their common political and security challenges, will define the bilateral relations between Tbilisi and Kyiv. Ukraine more than any other FSU state, will remain Georgia's closest strategic and economic partner in the short and medium term.

Notes

1   For a detailed discussion of this matter, see the introductory chapter by Stephen Jones.
2   For a comprehensive overview of these two imperatives of Georgian foreign policy, see the chapter by Kornely Kakachia and Tracey German 'Achieving Security as a Small State', in this volume.
3   Russia, Armenia, Azerbaijan and the Baltic States are intentionally excluded from the analysis. Other chapters in this book offer an in-depth look at relations between these countries and Georgia. On Georgia's Russia policies, see Ghia Nodia's chapter in this volume. David Aprasidze offers contextualization of relations with Armenia and Azerbaijan in terms of regional identity of Georgia; and support of Baltic States towards Georgia's foreign policy aspirations is analysed by Bidzina Lebanidze and Renata Skardžiūtė-Kereselidze.
4   Bidzina Lebanidze and Mariam Grigalashvili, 'Not EU's World? Putting Georgia's European Integration in Context', *Georgian Institute of Politics*, 2018, http://gip. ge/not-eus-world-putting-georgias-european-integration-in-context/ (accessed 17 September 2018).
5   See Levan Kakhishvili, 'Towards a Two-Dimensional Analytical Framework for Understanding Georgian Foreign Policy: How Party Competition Informs Foreign Policy Analysis', *Post-Soviet Affairs*, 37:2 (2021), pp. 174–97, doi:10.1080/106058 6X.2020.1869455.
6   The data used in the chapter has been officially provided by the Ministry of Foreign Affairs of Georgia as a response to a freedom of information request by the authors.
7   The documents analysed here include: 'Georgia, and the World: A Vision and Strategy for the Future', *Government of Georgia*, 2000, www.parliament.ge/files/1_886_192675_ nato_vision.pdf (accessed 6 January 2013). 'National Security Concept of Georgia', *Government of Georgia*, 2005, www.parliament.ge/files/292_880_927746_concept_ en.pdf (accessed 6 January 2013). 'Foreign Policy Strategy 2006–2009', *Government of Georgia*, 2006, www.mfa.gov.ge/files/35_9440_673620_11.pdf (accessed 6 January 2013). 'National Security Concept of Georgia', *Government of Georgia*, 2012, www. nsc.gov.ge/files/files/National%20Security%20Concept.pdf (accessed 6 January 2013). 'Foreign Policy Strategy 2015–2018', *Government of Georgia*, 2015, www.mfa.gov. ge/MainNav/ForeignPolicy/ForeignPolicyStrategy.aspx (accessed 12 April 2018). 'Foreign Policy Strategy 2019–2022', *Government of Georgia*, 2019, http://mfa.gov. ge/getattachment/MainNav/ForeignPolicy/ForeignPolicyStrategy/2019-2022-tslebis-sakartvelos-sagareo-politikis-strategia.pdf.aspx (accessed 24 April 2018).
8   GUAM was founded in 1997 in the form of Association Forum and has gone through a few stages of institutional development and was finally established in its current form in 2006 with the main goals of strengthening democracy, security and stability as well as deepening cooperation in the fields of economy, energy and transport. See 'About GUAM' *Guam-organization.org*, 2017, https://guam-organization.org/ en/about-the-organization-for-democracy-and-economic-development-guam/ (accessed 10 January 2019).
9   'Georgia and the World: A Vision and Strategy for the Future', *Government of Georgia*, 2000, www.parliament.ge/files/1_886_192675_nato_vision.pdf (accessed 6 January 2013).
10 'Georgia and the World: A Vision and Strategy for the Future', *Government of Georgia*, 2000, www.parliament.ge/files/1_886_192675_nato_vision.pdf (accessed 6 January 2013).

11 'Georgia and the World: A Vision and Strategy for the Future', *Government of Georgia*, 2000, www.parliament.ge/files/1_886_192675_nato_vision.pdf (accessed 6 January 2013).

12 See Barry Buzan, *People States and Fear*, 2nd ed. (London: Harvester Wheatsheaf, 1991).

13 'Tbilisi Seeks Saakashvili's Extradition from Ukraine', *Civil Georgia*, 5 September 2017, https://civil.ge/archives/218277 (accessed 10 January 2019).

14 'Ukraine Deports Mikheil Saakashvili to Poland', *Civil Georgia*, 12 February 2018, https://civil.ge/archives/219669 (accessed 10 January 2019).

15 'Mikheil Saakashvili Stripped of Ukrainian Citizenship', *The Economist Intelligence Unit*, 1 August 2017, http://country.eiu.com/article.aspx?articleid=365745420&Country=Ukraine&topic=Politics&subtopic=Forecast&subsubtopic=Political+stability (accessed 6 May 2019).

16 'Ukraine and Georgia to Co-Operate on EU and NATO Integration', *The Economist Intelligence Unit*, 21 July 2017, http://country.eiu.com/article.aspx?articleid=665703850&Country=Ukraine&topic=Politics&subtopic=Forecast&subsubtopic=International+relations&u=1&pid=965696680&oid=965696680&uid=1 (accessed 6 May 2019).

17 Joseph Larsen, 'Georgia–China Relations: The Geopolitics of the Belt and Road', *Georgian Institute of Politics*, 2017, http://gip.ge/georgia-china-relations-geopolitics-belt-road/ (accessed 11 January 2019).

18 Erica Marat, 'Reforming the Police in Post-Soviet States: Georgia and Kyrgyzstan', *The Letort Papers*, Strategic Studies Institute and US Army War College, 2013, www.globalsecurity.org/military/library/report/2013/ssi_marat.pdf (accessed 11 January 2019). See also Kornely Kakachia and Liam O'Shea, 'Why Does Police Reform Appear to Have Been More Successful in Georgia than in Kyrgyzstan or Russia?', *The Journal of Power Institutions in Post-Soviet Societies*, 13 (2012), https://journals.openedition.org/pipss/3964?lang=fr (accessed 11 January 2019).

19 'Georgia's Experience in Tax System Reform Relevant for Kyrgyzstan', *24.kg*, 17 July 2018, https://24.kg/english/91053_Georgias_experience_in_tax_system_reform_relevant_for_Kyrgyzstan/ (accessed 10 January 2019).

20 'Study Visit of Kyrgyzstan Delegation in Georgia', *Ministry of Internal Affairs of Georgia*, 18 October 2015, https://police.ge/en/shss-s-kirgizetis-delegatsia-estumra/8914 (accessed 10 January 2019).

21 'Representatives of the State Security Service of Georgia Held Meeting with the Kyrgyz Delegation to Georgia', *State Security Service of Georgia*, 17 October 2015, https://ssg.gov.ge/en/news/111/Representatives-of-the-State-Security-Service-of-Georgia-held-meeting-with-the-Kyrgyz-Delegation-to-Georgia (accessed 10 January 2019).

22 See Svante E. Cornell, 'Is Georgia Slipping Away?', *The American Interest*, 13 November 2014, www.the-american-interest.com/2014/11/13/is-georgia-slipping-away/ (accessed 9 August 2018). Valeriy Dzutsev, 'Georgia: The More Things Change … ', *Foreign Policy Journal*, 13 October 2012, www.foreignpolicyjournal.com/2012/10/13/georgia-the-more-things-change/ (accessed 9 August 2018). Kornely Kakachia, 'Georgia's Parliamentary Elections: The Start of the Peaceful Transfer of Power?', *Ponars Eurasia Policy Memo*, No. 230 (2012), www.gwu.edu/~ieresgwu/assets/docs/ponars/pepm_230_Kakachia_Sept2012.pdf (accessed 11 June 2015).

23 'Belarus President Starts First Official Visit to Georgia', *Civil Georgia*, 22 April 2015, https://civil.ge/archives/124542 (accessed 14 August 2018).

24 'Tbilisi – Belarus Won't Recognise Abkhazia and South Ossetia', *The Messenger,* 10 November 2009, www.messenger.com.ge/issues/1979_november_10_2009/1979_temo.html (accessed 14 August 2018). Also see 'Belarus to Consider Recognition of Abkhazia and South Ossetia', *Abkhaz World,* 5 November 2009, https://abkhazworld. com/aw/current-affairs/456-belarus-consider-recognition-nov5 (accessed 14 August 2018).

25 Evgeny Finkel and Yitzhak M. Brudny, 'No More Colour! Authoritarian Regimes and Colour Revolutions in Eurasia', in *Coloured Revolutions and Authoritarian Reactions,* ed. Evgeny Finkel and Yitzhak M. Brudny (London and New York: Routledge, 2014).

26 Bartek Tesławski, 'The "Eastern Partnership Plus" Is the EU's Failure', *New Eastern Europe,* 7 December 2017, http://neweasterneurope.eu/2017/12/07/eastern-partnership-plus-eus-failure/ (accessed 11 November 2018).

27 John Anderson, *Kyrgyzstan: Central Asia's Island of Democracy?* (Abingdon and New York: Routledge, 2013).

28 Shaun Walker, 'Turkmenistan Dictator Opens Golf Course – and Quickly Hits "Hole in One"', *Guardian,* 27 October 2017, www.theguardian.com/world/2017/oct/27/turkmenistan-dictator-gurbanguly-berdymukhamedov-opens-golf-course-hits-hole-in-one (accessed 7 November 2018).

29 Kornely Kakachia, 'European, Asian or Eurasian? Georgian Identity and the Struggle for Euro-Atlantic Integration', in *Georgian Foreign Policy: The Quest for Sustainable Security,* ed. Kornely Kakachia and Michael Cecire (Tbilisi: Konrad Adenauer Stiftung, 2013), p. 48.

30 President Giorgi Margvelashvili, 'Inauguration Speech of the President of Georgia Giorgi Margvelashvili', *The Administration of the President of Georgia,* 2014, www. president.gov.ge/ka-GE/prezidenti/inauguracia.aspx (accessed 14 August 2018).

31 'Inbound Tourism: Distribution of Monthly Average Number of Inbound Visitors of Age 15 and Older and Visits Made by Them by Country of Citizenship, Thousand', *GeoStat,* 2018, www.geostat.ge/cms/site_images/_files/english/Tourizm/InboudTourizm/Country%20of%20citizenship.xlsx (accessed 14 August 2018).

32 Bidzina Lebanidze and Mariam Grigalashvili, 'Not EU's World? Putting Georgia's European Integration in Context', *Georgian Institute of Politics,* 2018, http://gip. ge/not-eus-world-putting-georgias-european-integration-in-context/ (accessed 17 September 2018).

Part III

GEORGIA AND THE 'WEST'

Chapter 7

EU–GEORGIA: POLITICS, GEOGRAPHY AND IDENTITY

Natalie Sabanadze

The current state of play in relations between the European Union (EU) and Georgia can be summed up in one phrase: there is no consensus among EU Member States that Georgia should be given the prospect of joining the EU and neither is there a consensus that it should be denied such a prospect. This ambiguity is analytically fascinating, though politically frustrating. It generates contradictory signals from the EU, forcing Georgia to base its foreign policy and national security priorities on uncertainty. Alternatives to European and Euro-Atlantic integration are not seriously considered in Georgia since, in contrast to the EU, there exists a strong public consensus that the European Union is a cultural choice and a political destiny for Georgia.[1] This has led some commentators to identify a certain 'reciprocity deficit' in EU–Georgia relations, which leaves Georgia with contradictory choices. On the one hand, Tbilisi has to manage the expectations of its public on how much and how quickly progress on the path of European integration can be achieved; on the other hand, it has to rely on popular enthusiasm for the EU (as well as for NATO), in order to sustain its Western foreign policy which comes with heavy costs in the traditionally Russian-dominated region.

The purpose of this chapter is to explain why there is no consensus in the EU about Georgia's European perspective. This, despite the fact that the EU and Georgia have become politically close to each other, extending and deepening the scope of their cooperation. What are the main factors that prevent the building of the needed consensus? Are they of a systemic nature or circumstantial, contingent upon a specific yet transient set of events? Is there anything Georgia can do, to help generate the consensus and achieve its stated goal? Answers to these questions are important both from an analytical and policymaking point of view, revealing the nature of constraints limiting the foreign policy behaviour of small states in the regional context of power-political competition.

The chapter traces the evolution of Georgia's relations with the EU since the collapse of the Soviet Union, demonstrating Georgia's steady movement from the outer margins to the centre of the EU's Eastern neighbourhood. In this context, the signing of the Association Agreement including the DCFTA, and achieving visa liberalization for Georgian citizens, is particularly noteworthy as these represent the most important contributions to the narrowing of the 'reciprocity deficit'. The biggest challenge facing Georgia today is how to make a transition from association to that of integration when enlargement has lost its appeal for the EU and when sharing of the neighbourhood with Russia has become increasingly complicated.

There are three sets of factors which complicate the picture: geo-cultural, geopolitical and intra-European. While each factor is important and can be seen as a hurdle on Georgia's path to European integration, not every one of them is of the same nature. The EU is a union of states that are European in a geographic and cultural sense. But what constitutes 'European' as either a cultural or geographic category is complicated and contested. The definition of Europe is not set in stone but is rather a matter of perspective and subject to evolution. For this reason, promoting the 'Europeanness' of Georgian culture and identity has become a political project. Its aim is to legitimize Georgia's European and Euro-Atlantic aspirations notwithstanding the geographic distance and interrupted historical links. Geopolitical contestation, however, is a systemic factor and hence more of a constant in determining foreign policy choices and outcomes.

This chapter argues that the perceptions of geographic or cultural distance may change over time, and hence geo-cultural factors are less consistent than they appear. It is geopolitical contestation that is the most enduring and hence the most difficult hurdle for Georgia to overcome. It is exacerbated by domestic and intra-European divisions. The competitive nature of the international system favours strong unitary actors that have a clear perception of threats as well as national security interests. The EU is not such an actor. Opening up to countries like Georgia and Ukraine means growing confrontation with Russia, increasing the costs of its neighbourhood policy, and the exacerbation of internal divisions. Nevertheless, since the restoration of its independence, Georgia has managed to develop progressively closer relations with the EU and despite systemic and geographic constrains, has significantly reduced the political distance with Brussels. In the process, Georgia has become a more democratic state with a more open society, slowly overcoming the legacies of the past and demonstrating the value of its political choice despite the costs.

Three phases of approximation

The development of EU–Georgia relations can be divided into three major phases. The first begins with the restoration of independence after the collapse of the Soviet Union, when the EU found Georgia on the map and began providing humanitarian assistance. By this time, Georgia was in dire need of such aid. The EU supported Georgia's independence and sovereignty, but its engagement was limited as it still considered Georgia as part of Moscow's near abroad rather than in a common neighbourhood. The EU at the time focused its attention on former communist Eastern Europe and unified Germany.

The second phase lasted from the mid-1990s to 2008 and can be described as a partnership and cooperation phase, reflected in the title of the main agreement of the period, the PCA (Partnership and Cooperation Agreement). In this phase, a greater emphasis was placed on technical assistance and wide-ranging cooperation with the aim of consolidating democracy, boosting trade and investment, developing a market economy and establishing an enhanced political dialogue. PCAs were signed with all the countries of the former Soviet Union, with which the EU had no relations before. The PCAs with Ukraine, Russia and Moldova provided the prospect of future free trade deals, while the agreement with Georgia did not envisage this as a possibility.

The third phase – the current phase – can be defined as an Eastern Partnership (EaP) and association phase, which started with considerable intensification of EU–GE relations since 2003 and the introduction of the Eastern Partnership Initiative in 2009, which covered six former Soviet countries: Armenia, Azerbaijan, Belarus, Georgia, Moldova and Ukraine. The EaP offered partners an opportunity to pursue closer ties with the EU proportional to their ambition and commitment to respect common values. Georgia, Moldova and Ukraine took this opportunity and concluded Association Agreements, including Deep and Comprehensive Free Trade Areas (AA/DCFTA) in 2014. The full application of the AA/DCFTA began in July 2016 and a year later, in March of 2017 a decision on visa liberalization for short-term travel for Georgian citizens to the Schengen zone came into force.

In each phase, Georgia made one or two decisive steps that helped it slowly get closer to the EU both in the physical and political sense. Among these developments, some are particularly noteworthy. For example, with the signing of the PCA, Georgia established its first institutionalized mechanisms of cooperation with the EU, and developed relations across various fields – legislative, economic, social, financial, scientific, civil, technological and cultural. A Cooperation Council was set up as the highest body overseeing implementation of the agreement, which allowed Georgia to have regular meetings with EU officials. According to Gunnar Wiegand and Evelina Schulz, this agreement aimed at strengthening the democratic and economic development of partner countries through cooperation in selected policy areas and the creation of a regular framework for political dialogue.[2] While a breakthrough for institutionalized cooperation between the EU and Georgia, these agreements included mainly 'soft obligations' and lacked effective enforcement and dispute-settlement mechanisms.[3]

The PCA entered fully into force in 1999, the same year Georgia joined the Council of Europe. Georgia's membership in the Council of Europe was another important step taken towards Europe in the same period. Membership was a memorable moment, carrying symbolic as well as political significance. It symbolized Georgia's return to the European family of nations, a long-awaited sign of acceptance and recognition. Then chairman of the CoE Parliamentary Assembly, Lord Russell-Johnston greeted the Georgian delegation with the words 'Georgia, welcome back home!' The head of the Georgian delegation, the late Zurab Zhvania, concluded his speech by saying 'I am Georgian, therefore, I am European'. He spoke of Georgia's European aspirations and outlined Georgia's foreign policy priorities for the next decade.[4] True to his words, Georgia's relations with the EU intensified and after the 2003 Rose Revolution, gained further impetus. In 2003, the EU mentioned the South Caucasus in its security strategy (ESS) and established the post of EU Special Representative for Conflicts in the South Caucasus.

A decade after the signature of the PCAs, the borders of the EU changed dramatically. This led to Georgia's inclusion into the European Neighbourhood Policy (ENP). This was an important development in the context of shrinking the distance between Georgia and the EU. Two rounds of enlargement in 2004 and 2007 shifted the EU borders closer to the Black Sea. Consequently, the EU felt the need to come up with a new ENP, creating an 'arc of stability and prosperity' around the Union.[5] Georgia was not initially included in the ENP, but the shifting of the EU's borders, as well as comprehensive structural and democratic reforms ongoing within Georgia helped the government make the case for its inclusion in the ENP. Within the ENP framework, specific bilateral Action Plans were developed and their implementation monitored and reported in the form of annual Country Progress Reports. In order to support the implementation of Action Plans, the EU developed a dedicated financial instrument entitled the European Neighbourhood Partnership Instrument (ENPI).[6]

After the 2008 war between Russia and Georgia, which ended with an EU-mediated ceasefire led at the time by the French Presidency, the EU felt the urgency to strengthen the Eastern dimension of its neighbourhood policy.[7] Subsequently, Sweden and Poland proposed an Eastern Partnership (EaP) encompassing six former Soviet countries and representing a considerable step toward an even closer partnership. It offered the partners an opportunity to pursue closer ties with the EU proportional to their ambition and commitment to respect common EU values. Each partner was permitted to intensify relations with the EU at its own pace and according to its capacity. The European Commission called for upgrading contractual relations with partner countries by concluding a new generation of Association Agreements, and free trade deals. This could, in principle, lead to the creation of a Neighbourhood Economic Community and the easing of travel restrictions.

Georgia signed an Association Agreement, together with Moldova and Ukraine. These countries also received Visa Liberalization Action Plans (VLAP). Following their successful implementation, they were granted the long-awaited right for their citizens to travel to the EU visa-free. Achieving visa liberalization was probably the single most significant development in EU–Georgia relations which directly affected citizens of Georgia. For people who have been wishing to be part of the European space and to be seen and accepted as such, the right to travel without major hurdles was the most tangible sign of such recognition.

Signing of the AA/DCFTA can be singled out as the decisive step, which brought EU–Georgia relations into a qualitatively new stage of cooperation, making the third, *association phase* particularly significant in terms of approximation to the EU. This is due to the nature of the AA/DCFTA, which is a comprehensive agreement with an ambitious reform agenda and far-reaching scope. It moves away from the earlier 'cooperation' approach and establishes contractual relations between the EU and partner countries in the form of an 'association'. This means economic integration through a partial opening of the common market, and political approximation though a concrete reform agenda. Cooperation Councils were replaced by Association Councils as the highest decision-making body, underpinned by an Association Committee and numerous sub-committees. In Georgia's case, they meet on a yearly basis alternating between Brussels and Tbilisi.

Concluding the AA/DCFTA with the EU has symbolic, political and economic significance for Georgia. It can be described as the most tangible manifestation of Georgia's (as well as Ukraine's and Moldova's) political choice. This a legally binding commitment, not just a declaration of intent to pursue a European path of development. It is a roadmap to modernization of the economy according to the European model, with extensive commitments to regulatory norms and standards of the EU. Most importantly, AA/DCFTA is a reciprocal – as opposed to unilateral – commitment to Georgia's approximation and economic integration with the EU. To this end, the EU offers significant support both in terms of finance and expertise.

It is also an agreement that creates extensive institutional linkages. This includes all six sets of linkages identified by Steven Levitsky and Lucan Way: economic, intergovernmental, technocratic, social, informational and civil society linkages.[8] These are important for creating connections, people-to-people contacts and administrative links, but they also add up to effective leverage in the hands of the EU. In the absence of a perspective for accession (which could have been a strong leverage), the AA/DCFTA puts political pressure on the Georgian government to adhere to the European agenda; it strengthens the EU's role and influence and increases its leverage over partners such as Georgia. As argued by Levitsky and Way, linkages create domestic ownership of European norms and values. They reshape the domestic distribution of power and resources and reduce the likelihood of authoritarianism by creating local expectations for democracy and the rule of law.[9] In other words, through establishing these linkages, the AA/DCFTA can try and meet its transformative ambitions without the promise of accession.

The AA/DCFTAs concluded with Georgia, Moldova and Ukraine, were modelled on the Association and Stabilization agreements signed by the countries of South East Europe, and by the Association Agreements established with Central European countries. In the latter example, however, the aim of the agreements was to prepare the signatory states for future accession negotiations. In the case of Georgia, Moldova and Ukraine, there was no promise of the next step in the AA/DCFTAs, but neither was the idea ruled out.[10] Gunnar Wiegand and Evelina Schulz argue that the difference between the earlier Association Agreements and the new ones with Georgia, Ukraine and Moldova, was never adequately explained and answered. The question of accession was left open due to the lack of consensus among the EU Member States. While the European Neighbourhood Policy shares the logic of the enlargement policy,[11] in recent years Brussels has been maintaining that the two must be kept separate. The question is whether, as a result, EU–Georgia relations have hit a wall or whether there is room for further integration. Apart from the EEA countries (Norway, Lichtenstein and Iceland) and Western

Balkans candidate countries, this is the closest one can get to the EU both in terms of access to the market and in terms of approximation to the *acquis communitaire* – the body of common rights and obligations binding all the EU Member States.[12]

According to some reports, Georgia is outperforming candidate countries of the Western Balkans in a number of areas.[13] However, accession is not simply a question of fulfilling the criteria; it is also a question of identity, geography and geopolitics. The decision to put the accession of the Balkans onto the EU agenda was motivated by geostrategic considerations, but framed in terms of common history and geography, of shared identity and historical destiny.[14] Despite existing fatigue and disappointment with enlargement, there is a growing understanding in Brussels that the only way to stabilize the Balkans, reduce corruption, assist in state-building and minimize the risk of conflict, is by bringing these countries into the European Union. The EU's High Representative on Foreign Policy, Federica Mogherini, said before her tour of the region in April 2018 that the Western Balkans are Europe and they will be part of the future European Union. She underlined that the EU Member States and the Balkans have been connected through history and geography, and will build a common future.[15]

These factors which have helped return the Western Balkans to the EU agenda may be precisely those that keep Georgia off of it. Geography, history and culture together with the complicated geopolitics of the region in which Georgia is situated are among the main obstacles to Georgia's transition from an association to integration phase. In addition, internal challenges facing the EU today are numerous and make enlargement among the least attractive and most politically costly policy options. The question is whether these obstacles are of systemic and hence permanent nature, or are derived from a particular confluence of circumstances and are hence, transient. The rest of this chapter addresses this question by highlighting geo-cultural, geopolitical and intra-European factors affecting Georgia's European aspirations.

The relativity of geography

One often hears in the corridors of the European Commission that if only Georgia were located closer to the EU, if for example it was in place of Moldova, it might already have been a candidate for membership. This observation may or may not be true, but it is interesting as it indicates the enduring importance of geographic proximity. Georgia's perceived geo-cultural distance is, therefore, seen as one of the obstacles to securing its place in the EU.

Geography has no doubt played an important role in Georgia's political history and to this day, it determines its political destiny. In national imagery, it is portrayed as a country situated between East and West, a strategic borderland and a meeting point of two worlds. Among the most common images evoked when describing Georgia are those of a bridge, a junction, a crossroads. In theory, this could be a rare privilege which offers a choice: Georgia could go East or West or stay as a unique mix of the two worlds, benefiting from cultural wealth, trade routes and transit possibilities. In practice, however, this has meant continuous uncertainty and contestation on matters of identity and belonging and on how Georgia was and is perceived from outside. It has also meant that Georgia became a buffer zone, and a battlefield for influence.

In today's post-modern and globalized world, physical location, territorial boundaries and geographic indicators arguably matter less than at any given moment in history. We have moved away from the territorial confines of doing politics, building social relations and engaging in trade or business. Assisted by technological advances we have enlarged our social networks and areas of activities onto a global scale, way beyond the traditional boundaries of nation-states. De-territorialization of economic, social and political affairs is the defining feature of globalization. As the world is shrinking, geography should become increasingly irrelevant. This is a logical expectation stemming from processes of globalization and modern multinational business. When it comes to foreign policy, however, geography still holds power as illustrated by Georgia's attempts to go West (politically) while being located in the East (physically).

Yet culture and identity have been defined and redefined in today's Georgia in ways that serve its political ambitions against the odds of history and geography. Moreover, while physical geography cannot be altered, perspectives on what constitutes proximity and where the outer boundaries lie may change over time. The main challenge is not Georgia's geographic location, but rather the definition (or the lack therein) of the EU's geographic scope.

There are many different visions of the EU, its boundaries and its place in the world. The policy of enlargement was an attempt to expand and export the European model of integration on a larger scale, creating a rules-based, multilateral system of governance in the EU's neighbourhood. The EU wants new kinds of relations between and beyond states, on a global scale.[16] But the EU cannot go on expanding forever without dramatically changing and even losing its central vision of greater integration. When asked about the limits of enlargement, former EU Commissioner Romano Prodi declared there must be a debate on where EU borders end. Regarding Turkey's accession, he underlined that there are no geographic or cultural (for which read religious) factors hindering the process, Turkey simply needed to comply with the EU's criteria. When asked about countries like Georgia that feel European, he said: 'People in New Zealand also feel that they are European ... We cannot limit ourselves to historical roots. We also have to give a natural size to the EU.'[17]

Prodi's statement suggests that there is no internal EU-wide consensus on where Europe ends, especially in the East. Both Neil MacFarlane and Anand Menon write: 'the Union was reasonably clear that the countries of the southern Mediterranean littoral would not qualify for membership, since they were not in "Europe". The question was more difficult to the East: where did Europe end? The (European) Commission view was that although membership was not excluded, there needed to be a debate about the line.'[18] Europe is more than the EU, but being in Europe appears to be a precondition for membership. The question which concerns us, then follows: is Georgia in 'Europe'? Is it on the eastern frontier of the West or on the western frontier of the East? Or perhaps it is only a matter of perspective?

Historically, lines between the centre and periphery within Europe as well as between 'Europe' and 'Asia' have been shifting for centuries. Tony Judt recalls in his *Postwar: A History of Europe Since 1945* that by the eighteenth century, Hungarians and Bohemians were Catholic and often German speaking, but for enlightened Austrians, 'Asia' nevertheless began at the Landstrasse, the high road leading east out of Vienna. When Mozart headed west from Vienna to Prague in 1787, he envisaged himself crossing an oriental border. In the words of Judt, 'East and West, Asia and Europe, were always walls in the mind at least as much as lines on the earth'.[19]

Geography in this sense is a relative rather than absolute category. Nations that are seen today at the centre of Europe have been previously associated with its outer margins. Poles, Lithuanians and Ukrainians have all presented themselves in their literature and national narratives as guardians of the frontiers of Europe. The same can be said about Hungarians and Romanians, Serbs or Croats with each claiming borders that constitute the outer defence between civilized Europe and the rest. These narratives cannot all be true; they are often mutually exclusive and contradictory. But this is irrelevant, what matters is that belonging to Europe is a central pillar of their national narratives.[20] Europe offers a degree of security, a refuge and a promise of inclusion in a better, more civilized network of relations. Norman Davies reminds us that nations on the outskirts of Europe all attach great importance to inclusion in Europe and press it with urgency, both in their domestic national discourse and in external relations.

Georgia is no exception to Davies' observation. The established national narrative of modern Georgia is something like this: Christianity began first in Georgia and spread towards Europe from the Middle East. Georgia was the final stop along the Silk Road before the goods from Asia reached Europe. We were the first producers of wine in Europe (and the world); anchored in Europe, we are the bridge of the Western world with other worlds. This narrative asserts Georgia's proximity to, and significance for, Europe. Despite its geographic distance and interrupted historical ties, Georgia hopes with this narrative to shape boundaries in the minds of European decision makers, and to make Georgia's belonging to Europe uncontested.[21]

Cultural identity as a political choice

Georgia's historical connection with the West and Europe in particular has been repeatedly severed. After the fall of Byzantium in 1453, Georgian kingdoms fell under the influence of the Ottoman and Persian empires, excluded from the impacts of European cultural movements like the Renaissance and Reformation. Ghia Nodia argues that historically Georgia's experience of 'Western-ness' was minimal.[22] Nevertheless, the modern Georgian nation as conceived by its 'founding fathers' in the nineteenth century, who were under the influence of the ideas of the Enlightenment, was imagined according to the Western model. The West became a cultural, political and developmental choice for the Georgian intelligentsia. It became an inseparable part of the national narrative, reinforced by generations of Georgian intellectual and political elites. Noe Jordania, chairman/president of the First Georgian Democratic Republic, declared in front of the National Assembly in 1920 that 'our life today and our life in the future is ... indissolubly tied to the West, and no force can break this bond'. This sentiment has been echoed by successive Georgian leaders and shared by the majority of the Georgian public in a series of opinion polls since 1991.[23] It is underpinned by Georgian historiography which has constructed the notion of the 'Muslim' other, emphasizing Georgia's 'Westernness' through ancient Christian roots and cultural traditions that are at odds with its geographic location.

Georgia asserts its Europeanness not on historical or geographical grounds (it cannot do so), but rather as a defence against history and geography. Its national narrative is dominated by references to the 'return' of Georgia to the cultural and political space where it 'naturally' belongs.[24] According to Tracey German, 'Georgia's determination to emphasize its 'Europeanness' and to ensure a 'return to Europe' is an attempt to make a clear distinction between its past and its future, between the post-Soviet space and 'Europe'.[25] In that sense, 'European' national identity has both instrumental and cultural dimensions. It is not only about self-definition of the Georgian nation but about legitimizing a certain political and civilizational choice domestically and externally. For the majority of scholars, both Western and Georgian, Georgia's European and Euro-Atlantic aspirations are identity-driven and determined by ideational and cultural, as opposed to rational choice or realpolitik.[26]

Georgia is a country at a geographic and economic crossroads – it has experienced a diversity of cultural influences and a multiplicity of historical and cultural impacts. Georgians could have constructed a different national narrative, adjusted their political orientation accordingly, and made life easier for the struggling Georgian state. It could have identified itself with the Caucasus, emphasizing its ties with other Caucasian nations.[27] This was attempted from time to time and should not be ignored. Georgia might have adhered to ideas of Eurasianism, which has now become part of the legitimizing ideology of Putin's Eurasian Economic Union.[28] It could have allied itself with Russia, staying in the CIS and other post-Soviet political structures, perpetuating rather than breaking with the Soviet legacy. All of these options could have helped Georgia maintain its territorial integrity and avoid costly confrontation with Russia. But all these options were decidedly rejected by generations of Georgians, especially after 1991 when they were given the choice. This supports the argument that Georgia's pro-Western orientation stems largely from ideas and identity rather than from pragmatic or systemic factors.[29]

Alexandre Rondeli described Georgia's attempts to break with its past and integrate in European and Euro-Atlantic structures as strategic idealism.[30] This idea goes against the expectation that states behave as rational actors minimizing risks to their security and survival. The neo-realist paradigm, which prioritizes material and systemic factors, would suggest that any Georgian foreign policy behaviour which challenges Russia's interests in the region, is foolish and is bound to incur high costs. Nevertheless, there is a pragmatic logic in Georgia's choices, and a considerable degree of rationality, often defined as value rationality. If Georgia values political independence understood as freedom from domination; if it accepts democratic decision making, good governance and rule of law as fundamental to its national and human security, then there are no options other than pursuing the European model of social, political and economic development. Similar to many other peripheral nations, Europe for Georgia is associated with modernization, progress and prosperity, and the EU was a logical strategic choice for citizens and leaders alike. Georgia defines its national interest as one linked with Europe. European and Euro-Atlantic integration have no alternative.

But it is not sufficient to identify oneself as European in cultural and political terms. It is important to be recognized as such by the rest of the world, and most importantly by those who are today seen as the core Europeans. It is for this reason that the promotion of Georgia's European identity has become a political project and intensified greatly over the last decade as Georgia openly makes its bid to become a member of the EU and NATO. Recognition of Georgia's Europeanness is a precondition for accepting its European aspirations and for legitimizing ambitions for EU integration in the eyes of European decision makers. As Tony Judt observed, 'identification with Europe today is not about the common past, it is about asserting the claim, however flimsy and forlorn, about the common future'.[31]

The boundaries of the West have been changing from the Georgian perspective too. At the beginning of the eighteenth century, the closest thing to the West (understood as a culturally aligned and protective power), to which Georgia could reach out and seek protection from the Persians and Ottomans, was the Russian Empire. Moscow was seen from Georgia as an occidental power; it shared Georgians' Orthodox Christianity and could bring Georgia closer to Europe. Then as today, Georgians saw European civilization as progressive, highly developed and culturally close. Generations of Georgian students went to Russia's leading universities in the nineteenth century to discover Western intellectual trends and were inspired by the national liberation movements of Greece and Italy, which they could read about in Russian journals. A large part of the Georgian intellectual elite believed that Georgia's liberation could be obtained within and through Russia. It was only with the Bolshevik Revolution in October 1917 that the Georgian intelligentsia's intellectual and cultural links with Russia were broken.

In the first years of Bolshevik rule, Russia became disconnected from Europe, while Georgia chose the path of European social democracy and a Western model of development. Georgia's short-lived first republic of 1918–21, defined itself as progressive and European, promoting socialist ideals of equality and broad, participatory democracy. Georgia's ruling social democrats drew a clear line between themselves and Bolshevik Russia, which had established dictatorship and centralized the state system in the name of the proletariat. According to Malkhaz Matsaberidze, Bolshevism 'became marked as the "other", an "Asiatic" threat to

Georgia's European path'.[32] Thus Russia, from a window to Europe became a wall. In 1918–21, the government of the first republic sought alliance with Germany, and then Britain, to gain recognition of its independence. Only Western aid would allow Georgia to withstand the dual pressure of Turkey and Bolshevik Russia.

Ramsay MacDonald, who became the first Labour prime minister in the United Kingdom in 1924, visited the democratic republic of Georgia in 1920. He was impressed by its achievements and urged the allied governments to recognize Georgia as an anti-Bolshevik outpost which would guard the West's strategic interests in the Near East. Stephen Jones argues that for MacDonald there were at least three reasons why the British government should support Georgia. First, Georgia shared Europe's democratic aspirations; second, it occupied a precious geostrategic location adjacent to the Near East; and third, it was a transit hub for oil and freight.[33] Not everyone was convinced and, in the summer of 1920, British troops withdrew from Georgia. In February 1921, abandoned by European powers, Georgia fell victim to the Red Army.

MacDonald's writings on Georgia have a strikingly contemporary ring to them, reflecting the persistent nature of regional geopolitical constraints. Since Georgia regained its independence in 1991 after the Soviet collapse, it has been trying to gain Western recognition as a European state. It has been trying to convince Western powers of Georgia's political and strategic utility, urging a Western military presence in the country. For most of the 1990s, however, Georgia remained largely outside the European sphere of engagement. It was seen as an integral part of the Russian sphere of dominance and of little interest to the West in general and the EU in particular. In 1998, Bruno Coppieters observed that the EU does not really regard Georgia as a European nation but as a peripheral state, part of the region bridging Europe and Asia. He described the EU policies towards Georgia as a manifestation of 'benevolent indifference'.[34]

Twenty years later, the distance between the EU and Georgia has shrunk significantly. Georgia has moved up the EU's political agenda, joining the ranks of its closest neighbours, linked to the EU by association agreements. With the enlargement process, the boundaries of the EU shifted closer to Georgia and with the accession of Romania and Bulgaria, Georgia could now claim a maritime border with the EU. The same processes propelled the EU as an actor with a special role and importance in the region, allowing Georgia to gradually build up its connections with the EU. Today Georgia benefits from the DCFTA and visa-free travel, it participates in numerous EU programmes, including those linked to student and scientific exchanges (Erasmus + and Horizon Europe respectively); it contributes to the EU-led special missions and operations and it is not shy of presenting its membership ambitions at every available opportunity.

At the same time, however, Georgia's sovereign right to determine its alliances freely, join international structures of its choosing and to move away from the Russian sphere of influence has been met with resistance from Moscow and hence curtailed by the power-political competition in the region. The war with Georgia in 2008 and the Russian occupation of Georgia's regions of Abkhazia and South Ossetia, as well as the 2014 annexation of Crimea and the war in eastern Ukraine demonstrate that

Moscow is prepared to prevent the expansion of Western institutions into this part of the world by all means, including military. Moscow's responses to both Georgia and Ukraine made it evident that Russia looks at the world almost exclusively from the perspective of power-political competition, seeing the development of direct and meaningful links between the states in the region and the EU as contrary to its strategic interests. Moscow approaches the neighbourhood in zero-sum terms, claiming a special role and expecting others to recognize and respect this claim. From the Russian perspective, the EU's Eastern Partnership and its association agreements obscure the real intention of the EU to extend its influence into the East and challenge Russia's traditional dominance in the region.

The above analysis suggests that the question of Georgia's geographic distance from and cultural belonging to Europe is a matter of perception, subject to change rather than to immovable facts. Geo-cultural factors, while important, may not be taken as insurmountable obstacles to Georgia's European aspirations. When it comes to geopolitical competition, however, one may argue that this is a systemic and hence more durable factor that leads to certain, often undesirable outcomes. Different schools of international relations offer various explanations for the functioning of the international system. It was neo-liberalism, however, that was most frequently evoked in the context of the EU–Russia confrontation over the neighbourhood, which argues that the balance of power and inter-state competition are fundamentals of the international system and they determine what kind of room for manoeuvre states may or may not have. Normative principles such as sovereign equality and the freedom of choice lose their relevance in the context of international struggle for power and influence.

Georgia, EU and the 'return' of realpolitik

Neo-realism, which went out of vogue during the initial post-Cold War euphoria, has made a remarkable comeback in recent years, particularly as Russia has started to reassert itself in the neighbourhood and beyond. According to John Mearsheimer, the policy of turning Ukraine into a Western stronghold on the doorsteps of Russia was driven by 'liberal delusions' and should be seen as nothing short of reckless provocation. In his view, the world should accept that Russia acts in defence of its national security interests and abandon the idea of westernizing Ukraine, turning it instead into a neutral buffer. When it comes to the wishes of states such as Georgia and Ukraine and their ambition to make sovereign choices even if these contradict those of a big neighbour, Mearsheimer contends that this is a dangerous way for small states to think about their foreign policy options.

> The sad truth is that might often makes right when great-power politics are at play. Abstract rights such as self-determination are largely meaningless when powerful states get into brawls with weaker states. It is in the interest of small states to understand these basic facts of life and tread carefully when it comes to their more powerful neighbours.[35]

The EU did not intend to cause trouble with Moscow. It did not conceive of its policies for the Eastern neighbourhood, including the Eastern Partnership as a challenge to Russia and an invitation to renewed competition. Moscow, however, saw it exactly that way. According to Wiegand and Schulz, Moscow's fears were grossly exaggerated since the AA/DCFTA were not designed to lead to new dividing lines on this continent, but to promote additional economic opportunities without severing traditional ties.[36] Moscow, however, perceived it as a direct challenge and as Kadri Liik observed, this is precisely why Moscow spared no effort at preventing the EaP countries from signing association agreements with the EU.[37] It pressured Armenia into abandoning its association with the EU, and into joining the Eurasian Union.[38] Ukraine under Yanukovich was about to do the same until protests in Kyiv changed the course of events and the newly elected President, Petro Poroshenko, returned Ukraine to the association track with the EU. He did so against Moscow's warnings that the signing of the Association agreement and choosing the EU integration option would have 'catastrophic consequences'. Ukraine would no longer be Russia's strategic partner and it would lose its legal personality under international law.[39]

The Brussels 'realists' felt vindicated as a consensus began to emerge that the EU had misread Russia's intentions and its determination to pursue them. It was, they said, unforgivable to misjudge the huge strategic importance Ukraine had for Russia and not to take that into account. A *Spiegel* editorial concluded that Europeans failed to see how far Russia was willing to go to prevent a strong bond between Ukraine and the West. They did not take Russian concerns and warnings seriously enough because it did not fit into their own worldview. 'Russia and Europe talked past each other and misunderstood one another. It was a clash of two different foreign policy cultures.'[40] Moreover, it was a sign that Great Power competition did not disappear with the end of the Cold War and was still a factor to be reckoned with.

Nothing has changed from the perspective of Georgia and neither was the Russian response a surprise or a deterrent for Tbilisi. Georgia seeks integration with European and Euro-Atlantic structures precisely to get away from Russian domination and ensure its security, development and prosperity. Despite costs and risks attached to this policy, all other available alternatives are worse and incompatible with Georgia's historic and cultural choice. The weakness of the neo-realist approach is that it does not explain nor can it predict why states choose to behave in certain ways and not in others, often ignoring the realist logic. The international system may constrain and set limits to states' behaviour but it does not entirely determine policy choices they make. Neo-realism has a blind spot regarding internal processes and historically or culturally determined aspirations. It considers rationality as acontextual and instrumental. However, the behaviour of states and political actors can be driven by value rationality. The cause of European integration has so much intrinsic value in the current Georgian context that no political force can ignore it and yet remain relevant in the domestic political scene. Its value in turn is determined by the belief that the EU represents a non-dominating, non-threatening political entity based on multilateral cooperation and rules-based inter-state relations. For a small state like Georgia, belonging to such an entity is a survival strategy and historic necessity as well as a moral choice. It is therefore understandable why local elites pursue the cause of European integration and citizens are largely prepared to bear the costs.

The 2008 war between Russia and Georgia demonstrated clearly that the costs would be high as Moscow was ready to use force to defend its perceived geostrategic interests. However, many in Brussels as well as in other European capitals believed that the red line for Russia was NATO membership, while integration with the EU was a more acceptable option.[41] In other words, Georgia was seen as being reckless in testing the limits of Russian patience by pushing strongly for NATO membership. Consequently, the overall Western response to Russian aggression was timid and short-lived in the hope that it was a one-off event unlikely to be repeated elsewhere. Given the predominance of such views, Moscow's violent response to Ukraine's enhanced trade deal with the EU took many by surprise.[42] This time the EU responded by imposing sanctions on Russia, while Germany and France began to seek a solution to the conflict in the so-called Normandy Format.[43]

From the perspective of the EU, it became evident that the costs of confronting Russia while pursuing its neighbourhood policy had to be better calculated and assessed. There seems to be a growing consensus among European policymakers and commentators that Russia has to be factored in, if the neighbourhood policy, including the EaP, is to be successful. There is less of a consensus on how to do so, under what conditions, and according to which rules. With the invasion of Georgia in 2008, Russia successfully derailed Georgia's path to NATO membership and with the annexation of Crimea and the war in Eastern Ukraine, Moscow managed to put question marks on the EU's neighbourhood policy towards the East and reduced the chances of the EU membership for Georgia and Ukraine in the near future. In the cases of both Georgia and Ukraine, Russia contributed to the creation of unresolved territorial conflicts that have considerably complicated the path of integration for these countries into both the EU and NATO.

This leads to a conclusion that the biggest and the most real obstacle to Georgia's membership in the European and Euro-Atlantic structures is geopolitical, even if it may be framed in geographic and cultural terms. The EU and its members do not seem to agree on the need to support Georgia and its aspirations if this implies costly confrontation with Russia. However, the geopolitical obstacles facing Georgia are not only and not exclusively related to Russia. These also include the EU's own internal divisions and domestic challenges that complicate the definition of common interests for the union and lead to diverging understanding of its role as a global actor.

Conclusion: Georgia between association and (non)membership

The EU has traditionally defined itself as a normative power, supporting multilateralism in global affairs as well as promotion of norms and values in its foreign policy. In today's increasingly competitive world, where the EU has been facing challenges from Russia, China and even, to a certain extent, the United States, one can detect a shift away from values-based to more interests-based foreign policy. The two foreign policy documents put forward by the EU, the Global Strategy and the Review of Neighbourhood policy have both stepped away from the previous normative approach, towards one closer to Realpolitik.[44] Given the turmoil and conflict that has engulfed the EU's neighbourhood both from the East and from the South, the new documents focus on stabilization and security.

The ENP review emphasizes cooperation based on mutual interest with individual partners and moves away from a value-laden discourse, no longer attempting to transform the neighbourhood according to its own model. It acknowledges that some challenges need to be addressed with the involvement of other powers in the region and speaks of cooperation with 'neighbours of neighbours'. In the East, this means Russia and possibly Turkey. In addition, recent difficulties in relations with the United States after the election of President Trump also encouraged the EU to start thinking more profoundly on matters of its own defence and security and of its role as a global actor in the world where long-standing alliances and multilateralism are increasingly feeling the strain.

In the context of power-political competition, acting as a unitary actor with clearly defined national security interests is paramount. The EU, however, is a union of twenty-seven Member States all with different priorities, with their own domestic interest groups and varied types of leadership, which predictably makes the conduct of a common foreign and security policy complicated. Internal challenges ranging from the migration crisis to Brexit further exacerbated division. The EU often had to face the North–South divisions over economic matters. The recent migration crisis and disagreements on how to deal with migrants and refugees has particularly sharpened the East–West divide. Perceived backsliding on democratic standards and rule of law in some of the Central and East European Member States, has further exacerbated intra-EU tensions leading to a tacit reassessment of enlargement. As Stefan Lehn noted in relation to the enlargement policy, 'what used to be considered a historic achievement is now often viewed more critically. Many in Western Europe now think that the EU has extended too far and too quickly, and some are nostalgic for the earlier "Carolingian" union.'[45]

None of the above bodes well for Georgia's prospects of membership. In the context of increasing competitive global relations and internal divisions, it will be difficult to convince all Member States that Georgia's membership in the EU serves the interests of the union. In addition, the decision of the United Kingdom to leave the EU, as well as the growing popularity of euro-sceptical political forces in the Member States, has stimulated rethinking of the effectiveness and attractiveness of the European project first and foremost for European citizens. This may result in an increasingly inward-looking EU, which could further limit its global role and global ambitions. It also makes the EU particularly reluctant to consider further horizontal expansion when the discussions are ongoing about the shape of the current union after Brexit.

This leaves Georgia with European aspirations that are acknowledged but not reciprocated by the EU.[46] It is told to contend with political approximation and economic integration as offered by the Association Agreement and focus on its implementation. Some Member States favour expansion of the EU and support Georgia's European perspective; the European Parliament has expressed this view in its various resolutions. However, there is no unanimity for reasons ranging from geo-cultural to geopolitical and intra-European. Some of these reasons are determined by the current set of circumstances, while others are endemic to the EU and the international system. Nevertheless, this analysis demonstrates that Georgia has managed to move forward, closing the distance and further integrating with the EU against the odds. It would be logical to continue in this direction keeping in mind evolving circumstances as well as more permanent constraints.

Georgia should demonstrate its relevance and geopolitical utility to the EU, while simultaneously making the moral case for itself as a progressive European state. This would make it difficult for the EU to 'abandon' Georgia on normative grounds. This suggests a reversal of a traditional association-accession-transformation paradigm that was applied to the Central and East European states. In the case of Georgia, it should first make itself attractive to the EU by its own successful transformation, using tools like association and, if necessary, creating new bonds, before it can count on the promise of accession. The final outcome is hard to predict, but in the process, Georgia should consolidate itself as a European-style institutional democracy, which is in any case the ultimate goal of its efforts to join Europe.

Notes

1   Laura Thornton and Koba Turmanidze, *Public Attitudes in Georgia. Results of December 2019 survey carried out for NDI by CRRC Georgia, 2019*,www.ndi.org/sites/default/files/NDI%20Georgia_December%202019_Public%20Presentation_ENG VF.pdf (accessed 8 June 2020).

2   Gunnar Wiegand and Evelina Schulz, 'The EU and its Eastern Partnership: Political Association and Economic Integration in a Rough Neighborhood', in *Trade Policy between Law, Diplomacy and Scholarship Liber amicorum in memoriam Horst G. Krenzler*, ed. Christoph Hermann et al. (Cham: Springer International Publishing, 2015), pp. 321–58.

3   Ibid.

4   Natia Metsvirishvili and Maya Metsvirishvili, 'I am Georgian, therefore I am European: Re-searching the Europeanness of Georgia', *Central European Journal of International and Security* Studies, 14 (2020), pp. 52–64.

5   Former Commission President Romano Prodi, '*An Enlarged and More United Europe, a Global Player – Challenges and Opportunities in the New Century*', speech at College of Europe, Bruges, 12 November 2001, European Commission, http://europa.eu/rapid/press-release_SPEECH-01-528_en.htm?locale=en (accessed 8 June 2020).

6   This policy was based on the Commission's communication, 'Wider Europe – Neighbourhood: A New Framework for Relations with our Eastern and Southern Neighbours', adopted in March 2003. For a detailed analysis of the ENP in comparison to enlargement, see Deniz Devrim and Evelina Schulz, 'Enlargement

Fatigue in the European Union: From Enlargement to Many Unions', Real Instituto Elcano, 3 October 2009.

7   The 2008 French Presidency launched *Union pour la Méditerranée*, reinvigorating its relations with the South. Following this initiative, pressure also mounted to strengthen the eastern dimension of the ENP and the European Council had already adopted conclusions to this effect in June 2008. However, the Russo-Georgian War added urgency to this project and the Eastern Partnership was arguably developed as EU's policy response to this war. In December 2008, the Commission put forward the 'Communication on the EaP'.

8   Steven Levitsky and Lucan A. Way, 'Linkage versus Leverage. Rethinking the International Dimension of Regime Change', *Comparative Politics*, 38:4 (2006), pp. 379–400.

9   Ibid., pp. 380–85.

10 Association Agreement between the European Union and the European Atomic Energy Community and their Member States, of the one part, and Georgia, of the other part, *Official Journal of the European Union*, L 261, volume 57, 30 August 2014.

11 David Cadier, 'Is the European Neighbourhood Policy a Substitute for Enlargement?', in *The Crisis of EU Enlargement*, LSE IDEAS Special Report, 18 November 2013.

12 European Commission, European Neighbourhood Policy and Enlargement Negotiations, https://ec.europa.eu/neighbourhood-enlargement/policy/glossary/terms/acquis_en (accessed 8 June 2020).

13 Michael Emerson et al., *The Struggle for Good Governance in Eastern Europe* (London: Rowman & Littlefield International, 2018).

14 Speech by High Representative/Vice-President Federica Mogherini at the European Parliament Plenary Session on the Western Balkan Strategy, European External Action Service (EEAS), 6 February 2018, https://eeas.europa.eu/delegations/montenegro/39451/speech-high-representativevice-president-federica-mogherini-european-parliament-plenary_ga (accessed 8 June 2020).

15 Ibid.

16 Kalypso Nicolaidis and Robert Howse, '"This is my EUtopia": Narrative as Power', *Journal of Common Market Studies*, 4 (2002), pp. 767–92.

17 Cited in Neil McFarlane and Anand Menon, 'Of Wealth and Weakness', *Survival: Global Politics and Strategy*, 56 (2014), pp. 95–101.

18 Ibid.

19 Tony Judt, *Postwar: A History of Europe since* 1945 (New York: Penguin Press, 2005).

20 Margaret, Harvey, 'Europe after Wyclif', *Journal of Theological Studies*, 69:1 (2018), pp. 368–69.

21 Association Agreement between the European Union and the European Atomic Energy Community and their Member States, of the one part, and Georgia.

22 Ghia Nodia, 'Georgia: Dimensions of Insecurity', in *Statehood and Security: Georgia after the Rose Revolution*, ed. Bruno Coppieters and Robert Legvold (London: MIT Press, 2005).

23 Comprehensive databases of public opinion surveys in Georgia include The Caucasus Research Resource Centre, 'Caucasus Barometer' www.crrccenters.org/caucasusbarometer; International Republican Institute, 'Georgia' www.iri.org/country/georgia; National Democratic Institute, 'Library of NDI Georgia Public Opinion Research' www.ndi.org/georgia-polls.

24 *National Security Concept of Georgia*, adopted by parliament on 23 December 2011 (NSC 2011), www.mfa.gov.ge/index.php?lang_id=ENG&sec_id=12

25   Tracey German, 'Heading West? Georgia's Euro-Atlantic Path?', *International Affairs*, 91:3 (2015), pp. 601–14.

26   Kornely Kakachia, 'European, Asian, or Eurasian? Georgian Identity and the Struggle for Euro-Atlantic Integration'; Ghia Nodia, 'Divergent Interests: What Can and Cannot be Achieved in Georgia–Russian Relations', in *Georgian Foreign Policy: The Quest for Sustainable Security*, ed. Kornely Kakachia and Michael Cecire (Tbilisi: Konrad Adenauer Stiftung, 2013), pp. 175–89.

27   Martin McCauley, 'Obituary: Zviad Gamsakhurdia', *The Independent*, 25 February 1994.

28   Anton Shekhovtsov, 'Aleksandr Dugin's Neo-Eurasianism: The New Right à la Russe', *Religion Compass*, 4 (2009), pp. 697–716.

29   Kornely Kakachia and Salome Minesashvili, 'Identity Politics: Exploring Georgian Foreign Policy Behaviour', *Journal of Eurasian Studies*, 6:2 (2015), pp. 171–80.

30   Alexandre Rondeli, 'The Choice of Independent Georgia', in *The Security of the Caspian Sea Region*, ed. Gennady Chufrin (Oxford: Oxford University Press, 2001), p. 195.

31   Tony Judt, Postwar: A History of Europe Since 1945 (London: Pimlico 2007) p. 753.

32   Malkhaz Matsaberidze, 'The Democratic Republic of Georgia (1918–21) and the Search for the Georgian Model of Democracy', in *The Making of Modern Georgia, 1918–2012: The First Georgian Republic and its Successors*, 1st ed., ed. Stephen F. Jones (Abingdon: Routledge, 2016), p. 141.

33   Ibid.

34   Bruno Coppieters, 'Georgia in Europe: The Idea of Periphery in International Relations', in *Commonwealth and Independence in Post-Soviet Eurasia*, ed. Bruno Coppieters et al. (London: Frank Cass, 1998), p. 65.

35   John Mearsheimer, 'Why the Ukraine Crisis is the West's Fault', *Foreign Affairs*, September–October 2014, www.foreignaffairs.com/articles/russia-fsu/2014-08-18/why-ukraine-crisis-west-s-fault (accessed 8 June 2020).

36   Gunnar Wiegand and Evelina Schulz, 'The EU and Its Eastern Partnership: Political Association and Economic Integration in a Rough Neighbourhood', in *Trade Policy between Law, Diplomacy and Scholarship*, ed. Christoph Herrmann et al. (Cham: European Yearbook of International Economic Law, Springer, 2020).

37   Kadri Liik, 'How the EU Needs to Manage Relations with Its Eastern Neighbourhood', Carnegie Endowment for International Peace, 23 August 2017, https://carnegieendowment.org/2017/08/23/how-eu-needs-to-manage-relations-with-its-eastern-neighborhood-pub-72883 (accessed 8 June 2020).

38   Following the EU's increased engagement in its Eastern Neighbourhood, Russia launched a Eurasian Economic Area – a counterbalancing economic integration format inviting post-Soviet countries to join. Although Armenia successfully negotiated an Association Agreement with the EU, before the Vilnius Summit 2013, due to increased Russian pressure, Armenian President Serzh Sarkisian announced that Armenia would not sign the AA agreement with the EU and would instead join the Russia-led Customs Union.

39   The warning was issued by Sergei Glaziev, Putin's economic adviser, in August 2013. See *Spiegel online*; see also Glaziev's interview to *Kommersant*, 3 September 2013.

40   'How the EU Lost Russia over Ukraine', *Spiegel online*, 24 November 2014, www.spiegel.de/international/europe/war-in-ukraine-a-result-of-misunderstandings-between-europe-and-russia-a-1004706.html (accessed 8 June 2020).

41 This belief was not entirely unfounded since back in 2004, Putin reiterated his opposition to NATO expansion but spoke positively of the EU enlargement process. Press conference following talks with Spanish Prime Minister Zapatero, 10 December 2004 as cited in Wiegand and Schulz, p. 22.

42 For a detailed discussion of how the EU handled the Ukraine case in the run-up to the Vilnius summit, see a piece by *Spiegel* staff, 'How the EU lost Russia over Ukraine', *Spiegel online*, November 2014, www.spiegel.de/international/europe/war-in-ukraine-a-result-of-misunderstandings-between-europe-and-russia-a-1004706.html (accessed 8 June 2020).

43 The format was created on 6 June 2014, when French, German, Russian and Ukrainian leaders met on the margins of the seventieth anniversary of the D-Day allied landings in Normandy. This was the first meeting between Presidents Vladimir Putin of Russia and Petro Poroshenko of Ukraine since the crisis had erupted in Ukraine. The Normandy Format does not include the United States or the European Union, nor any other European countries beyond France and Germany.

44 Steven Blockmans, 'The Obsolescence of the European Neighbourhood Policy', Centre for European Policy Studies (CEPS), 9 October 2017, www.ceps.eu/ceps-publications/obsolescence-european-neighbourhood-policy/ (accessed 8 June 2020).

45 Stefan Lehne, 'Europe's East–West Divide: Myth or Reality?', Carnegie Europe, 11 April 2019, https://carnegieeurope.eu/2019/04/11/europe-s-east-west-divide-myth-or-reality-pub-78847 (accessed 8 June 2020).

46 Council of the European Union, Joint Declaration of the Eastern Partnership Summit, 24 November 2017, Brussels; Association Agreement between the European Union and the European Atomic Energy Community and their Member States, of the one part, and Georgia.

Chapter 8

SECURITY, SOLIDARITY, SPECIALIZATION: UNDERSTANDING BALTIC AND POLISH SUPPORT FOR GEORGIA'S EURO-ATLANTIC INTEGRATION

Bidzina Lebanidze and Renata Skardžiūtė-Kereselidze

This chapter is an attempt to trace the evolution of relations between Georgia and Poland and the Baltic States and to explain the reasons behind Polish and Baltic support for Georgia's Euro-Atlantic integration. We argue that the foreign policy strategy of Poland and the Baltic States towards Georgia is shaped by three interrelated and equally important factors: security considerations, ideational affinity and the desire to underline their influence and independence within the European Union (EU) and the North Atlantic Treaty Organization (NATO). The combination of these three factors explains why Poland and the Baltic States over time became the staunchest supporters of Georgia's Euro-Atlantic integration, as well as of its attempts to escape Russia's sphere of influence.

We devote a large part of our analysis to security considerations which in the case of the Baltic States are the most significant factors. Security interests and common threat perceptions are acknowledged to be one of the driving factors behind small (or medium) states' foreign policy in the academic literature as well as in studies on alliance formation.[1] Partly based on the logic of Stephen Walt's balance of threat theory,[2] we argue that the perception of Russia as a common enemy, and the need to balance it, motivates Poland and the Baltic States to look for allies and partners in the surrounding regions. According to Walt, weaker states tend to balance threatening powers by allying with the other states who share similar threat perceptions.[3] In this context, Georgia and the other pro-Western Eastern Partnership (EaP) countries[4] share the same expectations, the same foreign policy objectives and the same threat perceptions. They consider themselves to be natural allies. To support this argument, we will analyse how threat perceptions and alliance policies are constructed in the security and foreign policy documents and other primary sources of Poland and the Baltic States as well as of Georgia. Next to security considerations, Poland and the Baltic States' desire for a close partnership with Georgia is stimulated by their desire to improve their standing and relative strength in the EU and NATO. They wish to position themselves as key actors in the EaP region.[5] This is especially true for Poland, whose interests in the South Caucasus has always been shaped by the search for a political niche within the Western community. Therefore, as argued in the introductory chapter by Tracey German and Kornely Kakachia, status-seeking behaviour plays a significant role in shaping the foreign policy of small and medium states and this is also true for ties between Poland, the Baltic States and Georgia.[6] Finally, ideological affinities feature significantly in the security discourse of Poland and the Baltic States. European and liberal democratic values, which they share with Georgia, score highly in the foreign and security policy documents of both Poland and the Baltic States, which aim at widening the democratic space in Eastern Europe by including as many countries as possible. Georgia's positive embrace of Polish and Baltic support was dictated by the same factors: a perception of Russia as the principal source of threat, ideational affinity with Poland and especially with the Baltic States, and a desire to emulate their reform path to reach an economic and political transformation supported by other EU states.

Our research draws on qualitative content analysis of primary sources: the official documents of Poland, the Baltic States and Georgia such as foreign policy and national security strategies as well as speeches, interviews and statements by high-ranking governmental officials. We also use secondary sources in the form of academic articles, analytic and policy papers as well as materials from news agencies and newspapers. We review the evolution of relations between Georgia and Poland and the Baltic States, look at the factors that explain their close cooperation, and conclude with a discussion of the limitations and possible implications that can be drawn from our research.

The support of Poland and the Baltic States for Georgia

Polish and Baltic solidarity towards Georgia is based on deep historical roots. In 1918–21 when Georgia briefly gained independence from the Russian Empire, Poland and Georgia established close political and diplomatic ties and discussed the possibility of a military alliance.[7] Later, when Georgia was again annexed by Soviet Russia, Poland started to train Georgian military personnel at Polish military schools.[8] Among Georgian newcomers to Poland was Dmitri Shalikashvili – father of John Malkhaz Shalikashvili who later served as a US Army general and chairman of the Joint Chiefs of Staff.[9] Next to aspects of solidarity based on shared negative experience with Russia, Polish historical support for the Georgian military was also dictated by security considerations of containing the Soviet threat:

> The Poles hoped that in the case of military conflict with the Soviet Union, a strong allied Georgian army could be quickly formed at their side, with experienced commanders from lieutenant to general capable of leading it into combat.[10]

Security considerations are also key to explaining early attempts by Georgia's first republic (1918–21) to establish close relations and military alliances with as many European countries as possible. As Stephen Jones argues in the introductory chapter, Georgia was keen to attract 'Western protection and investment in the young state'.[11] Similarly, historical ties between the Baltic countries and Georgia were based on mutual solidarity and threat perceptions towards the Russian/ Soviet Empire. Baltic support for Georgia was particularly important during the late Soviet period when the Baltic National Fronts and other dissident groups supported Georgian dissidents and Georgia's battle for independence.[12] In particular, Baltic National Fronts acted as role models for Georgian dissidents to organize their own structures and activities aimed at Georgia's independence.[13]

Relations between Poland, the Baltic States and Georgia acquired a new dimension after the break-up of the Soviet Empire and independence of post-Socialist countries. Poland and the Baltic States, which succeeded in escaping Russia's sphere of influence and becoming part of the Western world, increased their support for Georgia and became staunch supporters of Georgia's membership of NATO and the EU.[14] For Poland and the Baltic States, European integration was associated with the idea of 'enlarging the area of stability in Europe and its surroundings' along with the enhancement of European security.[15] Their support for Georgia's Euro-Atlantic integration during the decisive 2008 NATO Summit in Bucharest culminated in both Poland and the Baltic States advocating strongly for the accession of both Georgia and Ukraine.[16] But despite the backing of the United States, they failed to persuade the Western European NATO members to grant the two post-Soviet states a Membership Action Plan (MAP) – the first stage of NATO membership. After this apparent failure of NATO's open-door policy at the Bucharest summit, which was followed by war between Russia and Georgia in August 2008, the Polish and Baltic approach towards Georgia and the post-Soviet area became more pragmatic. They did not abandon their support for Georgia's integration into Euro-Atlantic structures but accommodated the more cautious positions of the Western European states and switched to an incremental, step-by-step strategy towards inclusion of their eastern and southeastern neighbours into North Atlantic security structures.

In 2009, a year after the Bucharest NATO summit and the subsequent Russo-Georgian war, Poland, together with Sweden, initiated the Eastern Partnership (EaP) initiative, which was launched as an eastern dimension of the European Neighbourhood Policy (ENP). Since then, the EaP has served as the main framework for EU relations with former Soviet states. Poland had more ambitious ideas in mind regarding the EU's relations with its new Eastern neighbours; however, as resistance to enlargement in the EU and NATO strengthened, Warsaw was forced to make adjustments. It realized that offering the prospect of rapid membership to the post-Soviet countries and deviating from the overarching framework of the ENP would reduce the chances of EU-wide support.[17] Swedish involvement had a positive impact; Swedish advice led Poland to reduce its ambitious proposals, which enhanced the chances of their acceptance by EU institutions and sceptical Member States. According to one source from the European Commission (EC), the Swedes 'translated the EaP into the language of the EU'.[18] Yet ironically, the 2008 Russo-Georgian War was the catalyst that turned the Polish–Swedish initiative into the EaP.[19]

Unlike the Western European EU Member States, Poland and the Baltic countries saw the EaP as a first stage in Georgia's potential EU membership.[20] Yet both Poland and the Baltic States were aware of the enlargement fatigue that existed in Western Europe and struck a more moderate tone by rooting for modernization and further improvement of the cooperation frameworks with Georgia instead of a full membership campaign.[21] Poland and the Baltic States have been attempting for some considerable time to include a 'European perspective'[22] on Georgia and other EaP states in EU documents, especially in the communiqués of EaP summits. They achieved acknowledgement by the EU of 'the European aspirations and European choice' of Georgia, Moldova and Ukraine – the three EaP countries that signed the Association Agreements.[23] But Poland and the Baltic States were unable to successfully challenge enlargement fatigue within NATO. They had to switch to a pragmatic step-by-step approach towards Georgia's NATO integration – de facto integrating it into NATO structures without formal membership.[24] Poland and the Baltic States have shown consistent support for Georgia's Euro-Atlantic aspirations, especially since 2008. They have identified themselves as a significant lobby group within the EU and NATO for Georgia and the other EaP countries. What other reasons are behind their support? We argue that both pragmatic considerations and ideational affinities contribute to strong bonds between Georgia and Poland, and the Baltic States.

A common enemy makes for close friends

Common threat perception and a similar understanding of the geopolitical environment explains a big part of the close relations between Georgia and Poland and the Baltic States. The literature on alliance formation among small (and medium) states[25] and their foreign policy behaviour provides theoretical insights, and can help us understand why Poland and the Baltic States are so keen on having Georgia, together with Ukraine, as full members of NATO and the EU. Stephen Walt in his balance of threat theory, argues that states try to balance the threatening power, which is geographically close, has offensive capabilities and aggressive intentions (as perceived by the balancing states).[26] The chances of balancing behaviour increase if the threatening state appears to be non-appeaseable.[27] Russia fulfils these criteria: it is the biggest and the most threatening neighbour of Poland and the Baltic States, has offensive military capabilities deployed on their borders, and displays little intention of accommodating either Poland's or the Baltic States' security-related concerns.

Both Poland and the Baltic countries are naturally interested in having as many allies as possible. The EU, on the other hand, sees itself as a post-modern actor or a civilian power[28] which eschews the traditional understanding of international politics and defies realist logic based on balance of threat or balance of power. But realism as a way of thinking about foreign policy has not been abandoned in Eastern Europe. Overall, Poland's foreign policy documents read like texts written by realist International Relations scholars, with a pessimistic worldview and a traditional preference for high politics and hard security. Poland's 2017 Foreign Policy Strategy concludes, 'the fundamental premise of Polish foreign policy is political realism'.[29] The majority of strategic documents are written in this spirit. The 2007 National Security Strategy maintains, 'fundamental national interests do not change and are based on an overall concept of state security'.[30] The Polish understanding of world politics deviates significantly from the post-modern vocabulary of the EU. For Poland 'ensuring adequate levels of defence spending' has always been central to national security.[31] Poland defines its national interests in terms of territorial defence and hard security. The 2007 Polish National Security Strategy describes the principal national interest of Poland to be 'guaranteeing the survival of the state and its citizens'.[32] This includes 'the need to preserve state independence and sovereignty, its territorial integrity and the inviolability of its borders'.[33] The worldview of hard security in Poland's foreign policy has been shaped by the country's negative historical experience, which is closely linked to Russia. According to its 2017 Foreign Policy Strategy, the main danger the Polish government associates with Russia is explained by Russia's push for dominance in the post-Soviet area:[34]

> The failure to respond to Russia's aggressive drive for domination over ex-Soviet territories revealed the West's weakness. This ultimately led to war in Ukraine and undermined Europe's security architecture.[35]

The official Polish discourse on Russia has not always been so damning. The 2012 Foreign Policy Strategy – which was drafted by a moderate government led by Donald Tusk – did not explicitly mention Russia as an external threat. Neither did the 2007 National Security Strategy. However, in all documents, both moderate and radical, Russia is seen as an integral part of the challenge faced by the current international order dominated by the West.[36] A consistent guiding principle of Polish foreign policy has been to balance the Russian threat.

Membership of NATO and the EU was seen as one solution to Poland's vulnerable security.[37] But even after joining NATO and the EU, Poland continued to view Russia as the principal danger to its national security and became very sensitive to the close cooperation emerging between Germany and Russia, especially in the energy field. The controversial gas pipelines Nordstream and Nordstream II, which bypass Poland and other Eastern European transit countries, have long been a matter of concern in Poland. In 2005 the Polish magazine *Gazeta Wyborcza* named the first Nordstream project, launched by then-chancellor Gerhard Schröder and Russian President Vladimir Putin, the 'Schröder-Putin pact', an allusion to the agreement between Adolf Hitler and Josef Stalin dividing Poland in 1938.[38] Since then, energy cooperation between Russia and Germany has deepened, as have Polish concerns.[39] NATO membership is not seen as an adequate guarantee of protection against external threats. As one observer put it, Poland and the Baltic States belong to 'a grey area of second-class membership' which will not 'be immediately defended by NATO forces if attacked' but 'would most likely be ravaged for weeks or months before NATO forces made an appearance'.[40] Polish anxieties are strengthened by massive Russian military exercises close to Poland's borders and the augmentation of military equipment in the Russian enclave of Kaliningrad.[41]

The foreign and security policy discourse in the Baltic States reflects Poland's concerns. Like Poland, the Baltic States have a realist understanding of security largely because of the resurgent role of Russia. The Lithuanian approach is straightforward. Its 2016 National Security Strategy speaks of 'conventional military threats' which are 'no longer theoretical.'[42] The document continues, 'military and non-military measures ... against the national security of ... Lithuania may be used concurrently, seeking to affect the most vulnerable areas of the state.'[43] In the report on national threat assessment issued by the State Security Department of Lithuania in 2017, five out of six major threats to national security were directly related to Russia: Russia's aggressive foreign policies to undermine Western unity, Belarus' dependence on Russia, energy security, propaganda and fake news, and Russia's instrumentalization of national minorities in third countries.[44] Similarly, Latvia's national security concept in 2015 acknowledged that 'being a member of NATO does not solve all issues regarding national security ... and does not provide defence against several significant threats'. According to the document, Russian actions (in Ukraine) worsened 'the security within the Euro-Atlantic area' and created 'long-term effects on the national security [of Latvia]'.[45] In traditional security terms, Latvia regards its eastern borders with Russia as 'the first line of defence which comes into contact with an external threat' and does not exclude 'open aggression' towards the current state authority in Latvia.[46] Estonia's 2017 national security concept considers 'Russia's unpredictable, aggressive and provocative activity' and its interest in 'restoring its position as a great power' as the main danger to the security of both Estonia and the EU.[47] The document does not rule out 'the possibility of a military attack on Estonia' and warns against increased 'military coercion and the probability of military deployment against Estonia or another state in the Baltic Sea region'.[48] The strategic documents of all three Baltic States link Russia, explicitly or implicitly, not just to a military threat but also to a range of other types of risks including economic, demographic and ethnic threats as well as cyber security and hybrid warfare.[49]

Poland, the Baltic States and Georgia

The EaP states are seen as the best potential allies to balance the Russian threat. The enthusiastic support of Poland and the Baltic States for Georgia and other EaP countries should be understood in this context. For them, Russia's assertiveness in the Eastern neighbourhood countries is the region's major security challenge. According to the Polish Foreign Minister, Witold Waszczykowski:

> Russia's leaders still seem to be guided in their thinking about neighbouring countries by a kind of modern version of Brezhnev's doctrine, assuming their limited – tailored to Moscow's interests – sovereignty.[50]

In 2014, Ukraine symbolized the Eastern neighbourhood's most serious vulnerability. According to former Polish Prime Minister Donald Tusk, 'everyone who wants a secure Poland within a united Europe has to keep his fingers crossed for Ukraine'.[51] Sławomir Sierakowski, a Polish sociologist, summarized the importance of Ukraine for Poland's security in the following way:

> If Ukraine survives in its current shape … and enters a path similar to that followed by Poland, the human and economic potential of both countries, strengthened by ad hoc alliances within the European Union, will allow the realization of Poland's historical dream to balance Russia's role in the region and ensure a significant position for Eastern Europe within the West.[52]

The interest of the Baltic States in the Eastern Partnership is driven by a desire to have more like-minded countries focused on countering Russia's influence. In 2014, the Latvian MFA designated 'support for Ukraine and other Eastern Partnership countries' as one of the key lines of activities 'to ensure stability and security in the Euro-Atlantic space'.[53] Similarly, in 2015, the annual report of the Latvian MFA identified 'Russia's aggression in Ukraine' as 'a genuine threat to both European security and Latvia's national security'.[54] The 2016 National Security Strategy of Lithuania describes the 'aggressive actions of the Russian Federation violating the security architecture based on universal rules and principles of international law and peaceful co-existence' as 'the main threat for security'.[55]

Due to its size and location, Georgia is arguably a less important country to Poland and the Baltic States than Ukraine,[56] but Polish and Baltic support for Georgia should be understood in a similar spirit. These countries, on the EU's northwestern borders with Russia, view Georgia's close integration into the Euro-Atlantic structures and its membership in these organizations as an additional means to counterbalance Russian dominance, as well as to strengthen the Eastern European position within these organizations. According to the Polish Foreign Policy Strategy 2017–21, Poland's security is negatively affected by 'the failure [of the West] to adequately respond to Russia's revisionist policy, dating back at least to 2007–2008'.[57] This was a deliberate reference, as 2008 refers to the Russo-Georgian War. Poland and the Baltic States have a systemic, holistic view of Russia's geopolitical challenge and Georgia is an integral part of this geopolitical understanding. The conflict in Ukraine, which is seen in Warsaw as the main geopolitical challenge and main danger to Poland's security, is considered a continuation of the 2008 Russo-Georgian War:

> The armed conflict in Ukraine was preceded by the war with Georgia and the international community's blind eye to Russia's support for the secession of South Ossetia, Abkhazia, and Transnistria.[58]

In the 2017 Foreign Policy Strategy of Poland, Georgia (along with Ukraine but interestingly not Moldova) is included in the group of Poland's 'neighbours that share the Polish view of Eastern European challenges [and] will play a prominent role in shaping Poland's security policy'.[59] In a 2017 interview, the Polish Foreign Minister, Witold Waszczykowski, underlined the importance of similar threat perceptions between the two countries, saying '[w]e must face up to similar challenges, and we have a similar perception of the threats in the region'.[60]

Poland pays much attention to cooperation in the areas of security and defence. Polish officials have often criticized the 'faulty construction of the ENP' as being 'deprived of so-called hard security elements'.[61] Poland's and the Baltic States' security-driven approach, unlike many Western European countries, is reflected by support for China's rising influence in the region. They urge cooperation with Georgia within the Belt and Road framework.[62] The Chinese presence is viewed as a balancing factor against Russian influence as well as an additional source of economic growth.[63] According to the Polish Foreign Minister, Georgia's signing of both the DCFTA with the EU and the FTA with China, make Georgia 'ideally placed to become a hub for EU and China investments'.[64] The Baltic States also see a close connection between the Russian invasion of Georgia in 2008 and Ukraine in 2014, and their own vulnerable security. In 2015, the Defence Minister of Lithuania Juozas Olekas did not exclude a repetition of a similar war scenario in his country:

> The examples of Georgia and Ukraine, which both lost a part of their territory, show us that we cannot rule out a similar kind of situation here, and that we should be ready.[65]

In a recent interview, Estonia's President Kersti Kaljulaid reiterated the position pronounced by many Baltic politicians that the West's weak reaction to the 2008 Russo-Georgian War led to the annexation of the Crimea a few years later and that a solid response was needed to deter Russia.[66] The 2008 Russo-Georgian War acted as a bellwether for the Baltic countries, leading them to reassess their approach to foreign and security policy and to significantly strengthen their military and defence policy despite the EU. The Baltic States integrated the lessons of the 2008 war as best practices into their defence and security strategies.[67] The lessons of the war played a key role in the acquisition of anti-tank weapons and ammunition by the Baltic States. As in the case of Poland, the Baltic States are not entirely convinced that NATO can deter Russia's potential aggression. According to one analyst, 'Putin does not believe NATO will defend such, in his view, unimportant countries, risking nuclear confrontation'.[68]

Our content analysis of strategic documents and other primary sources of Poland's and the Baltic States' foreign policy establishment underlines their security-driven approach towards the EaP, and helps explain their support of Georgia. Their support for Georgia is driven by a need to balance Russia, which has become an existential threat to the national security of Eastern European countries. Balancing the main source of threat has been one of the key motives behind the support of Poland and the three Baltic States for Georgia. In 2008, Georgia gave a warm reception to Polish and Baltic support for the Saakashvili administration after the war ended. Georgia's political elites have always regarded Russia as the main threat to its national sovereignty and territorial integrity. Georgia's strategic documents constantly refer to Russia, and specifically to Russia's policy in Abkhazia and South Ossetia, as a major threat to Georgia's sovereignty. Yet the tone and wording has varied depending on the expectations and motivations of various Georgian governments. The 2005 National Security Concept of Georgia, for example, coincided with the attempts of Mikheil Saakashvili's government to normalize relations with Russia and also with some initial optimistic expectations about Russia's role with regard to territorial conflicts. The document was more moderate in tone and optimistic about the potential of de-escalation and cooperation between Georgia and Russia.[69] However, the concept described the presence of the Russian military bases in Georgia as a risk to Georgia's stability and security.[70] Other elements of threat included the 'granting of Russian citizenship to residents of the breakaway regions of Georgia' as well as the lack of control of state borders between Georgia and Russia.[71] The 2012 National Security Strategy, by contrast, lost its moderate tone regarding Russia's role. The document mentioned Russia eighty-six times, mostly in a negative context.[72] The occupation of Georgian territories and terrorist acts organized by Russia from the occupied territories is considered as the number one threat to Georgia's security.[73] Russia is explicitly mentioned in at least seven out of twelve national security threat categories listed in the document (occupation of Georgian territories, the risk of renewed military aggression, violation of the rights of internally displaced persons and conflicts in the Caucasus, cyber security, environment and demography).[74]

The Foreign Policy Strategy 2019–22 released in 2019 by the 'Georgian Dream' government was criticized for taking a too accommodating approach towards Russia, although it refers to Russia's detrimental impact on Georgia's security environment and national sovereignty.[75] The new strategy sees the support of Poland and Baltic States in the security and political spheres, as well as in the process of Euro-Atlantic integration, as critical. The 2019 Strategy document emphasizes the attempt of the Baltic States to consolidate support for Georgia in the international arena as well as their assistance to Georgia's security, territorial integrity and experience with regard to NATO integration.[76] Georgian politicians have frequently hailed the support of Poland and the Baltic States for Georgia's integration into NATO as a way to contain the Russian threat.[77] Overall, Georgia's fragile security situation and the sceptical attitude of Western European countries towards Georgia's Euro-Atlantic integration leaves Georgia somewhat reliant on Polish and Baltic support.

Poland and the Baltic States: profile-boosting

The motive behind Polish and Baltic support for Georgia's Euro-Atlantic integration is to strengthen opposition to Russia's assertive foreign policy. At the same time, these states wish to strengthen their own position in Western institutions by defining their own active engagement in the EaP region. They attempt to paint Eastern Europe, including Georgia, as an area of their particular competence and concern. It is a strategy aimed at increasing 'intra-EU visibility'[78] or the creation of a 'niche policy'.[79] According to one author, finding one's own niche and increasing intra-EU visibility leads to 'greater intra-EU prestige' which may improve the overall financial and political position of a Member State.[80] This is noticeable when we look at how EaP policy is constructed in the official narratives of Poland and the Baltic States. In Polish formal documents this is called a 'brand' policy or a 'high standing' policy, which Polish Foreign Policy Strategy defines as 'shaping a positive image of Poland and bolstering its credibility in Europe, and globally'.[81] According to Poland's Foreign Policy Strategy 2017–21, achieving 'high standing' is among the top three foreign policy objectives, alongside growth and security. Poland's 'high standing' approach is driven by a desire to act as 'a responsible player in global politics', and as a 'provider of "international public goods" such as stability and the knowledge of how to conduct effective reforms'.[82]

Poland shares a similar historical legacy and the same foreign policy objectives as its Eastern European neighbours, including Georgia. This allows Poland to emphasize 'its experience of uneasy systemic transformation'[83] and to present itself as part of the avant-garde of the EU's good governance agenda in the region. Poland's leaders feel they have played a leadership role in the EU's past engagement in the region. The Polish Foreign Minister Witold Waszczykowski, designated Poland's achievements within the EaP, such as the signing of the AA and the DCFTA and the launching of visa-free regimes with the three partner countries as 'genuine successes of Polish diplomacy in the EU'.[84] Poland, as a founder of the EaP, is proud of playing 'a leading role in its implementation and promotion'.[85] According to one author, the active engagement of Poland in the EaP region contributes to a strengthening of 'its international position, especially compared with the rest of the European Union'.[86] The Baltic States, too, have been trying to leverage their own role in the EaP to improve their standing and prestige within the EU and the NATO. The EaP is presented as 'one of the main priorities and foreign policy niches' of Latvia.[87] According to one author, Latvia tried 'to establish itself within the EU as an expert on this region'.[88] Latvia also considers the EaP to be 'a strategic region' in Latvia's development assistance strategy.[89] It directs much of its policy resources, including the promotion of good governance, towards the EaP states. Estonia's developmental policy, likewise, is based on sharing its 'transition experience' with 'other countries that share a similar past with the country'.[90] Estonia considers its 'ability to provide value added through its activities' to be among the highest in the EaP countries.[91] Since 2006 Georgia, as one of the more committed and successful of the ENP/EaP partners, has been among the priority partner countries for Estonia's developmental policy.[92] Since 2016 Estonia has had a separate development cooperation country strategy for Georgia.[93]

Lithuania's development policy has followed a similar path. 'The transfer of transition experience to the EaP countries' has become a priority of the Lithuanian government.[94] According to one author, the success stories of cooperation with the EaP countries 'contributes to a more positive image of Lithuania within the international community of donors and among the recipient countries'.[95] One of the earlier manifestations of both the security-driven approach and the profile-boosting strategy was the establishment of the New Group of Friends of Georgia in 2004.[96] The three Baltic States together with Poland were the founding members of the group. Since its establishment, the main objective of the group has been to assist Georgia's Euro-Atlantic integration attempts 'by putting to good use the experience of the Group's members'.[97] The group has been providing political and diplomatic support to Georgia. It issues statements of support for Georgia's territorial integrity and criticizes Russia for its aggressive actions.[98] Like Poland, the three Baltic States have been using their active engagement in the EaP region to boost their own profiles within Western organizations in order to establish themselves as promoters of Western developmental policy.

The Polish and Baltic policy of solidarity with Georgia is based on enlightened self-interest. It is also rooted in a shared negative historical experience, a shared pessimistic worldview, and a common identification with European civilization. Poland and the Baltic States share a negative view of Russia's role in the region with Georgia. According to the Polish Foreign Policy Strategy of 2017, 'standing in solidarity with both closer and more distant neighbours is a moral imperative, which also serves the best interests of the Republic of Poland'.[99] The policy of solidarity is based on ideational affinity and a values-based understanding of foreign policy.[100] For Poland and the Baltic States, the West, as a cultural community, represents a civilizational purpose and a preferred social order. This is identical to the Georgian position. The enlargement of the EU and NATO will make these Eastern European states more secure in civilizational terms. According to the 2012 Foreign Policy Strategy of Poland, 'In civilizational terms, it is worthwhile having partners who espouse the same values on both sides of the Polish border'.[101] The normative component is expressed even more strongly in the foreign policy documents of the Baltic States. According to the new Lithuanian security concept of 2016, 'contributing to the promotion of democratic values in the Eastern neighbourhood' is one of the main goals of Lithuanian foreign policy priorities.[102] Similarly, Estonian and Latvian security and foreign policy documents underline the role of the democratic and rules-based community for ensuring international peace and stability. The normative component in the Baltic and Polish approach towards Georgia and Eastern Partnership countries parallels the signals we are getting from the new Biden presidential administration, elected in November 2020, which seems determined to bolster democratic coalitions around the world and oppose authoritarian adversaries such as Russia and China.

Georgia has warmly welcomed the Polish and Baltic engagement in Georgia's reform process. Georgia's political establishment considers both Poland and the Baltic States as able to provide Georgia with expertise and know-how in the process of economic and political transformation, and in the strategies of Euro-Atlantic integration. The 2012 National Security Concept of Georgia underlined the importance of 'sharing the experience of the Baltic States in European and Euro-Atlantic integration'.[103] The 2019 Foreign Policy Strategy reiterates the importance of sharing experience with the Baltic States with regard to EU and NATO integration along with their history of institutionalizing democratic reforms.[104] The representatives of the Georgian government often refer to the Baltic States and Poland as role models for Georgia. In 2015, Georgian President

Giorgi Margvelashvili called Lithuania 'an important and impressive role model to be followed'.[105] The newly elected President Salome Zurabishvili hailed Poland as a successful model for employment, post-socialist economic transformation and regional development.[106] The active exchange of expertise and know-how between Poland, the Baltic States and Georgia, which began under Georgian President Eduard Shevardnadze, reached its peak during Mikheil Saakashvili's administration (2003–13). A clear example of cooperation and experience sharing was the appointment of the president of the National Bank of Poland Leszek Balcerowicz as a special adviser on economic issues to then-President of Georgia Eduard Shevardnadze in 2000. Similarly, in 2006 former Prime Minister of Estonia Mart Laar was invited as an aide for reform issues by Mikheil Saakashvili's government.[107] The status-seeking policies of the Baltic States and Poland in Georgia is a two-way street. On the supply side, Poland and the Baltic States boost their profile and find their niche within the EU. On the demand side, by embracing its Polish and Baltic engagement, Georgia benefits from their know-how and expertise.

Conclusion

This chapter explored the reasons behind the exceptional support of Poland and the three Baltic States for Georgia's attempt to integrate with NATO and the EU and to counter Russian influence. We identified three main interrelated factors: security considerations, credibility boosting and ideational affinity. Based on the analysis of official documents of Poland and the three Baltic States we identified a common threat perception and security-driven discourse towards the EaP countries and Russia in particular, but also more generally in their foreign and security policy. Poland and Lithuania have always nurtured a sceptical approach towards Russia. Estonia and Latvia initially used to have a more reserved and accommodating policy towards Russia, but their positions hardened once Russian revanchism took concrete form during the 2008 Russo-Georgian War and the 2014 annexation of Crimea and invasion of eastern Ukraine. Supporting Georgia and other EaP states became an important instrument for strengthening their own security and containing Russia's expansionism – or in Walt's terms – balancing the source of the threat.[108] Close association with European security structures, or EaP states' membership of the EU and NATO was seen as significantly improving the security of Baltic States and Poland vis-à-vis Russia. The accession of Georgia, along with Ukraine and Moldova, to the EU and NATO would alter the in-group dynamics within both organizations, strengthening the Polish and Baltic positions and boosting their profile within the EU.

A powerful motivation behind Baltic and Polish support to Georgia has been the strengthening of their own credibility inside the EU and the NATO. The analysis of primary sources has shown that both Poland and the Baltic States have made the EaP region the centrepiece of their respective developmental policies. Poland and especially the Baltic States have a strong comparative advantage in the

EaP region based on the experience of transition they went through when they joined the EU and NATO. As a result, they have leveraged their unique expertise in the EaP countries in order to become a more central part of the Western donor community, and to prove their usefulness as providers of public goods on an international scale.

Finally, we can also speak of ideational reasons behind the Polish and Baltic States' approach towards Georgia. Ideational affinities are closely related to both security considerations and prestige politics. To some extent they are even parts of their security discourses as both Poland and the Baltic States consider the promotion of democracy and rule of law as having a positive impact on their security environment. Stephan Walt's 'balance of threat' is helpful in understanding the Polish and the Baltic States' strategic behaviour towards Georgia. The foreign policies of the Baltic States, Poland and Georgia have been explored separately by many authors with different theoretical frameworks.[109] The multidimensionality and complexity of relations between Georgia, Poland and the Baltic States offers a rich laboratory to anyone who wants to test or generate theoretical models on what motivates relations between small (and medium) states.

Notes

1   For the foreign policy behaviour of small states, see Kenneth N. Waltz, *Theory of International Politics* (Long Grove, IL: Waveland Press, 2010); Robert Jervis, 'Cooperation under the Security Dilemma', *World Politics*, 30: 2 (1978), pp. 172–73; Robert O. Keohane, 'Lilliputians' Dilemmas: Small States in International Politics', *International Organisation*, 23:2 (1969), pp. 291–310; Robert L. Rothstein (1968) *Alliances and Small Powers* (New York: Columbia University Press, 1968); David Vital, *The Inequality of States* (Oxford: Oxford University Press, 1968).

2   Stephen M. Walt, 'Testing Theories of Alliance Formation: The Case of Southwest Asia', *International Organization*, 42:2 (1988), pp. 275–316; Stephen M. Walt, *The Origins of Alliances* (Ithaca, NY: Cornell University Press, 1990); Stephen M. Walt, 'Why Alliances Endure or Collapse', *Survival*, 39: 1 (1997), pp. 156–179; Stephen M. Walt, 'Alliances in a Unipolar World', *World Politics*, 61: 1 (2009), pp. 86–120.

3   Walt (1988).

4   The EaP was launched in 2009. It has been the EU's instrument to establish close political, economic partnerships with its Eastern neighbourhood countries.

5   In fact, this argument, in many variations is reiterated by many authors. See, for instance: Mariam Apriashvili, 'Baltic Support for Georgia: Solidarity, Niche, and Security Policies', *Research Paper Series No. 4* (Tbilisi: Georgian Institute of Politics, 2017); Vahur Made, Shining in Brussels? The Eastern Partnership in Estonia's Foreign Policy, *Perspectives*, 19: 2 (2011), pp. 67–79.

6   Kakachia Kornely and Tracey German, 'Georgia: Achieving Security as a Small State', in *Georgia's Foreign Policy in the 21st Century: Challenges for a Small State*, pp. 28–49.

7   Andriy Rukkas, 'Georgian Servicemen in the Polish Armed Forces (1922–39)', *The Journal of Slavic Military Studies*, 14: 3 (2001), pp. 93–106.

8   Rukkas, p. 93.

9   Rukkas, p. 94.

10   Rukkas, p. 95.
11   Stephen Jones, 'Introduction', in *Georgia's Foreign Policy in the 21st Century: Challenges for a Small State*, pp. 13–28.
12   Nils R. Muiznieks, 'The Influence of the Baltic Popular Movements on the Process of Soviet Disintegration', *Europe-Asia Studies* 47: 1 (1995), pp. 3–25.
13   Muiznieks (1995).
14   Poland Joined NATO in 1999 and the EU in 2004. The Baltic States joined both the NATO and the EU in 2004.
15   Ministry of Foreign Affairs of the Republic of Poland, 'Polish Foreign Policy Priorities 2012–2016', March 2012, www.msz.gov.pl/resource/d31571cf-d24f-4479-af09-c9a46cc85cf6:JCR (accessed 17 March 2018).
16   For instance, Ronald Asmus in his book on Russia–Georgia War offers a detailed analysis of the behind-the-scenes negotiations at the Bucharest summit. According to him, Poland and the Baltic States retained their staunch position until the end of the summit. For more information, see Ronald Asmus, *A Little War that Changed the World: Georgia, Russia, and the Future of the West* (New York: Palgrave Macmillan, 2010).
17   Nathaniel Copsey and Karolina Pomorska, 'The Influence of Newer Member States in the European Union: The Case of Poland and the Eastern Partnership', *Europe-Asia Studies*, 66: 3 (2014), pp. 421–43.
18   Copsey and Pomorska, p. 433.
19   Copsey and Pomorska, p. 436.
20   Ministry of Foreign Affairs of the Republic of Poland, 'Foreign Minister on Providing Eastern Partners with Prospects for EU Membership', 20 October 2017, www.msz.gov.pl/en/foreign_policy/eastern_partnership/foreign_minister_on_providing_eastern_partners_with_prospects_for_eu_membership_eap (accessed 18 March 2018).
21   Ministry of Foreign Affairs Republic of the Republic Poland (2017). Change is visible in the rhetoric of Polish and Baltic politicians. Whereas they still support Georgia's full membership into the EU and NATO they put greater emphasis on continuing the reform process as an end itself, which replicates the position long held by enlargement-sceptic Western EU Member States. They also underline the significance of economic and sectoral cooperation. For some of the examples of the changing rhetoric see: *Civil Georgia*, 'Georgian, Lithuanian FMs Discuss EU, NATO Integration', *Civil Georgia*, 23 October 2018, https://civil.ge/archives/260479 (accessed 26 January 2019); Thea Morrison, 'Estonia's Kaljulaid: Georgia is Eastern Partnership Torchbearer', *Georgia Today*, 14 September 2018, http://georgiatoday.ge/news/12284/Estonia%E2%80%99s-Kaljulaid%3A-Georgia-Is-Eastern-Partnership-Torchbearer (accessed 26 January 2019); MFA Estonia, 'Estonia Continues to Support Georgia on its Course towards Europe and NATO', *MFA Estonia*, 9 November 2016, https://vm.ee/en/news/estonia-continues-support-georgia-its-course-towards-europe-and-nato (accessed 26 January 2019); MFA Estonia, 'The Prime Minister: Estonia Supports Georgia on their Way to the European Union', MFA Estonia, 19 December 2018, www.valitsus.ee/en/news/prime-minister-estonia-supports-georgia-their-way-european-union (accessed 26 January 2019); Polish Press Agency, 'Poland Supports Georgia's Aspirations to join EU and NATO – FM', Polish Press Agency, 24 October 2018, www.pap.pl/en/news/news%2C346993%2Cpoland-supports-georgias-aspirations-join-eu-and-nato-fm.html (accessed 26 January 2019); *The Baltic Times*, 'Lithuania and Georgia Would Like to Strengthen Economic Ties, PMs Say', *The Baltic*

Times, 21 January 2019, www.baltictimes.com/lithuania_and_georgia_would_like_
to_strengthen_economic_ties__pms_say/ (accessed 26 January 2019).

22   For instance, the preamble of the AA refers to Georgia as an 'Eastern European
country' to avoid any reference to Article 49 of the Treaty Establishing the European
Union (TEU). Article 49 states that 'any European State which respects the principles
set out in Article 6(1) may apply to become a member of the Union'. Source: Vano
Chkhikvadze, 'The Eastern Partnership: What's next for Georgia?' *Heinrich-Böll-
Stiftung*, 12 September 2019, https://ge.boell.org/en/2019/09/12/eastern-partnership-
whats-next-georgia (accessed 20 February 2020).

23   Council of the European Union, 'Joint Declaration of the Eastern Partnership
Summit', 24 November 2017, www.consilium.europa.eu/media/31758/final-
statement-st14821en17.pdf (accessed 19 March 2018), p. 4.

24   Bidzina Lebanidze, 'NATO and Georgia: Waiting the Winter Out', *ISPI*, 7 August
2018, www.ispionline.it/en/pubblicazione/nato-and-georgia-waiting-winter-
out-21098+ (accessed 24 January 2019).

25   We include the term 'medium state' since characterizing Poland as a small state
may be problematic for many reasons. Nevertheless, in contrast to Russia, Poland
may still be a relatively weak or easily vulnerable state – at least in terms of military
capabilities, energy dependency and security-related vulnerability.

26   Walt (1988), pp. 280–1.

27   Walt (1988), p. 314.

28   Karen Smith, 'Beyond the Civilian Power EU Debate', *Politique européenne*, 3 (2005),
pp. 63–82.

29   Ministry of Foreign Affairs of the Republic of Poland, 'Foreign Minister on Providing
Eastern Partners with Prospects for EU Membership', 20 October 2017, www.msz.
gov.pl/en/foreign_policy/eastern_partnership/foreign_minister_on_providing_
eastern_partners_with_prospects_for_eu_membership_eap (accessed 18 March
2018), p. 20.

30   NSB Poland, 'National Security Strategy of the Republic of Poland', *NSB Poland*,
2007, www.files.ethz.ch/isn/156796/Poland-2007-eng.pdf (accessed 17 March 2018),
p. 4.

31   Ministry of Foreign Affairs of the Republic of Poland, 'Polish Foreign Policy
Priorities 2012–2016', 2012, www.msz.gov.pl/resource/d31571cf-d24f-4479-af09-
c9a46cc85cf6:JCR (accessed 17 March 2018).

32   NSB Poland (2007), p. 4.

33   Ibid.

34   Ministry of Foreign Affairs of the Republic of Poland, 'Foreign Minister on
Providing Eastern Partners with Prospects for EU Membership', 20 October 2017,
www.msz.gov.pl/en/foreign_policy/eastern_partnership/foreign_minister_on_
providing_eastern_partners_with_prospects_for_eu_membership_eap (accessed 18
March 2018), p. 2.

35   Ministry of Foreign Affairs of the Republic of Poland, 'Polish Foreign Policy Strategy
2017–2021', MFA Poland, 2017, http://www.msz.gov.pl/resource/0c98c3b2-9c5d-
4c42-8761-f7827134ee76:JCR (accessed 17 March 2018), p. 2.

36   Ministry of Foreign Affairs of the Republic of Poland (2012), p. 3; NSB Poland (2007),
p. 6.

37   NSB Poland (2007), p. 4.

38   Stephan Raabe, 'The Dispute over the Baltic Gas Pipeline: A Threat or a Necessary
Supply Project?', *Konrad-Adenauer-Stiftung*, International Reports, no. 2, 6 April 2009,

www.kas.de/wf/doc/kas_16137-544-2-30.pdf?090406132317 (accessed 18 March 2018), p. 1.

39 Jo Harper, 'Nordstream II gas Pipeline in Deep Water', *Deutsche Welle,* 14 November 2017, www.dw.com/en/nordstream-ii-gas-pipeline-in-deep-water/a-41372833 (accessed 18 March 2018).

40 Slawomir Sierakowski, 'NATO's Second-Class Members', *New York Times*, 22 August 2014, www.nytimes.com/2014/08/23/opinion/slawomir-sierakowski-natos-second-class-members.html?rref=collection%2Fcolumn%2FSlawomir%20Sierakowski (accessed 18 March 2018).

41 Jerry Hendrix, 'In a Chess Game with Putin, the Polish City of Gdansk is Our Queen', *The National Review*, 20 December 2017, www.nationalreview.com/2017/12/gdansk-poland-defending-baltic-putin-russia/ (accessed 18 March 2018).

42 Ministry of National Defence of the Republic of Lithuania, 'National Security Strategy of the Republic of Lithuania', 2017, https://kam.lt/download/57457/2017-nacsaugstrategijaen.pdf (accessed 14 June 2018), p. 5.

43 Ministry of National Defence of the Republic of Lithuania (2016), p. 5.

44 BNN, 'Lithuanian intelligence Singles out Six Major Threats to National Security', *BNN*, 7 April 2017, http://bnn-news.com/lithuanian-intelligence-singles-out-six-major-threats-to-national-security-163571 (accessed 18 June 2018).

45 Ministry of Defence of Latvia, 'The National Security Concept', 2015, www.mod.gov.lv/sites/mod/files/document/NDK_ENG_final.pdf (accessed 14 June 2018): 3

46 Ministry of Defence of Latvia (2015), p. 6.

47 Parliament of Estonia, 'National Security Concept', 2017, https://riigikantselei.ee/sites/default/files/content-editors/Failid/national_security_concept_2017.pdf (accessed 25 June 2018), p. 4

48 Parliament of Estonia (2017), p. 4.

49 BNN (2017); Ministry of Defence of Latvia (2015); Parliament of Estonia (2017).

50 Ministry of Foreign Affairs of Poland, 'Polish FM: European Integration of Eastern Partnership Countries is a Success of Polish Diplomacy', 2017, www.msz.gov.pl/en/foreign_policy/eastern_partnership/polish_fm__european_integration_of_eastern_partnership_countries_is_a_success_of_polish_diplomacy__interview_eap;jsessionid=9B81479CFB3BFB529F9EB5296183E581.cmsap1p (accessed 17 March 2018).

51 Slawomir Sierakowski, 'Why Poland Loves Ukraine … For Now', *New York Times*, 28 March 2014, www.nytimes.com/2014/03/29/opinion/sierakowski-why-poland-loves-ukraine-for-now.html (accessed 18 March 2018).

52 Sierakowski (2014).

53 Ministry of Foreign Affairs of Latvia, 'Annual Report by the Minister of Foreign Affairs on Accomplishments and Activities Planned with Respect to National Foreign Policy and the European Union, 2014–2015', 2014, www.mfa.gov.lv/images/zinojums_FINAL_FINAL_ENG.pdf (accessed 17 June 2018).

54 Ministry of Foreign Affairs of Latvia (2014), p. 3.

55 Ministry of Defence of Lithuania, 'National Security Strategy of the Republic of Lithuania', 2016, https://kam.lt/download/57457/2017-nacsaugstrategijaen.pdf (accessed 14 June 2018), p. 4.

56 Georgia is many times smaller in terms of population, territory, GDP, market size and industrial output and is geographically more distant from the EU.

57 Ministry of Foreign Affairs of the Republic of Poland, 'Polish Foreign Policy Strategy 2017–2021', MFA Poland, 2017, http://www.msz.gov.pl/resource/0c98c3b2-9c5d-4c42-8761-f7827134ee76:JCR (accessed 17 March 2018), p. 2.

58 Ministry of Foreign Affairs of the Republic of Poland (2017), p. 6.

59 Ministry of Foreign Affairs of the Republic of Poland (2017), p. 10.

60 Ministry of Foreign Affairs of Poland, 'Polish FM: European Integration of Eastern Partnership Countries is a Success of Polish Diplomacy', 2017, www.msz.gov.pl/en/ foreign_policy/eastern_partnership/polish_fm__european_integration_of_eastern_ partnership_countries_is_a_success_of_polish_diplomacy__interview_eap;jsessionid =9B81479CFB3BFB529F9EB5296183E581.cmsap1p (accessed 17 March 2018).

61 Ministry of Foreign Affairs of Poland, 'Polish FM: European Integration of Eastern Partnership Countries is a Success of Polish Diplomacy', 2017, www.msz.gov.pl/en/ foreign_policy/eastern_partnership/polish_fm__european_integration_of_eastern_ partnership_countries_is_a_success_of_polish_diplomacy__interview_eap;jsessionid =9B81479CFB3BFB529F9EB5296183E581.cmsap1p (accessed 17 March 2018).

62 Ministry of Foreign Affairs of Poland, 'Foreign Ministers of Poland and Sweden Discuss Eastern Partnership in Georgia', 2017, www.msz.gov.pl/en/foreign_policy/ eastern_partnership/foreign_ministers_of_poland_and_sweden_discuss_eastern_ partnership_in_georgia_eap;jsessionid=CB46ECCE402831FD320B2A8532936BF9. cmsap2p (accessed 17 March 2018).

63 Piotr Buras and Adam Balcer, 'An Unpredictable Russia: The Impact on Poland', *European Council on Foreign Relations,* 15 July 2016, www.ecfr.eu/article/ commentary_an_unpredictable_russia_the_impact_on_poland (accessed 18 March 2018).

64 Ministry of Foreign Affairs of Poland, 'Foreign Ministers of Poland and Sweden Discuss Eastern Partnership in Georgia', 2017, www.msz.gov.pl/en/foreign_policy/ eastern_partnership/foreign_ministers_of_poland_and_sweden_discuss_eastern_ partnership_in_georgia_eap;jsessionid=CB46ECCE402831FD320B2A8532936BF9. cmsap2p (accessed 17 March 2018). Certainly for Poland itself increasing the Chinese presence in Europe may present a chance of becoming an economic and trade hub. In this context, a route from China bypassing Russia (i.e. via South Caucasus) will be more favoured.

65 Andrius Sytas, 'Worried about Russia? Lithuania says "Keep Calm and Read the War Manual', Reuters, 15 January 2015, www.reuters.com/article/us-lithuania-manual- idUSKBN0KO0XZ20150115 (accessed 17 March 2018).

66 EurActiv, 'Estonia Calls for Deployment of US Troops, Patriot Missiles', 5 April 2018, www.euractiv.com/section/defence-and-security/news/estonia-calls-for-deployment- of-us-troops-patriot-missiles/ (accessed 25 June 2018).

67 Robert Beckhusen, 'To Beat Russian Tanks, the Baltic States Are Studying the Georgia War: 2008 Conflict with Russia Proves that Anti-tank Missiles Rule', 29 October 2014, www.realcleardefense.com/articles/2014/10/29/to_beat_russian_tanks_the_baltic_ states_are_studying_the_georgia_war_107518.html (accessed 25 June 2018).

68 Ola Cichowlas, 'Lithuania Prepares for a Feared Russian Invasion', *Reuters,* 16 March 2015, http://blogs.reuters.com/great-debate/2015/03/15/lithuania-prepares-for-a- feared-russian-invasion/ (accessed 25 June 2018).

69 Parliament of Georgia, 'National Security Concept of Georgia', 2005, www.parliament. ge/files/292_880_927746_concept_en.pdf (accessed 20 February 2020).

70 Parliament of Georgia (2005), pp. 3–4.

71 Parliament of Georgia (2005), p. 3.

72 Ministry of Foreign Affairs of Georgia, 'National Security Concept of Georgia', 2012, www.mfa.gov.ge/MainNav/ForeignPolicy/NationalSecurityConcept.aspx?lang=en-US (accessed 10 April 2017).

73   Ministry of Foreign Affairs of Georgia (2012), p. 7.

74   Ministry of Foreign Affairs of Georgia (2012), pp. 7–10.

75   Ministry of Foreign Affairs of Georgia, 'The Foreign Policy Strategy 2019–2022', 2019, http://mfa.gov.ge/MainNav/ForeignPolicy/ForeignPolicyStrategy.aspx?lang=en-US (accessed 20 February 2020).

76   Ministry of Foreign Affairs of Georgia (2019), p. 13.

77   President of Georgia, 'President Zourabichvili: More Europe, More NATO, and More Poland in Georgia!', 2019, www.president.gov.ge/eng/pressamsakhuri/siakhleebi/salome-zurabishvili-meti-evropa,-meti-nato-da-meti.aspx (accessed 20 February 2020).

78   Vahur Made, 'Shining in Brussels? The Eastern Partnership in Estonia's Foreign Policy', *Perspectives*, 19:2 (2011), pp. 67–79.

79   Mariam Apriashvili, 'Baltic Support for Georgia: Solidarity, Niche, and Security Policies', Research Paper no. 4 (2017), Tbilisi: Georgian Institute of Politics.

80   Made (2011), p. 68.

81   Ministry of Foreign Affairs of the Republic of Poland, 'Polish Foreign Policy Strategy 2017–2021', MFA Poland, 2017. http://www.msz.gov.pl/resoue/0c98c3b2-9c5d-4c42-8761-f7827134ee76:JCR (accessed 17 March 2018), p. 5.

82   Ministry of Foreign Affairs of the Republic of Poland (2017), p. 20.

83   Ministry of Foreign Affairs of the Republic of Poland (2017), p. 17.

84   Ministry of Foreign Affairs of the Republic of Poland (2017), p. 18.

85   Ibid.

86   Slawomir Sierakowski, 'Why Poland Loves Ukraine … For Now', *New York Times*, 28 March 2014, www.nytimes.com/2014/03/29/opinion/sierakowski-why-poland-loves-ukraine-for-now.html (accessed 18 March 2018).

87   Diana Potjomkina, 'Peace, Trade, and European Resources: Latvia and the Eastern Partners in 2015–2016', in *Latvian Foreign and Security Policy. Yearbook*, ed. A. Sprūds and I. Bruģe (Zinātne, 2016), pp. 43–59.

88   J. Poikāns, 'The Eastern Partnership – Latvia's Contribution', in A. Sprūds and I. Bruģe ed. ibid., p. 37.

89   MFA Latvia, 'Annual Report by the Minister of Foreign Affairs on Accomplishments and Activities Planned with Respect to National Foreign Policy and the European Union, 2014–2015', 2014, www.mfa.gov.lv/images/zinojums_FINAL_FINAL_ENG.pdf (accessed 17 June 2018), p. 22.

90   Evelin Andrespok, 'Estonian e-Tiger Leaping to Georgia: Added Value of Estonian Development Cooperation', 2014, https://helda.helsinki.fi/bitstream/handle/10138/135426/Masters%20thesis_eTiger%20leaping%20to%20Georgia_Evelin%20Andrespok.pdf (accessed 17 June 2018), p. 1.

91   MFA Estonia, 'National Security Strategy of Estonia', 2010, http://vm.ee/sites/default/files/content-editors/JPA_2010_ENG.pdf (accessed 14 June 2018), p. 18.

92   MFA Estonia, 'Estonian Development Cooperation Country Strategy Paper Georgia 2016–2018', 2015, http://vm.ee/sites/default/files/content-editors/development-cooperation/gruusia_maastrateegia_2016_2018_eng.pdf (accessed 17 June 2018).

93   MFA Estonia, 'Estonian Development Cooperation Country Strategy Paper Georgia 2016–2018', 2015, http://vm.ee/sites/default/files/content-editors/development-cooperation/gruusia_maastrateegia_2016_2018_eng.pdf (accessed 17 June 2018).

94   Anastasija Panasevič, 'Lithuanian Development Cooperation: 10 Years for Finding a Place in the Donors' Community', *Latvia's Interests in the European Union*, 3 (2014), pp. 32–45.

95 Panasevič (2014), p. 44.

96 The functionality of the initial 'Group of Friends of Georgia' which was founded by
    France in 1993 and included the United States, Germany and Britain, was essentially
    compromised after 2004 when it was renamed the 'UN Secretary-General's Group
    of Friends of Georgia' and was joined by Russia which as a veto actor paralysed
    the activities of the group. For more information see: Vladimir Socor (2005), 'New
    Group of Georgia's Friends Founded', in *Eurasia Daily Monitor* 2 (26), checked on
    25 June 2018; Teresa Whitfield, (2007)', Friends Indeed? The United Nations, Groups
    of Friends, and the Resolution of Conflict' US Institute of Peace Press.

97 MFA Romania, 'Minister Teodor Baconschi co-chaired New Group of Friends of
    Georgia meeting', 2011, www.mae.ro/en/node/8330 (accessed 25 June 2018).

98 *Civil Georgia*, 'Friends of Georgia Group Stresses Support in the Face of Russian
    Occupation', 9 December 2017, https://old.civil.ge/eng/article.php?id=30716
    (accessed 25 June 2018).

99 Ministry of Foreign Affairs of Poland, 'Polish Foreign Policy Strategy 2017–2021',
    2017, www.msz.gov.pl/resource/0c98c3b2-9c5d-4c42-8761-f7827134ee76:JCR
    (accessed 17 March 2018), p. 5

100 On the role of ideas in foreign policy see E. Adler, 'Seizing the Middle Ground:
    Constructivism in World Politics', *European Journal of International Relations*
    3:3 (1997), pp. 319–63; J. Goldstein and R. Keohane, *Ideas and Foreign Policy:
    Beliefs, Institutions, and Political Change* (New York: Cornell University Press,
    1993); Ted Hopf, 'The Promise of Constructivism in International Relations
    Theory', *International Security* 23:1 (1998), pp. 171–200; Frank Schimmelfennig,
    'Nato Enlargement: A Constructivist Explanation', *Security Studies* 8: 2–3 (1998),
    pp. 198–234; Alexander Wendt, 'Anarchy is What States Make of it: The Social
    Construction of Power Politics', *International Organization*, 46:2 (1992), pp.
    391–425; Alexander Wendt, *Social Theory of International Relations* (Cambridge:
    Cambridge University Press, 1999).

101 Ministry of Foreign Affairs of Poland, 'Polish Foreign Policy Priorities 2012–2016',
    2012, www.msz.gov.pl/resource/d31571cf-d24f-4479-af09-c9a46cc85cf6:JCR
    (accessed 17 March 2018), p. 17.

102 Ministry of Defence of Lithuania, 'National Security Strategy of the Republic of
    Lithuania', 2016, https://kam.lt/download/57457/2017-nacsaugstrategijaen.pdf
    (accessed 14 June 2018), p. 10.

103 MFA Georgia, 'National Security Concept of Georgia', 2012, www.mfa.gov.ge/
    MainNav/ForeignPolicy/NationalSecurityConcept.aspx?lang=en-US (accessed 10
    April 2017), p. 20.

104 MFA Georgia, 'The Foreign Policy Strategy 2019–2022', 2019, http://mfa.gov.ge/
    MainNav/ForeignPolicy/ForeignPolicyStrategy.aspx?lang=en-US (accessed 20
    February 2020), p. 13.

105 Government of Lithuania, 'Prime Minister in Tbilisi: We Are Committed to Help
    Georgia on its Path of Democracy', 2015, https://lrv.lt/en/news/prime-minister-
    intbilisi-we-are-committed-to-help-georgia-on-its-path-of-democracy (accessed 20
    February 2020).

106 Polandin, 'Salome Zourabichvili, the President of Georgia, said in a special interview
    with the Polish public broadcaster TVP that Poland is a very good partner of this
    country', 8 May 2019, https://polandin.com/42531470/poland-can-be-a-bridge-
    between-georgia-and-europe-georgian-president (accessed 20 February 2020).

107 *Civil.ge*, 'Saakashvili's New Aide for Reforms Visits Georgia', 24 May 2006, https://civil.ge/archives/110656 (accessed 20 February 2020).
108 Walt (1988).
109 Giorgi Gvalia, Bidzina Lebanidze and David Siroky, 'Neoclassical Realism and Small States: Systemic Constraints and Domestic Filters in Georgia's Foreign Policy', *East European Politics*, 35:1 (2019), pp. 21–51; M. Mälksoo, 'From Existential Politics towards Normal Politics? The Baltic States in the Enlarged Europe', *Security Dialogue*, 37:3 (2006), pp. 275–97; Kevork Oskanian, 'The Balance Strikes Back: Power, Perceptions, and Ideology in Georgian Foreign Policy, 1992–2014', *Foreign Policy Analysis*, 12:4 (2016), pp. 628–52.

Chapter 9

GEORGIA'S ALLIANCE WITH – NOT IN – NATO: EXTERNAL BALANCING, AUTONOMY AND COMMUNITY

Michael Hikari Cecire

This chapter explores Georgia–NATO relations in the context of Georgian national identity, politics and especially state insecurity, with a concluding emphasis on contemporary and emergent issues surrounding Georgia–NATO relations. Georgia privileges a Euro-Atlantic strategic orientation as a centrepiece of its national security and foreign relations policies, particularly in its ties with NATO. As a result, Georgia–NATO ties have steadily developed in intensity and sophistication since independence, and Georgia is arguably the most NATO-engaged and -integrated state outside formal membership, and by certain measures functions as a model for non-member external engagement.

However, extended Georgian dissatisfaction with the terms of nominally excellent relations suggests a limit to the transferability of Georgia's case. Georgians' Euro-Atlantic leanings enjoy durable public support, potentially as a function of broad perceptions of Georgian 'civilizational' affinities to Europe and the Euro-Atlantic West. The political dimension of Georgia's Euro-Atlantic consensus is predominantly utilitarian, and attributable to an interests-based bid to maximize strategic autonomy in the face of stark power asymmetry with respect to the regional hegemon, Russia. With evidence of growing public apathy towards NATO in Georgia and a perceived recession of Euro-Atlantic functional influence (i.e. the limitations of an integration strategy absent viable pathways for membership), a Euro-Atlantic-centric strategy may not necessarily be indefinitely tenable or viable.

Georgia–NATO in context

Euro-Atlantic integration, and NATO in particular, has long been a centrepiece of Georgian foreign policy and national security thinking.[1] While the immediate aftermath of Georgian independence was characterized by internal political and ethnic conflict, Georgian foreign policymaking quickly embraced the Euro-Atlantic vector. Georgia joined NATO's Partnership for Peace programme in 1994. This followed the accession of Eduard Shevardnadze to leadership in 1992, and the ceasefire that ended active armed hostilities during the 1992–93 Georgian–Abkhazian war.

Like several other states of the former Soviet Union, Georgia and NATO saw gradual advances in relations in the 1990s, with Tbilisi joining the Euro-Atlantic Partnership Council in 1997, and Georgia and NATO establishing formal relations in 1998. Although notably incremental compared to the 2003 Rose Revolution and the 2012 democratic transition, this period could be regarded as relatively momentous given the need to repair Georgia's state development, which was only a few years out from successive ethnic conflicts and a civil war. In the 1990s, Georgia continued to be plagued by warlordism, endemic corruption and state weakness.[2]

In 2002, then-President Shevardnadze announced his government's intention to join NATO and the EU, which coincided with Georgian military deployments to NATO peacekeeping missions in Kosovo, and later, participation in coalition activities in Afghanistan and Iraq, representing a broad-based advance in Georgian military relations with the West. In 2002, Georgia was the beneficiary of the US-proffered Georgia Train and Equip Program, which aimed to increase the security capabilities of Georgian forces, and led to a succession of additional cooperative military support programmes. While the US programmes aimed to counter criminal and militant extremist elements in the country, they had a catalyzing effect on Georgian military relations with Western partners, particularly with the US and NATO as a whole.[3]

Georgia–NATO cooperation saw rapid advancement in the aftermath of the 2003 Rose Revolution and the accession of Mikheil Saakashvili and his United National Movement to power. While NATO and Euro Atlantic integration was an increasingly prioritized foreign policy vector under the Shevardnadze government, particularly in the latter years, Saakashvili's government privileged Euro-Atlantic integration as a focal element of both his party's political line, and Georgia's national strategy. NATO integration, in particular, became a central component of this approach, as it signalled a clear break from Georgian post-Soviet associations and announced a civilizational affinity with the West.[4] The 2005 National Security Concept explicitly tethered Georgian–NATO aspirations to the notion of Georgia's longstanding European identity. It declares:

> Georgia, as a Black Sea and South-Eastern European state, has historically been a geographic, political and cultural part of Europe. Therefore, integration into European and Euro-Atlantic political, economic and security systems is the firm will of Georgian people. Georgia welcomes NATO and EU enlargement and believes that integration of the Black Sea states into NATO and the EU will significantly reinforce the security of the Black Sea region as the South-Eastern border of Europe. Integration into NATO and the EU represents a top priority of Georgian foreign and security policy.[5]

Similar language was contained in other national security and foreign policy documents under Saakashvili's government, and under subsequent governments led by Georgian Dream.[6] Saakashvili and the UNM's 2003–12 governments advanced Georgia's ties with NATO. Swift internal reforms and a new policy agenda sought to align military and political processes to NATO and Euro-Atlantic standards. While no political consensus was achieved among NATO members on a Membership Action Plan (MAP) for Georgia during the 2008 Bucharest summit, language promising eventual Georgian membership was adopted, though without clear benchmarks or a date or for accession. Georgia's 2008 war with Russia deepened the differences among NATO member states, who variously regarded the war as evidence of the merits of Georgian membership or the wisdom of its continued rejection. Extended controversy over 'blame' for the war, and the detailed conclusions of veteran Swiss diplomat Heidi Tagliavini's EU-commissioned *Independent International Fact-Finding Mission on the Conflict in Georgia* (2009), did little to dispel such differences of opinion.

Nonetheless, the war lent new impetus to additional Georgia–NATO technical integration measures, including the launch of the NATO–Georgia Commission and the Annual National Programme. These offered mechanisms that were functionally equivalent to the coveted MAP – a benchmark-oriented pathway to prepare a candidate for membership – but lacked the formal commitment or positive conditionality represented by the MAP process. In 2010, a NATO liaison office was opened in Tbilisi, which provided a permanent coordinating delegation to assist with Georgian reforms in service of NATO cooperation and integration.

In the aftermath of the 2012 parliamentary elections and the democratic transition of power, Georgia's ruling Georgian Dream coalition continued its predecessors' policies privileging Euro-Atlantic integration. Certain reform processes, which were regarded as stalled in the latter period of UNM rule, were renewed. In recognition of the Georgian armed forces' technical progress, and in light of Russian military interventions in Ukraine, NATO awarded Georgia a 'substantial package' during the 2014 NATO summit in Wales, which significantly expanded the NATO Liaison Office in Tbilisi, launched an array of integrated advisory programmes, and saw the establishment of permanent NATO facilities on Georgian soil.[7] Georgian forces also continued to receive NATO training and experience as part of their contributions to the International Security Assistance Force, including the NATO-led Resolute Support advisory mission after 2014.[8] In 2015, Georgia committed forces to the NATO Response Force (NRF), an operational high-readiness unit developed as a rapid reaction force, and designed to respond to threats to NATO member states. At the 2014 NATO Summit in Wales, the NRF was restructured to respond to Russian 'hybrid' operations of the kind demonstrated in Ukraine in 2014.[9] In the latter half of the decade, with the structural elements of Georgia–NATO cooperation largely maximized, and few remaining potential frontiers for integration short of a direct pathway to membership, emphases shifted to increasingly large and complex functional collaborations, particularly multinational exercises.[10]

NATO as centrepiece

Why does Georgia privilege Euro-Atlantic integration and NATO in particular? Kakachia and Minesashvili argue that Georgian affiliation with the Euro-Atlantic West is an identity-driven and even a civilizational imperative.[11] By contrast, Kevork Oskanian suggests a neoclassical realist reading of contemporary Georgian foreign policy, in which ideology serves as a critical intervening variable in Tbilisi's formulation and conduct of foreign policy, including its prioritization of Euro-Atlanticism and the liberal narrative it evokes.[12] Anders Wivel takes an alternative approach to Georgia's foreign policymaking, using an adaptation of the Waltian realist balance of threat theory to explain variations in Georgian foreign policy approaches to its neighbourhood.[13]

There are merits to all of these approaches, which variously offer credible explanations for Georgian foreign policymaking, and why it favours the Euro-Atlantic West. However, without minimizing the potential utility of other analytical frameworks, there may be a more straightforward approach to explaining Georgian strategic choices in the context of relative power asymmetry, particularly when compared to its chief rival and regional hegemon, Russia. In this more utilitarian reading, Georgia's prioritization of NATO and the Euro-Atlantic West is an effort to attenuate its own weakness relative to Russia. The literature on alliance formation suggests that this is a natural outgrowth of Georgia's precarious strategic position. Georgia's behaviour could be described as an example of Waltian external balancing in response to the strategic challenge of Russian military and economic power. This is not to say that Georgia is responding solely to perceived power imbalances, or balancing threats without endogenous considerations – after all, there is no single rule governing a rational actor's threat perceptions.[14] In Georgia's intricate internal politics, riddled with metaphors and symbols, threat perceptions are a fluctuating and discursive arena.

At the same time, evidence of an existing imbalance of power and a reasonable perception of material threat from Russia, is clear. This was evident well before the 2008 war, as Georgia's relative weakness vis-à-vis Russia was never in doubt, despite Russia's own weaknesses in the 1990s. The post-independence period led to intense acrimony between the two states. Although Russia could not be said to have been internally monolithic in its deliberations, Russia's role as a participant in the Abkhazian and South Ossetian separatist conflicts has been well documented.[15] Russian involvement as backers or participants in the South Ossetian and Abkhazian conflicts led to Georgia's territorial fragmentation; and other forms of military incursions (such as in the Pankisi Gorge), contributed to the broad perception in Georgia of Russian hostility and its own relative military weakness. This narrative of Russian threat perceptions only crystallized following Russia's overwhelming military victory in the 2008 war and in the ongoing territorial occupation of Georgia.[16]

Despite relatively rapid economic and political development since the 2003 Rose Revolution, the regional balance of power in Georgia's immediate environment has not changed. Russia remains the leading regional power and, by some reckoning, may have only increased in relative strength.[17] With such a strident strategic imbalance, Georgian governments have sought to utilize external balancing as a means of maximizing autonomy. While issues of identity, culture, ideology and threat perception may have contributed to the relative success and extended durability of a pro-Western consensus, Georgia–NATO relations might be best considered within the context of Georgia engaging in autonomy-maximizing behaviour in response to stark power asymmetry with respect to Russia. This may explain otherwise counterintuitive examples of Georgian foreign policy decisions, which embraced alternative 'candidates' as external balancers, such as Turkey, Iran and China.[18]

Euro-Atlantic institutions and states embraced Georgia amid NATO's pivot to a more globally engaged and expeditionary mission orientation. This intensified following the US-led invasions of Afghanistan (and the ensuing need for alternative supply routes) and Iraq. US and Euro-Atlantic fixations on validations to its so-called democracy agenda, led to initial – if short-lived – optimism about NATO expansion to and beyond the Black Sea basin. Such factors accelerated the development of Georgia–NATO relations to advanced levels of integration and cooperation that persist today. However, they have also exposed divergences in expectations and goals.

Even so, NATO's willingness to integrate so deeply with Georgia suggests there is some utility derived from its relationship with Georgia. James Morrow describes this arrangement as an asymmetrical relationship whereby the stronger power (in this case, NATO) derives 'autonomy', or greater operational flexibility, by extending security benefits to the weaker power – Georgia (1991). This is an arrangement not unlike NATO itself, which periodically purports to be based on a symmetrical model of capability integration, but is in fact an asymmetrical relationship between a single military superpower, a few major military powers and a much larger grouping of third-rate military powers. The public debate regarding the 2 per cent GDP defence-spending target is emblematic of this faulty logic; even strict adherence would do little, if anything, to overturn sharp capability asymmetries between members.[19] More importantly, devotion to the ancient religion of capability symmetry pleaded ignorance to NATO's founding purpose as an extension of post-1945 US political and strategic goals. NATO was designed to enhance the US role as Atlantic hegemon, European security provider and architect of a rules-based international order favouring its own interests.

Similarly, Georgia's relationship with NATO confers mutual benefits, albeit of varying kinds. Today, Georgia occupies a unique position in NATO's orbit. Neither a full alliance member nor a mere partner, Georgia can justifiably be described as being both deeply integrated with the Atlantic alliance in important respects, as well as markedly removed, in that it is unlikely to achieve full membership in the near to medium term. In some ways, Georgia's extensive integration and cooperation with NATO as an institution could be justifiably described as an alliance *with* NATO – perhaps in the classical sense of Georgia subsisting within the NATO alliance system, albeit in a deeper orbit, but lacking full integration within the NATO treaty and mutual defence architecture. NATO and Georgia are closely synchronized in most meaningful activities and outlook, yet in an arrangement external to the formal treaty alliance itself – a fine but crucial distinction.

Georgia's position renders it exceedingly close to NATO in most respects, but its security is ultimately unfulfilled in ways that perhaps matter most. The nomenclature and discursive frontiers describing Georgia–NATO relations can be contested; they are controversial, with competing narratives regarding the nature and likely end-goal of Georgia–NATO relations. However, a rough consensus does exist: Georgia is deeply integrated with NATO, and perhaps more so than any other non-NATO member, but it is also extremely unlikely to formally join the alliance in the foreseeable future.

While rapid changes in international and regional strategic dynamics may upset this prognostication, few observers regard Georgian accession as anything other than a remote possibility.[20] This is attributable to two factors: first, the risk of Georgian accession triggering a great power conflict with Russia; and second, an extended lack of consensus among NATO members regarding the efficacy of Georgian accession, given the necessity of unanimity between member states for expansion. However, a consensus appears to exist within NATO to invite and incentivize Georgia's ever-deepening integration with the Atlantic alliance and other Euro-Atlantic structures. While de facto, NATO injunctions on Georgian accession and NATO integration are fundamentally outcome-divergent, they are also largely complementary and convergent in terms of the process. As a result, deepening Georgia–NATO integration may be incorrectly interpreted as demonstrating progress towards accession, despite the latter being a political and, ultimately, a non-technical decision.

This is further complicated by Georgia's relative position to comparable states in its neighbourhood, as Georgian integration into EU and NATO structures provides it with unique access to Euro-Atlantic markets, political structures and aid packages. By some measures, Georgia receives more material benefits as a non-formal ally than other states may receive in other formal alliance structures. For example, US designations of 'major non-NATO ally' confer no mutual defence obligations or aid authorizations. States in the Russia-led Collective Security Treaty Organization (CSTO), rarely achieve similar material benefits in nominal terms as Georgia does from its informal alliance with the Euro-Atlantic space.

Georgia: The model

In purely technical terms, Georgia–NATO cooperation might be considered a potent model for NATO's external engagement. The Georgia–NATO 'alliance' evokes an 'associate membership' model that confers limited benefits that are material and moral. In some sense, this presents a robust model for NATO engagement outside its membership, particularly in an era of increasingly strident opposition to continued expansion of the Alliance.

A wayfarer in every way, even without membership, Georgia offers NATO many of the benefits of a member state with fewer obvious strategic liabilities to the Atlantic alliance. For its part, Georgia is generally an open and enthusiastic proponent of rules-based liberal international norms, an advocate of the prevailing Euro-Atlantic security architecture, a willing and generous purveyor of competent troops for reassurance and stabilization missions, a functioning democracy of sorts, and, at least for the better part of the past decade, a state which exercises a mostly cautious and pragmatic foreign policy. In exchange, Georgia receives much less in terms of concrete security benefits, even if its prospects for full membership are broadly regarded to be indefinitely, if not permanently, foreclosed.

That said, the relationship is hardly one-sided, as Georgia receives many benefits from the arrangement. For one, the regular and frequent engagement by NATO and Euro-Atlantic partners evinces a strong diplomatic commitment to Georgia by Western capitals. This suggests certain consequences for any would-be aggressor – even if NATO or Western states are not necessarily willing to provide hard security guarantees. In addition, frequent technical assistance in economic, military and political spheres provides Georgia with an array of resources that benefit national security and development in a variety of other ways.

Yet the 'associate member' model is inherently hamstrung in Georgia's case by the original expectation, still reinforced, that full membership is in the offing. This model might be more appropriate if it had been originally structured as an integration pathway without the possibility of eventual membership. That said, a major incentive of integration is the technical possibility of full membership, which NATO continues to tout in its insistence on the continuation of its 'open door' policy. If that idea is foreclosed, it jeopardizes the viability of the model.

NATO–Georgia relations are torn between an official narrative of eventual Georgian membership, and an integration model that effectively obviates the likelihood of it occurring at any point in the future. While both NATO and Georgia see their partnership as a fruitful one, the maintenance of high levels of Georgia–NATO relations is dependent on both sides deriving significant utility from the arrangement in spite of misgivings they might have about the exact terms of that relationship. However, the exhaustion of additional avenues for meaningful Georgia–NATO integration could very well sap momentum for the project, particularly if other workable alternatives to address Georgia's power asymmetry reveal themselves over time.

Limits of the model

While Georgia may be an exemplary model of external engagement for NATO, and NATO a demonstrably important partner for Georgia even absent security guarantees, Georgia–NATO relations are curtailed and perhaps degraded by divergences in goals and expectations. The question of Georgia's membership – from its technical readiness to the receptiveness of NATO members – hangs over and dictates the terms of Georgia–NATO relations. While NATO membership would likely serve as kind of a moral benefit to Georgia and its population, its most profound impact would be to cement an ultimate strategic reinsurance policy for Georgian statehood and independence, which would be a considerable accomplishment given the relatively recent nature (and broadly understood precarity) of both. Of course, NATO membership does not substitute for a national security policy, and as discourses among and within Eastern European states that are part of NATO show, NATO membership does not necessarily solve security concerns, but may only reveal anxieties of a different sort.[21]

However, the difference between NATO membership and its absence is qualitatively significant. Security planning with the expectation of collective security guarantees from a uniquely powerful and successful alliance system like NATO is a fundamentally different exercise than one without. This does not detract from the need for independent contingency planning, including those scenarios in which the alliance fails to act, or fails to act successfully, but the alliance system serves as a cornerstone for navigating regional threats and relationships. In Georgia's case, NATO membership would offer significant ballast to the country's balance of threats perceptions, and would force Russia to shape its regional strategy to the reality of permanent NATO interests.

One conceivable Russian reaction to such an outcome would be to test NATO guarantees and solidarity by openly undermining Georgia through economic, political, or even military provocations. Georgia would be among the most strategically exposed of states in the alliance if it acceded. It is a low-probability but high-risk proposition that could conceivably trigger a series of events that would end in the destabilization or even fracturing of the alliance. At the same time, the aggressor's power in this scenario may be overstated. Mindful of the stakes, the aggressor's miscalculation could lead to an overwhelming NATO response rather than quiescence, which could more profoundly and permanently upset the regional balance of power, weakening Russia's role as a primary regional player. Even if the traditional hegemon retains the upper hand, unforeseen externalities of the conflict could lead to a net-detraction in strategic gain or regime stability. In certain scenarios of Russian victory, the collapse of NATO could provoke a power vacuum with other kinds of strategic consequences that could also be detrimental to regional stability as a whole.

Georgian elites have thus perhaps justifiably prioritized Euro-Atlantic integration, and especially NATO membership, as a means of balancing Russian regional dominance. The Georgian population has lent firm and ongoing backing to Georgian membership. Polling by the US-funded National Democratic Institute (NDI), which has engaged in public policy polling in Georgia for many years (in cooperation with the Caucasus Research Resource Center, or CRRC), is regularly cited as evidence of Georgia's pro-Western leanings. Since 2014, in the immediate aftermath of the 2014 Ukraine crisis, pro-NATO sentiments in Georgia have appeared robust, with majorities consistently in the 1960s and 1970s in terms of percentages (see Table 9.1). This, by any definition, appears to demonstrate both the strength and durability of public support for NATO integration.

However, the conventional emphasis on top-line levels of reported support elides more substantial questions regarding the depth of public support. In the same set of polls, for example, NATO is consistently ranked among the lowest of priorities for respondents, with the alliance only achieving double digits once in

Table 9.1 Percentage support for NATO membership (NDI, 2014–20)

	Approve	Disapprove	DK/RA
April 2014	72	15	12
April 2015	65	20	15
November 2015	69	21	10
March 2016	68	19	13
June 2016	64	22	14
November 2016	61	25	14
April 2017	68	21	12
June 2017	66	23	11
December 2017	64	26	9
March 2018	65	20	15
June 2018	75	17	9
December 2018	78	13	9
April 2019	74	15	10
July 2019	71	17	12
December 2019	74	14	12
June 2020	69	11	21
August 2020	–	–	–
December 2020	74	9	16

Source: CRRC Caucasus Barometer Online Data Analysis.

Notes: In some cases, 'Don't Know' (DK) and 'Refuse to Answer' (RA) were reported separately, but are combined here for consistency and readability. NDI advises that some cases the percentages do not exactly equal 100 due to rounding decimal points.

the 2014–18 timespan (11 per cent in the aftermath of the Russian annexation of Crimea). Public support for NATO may be reasonably high, but it is ultimately a minor issue for all but a decided minority of the population (see Table 9.2).

A more contextualized view of NATO support requires further inquiry into Georgians' sentiments regarding Georgia–NATO relations. In the 2014–19 period, NDI asked Georgians their views on the likelihood of Georgian accession. While the exact questioning is inconsistent, the polling is broadly comparable and the results offer additional insights into the Georgian public's views of NATO's place in their country. Consistently, and notably, a strong plurality of respondents declared that Georgia would either 'never' join NATO, or that they 'did not know' or refused to respond (see Table 9.3).

This data runs contrary to typical depictions of pro-NATO sentiment in Georgia as an immutable, unceasingly enthusiastic enterprise. Views of NATO in Georgia might be better considered to be apathetic, or even fatalistic, when considering the low priority that respondents gave to NATO integration, on one hand, and their views on the likely timeline of accession, on the other. NATO representatives have periodically counselled the Georgian government to temper expectations among the population regarding the likelihood of near-term accession – perhaps as a response to the widespread view that the government during the Saakashvili era essentially depicted NATO as being a near-term proposition – but this data suggests that such entreaties are hardly necessary.

Table 9.2 Percentage believing NATO membership is among most important national issues (NDI, 2014–20)

	NATO mentioned	**NATO not mentioned**	**DK/RA**
April 2014	11	89	0
April 2015	5	94	1
November 2015	5	95	0
March 2016	6	94	0
June 2016	6	94	0
November 2016	3	96	0
April 2017	–	–	–
June 2017	5	95	0
December 2017	3	97	0
March 2018	–	–	–
June 2018	4	96	1
December 2018	4	96	0
April 2019	–	–	–
July 2019	6	93	1
December 2019	–	–	–
June 2020	–	–	–
August 2020	3	95	3
December 2020	2	95	4

Source: CRRC Caucasus Barometer Online Data Analysis.

Notes: For consistency, the same polls are included in this table, although several did not ask this particular question. NDI advises that some cases the percentages do not exactly equal 100 due to rounding decimal points.

Table 9.3 Percentage views on the likelihood of NATO accession (NDI: 2014, 2015, 2017, 2019)

	Next 5 years	**5–10 years**	**After 10 years**	**Never**	**DK/RA**
April 2019	19	17	15	14	43
April 2017	12	15	20	16	38
	Next 3 Years	**After 2018**	–	**Never**	**DK/RA**
Nov 2015	8	31	–	24	37
	Next 3 Years	**After 2018**	–	**Never**	**DK/RA**
April 2014	14	24	–	21	40

Source: CRRC Caucasus Barometer Online Data Analysis.

Additional details of Georgian public opinion towards NATO suggest that even the top-line levels of support are hardly unconditional. According to polls conducted as part of CRRC's Caucasus Barometer, more detailed queries regarding NATO support elicit a more nuanced picture than otherwise lofty levels of support would indicate (see Table 9.4).

Although one reading of this data suggests that pro-NATO sentiments are reasonably well distributed, they are also far more qualified and potentially contingent than the top-line figures reported in NDI polling would suggest. While questions regarding the depth and staying power of pro-NATO sentiments can

Table 9.4 Percentage views of NATO (CRRC: 2013, 2015, 2017, 2019, 2020)

	Don't support at all	Rather not support	Equally support and do not support	Rather support	Fully support	DK/RA
2020	4	3	12	29	42	9
2019	7	7	23	26	24	11
2017	7	5	19	29	29	11
2015	10	10	27	21	17	15
2013	12	8	26	25	16	13

Source: CRRC Caucasus Barometer Online Data Analysis.

be identified in the NDI data readily enough, it requires an examination of other non-NATO-specific questions and less frequent reports of accession confidence. By contrast, the CRRC data suggests that while pro-NATO sentiments are broad, they unmistakably coexist alongside certain reservations, as depicted by more qualified responses of support.

This data does not undermine the view that Georgia favours NATO integration. It is likely that any detailed treatment of NATO in a given country's opinion polling (including in many member states) would produce a similar range of reported sentiments in various other contexts. However, this data does reveal that pro-NATO views in Georgia are not monolithic; Georgians are capable of being swayed by changing conditions. A justifiable contingent hypothesis might even be that as the horizon for NATO accession extends, enthusiasm for NATO stagnates. This does not mean that Georgians would oppose membership if it were on offer, but in its absence – or the unlikelihood of membership as a realistic outcome – it may result in calculations of diminishing utility.

At the elite level, a similar hypothesis might be offered. As the frontiers of Euro-Atlantic technical conditionality were gradually met and even in some cases surpassed, motivations for the enterprise gradually stalled. Evidence of democratic stagnation and even decline in recent years might be considered in this context. Indeed, what is the marginal utility of a 0.2 point increase in Georgia's democracy score in one direction or another? The West has limited means to incentivize the Georgian government, and having achieved a kind of precarious equilibrium in its dealings with Russia, the Georgian government's perceived and measured momentum toward further democratization has slowed or even stalled.[22] This is not to absolve the Georgian elite for the uncertain future of their democracy. However, it is widely acknowledged that weakening political conditionality – amid rollback in democratic norms and standards in the United States and Europe – plays an appreciable role in Georgia's 'middle regime trap'.

Even so, Georgia remains a regional leader in both its political development and suitability as a Euro-Atlantic partner, and continues mutual cooperation with NATO and the EU. But even if ties remain strong, it could be a matter of inertia rather than any particular positive momentum on either technical reform or political advance. Over time, such an arrangement could resemble a transactional relationship, one maintained on a utility-based exchange, rather than one defined by mutual interests.

In such a scenario, if Georgian efforts at external balancing are reduced to utility maximization, Georgia may turn elsewhere in cultivating external balancing against Russia as new potential candidates emerge. One potential example is China. In recent years, Georgia has sought to position itself as a key part of China's regional strategy, and it is not beyond the realms of possibility that Georgia could pivot towards an external balancing strategy that is more oriented towards Beijing rather than Washington or Brussels.[23] This is not to say that Beijing is an obvious or even likely alternative external balancer for Tbilisi, but it is a credible candidate given its own global power, its presence in the broader region, and its increasing interest in Georgian overtures.

Another possibility is bandwagoning, when the regional calculus is deemed overwhelming, and external balancing opportunities are regarded as faint or unworkable. In this case, a policy of concerted accommodation might be regarded as the best decision. While the Waltian model of balance of threats suggests bandwagoning is rare, it may be seen as a preferable alternative to outright capitulation to the regional hegemon. The likelihood of this scenario is context dependent, but if there is a sense that the United States and Euro-Atlantic West are no longer the leading global powers, and have limited influence regionally, then bandwagoning with Russia may be seen as a reasonable utilitarian alternative. A variation of this scenario is Georgian bandwagoning with a regional challenger to Russian primacy. In this, Turkey may be the most viable candidate, given its relative success in revising Russian positions in Libya, Syria and most recently in Nagorno-Karabagh to be more consistent with its perceived interests.[24] Georgia is already structurally aligned with Turkey through a bevy of bilateral agreements, and a durable trilateral cooperation platform with Azerbaijan and Turkey.

Although these represent scenarios in which Georgia–NATO ties are perhaps implied to gradually atrophy and reverse, that is not necessarily the case. It is far likelier that the Georgia–NATO partnership will continue into the foreseeable future. Barring major structural changes in the international system – although this is no longer in the realm of the unthinkable given the shifts in relations between the United States and the EU in recent years – NATO will likely seek to maintain its local relationships even if it conceded the impossibility of Georgian accession. At that point, however, NATO's utility to Georgia would be reduced to an entirely technical one, which may trigger broader strategic questions as to whether Georgia's Euro-Atlantic moorings are a net-contributor to its national security or, whether it is simply an autonomy-enhancing relationship subject to change.[25]

Conclusion

Georgia–NATO ties are strong, but they are also products of divergent goals and perceptions that place the relationship at risk. Georgia's moorings to the Euro-Atlantic West are largely attributable to its own weakness in the face of a large and relatively aggressive regional hegemon. Seeking to maximize its own autonomy, Georgia has cultivated a relationship with NATO and devoted considerable national resources to service that relationship in the hope that it will eventually provide security guarantees with regard to Russia. Yet, as Georgian integration has deepened with Euro-Atlantic institutions such as NATO, the possibility of accession to the alliance has grown more remote. Georgia's need for external balancing suggests that whatever the identity-driven basis for pro-NATO sentiments, Georgia may seek to take advantage of other opportunities to maximize its own autonomy – even if it comes at a cost to its relationship with NATO.

One way to forestall such an eventuality would be to provide Georgia with the technical and political mechanisms necessary to accede. However, this is among the least likely scenarios, given the continued reticence among NATO members to accept full Georgian membership. Georgia's security dilemma will continue to be a motivating factor in its foreign policy and strategic outlook. Georgia–NATO relations are currently robust, but they may represent a peak. At the same time, relations could continue to improve if new means of integration are developed and put into action. This would contribute to a sense of forward momentum. But with Georgia–NATO integration already functionally advanced, there are few other pathways at NATO's disposal. Continued half-measures of integration over time appear to resemble a kind of NATO integration version of Zeno's dichotomy paradox, which effectively render no breakthrough despite the consistent appearance of progress. That said, such a status quo scenario may be viable as long as: (1) the alliance itself remains content with such an arrangement; (2) Georgia is content with the status quo, and NATO continues to be seen as a net asset; and (3) NATO continues to serve as an effective means to maximize Georgian autonomy vis-à-vis Russia.

NATO's ties with Georgia are, by many measures, a success story. They show the organization's outreach and power of attraction. But the Georgian case also exposes the hard limits on such a model and raises issues regarding future forms of extra-regional engagement by NATO. Without the explicit or even implicit conditionality of membership, which was codified in the 2008 Bucharest Summit, it is likely that Georgian reforms would have been less effective. But Georgia is not necessarily a model repeatable elsewhere, and if practical incentives are exhausted, prospects for accession will lose their credibility, sapping NATO's role as both a cultural force and as a utility-maximizing one in the Black Sea region. This could lead to the diminution of NATO's role in Georgia, and to a Georgian shift in favour of an alternative external balancer, were a viable candidate to emerge.

There is another potential scenario where NATO's longstanding role in Georgia cultivates an organic association between democracy and security, and an implicit form of conditionality that propels Georgia toward further liberal democratic norms, even absent formal pathways. In this scenario, Georgia may yet recognize that it does not need an official charter or formal membership to achieve security, prosperity or democracy. In other words, the autonomy gains that Tbilisi derives from its close relationship with NATO could be seen as real and even measurable, and which includes Euro-Atlantic advocacy on its behalf, the promise of membership, and assistance with the technical wherewithal to get there. Yet, even in the foreclosure of its accession prospects, Georgia may identify means to achieve similar goals endogenously, or without the need for Western or Euro-Atlantic 'certification'.

In certain respects, in line with Kakachia and Minashvili's characterizations of Georgian civilizational affinities, significant aspects of Georgia's relationship with NATO (and other Euro-Atlantic institutions) provide Georgians with the sensation of being part of a defined community of nations.[26] However, a Georgia that can navigate its way out of its regular cycles of political upheaval and can achieve a semblance of predictable, democratic stability may be a better signal of its kinship with its Euro-Atlantic partners than a hybrid regime toiling through the MAP process. Likewise, a Georgia that can effectively manage the regional hegemon's provocations, sensitivities and red lines, as well as the more general tumult of its neighbourhood – if paired with a more credible indigenous national security strategy – may be more sure-footed regionally than a NATO member prone to external and internal crises.

Even in the absence of Georgian accession, an enduring aspect of Georgia–NATO ties may be the transmission and internalization of the technical characteristics of Euro-Atlantic integration, which serve as waypoints in a longer process that does not end with membership. To that end, Georgia may still pursue and achieve many of the attributes it seeks – democracy, security, prosperity – even without the formal edifices of NATO and Euro-Atlantic membership. If this is even an approximate outcome of the longstanding Georgia–NATO partnership, it will likely be regarded as worthwhile and mutually beneficial endeavour.

Notes

1 Michael Cecire, 'Georgia's 2012 Elections and Lessons for Democracy Promotion', *Orbis* 57:2 (2013), pp. 232–50; Kornely Kakachia and Salome Minesashvili, 'Identity Politics: Exploring Georgian Foreign Policy Behaviour', *Journal of Eurasian Studies*, 6:2 (2015), pp. 171–80.

2 Fawn provides an extensive account of Georgia's security position, particularly with regard to the US 'War on Terror' after the events of 11 September 2001. His paper offers considerable context regarding issues of Georgian state weakness and insecurity. Rick Fawn, 'Russia's Reluctant Retreat from the Caucasus: Abkhazia, Georgia and the US after 11 September 2001', *European Security*, 11: 4 (2002), pp. 131–50. David Phillipps, in the early days of Saakashvili's government, also provides an ample snapshot of the state's frailties and significant regional challenges. David L. Phillips, 'Stability, Security, and Sovereignty in the Republic of Georgia', *Council on Foreign Relations, Washington DC*, 15 January 2004. Closson examines state weakness manifesting in the Georgian energy sector. Mitchell, however, considers Georgian state weakness from a retrospective position, in the context of Saakashvili's reforms to ameliorate them. Stacy Closson, 'State Weakness in Perspective: Strong Politico-economic Networks in Georgia's Energy Sector', *Europe-Asia Studies*, 61:5 (2009), pp. 759–78.

3   For a contemporaneous account of GTEP as it was unveiled, see www.nytimes. com/2002/05/20/world/green-berets-land-in-georgia-for-2-year-training-program. html. See also Fawn, 2002. For a broader discussion of GTEP, see Jennifer D.P. Moroney, Beth Grill, Joe Hogler, Lianne Kennedy-Boudali and Christopher Paul, 'How Successful are US Efforts to Build Capacity in Developing Countries?: A Framework to Assess the Global Train and Equip', Rand Corporation (2011).

4   See Donnacha Ó Beacháin and Frederik Coene, 'Go West: Georgia's European Identity and its Role in Domestic Politics and Foreign Policy Objectives', *Nationalities Papers*, 42:6 (2014), pp. 923–41; Kornely Kakachia and Salome Minesashvili, 'Identity Politics: Exploring Georgian Foreign Policy Behavior', *Journal of Eurasian Studies*, 6:2 (2015), pp. 171–80; Salome Minesashvili, 'Narrating Identity: Belongingness and Alterity in Georgia's Foreign Policy', *Values and Identity as Sources of Foreign Policy in Armenia and Georgia*, (2016), pp. 1770.

5   See National Security Concept of Georgia, www.parliament.ge/files/292_880_927746_ concept_en.pdf.

6   See, for example, Saakashvili's speech to the Parliamentary Assembly of the Council of Europe in 2013, www.assembly.coe.int/nw/xml/Speeches/Speech-XML2HTML-EN. asp?SpeechID=192; and statements from Prime Minister Gharibashvili, www.reuters.com/ article/us-eu-georgia/georgian-leader-tells-eu-nato-he-remains-on-pro-western-path- idUSKCN0J12AC20141117, and Bakhtadze in 2014 and 2019, www.cnbc.com/2019/01/22/ russia-is-still-occupying-20percent-of-our-country-georgias-leader-says.html

7   For more information on the Substantial NATO–Georgia Package (SNGP), see www. nato.int/nato_static_fl2014/assets/pdf/pdf_2016_02/160209-factsheet-sngp-en.pdf

8   At its peak, Georgian troops represented nearly 1,600 troops in Afghanistan, and nearly 900 during the Resolute Support mission.

9   See NATO Response Force, https://jfcnaples.nato.int/page6734927.aspx

10 See, for example: https://agenda.ge/en/news/2016/2801; www.reuters.com/article/ us-georgia-exercises/georgia-begins-u-s-led-military-exercise-a-day-before-vice- president-pence-visit-idUSKBN1AF0G6; www.act.nato.int/articles/georgian-defence- forces-lead-nato-georgia-exercise-2019; and www.dw.com/en/georgia-launches-joint- military-drills-with-nato-countries/a-54846498

11 Kakachia and Minesashvili, 2015.

12 Kevork Oskanian, 'The Balance Strikes Back: Power, Perceptions, and Ideology in Georgian Foreign Policy, 1992–2014', *Foreign Policy Analysis*, 12:4 (2016), pp. 628–52.

13 Anders Wivel, 'Living on the Edge: Georgian Foreign Policy between the West and the Rest', *Third World Thematics: A TWQ Journal*, 1:1 (2016), pp. 92–109.

14 Stephen M. Walt, 'Alliance Formation and the Balance of World Power', *International Security*, 9:4 (1985), pp. 3–43; Kenneth N. Waltz, *Theory of International Politics* (Reading, MA: Addison-Wesley, 1979).

15 See, for example, E.M. Kozhokin, Georgia–Abkhazia, *US and Russian Policymaking with Respect to the Use of Force* (*Santa Monica*, CA: RAND Corporation, CF-129- CRES, 1996), pp.75–83; Dennis Sammut and Nikola Dvetkovski, *The Georgia–South Ossetia Conflict* (Verification Technology Information Centre, 1996); Rick Fawn, 'Russia's Reluctant Retreat from the Caucasus: Abkhazia, Georgia and the US after 11 September 2001', *European Security*, 11:4 (2002), pp. 131–50; Christoph Zürcher, Pavel Baev and Jan Koehler, 'Civil Wars in the Caucasus', *Understanding Civil War*, 2 (2005), pp. 259–98; Tracey German, 'Securing the South Caucasus: Military Aspects of Russian Policy towards the Region since 2008', *Europe-Asia Studies*, 64: 9 (2012), pp. 1650–66.

16　The dominant perception of Russia as the prevailing threat to Georgia is a rational narrative, as shown by Russian participation in local separatist projects and other forms of regular military, economic and political interventions. However, the intervening variables that contribute to elite decision making favouring external balancing (in the form of NATO, for example) versus bandwagoning is less clear, and beyond the immediate scope of this chapter.

17　Pavel K. Baev, 'The Military Dimension of Russia's Connection with Europe', *European Security*, 27:1 (2018), pp. 82–97; Dmitry Adamsky, 'From Moscow with Coercion: Russian Deterrence Theory and Strategic Culture', *Journal of Strategic Studies*, 41:1–2 (2018), pp. 33–60.

18　In this context, external balancing is understood broadly, encompassing aspects that go beyond pure security dimensions, and include critical masses of economic infrastructure and strategic interests. In this sense, Turkey, China and Iran are not courted explicitly to provide security guarantees to Georgia – which is at best a very long-term prospect with regard to Georgia and NATO as well – but to be diplomatically or otherwise invested sufficiently as to deter, oppose and/or preempt Russian adventurism in Georgia. For more on Georgia's relations with these states in the context of regional balance, see Alexander Iskandaryan, Murad Ismayilov and Michael Cecire, 'Russia's Relations with the South Caucasus', *Russian Analytical Digest, (RAD)* 232 (2019).

19　For additional discussion of this issue, see, for example: www.washingtonpost.com/news/monkey-cage/wp/2017/02/27/3-things-to-know-about-the-trump-administrations-warning-shots-on-nato/

20　Tracey German, 'NATO and the Enlargement Debate: Enhancing Euro-Atlantic Security or Inciting Confrontation?', *International Affairs*, 93:2 (2017), pp. 291–308; Andrew T. Wolff, 'The Future of NATO Enlargement after the Ukraine Crisis', *International Affairs*, 91:5 (2015), pp. 1103–21.

21　For example, see David A. Shlapak and Michael W. Johnson, *Reinforcing Deterrence on NATO's Eastern Flank: Wargaming the Defense of the Baltics* (Santa Monica, CA: RAND Arroyo Centre, 2016).

22　Michael Cecire, 'Nations in Transit 2016–Georgia', *Freedom House,* 2016.

23　Were Georgia to retreat from a position seeking Euro-Atlantic integration – or at least effectively so – it is presumed here that other qualitatively similar bilateral arrangements, such as a mutual defence treaty with the United States, would also be unlikely. One alternative that has been discussed variously is the possibility of Tbilisi seeking major non-NATO ally status with the United States, while this may provide some semblance of moral significance, but such a designation on its own confers no promise of mutual defence, and may even increase the risk of conflict in deterrence terms.

24　See, for example: www.mei.edu/publications/escalation-and-regional-risks-new-karabakh-war

25　One under-discussed realm of Georgia–NATO relations is the degree to which Georgia's Euro-Atlantic choices potentially invite acrimony from the regional hegemon, Russia. This is not to discount Georgia's sovereign choices of alliance or partnership, but interrogates the degree to which Tbilisi's elite consensus in favour of pro-West policies make Georgia more and not less likely to be in conflict with Russia. This chapter argues that it has been a net benefit for Georgia, and autonomy maximizing in the final calculus, but this may not always be the case.

26　Kornely Kakachia and Salome Minesashvili. 'Identity Politics: Exploring Georgian Foreign Policy Behaviour', Journal of Eurasian Studies 6:2 (2015), pp. 171–80.

Part IV

GEORGIA AND THE GREAT POWERS

Chapter 10

THE STORY OF TWO TRIANGLES: GEORGIA'S RUSSIA POLICIES

Ghia Nodia

Since independence in 1991, Russia has been the main point of reference for Georgia's foreign policy and it could hardly be otherwise. For Georgia, relations with Russia have been more than a foreign policy issue in the narrow sense of determining the terms of relations between two countries. Rather, they are related to the definition of its identity, and its survival as a state. In both dimensions, this point of reference was negative: Georgia's identity was to be defined in contrast to Russia, and Georgia's survival depended on its capacity to defend itself from Russia's infringements on its sovereignty. Hence, the most stable feature of Georgian–Russian relations throughout almost all the years since 1991 was that they were bad, but that the intensity of tensions varied at different periods.

Neither country considers their relations to be truly bilateral. In this chapter, they will be discussed within the context of two triangular conflicts. The larger triangle is that which includes Georgia, Russia and the West.[1] The West has always been implied in any issue that emerged from Georgian–Russian relations, and the Russian factor was always looming in any contacts between Georgia and Western actors. On the other hand, Russia has always been a party to Georgia's domestic conflicts with the separatist Abkhazia and South Ossetia regions. This constitutes the second, smaller triangle. Georgia never considered these as purely domestic conflicts: they could only be understood, and respective policies developed, in the context of Georgian–Russian relations.

Methodologically, this article will tilt towards a constructivist approach: it will be based on an assumption that a country's identity (or, to be more precise, the way in which its political and intellectual elites define its identity) determines the general direction of its foreign policies.[2] This does not exclude the importance of 'hard' factors such as geographical location, size, the level of economic development, and military capabilities. However, all these factors are to be seen through the prism of identity: they influence the way national elites define their nation and its interests.[3] In order to understand Russia's role in modern Georgia's identity construction, it is useful to take a *longue durée* approach, that is to examine the historical background of Georgian attitudes towards Russia, because this background is often invoked in contemporary discussions of Georgia's foreign policy choices, and influences the ways in which all the relevant actors approach these relationships.

History and background: Georgia's image of Russia

Georgia's attitudes to Russia are historically ambivalent, and this ambivalence continues to be relevant. The initial image of Russia was extremely positive; it emerged somewhere around the sixteenth century, when Orthodox Christian Georgia (or rather, different Georgian principalities, of which the Kingdom of Kartl'Kakheti was the strongest), was involved in a struggle for survival with its eastern and southern Islamic neighbours, like Persia and the Ottoman Empire. Georgia started to view its increasingly powerful northern co-religionist state, Russia, as a potential saviour. Initially, Russia's reception was lukewarm, but in the second half of the eighteenth century, as its ambitions expanded to the Black Sea region, Russia started to show greater interest towards the small kingdom to its south. In 1783, the *Georgievskii Traktat*, a bilateral agreement, was signed, according to which Georgia gave up its sovereignty in foreign policy hoping for Russian protection from the Islamic empires. However, Georgian and Russian perceptions and expectations turned out to be grossly asymmetrical: while Georgia was looking for an arrangement defined by a bilateral agreement, Russia decided to fully incorporate the Kingdom of Kartl'Kakheti,[4] based on a unilateral Tsarist manifesto published in September 1801.[5] It was only after this that the Russian security shield really extended to Georgia – but there was no longer any Georgia as a political unit, only a province within the Russian Empire.[6] Georgia as a polity only existed in historical memory, or in the political imagination of educated Georgians.

This created fundamental ambiguity. According to the official discourse of the Russian and Soviet Empires, Georgia had voluntarily joined Russia, while in reality it was incorporated into an empire based on a unilateral decision. On the other hand, there was a kernel of truth in the official version: Georgia had really sought Russia's protection and the majority of its ruling class did not protest against the establishment of Russian rule.[7] In effect, it was a trade-off: Georgia got peace and protection, a higher level of development, and unification of most of its historical lands under a single political umbrella, but it lost its political identity and – as many Georgians feared – was on the way to losing its cultural identity as well.

During the 1860s, a group of *tergdaleulebi* (mostly Georgian graduates of Russian and European universities) under the leadership of Ilia Chavchavadze, started a movement of Georgian national revival, though its activities were cultural and educational rather than political, and it never dared to become openly anti-Russian.[8] In part, this could be explained by the fear of repression from the Tsarist autocracy, but this is not the only explanation. In the 1890s, when independent political movements started to spread, it was social democrats (who never seriously discussed the prospect of independence) rather than nationalists who became the most influential and organized political group. This indicated that at that moment, most Georgians tacitly accepted the trade-off, though they were not happy with its terms.

The brief period of Georgia's independence in 1918–21 was a turning point. After the breakdown of the Tsarist regime and the Bolshevik coup, Georgia came to be ruled by social democrats who considered themselves part of the European social democratic family and would not accept domination by Russia's autocratic Bolsheviks.[9] This not only prompted Georgia's social democrats to proclaim independence, but also laid the ground for a new narrative: Georgia was an essentially European nation defined by a taste for freedom, but it was threatened by an Oriental despotism embodied by Russian Bolsheviks.[10] A new Georgian political nationalism was born, simultaneously pro-European and anti-Russian.[11]

Georgia's independence under the social democrats proved short-lived: in February 1921, it fell prey to the Russian Bolshevik military invasion. This time Georgians actually fought Russia, though they were overpowered. While the republic hoped for support from the West, no help came. Great Britain, the power with the heaviest presence in the region at the time, decided that defending Transcaucasia from the Bolsheviks was not worth it.[12] But the new narrative born during this short period survived the era of Soviet ideological domination and resurfaced in the twilight of Soviet Empire, when Gorbachev's liberalization led to the creation of a chaotic but powerful national independence movement in Georgia. The difference was that it was strongly nationalist to start with, while the socialist ideology of the First Republic was rejected (as something close to the dominant Soviet ideology). Still, the slogan was not just to gain independence, but to reinstate the 1918–21 republic that had been unlawfully ended by Soviet occupation. Georgian nationalists presumed that the West had a moral and political obligation to support Georgia's independence, because Georgia represented democracy in a fight against Russian–Soviet imperialism and despotism.

This continued to be the dominant narrative in independent Georgia. However, it is not the only possible one. There is also an alternative theme of co-religionist Russia as a benevolent hegemon that protected Georgia from annihilation by hostile Muslim hordes and contributed to modernizing the country. The only thing it requests in return is loyalty. In this sense, Georgia's pro-Western policies constitute acts of ingratitude and treason and the Georgian political elite shares responsibility for the breakdown of its relations with its northern neighbour. The Georgian origin of Joseph Stalin, who was at the helm of the Soviet Russian Empire at the summit of its global power, also underlined the psychological link between Georgian nationalism and Russian imperialism. In this narrative, the culturally alien and imperial West is trying to instrumentalize Georgia in its efforts to weaken Russia, and this became the real reason for the breakdown of relations between the two brotherly peoples. Moreover, the West is undermining true Georgian identity and culture based on Orthodox Christian tradition. This narrative defines Russian policies towards Georgia; it exists in Georgia too and has become stronger in recent years,[13] although it has never defined Georgia's foreign policies.

The big triangle

This tension between Russia and the West may be considered a foundational principle of Georgia's modern political vision. Supporting a sovereign Georgia implies resistance to Russian pressure and orienting oneself to the West. It implies that the West is the best hope for Georgia to maintain its true sovereignty. On the other hand, resentment of Westernization has become the main motive for the forces that want Georgia to stay closer to Russia. However, in practice, this latter strategy looks rather like partial abrogation of Georgia's sovereignty and is based on a neo-Soviet vision of a peaceful, stable and culturally authentic Georgia under a Russian political umbrella.

The West tends not to support this dramatic either/or vision. Such an attitude is contrary to Western political interests because it makes a small (and, arguably, insignificant) country like Georgia a spoiler in Western efforts to find a *modus vivendi* with Russia, which is a rather difficult task. Moreover, until 2014 when Russia violated the territorial integrity of Ukraine and reportedly began meddling in the internal processes of Western democracies, the West considered Russia a difficult and volatile partner but not an adversary. Western strategists continued to hope (some still do) that they just needed to be a little bit more creative and flexible in order to find some kind of satisfactory accommodation with Russia (the 2008 Russo-Georgian War was not sufficient to change that mindset). Some of them blamed Western policies, such as NATO (and maybe also EU) enlargement for unnecessarily alienating Russia. But even those who supported policies of double enlargements, usually sought accommodation rather than competition with Russia.

This ran contrary to the Georgian (probably, generally eastern European and post-Soviet) propensity to see Russia and the West as mutual adversaries involved in a zero-sum game. Because of this, Western observers sometimes saw Georgia's attitudes to Russia as obsessive, paranoid and immature.[14] Western politicians were annoyed that Georgia expected them to deal with Russia instead of Georgians trying to find accommodation with their northern neighbour on their own. The West condemned Russia's invasion in Georgia in 2008 and made efforts to contain the results of the invasion through mediation led by French President Nicolas Sarkozy on behalf of the European Union. EU leaders more or less evenly divided the blame for this violent episode between Russia and Georgia, accusing the latter's leadership for being too provocative with regard to Russia, or for falling for its provocation.[15]

Russia under Putin eventually vindicated Georgia's perception that it really is a committed adversary of the West. Russia's pro-Western neighbours, such as Georgia and Ukraine, became the arena of this rivalry. Putin decided that inclusion of these countries into a Western orbit (expressed by membership of or close cooperation with NATO and/or the EU) was crossing a red line he would not tolerate, and he had to respond with military action. From Russia's point of view, its relations with Georgia (as well as Ukraine) were a corollary of its contest with the West, which denied Russia its right to have proper 'zones of influence' or 'zones of responsibility'. In that sense, the Russian perspective on its relations with Georgia is closer to the Georgian perspective. It sees Georgia as part of the same triangle with the West, but the most important difference is that Russia hardly considers Georgia as an independent political actor, but as an extension of Western influence in its neighbourhood. This presumption of 'non-actorness' also extends to the internal politics of these countries. According to the Russian point of view, neither the coloured revolutions in Georgia and Ukraine (2003 and 2004), nor the 2014 Euromaidan revolution in Ukraine can be seen as truly internal events, but were masterminded by the United States in order to install pro-Western political regimes there.[16]

This 'triangularization' of bilateral relations cannot be explained solely by idiosyncratic views that happen to be popular in some nations. Georgia is pragmatic when it relies on Western support for guarantees of its sovereign existence, because small and vulnerable countries have a much better chance of maintaining a modicum of sovereignty within a liberal international order supported by the West. A lot has been written – especially after the election of Donald Trump – about what such order implies (or implied, as more sceptical observers would prefer to say) and how real and sustainable it is.[17] The main idea of this order is that Western powers (led by the United States) attach considerable value to the existence of rules-based relations between states, big or small, and prioritize their preservation. The West maintained this order through a number of international and regional institutions (such as the UN, NATO, the Bretton Woods institutions, the EU), and also by trying to pressure and punish the offenders who defied these rules. To be sure, the West and, specifically the United States, has never been fully consistent in living up to these rules, and their very substance was often open for debate. The West was never powerful enough to enforce such an order globally. However, the 'long peace' since the Second World War (at least within the area where the West dominated) was largely the result of the consensus around the main principles of the liberal world order. The end of communism created expectations that the rules of this order would now extend to this part of the world as well – and, if Cold War former adversaries joined forces, could be applied universally. The successful international operation to liberate Kuwait in 1991 was probably the highest point of optimism about global liberal international order.

The comparison between the effects of the two Russian military invasions of Georgia (in 1921 and 2008) is a good illustration of the value of the liberal international order – however limited and imperfect – for a small state. Georgia could not survive in 1921 because there was no such order at that time. However, despite losses, it did survive the 2008 Russian intervention, maintaining genuine sovereignty and being able to pursue the same foreign policies as it had before. Even if the West did not support Georgia as vigorously as Georgians (and some of its Western friends) would have liked,[18] it did consider the security of a small state as a value worth supporting, and that made an important difference in limiting the tangible results of Russian military action to the occupation of Abkhazia and South Ossetia.

Russia explicitly opposes the idea of a liberal international order as it equates it with Western domination.[19] The principles of such order – which some Russian analysts describe as 'liberal fundamentalism'[20] – allegedly threaten Russia because they enable countries like Georgia or Ukraine, which 'naturally' fall into Russia's zone of influence, to make their own choices, often contrary to Russia's designs. Arrangements like the Vienna Congress (an agreement between European great powers negotiated in 1814–15 after the Napoleonic Wars), or the 1945 Yalta agreement that divided post-Second World War Europe between the Soviet Union and Western powers, are much more to its liking.[21] Under such an arrangement, the notional sovereignty of countries like Georgia might still be possible, but they would have to accept the fate of being the satellites of big powers – without claiming a right to choose the patron-state themselves. In this vision, Georgia would naturally fall into Russia's zone of influence.

The rise of NATO- and Eurosceptic populism in Europe, and the election of Donald Trump in the United States raised questions about whether the West would remain committed and maintain the capacity to continue upholding such an order. But so far, Georgia's policy towards Russia is based on an assumption that the West still maintains some commitment to some kind of liberal international order, and it is within this order that Georgia has the best chance of surviving as an independent nation.

When Joe Biden, a politician known for his commitment to liberal internationalism, won the 2020 presidential elections in the United States, it revived Georgia's hopes of greater support from the US administration. His early statements have shown – in contrast to President Trump – a readiness to confront Russia's revisionist policies in the South Caucasus and elsewhere. The United States has already begun to seek greater coordination with its European partners.[22] This suggests that relations between Russia and the United States (and the West more generally) will continue to be adversarial. In this context, any Georgian accommodation with its northern neighbour should not be expected.

The second triangle

Georgia's difficult relations with Russia are locked in another triangle created by the territorial conflicts of Abkhazia and South Ossetia. There are two misleading narratives about these conflicts.[23] One of them is predominantly Georgian and says that these conflicts can be fully explained by Russia's instigation and would not have happened without external manipulation. Another (Russian and partly Western) is that these conflicts emerged as a reaction from ethnic minorities towards aggressive Georgian nationalism. Russia is an external power which tries to establish a just peace (the Russian version) or uses these conflicts for its own political advantage (the version more popular among Western analysts).

In fact, conflicts of this kind that emerge in the context of a break-up of multinational empires, are usually triangular in character. To be sure, there would be no conflict unless the Georgians and the Abkhazians, as well as the Georgians and the Ossetians living in South Ossetia did not have fundamentally different visions of their respective futures. In the period before the Soviet break-up, Georgian nationalists envisioned their country being sovereign within the borders of Soviet Georgia, while Abkhazian and Ossetian nationalists saw the future of their nations outside it.[24] Russia did not need to invent this discord. Following their effective separation as a result of wars in the early 1990s,[25] the two communities have had no contacts with other parts of Georgia for a quarter of century. They are now even more confident in their belief that their fate is independent of Georgia's.

On the other hand, the Kremlin was a full participant in both conflicts from the very beginning. There has been no moment when the conflicts' dynamics could be understood without factoring in Russia. The latter was decisive in their actual outcomes. The conflicts started not *after* Georgia became independent (as some observers imagined), but *while* nationalist movements emerged in different parts of the Soviet Union (in 1988–89), including in Tbilisi, Sokhumi and Tskhinvali. These conflicts became part of a much bigger game on which the still unclear fate of the Soviet Union depended. The Kremlin naturally wanted to maintain the Union and considered national independence movements in the Union republics (including the one in Georgia) to be a major threat to state integrity. It had a direct interest in encouraging the separatist aspirations of Abkhazians and Ossetians in order to weaken and discredit its enemy (it pursued similar strategies in all of its independence-inclined constituent republics from the Union).

After the Soviet break-up, the situation changed, but commonalities of interest continued. Moscow maintained its interest in the formerly Soviet 'near abroad', and the separatist entities served as their natural allies: a weaker Georgia would be easier to dominate. The leading role in managing 'frozen' conflicts became the main trump card Russia had to influence its southern neighbours. While at this point Russia was very weak as an international player, its power (especially its military) still looked immense for local actors in the Caucasus. When Georgian, Abkhazian or Ossetian nationalists planned their next steps, they based them on calculations (or miscalculations) of Russia's expected reactions. This is what makes these conflicts triangular: they cannot be adequately understood either as stand-offs between two pairs of ethnic communities (Georgians and Abkhazians, Georgians and Ossetians), nor simply as a corollary to a larger Georgian–Russian dispute.

The outcome of the military stages of the conflicts led to the creation and partial consolidation of two de facto states. The positions of all three parties hardened into intractable and mutually exclusive stands. After the 2008 war, their space for manoeuvre narrowed even more. Both conflicts are 'frozen' in the sense that all sides tacitly recognize the status quo and accept that they cannot, and should not, try to change it by force. But the terms of the precarious peace, and especially Russia's role in it, were different before and after 2008. Until 2008, Russia, at least formally, acted as a neutral mediator, and that left space open for a negotiated solution, at least theoretically. The 'new reality' created after the war, and Russian recognition of the de facto states, removes all hope of a negotiated solution for the distant future. Georgia cannot possibly accept the independence of the secessionist territories; hence it cannot stop considering Russia other than as a hostile (occupying) power. Once Georgia decided to sever diplomatic relations, it is very difficult to find a face-saving way to restore them. Even a modest step suggesting that Georgia is reconciling itself to the 'new realities' might be politically suicidal for a government that undertakes it. At the same time, it is difficult to imagine Russia reversing its recognition of Abkhazia and South Ossetia, or Sokhumi and Tskhinvali accepting any kind of arrangement with Georgia short of formalizing their full separation (at least, until they enjoy Russian protection).

What is the way out of this deadlock? The position of Russia, as well as that of the de facto governments is that both conflicts are actually over: there are two new states, and Georgia and the rest of the world have to reconcile themselves to these 'new realities'.[26] But as long as the 'new realities' stay unrecognized, the two de facto states cannot be considered 'normal' parts of the international system, and this abnormality will affect the lives of the people who live there. Until some internationally valid agreement is achieved, there can be no closure. However, the status quo appears quite satisfactory for Russia which can actually draw benefits from the unrecognized character of these entities: they exclusively depend on their political patron and can safely be used as a Russian strategic outpost to the south of the Caucasus mountain range. Russia has another option: it can launch a full Crimea-like annexation of both regions. South Ossetia (though not Abkhazia) is quite eager to pursue that path.[27] This may happen at some point, though Russia has no strong reason to opt for that scenario. There are no obvious benefits it can draw from an annexation, and hypothetically, it can use the status of both territories as a bargaining chip with Georgia. Russia is quite prepared to treat the status quo as final without the need for further international legitimation.

Georgia's position is more difficult. It has to exercise 'strategic patience', which is a polite phrase for doing nothing, and wait for an undefined regional game-changer that may create some new opportunities. In the meantime, its actual interest is also to preserve the status quo, which in this case means prevention of further recognition of Abkhazia and South Ossetia. Georgia has been quite successful in doing so.[28] It also faces the difficult task of containing damage from destabilizing developments across the administrative boundary lines between Abkhazia and Tskhinvali regions on the one hand and Georgia proper on the other. Russia, as well as the de facto authorities of Sokhumi and Tskhinvali, consider these lines to be international borders, while Georgia (as well as the international community) does not. The resulting uncertainty leads to numerous problems related to 'borderization' (the arbitrary demarcation of the 'border' which often leaves some land plots out of reach of their owners, or results in people being detained for violating the border regime).[29]

For internal political reasons, the government cannot be seen as doing nothing, so it comes up with new initiatives to handle the conflict issue. For instance, since 2012, the government has publicized efforts to establish direct dialogue with the Sokhumi and Tskhinvali authorities, even though the latter have made it clear that they are not interested in any such contacts unless they are promised a prospect of recognition. In December 2020, the tables were reversed when the Abkhaz de facto leaders proposed new dialogue, but Tbilisi showed no interest.[30] There appears to be a tacit consensus that nothing can and will change for the time being. While this situation is uncomfortable for Georgia, it can only maintain some form of damage control.

Interrelations between the two triangular conflicts

Which of these triangular conflicts in which Georgia and Russia are involved are more important? How are they interconnected? Is Georgia's conflict with Russia primarily caused by divergent positions on separatist conflicts, or is the role that Russia plays in them motivated by its resentment of Georgia's pro-Western leanings? This is not obvious. One logical argument may be that it was disagreements on the issues of Abkhazia and South Ossetia that soured Russian–Georgian relations in the first place; afterwards, as Georgia was involved in an unequal conflict with its northern neighbour, it started to look towards the West for protection. Still later, these pro-Western policies of Georgia, and the West's generally benevolent, if also lukewarm and inconsistent response, further exacerbated the existing tensions between the two countries.

This narrative sounds logical, but there is another framework of analysis. From both Georgia's and Russia's perspectives (though not necessarily from a Western one), Georgia's agenda of independence from Russia and its linkage to the West are two sides of the same coin. As the national independence movement started to take shape in Georgia as early as 1988, it presumed that it was entitled to Western support, and actually expected it.[31] This assumption was based on continuity with Georgia's position in 1918–1921: at that time, Georgia presumed Russia was a threat and the West (first Germany, then the United Kingdom) was an ally, even if an ineffective one. It was hard for the Georgians to understand why the West supported the independence of the Baltic States, but not of Georgia; after all, independent Georgia had also been unlawfully annexed by Bolshevik Russia, although it happened earlier than in the Baltic States. During the April 1989 pro-independence demonstrations in Tbilisi, some speakers claimed that as soon as Georgia became independent from the Soviet Union, it would become a member of NATO.[32] At the time, such assumptions looked extremely naive – in fact, the West did not support Georgia's independence until the Soviet Union actually broke up in December 1991. However, there was a certain logic to this line of Georgian thinking that eventually proved prescient. The West supported democracy, but the democratic transformation of the Soviet regime made it impossible to preserve the integrity of the Soviet Union without giving up on democratic reforms (even if most Western politicians and Soviet Studies experts did not appreciate this connection). All popular democratic movements outside Russia were at the same time movements for independence – even the Russian Federation itself was part of this pattern, however strange it might have looked. This pro-independence tide could not possibly be reversed without large-scale violence and the re-establishing of extremely repressive regimes (something that conspirators behind the August 1991 Moscow putsch probably intended to do) – which the West could not possibly have supported. Hence, whatever calculations George H. Bush or Helmut Kohl might have had, by supporting any movement towards the liberalization of the Soviet regime or democratic movements, they were unwittingly supporting the Soviet demise (which included Georgia's independence). Support for democracy made the West into an effective ally of Georgian nationalists.

Once former Soviet republics became independent and the international community recognized them, it was in the interest of the West to support a new configuration of states. The principles of the post-Second World War liberal international order that now extended to the formerly communist world became the best hope for survival of small and vulnerable states like Georgia. But this order was sponsored and protected by the West (often referred to under the alias of 'the international community'). On the other hand, Russia considered the fact that norms of liberal international order now extended to its 'near abroad' to be a sign of its defeat, a status it never really accepted. To be sure, Russia contributed, through its democratic movement and the leadership of Boris Yeltsin, to former Union Republics becoming internationally recognized sovereign states. However, Yeltsin's Russia accepted the Soviet break-up in a fit of absent-mindedness, while being involved in a conflict for control of the Kremlin with Gorbachev.[33] As events showed, the Russian political elite never meant to accept the new nations as truly sovereign, hoping for some kind of 'reintegration'. Therefore, a country like Georgia could only consolidate its sovereignty within the Western-promoted liberal international order, while Russia considered the expansion of the norms of this order as the West's attempt to squeeze Russia out of its own zone of influence. By supporting the independence of Georgia and other post-Soviet countries, the West inevitably drew itself into a conflict with Russia, whether or not its political leaders were ready to admit this.

If this is true, the larger conflictual triangle between Georgia, Russia and the West superseded in its importance the territorial conflicts of Abkhazia and South Ossetia, even if most Georgians would consider the latter more emotionally painful. By the time of the 2008 war, this became clear, at least for Russians and Georgians (though not for all Westerners). While the Kremlin formally justified its intervention as protecting the peaceful population of South Ossetia and 'coercing Georgia into peace',[34] other statements of Russian officials show,[35] and most sober analysts agree, that the main motive of Russia's actions in August 2008 was to prevent Western (in particular, NATO) expansion to Russia's southern borders.[36] Because territorial conflicts constitute Georgia's main vulnerability, they became (at least, from the Russian perspective) an arena of geopolitical competition between itself and the West. This is a hard pill to swallow for the Abkhazians and the Ossetians who think they have their own accounts to settle with Georgia. However the problems started historically, they eventually became secondary to Georgia's triangular relations with Russia and the West. Admittedly, this is not the first time that small, local conflicts in the debris of a decaying empire have become part of great powers' geopolitical games.

How Georgia's Russia policy evolved

These overlapping conflicts have defined Georgian–Russian relations for the whole period of Georgian independence. However, they have also evolved over time. While the positions of the parties hardened in the 2000s, it was not like this all the time. At some points, there was genuine hope that things could develop in a different direction. Obviously, perpetual tension with Russia is extremely uncomfortable for Georgia and it has a strong interest in finding accommodation with its northern neighbour. Commentators may express suspicions that this or that political leader instrumentalizes the Russian threat in order to increase his popularity or discredit the opposition by calling it pro-Russian, therefore unpatriotic.[37] Occasionally, there may be some ground for such contentions. However, even if such instrumentalization may work in the short run, the benefits of the normalization of relations with Russia are too obvious for the public, so by improving relations with Russia not only would any Georgian government advance the national interest of its country, but it would also reap important benefits domestically.

This may explain a notable cyclical regularity in Georgia's Russia policies. Any new Georgian government accuses its predecessor of unnecessarily contributing to the deterioration in Georgian–Russian relations and promises to find ways of improving them. In each case, however, an initial rapprochement leads to eventual disappointment, and sometimes to periods of crisis. Eduard Shevardnadze's tenure (1992–2003)[38] is an obvious example of such dynamics. When he was brought back to Georgia after a bloody coup against his predecessor, he was presented as someone who could both improve relations with Russia (he came back after spending several years in Moscow as the Foreign Minister of the Soviet Union, and had good connections in the Russian political elite) and attract the support of the West (where he also had excellent connections and an image of a democratic reformer, due to his role in the unification of Germany and the dismantling of the Soviet outer empire in Eastern Europe). Initially, Shevardnadze was careful not to prioritize relations with Russia too much as Gamsakhurdia's supporters portrayed him as Russia's stooge, but he and many of his supporters believed that Georgia's fate, especially the outcome of the violent territorial conflicts that were underway at the time, depended on gaining Russia's goodwill. He was probably encouraged to think like that by his Western partners, as the early years of Yeltsin's presidency were a honeymoon in relations between Russia and the West, where the view was almost universally shared that Russia was a nascent democracy and could become a promising ally. So, stabilizing the new Russian democratic government was an unquestionable priority in the post-Soviet space. The West supported consolidation of the new smaller post-Soviet states as well, but not at the expense of spoiling relations with Russia (or so it was hoped).

As a result, the first half of the 1990s was probably the best, or rather the least bad period in Georgian–Russian relations. Relations could not be called good because Georgia quite openly accused Russia of siding with the separatist forces in its internal conflicts, and argued that Russia was the main reason why Georgia lost them. However, this was also a period when commentators agreed that there was no single centre defining Russia's policies towards its 'near abroad,' and it was popular to talk about 'two Russias,' a good, democratic one represented by Yeltsin and his supporters, and a bad one represented by conservative enemies of reforms, including those within Yeltsin's own government.[39]

Against this background, however, Georgia made important steps to normalize relations with its northern neighbour. While initially it refused to join the Russia-led Commonwealth of Independent States, in October 1993, immediately after its defeat in the Abkhazian war and facing an insurgency of supporters of the former president, Georgia yielded to Russian pressure and joined the organization. Even more importantly, in 1994 Georgia joined the Russia-led Collective Security Treaty Organization (CSTO), and in 1995 signed an agreement on hosting four Russian military bases in Georgia. This created the perception that Georgia had made a strategic choice in favour of 'bandwagoning'; that is, it decided to reduce threats coming from Russia by formalizing the latter's dominant position in bilateral relations.[40]

However, this decision proved short-lived. In return for its concessions, Georgia expected some tangible benefits in economic and security areas but did not receive them. To be precise, Shevardnadze did get some backing immediately after he declared its decision to join the CIS. When in September–October 1993, in the wake of Georgia's military defeat in Abkhazia, his government faced a military rebellion of supporters of the deposed president Zviad Gamsakhurdia in Western Georgia, the Russian demonstration of military support to the standing government (by sending a ship from its Black Sea Fleet to the port of Poti) may have played an important role in defeating the insurgents. However, Georgia did not get the most important thing it expected – Russian support for the restoration of its territorial integrity. The initial version of the treaty on the Russian military bases in Georgia included a clause saying that the treaty would come into force after the restoration of Georgia's territorial integrity. However, no progress was achieved on that account. Expectations of economic benefits did not materialize either: the dysfunctional Russian economy could not possibly work as a role model and magnet for Georgia.

As a result, gradually and almost imperceptibly, Shevardnadze's Georgia started to drift westwards in its policy orientation.[41] There were several expressions of this change: in 1999, Georgia quit its membership in the Collective Security Treaty Organization (CSTO), and following the agreement achieved at the 1999 OSCE Istanbul summit, started a process of dismantling Russian military bases on Georgian territory.[42] In contrast to the first 1994–96 Chechen War when Georgia strongly supported Russia's official position, in the second war that started in 1999, Georgia took a lukewarm or neutral stance, and even hosted Chechen refugees from the conflict in its Pankisi Gorge. Russia accused it of harbouring terrorists. Georgia mounted its cooperation with NATO and during the 2002 Prague summit of that organization, made a formal bid to join NATO. All this led to a sharp deterioration of relations with Russia, which reached a crisis point over the Pankisi issue.[43]

Mikheil Saakashvili, a US-educated lawyer who came to power as a result of the November 2003 'Rose Revolution', is mostly remembered as an anti-Russian firebrand whose policies may have been partly responsible for the direct military conflict with Russia in 2008. Not many people remember, however, that initially, he sharply criticized his predecessor for unnecessarily moving strategically important relations with Russia to a point of crisis, and promised to find an understanding with President Putin.[44] Saakashvili started by 'extending his hand to Putin' and tried to strike a deal by opening the doors to Russian business in Georgia, and going after Chechen fighters who happened to be in his country.[45] In return, Russia was expected not to oppose Georgia's efforts to solve its territorial conflicts, and advance on the way to European and Euro-Atlantic integration. As in Shevardnadze's case, Saakashvili's government drew some initial benefit: Russia did not try to stop Georgia from ousting Aslan Abashidze, an autocratic but also openly pro-Russian leader of the autonomous republic of Achara – even though it had a military base there.[46] The withdrawal of the Russian military bases from Georgian territory was another important landmark in bilateral relations that could not have been achieved without a modicum of cooperation between the two countries.[47]

But this honeymoon proved even more short-lived than in Shevardnadze's case. The story is well known and does not need lengthy recapitulation. The souring of relations started from Georgia's attempt to re-establish control over South Ossetia in July–August 2004,[48] and peaked in a Russian military invasion in August 2008. Many commentators believe that Georgia's progress in its relations with NATO and the ambiguous decision of the April 2008 NATO Bucharest summit where Georgia was denied a Membership Action Plan but promised eventual membership at some undefined point in the future, was the root cause of the conflict.[49] In the final period of Saakashvili's rule (until October 2012),[50] relations with Russia remained frozen at an extremely low point, with Georgia having severed diplomatic relations with its neighbour in the wake of the August 2008 war, and routinely referring to Russia as an 'occupying power' in Abkhazia and South Ossetia.

The next Georgian government of Georgian Dream, a party (initially also a coalition of parties) created by a Georgian billionaire turned politician, Bidzina Ivanishvili, started with a similar message. It blamed Saakashvili's allegedly irresponsible policies for the deterioration in Georgia–Russia relations that led to the August War, and promised to normalize them. This was probably one of the most important promises of its pre-election campaign,[51] and could have contributed to its victory as many voters might be afraid that Saakashvili's uncompromising stance could lead to more complications with its northern neighbour. Georgian Dream considerably softened Georgia's anti-Russian rhetoric and created the position of Special Envoy for relations with Russia, entrusting it to a seasoned diplomat, Zurab Abashidze.[52] The result was the creation of the so-called Karasin-Abashidze format, a series of direct meetings between Abashidze and his Russian counterpart Grigory Karasin, deputy Minister of Foreign Relations. In its rhetoric, the new Georgian government was extremely cautious not to incite Russian wrath. For instance, it abstained from shows of solidarity with Ukraine during its conflict with Russia which began in 2014, in spite of obvious similarities and links to Georgia's own conflict with Russia in 2008. Despite this, however, Georgia did not go as far as restoring diplomatic relations, reiterating the position of the previous government that Russia already has two embassies in Georgia (in Abkhazia and South Ossetia), which has made the opening of a third one impossible. It continued to formally refer to Russia as an 'occupying power' in Abkhazia and South Ossetia, though it did not use this term as frequently. Zurab Abashidze's mandate only included discussing economic and humanitarian cooperation with Russia. The greatest benefit Georgia got from this new rapprochement was the lifting of Russia's blockade against the import of Georgian agricultural produce to Russia. Russian tourism to Georgia also increased dramatically – but that trend had already started under Saakashvili's government, which unilaterally lifted the visa regime for Russian citizens (Georgian travellers to Russia do not have that same privilege).[53]

There are still no tangible signs of further improvements in Georgia–Russia relations.[54] There is no deterioration that could be compared to Shevardnadze's and Saakashvili's period either, although the general dynamics are not necessarily positive. In March 2018, following a series of episodes when Georgian citizens were arrested and in some cases killed for alleged violations of the visa regime between the de facto states and Georgia proper, the Georgian parliament adopted a law on creating a 'Otkhozoria-Tatunashvili list' that obliges the government to blacklist officials of Russian, as well as de facto Abkhazian and South Ossetian governments involved in the death, kidnapping, torture or mistreatment of Georgian citizens on the occupied territories of Abkhazia and South Ossetia.[55] Later, in the wake of a former Russian security operative and his daughter being poisoned in the United Kingdom, Georgia showed solidarity with Western nations by expelling one Russian diplomat from a Russian section of the Swiss embassy in Georgia.[56]

This does not imply that Georgian–Russian relations are doomed to deteriorate to the low point they reached during the time of Shevardnadze and Saakashvili. The Georgian Dream government appears to be more committed than its predecessors to prevent this and appears to be giving greater priority to improving bilateral relations. Its failure to achieve substantive progress despite an obvious wish to do so demonstrates, however, that as long as any Georgian government pursues the traditional policy of European and Euro-Atlantic integration, the future of Georgian–Russian relations will remain murky.

Alternatives and prospects

Are Georgian–Russian relations doomed to remain antagonistic? Can there be any genuine game-changing event in this area? If not, how can Georgia proceed from this point, when it comes to relations with its most powerful neighbour? As I hope to have shown, Georgia's insistence on its pro-Western course, the West's encouragement of such policies (even if cautious and often half-hearted) and Russia's resentment of this constitute the core reasons for the conflict. At least one side of this triangle has to change its policies and approaches in an essential way in order to change the dynamics. Possible scenarios within the smaller triangle – related to Georgia's territorial conflicts – should also be considered in order to properly establish the future of bilateral relations.

Hypothetically, Georgia could change its attitudes in two ways. The first is the issue of Abkhazia and South Ossetia. Could Georgia at some point decide to cut its losses and accept the 'new realities', that is, recognize the independence of its lost provinces? Russia openly encourages her to do so, while some Western friends may also informally give similar advice. Such a turn would probably take the extremely painful and emotional element out of Georgian–Russian relations. However, at this point, this kind of reversal in Georgia's policy appears quite unthinkable and is never even discussed. This is despite the August 2008 war and Georgians' acceptance of the fact that the prospect of restoring territorial integrity is very remote. There is no political party or even civic organization of any influence which advocates solving the conflict through official recognition of the breakaway regions. It would be an extraordinary precedent in international politics. Despite harsh criticism of its predecessors' policies with regards to territorial conflict, in effect Georgian Dream follows the same policies.[57] One can also imagine a fundamental shift in public attitudes that would make it possible for Georgia to discuss the possibility of major concessions on this issue. However, there would have to be great and tangible benefits for Georgia if it opts for such a reversal – and no such benefits are in sight. If we are right in contending that it is Russia's opposition to Georgia's policies of Western integration that is the core reason for tension, at this point there are no guarantees that even a dramatic change of direction in Georgian policies on the territorial issue would bring genuinely substantive improvement to bilateral relations.

One can imagine another fundamental reversal of direction in Georgia's policies, which would be dropping its pro-Western policies in favour of neutrality or direct association with the Russia-led Eurasian Union. While discussing recognition of lost territories remains a taboo, there is an increasing number of political groups, civil society and media organizations that support such a change of policy: some of them oppose both European and Euro-Atlantic integration; others only oppose the insistence on NATO membership. The number proliferated after the 2008 war, and this may be explained not only by a perception that the West did not support Georgia in the face of Russian aggression, but also by Russia's much more direct support of anti-Western populist forces everywhere, including Georgia.[58] The arguments of the anti-Western forces are related to both security (allegedly, Georgia unnecessarily spoiled its relations with Russia when it opted for the West – even though the latter does not really support Georgia), and culture. The latter argument is that Westernization undermines Georgian identity by promoting 'immorality' (like homosexuality), and co-religionist Russia has the best chance to protect Georgia from this pernicious influence.

This active populist propaganda has worked to some extent. Following the 2016 parliamentary elections, the first populist anti-Western party, the *Alliance of Patriots, Georgia,* cleared the barrier to enter parliament – but only with 5 per cent of the vote. According to some recent polls, support for Georgia joining the Russian-led Eurasian Economic Union is now over 20 per cent (reaching 25 per cent in some polls).[59] Those changes have become the source of serious concern for those who are committed to a European Georgia. However, so far these trends have not reached any critical level. Public support for EU and NATO integration is still solid – the same polls show it to stand in the vicinity of 60–70 per cent. Fears that a party created by Bidzina Ivanishvili, a reclusive billionaire who enriched himself in Russia in the 1990s, would reverse Georgia's political course, did not materialize. A large majority of the political elite remains committed to a pro-Western course. This does not mean that public attitudes, or Georgian policies, may not change in the future – at this point we can only say that they have been fairly stable.

What about the two other sides of the triangle? Can we imagine any fundamental change in Russia's policies, for instance, after the political demise of Vladimir Putin? Nothing can be precluded here either. However, the perception of the West as Russia's enemy appears to be rooted in the Russian political elite and the public, with most political groups of any influence sharing it. It is especially hard to imagine that any of Putin's successors would step back from Russia's recognition of Abkhazia and South Ossetia. That makes any forthcoming substantive change in Russia's policies towards Georgia and the West fairly unlikely.

The last hypothetical scenario would be the West giving up any support of liberal international order and, in particular, accepting Russia's view of a tacit division of the world into great power zones of influence – with Georgia becoming part of the Russian share. This is a recurrent fear of small countries like Georgia, that they will be short-changed in some big international deal between great powers. As mentioned above, the election of Donald Trump and the successes of right- and left-wing populist parties in Europe that all question some fundamental assumptions behind the liberal international order, put the sustainability of the latter under question. This might imply that Georgia will lose the existing level of Western support that had enabled it to follow a fairly independent foreign policy.

Again, nothing can be excluded here, although expectations may have proved exaggerated. The policies of the Trump administration towards Russia proved more muscular, and Georgia actually got greater support in matters of security than it did in the period of the Obama administration – for instance, through sales of Javelin missiles to Georgia.[60] On the other side of the Atlantic, populist anti-establishment parties (who also tend to be more accommodating to Putin's Russia) have achieved important gains in several European countries, but no fundamental changes in relations to Russia (such as the lifting of sanctions, for instance) ensued. There is no doubt that international order has become even more precarious and unpredictable, but it is too early to speak about the principles of liberal international order in the past tense. As noted above, Joe Biden's victory in 2020 will lead to a change in US policy toward a more consistently rules-based international order.

This means that at this point Georgia has no specific incentives to change its Russia policies. It suffered from bad relations with Russia: it lost 20 per cent of its territory, and is in an unstable region bordering an unpredictable Russia (as well as an increasingly unpredictable Turkey). This has hardly been conducive to the country's security, or its political and economic development. However, one can also summarize the story in a positive light: Georgia not only survived these misfortunes, but progressed in many ways and has established itself as a fairly stable and successful country. Why change tack?

Notes

1. The West in this chapter is defined as the states of western Europe and North America, as well as the key organizations associated with the post-Second World War international order, most importantly NATO and the European Union.
2. P.J. Katzenstein (ed.), *The Culture of National Security: Norms and Identity in World Politics* (New York: Columbia University Press, 1996).
3. For a similar approach, though with different conclusions, see A.P. Tsygankov and T. Marver-Wahlquist, 'Duelling Honors: Power, Identity and the Russia–Georgia Divide', *Foreign Policy Analysis*, 5:4 (October 2009).
4. Other parts of today's Georgia were gradually incorporated from the Russian Empire, or annexed after the Russian–Ottoman wars, during the nineteenth century.
5. Z. Avalov, *Prisoedinenie Gruzii k Rosssii* [The Joining of Georgia to Russia] (St Peterburg: A. Souvorine Publishers, 1901); D. Rayfield, *Edge of Empires: A History of Georgia* (London: Reaktion Books, 2012).
6. The territory of today's Georgia included Tbilisi and Kutaisi gubernias (provinces) and Sukhumskii Okrug (more or less today's Abkhazia).
7. There were anti-Russian rebellions and conspiracies in later years, but not in the immediate aftermath of the annexation – see Rayfield, *Edge of Empires,* pp. 258–264.
8. O. Reisner, *Die Schule der Georgischen Nation* [The Schooling of the Georgian Nation] (Wiesbaden: Reichert Verlag, 2004). The *tergdaleulebi* got their name from the symbolic crossing of the river Terek in Georgia's north into Russia, and by extension, Europe. Literally, the term refers to 'those who had drunk from the river Terek'.
9. E. Lee, *Experiment: Georgia's Forgotten Revolution 1918–1921* (London: ZED books, 2017).
10. The concept of Georgia's European identity can already be found in the *Tergdaleulebi*, but until the Bolshevik coup, Georgian elites still considered Russia as a broadly Europeanizing power for Georgia.
11. I have developed this point in 'The Georgian Perception of the West', in *Commonwealth and Independence in Post-Soviet Eurasia* ed. B. Coppieters, A. Zverev and D. Trenin (London and Portland, OR: Frank Cass, 1998), pp. 12–43.
12. Rayfield, *Edge of Empires*, pp. 323–38; Lee, *The Experiment*, pp. 195–215.
13. See, for instance, L. Vasadze, 'Eri da sakhelmtsipo' (Nation and State), 18 March 2005, www.kvirispalitra.ge/politic/16259- ... helmtsifoq.html?start=8 (accessed 18 December 2018).
14. This was rather expressed in private.
15. The so-called Tagliavini report became the official representation of this Western view – see *Independent International Fact-Finding Mission on the Conflict in*

Georgia: Report, 2009, www.mpil.de/en/pub/publications/archive/independent_international_fact.cfm (accessed 18 December 2018). See also C. Welt, 'After the EU War Report: Can There Be a "Reset" in Russian–Georgian Relations?', *Russian Analytical Digest,* 68:9 November 2009).

16 G.W. Lapidus, 'Insecurity: Russian Elite Attitudes and the Russia–Georgia Crisis', *Post-Soviet Affairs,* 23:2 (2007).

17 See 'What Was the Liberal Order: The World We May Be Losing', *Foreign Affairs,* Special Issue March 2017.

18 K. Bennett, 'Georgia's Dilemma', *The American Interest,* July 2007, www.the-american-interest.com/2017/07/10/georgias-dilemma/ (accessed 18 December 2018).

19 Some Western analysts agree – see, for instance, J.J. Mearsheimer, 'Why the Ukraine Crisis is the West's Fault: The Liberal Delusions that Provoked Putin', *Foreign Affairs,* September–October 2014; G. Allison, 'The Myth of the Liberal Order: From Historical Accident to Conventional Wisdom', *Foreign Affairs,* July/August 2018.

20 B. Mezhuev, 'O realizme i beregakh tsivilizatsii' [On Realism and the Shores of Civilization] *Vzglyad* newspaper, 13 January 2017, https://vz.ru/columns/2017/1/13/853243.html (accessed 18 December 2018).

21 See, for instance, S. Karaganov, '2016 – A Victory of Conservative Realism', *Russia in Global Affairs,* February 2017, http://eng.globalaffairs.ru/number/2016–A-Victory-of-Conservative-Realism-18585 (accessed 18 December 2018).

22 E. Rumer and A. Weiss, *Back to Basics on Russia Policy,* Carnegie Endowment for International Peace, March 2021, https://carnegieendowment.org/2021/03/09/back-to-basics-on-russia-policy-pub-84016 (accessed 19 March 2021).

23 The conflicts in Abkhazia and South Ossetia are also different from each other, but in this context these differences may be ignored.

24 Initially, Abkhazians and southern Ossetians might have accepted some kind of loose union with Georgia, but this was a tactical move: full separation was always preferable.

25 The Georgian–Ossetian conflict ended in July 1992 with the Dagomys agreement, while the Georgian–Abkhazian war was effectively ended in September 1993, though the terms of the ceasefire were formally defined by the April 1994 Moscow Agreement.

26 See, for instance, 'Karasin: abkhaziia i iuzhnaia ossetiia sostoialis kak suverennie gosudarstva', *RIA Novosti,* 7 August 2018, https://ria.ru/world/20180807/1526059192.html (accessed 18 December 2018).

27 P. Gaprindashvili, 'How to Improve Georgia-Russia Talks?' in *Georgia and Russia: in Search of Ways for Normalization* (Tbilisi: Georgian Foundation for Strategic and International Studies, 2017).

28 Venezuela, Nicaragua and Nauru are the three states apart from Russia that recognized Abkhazia and South Ossetia (between September 2008 and December 2009). In 2011, Tuvalu and Vanuatu, two tiny Pacific island states, also recognized them, but subsequently withdrew their recognition. Since that time only Syria, whose regime fully depends on Russia, joined the club by recognizing both entities in May 2018.

29 See E. Boyle, 'Borderization in Georgia: Sovereignty Materialized', *Eurasia Border Review,* 2018, http://src-h.slav.hokudai.ac.jp/publictn/eurasia_border_review/Vol71/01-Boyle.pdf (accessed 18 December 2018); K. Kakachia, 'How the West Should Respond to Russia's "Borderization" in Georgia', *PONARS Eurasia Policy Memo No. 523,* April 2018.

30 *Civil Georgia,* 'Abkhazia's Shamba Tells Tbilisi: "We Are Ready to Talk"', 21 December 2020, https://civil.ge/archives/388091, accessed 3 March 2021.

31 Respective assumptions were often made during speeches at rallies which this author attended then, and discussion in which he took part.

32 Soviet leader Mikhail Gorbachev later justified violent suppression of this demonstration by the impossibility to tolerate such outrageously 'irresponsible' statements. See C. Neef, 'The Gorbachev Files: Secret Papers Reveal Truth behind Soviet Collapse', *Spiegel Online*, 11 April 2011, www.spiegel.de/international/europe/the-gorbachev-files-secret-papers-reveal-truth-behind-soviet-collapse-a-779277.html (accessed 18 December 2018).

33 S. Plokhy, *The Last Empire: The Final Days of the Soviet Union* (New York: Basic Books, 2014).

34 D. Medvedev, *Address to the Federal Assembly of the Russian Federation*, 5 November 2008, http://en.kremlin.ru/events/president/transcripts/1968 (accessed 18 December 2018).

35 'Medvedev: esli by ne voina s Gruziei, v NATO priniali by neskolko stran, vopreki pozitsii Rossii' [Medvedev: if it wasn't for the war with Georgia, a number of countries would have been taken into NATO, despite the position of Russia] gazeta.ru, 21 November 2011, www.gazeta.ru/news/lenta/2011/11/21/n_2104434.shtml (accessed 18 December 2018).

36 R. Asmus, *A Little War that Shook the World: Georgia, Russia, and the Future of the West* (New York: Palgrave Macmillan, 2010); S.E. Cornell and F. Starr (eds), *The Guns of August 2008: Russia's War in Georgia* (London: M.E. Sharpe, 2009); R. Allison, 'Russia Resurgent? Moscow's Campaign to "Coerce Georgia to Peace"', *International Affairs*, 84:6 (2008); M. Van Herpen, *Putin's Wars: The Rise of Russia's New Imperialism* (Lanham, MD: Rowman & Littlefield, 2015).

37 Mikheil Saakashvili was more often the object of such criticism, though the anti-Russian card might have been played by other political leaders as well. See, for instance, G. Khelashvili, 'Georgia's Foreign Policy Impasse: Is Consensus Crumbling?' – *PONARS Eurasia Policy Memo* No. 187, September 2011, www.ponarseurasia.org/sites/default/files/policy-memos-pdf/pepm_187.pdf (accessed 18 December 2018).

38 Shevardnadze served as the chairman of parliament and the head of state (1992–95), and later as the president.

39 See on this R. Koiava, E. Baghaturia and Y. Nikitina, *Georgia and Russia: Bilateral View on the Quarter Century Relations*, Research Report (Tbilisi: Caucasian House, 2017), p. 13.

40 H. Frazer, *A Case of Bandwagoning? Georgian Foreign Policy and Relations with Russia* (University of Oxford. MPhil in International Relations, 1997).

41 For the best source on the evolution of Shevardnadze's foreign policy, see the memoirs of his long-time foreign policy adviser: Gela Charkviani, *Natsnob Kimerata perkhuli* (in Georgian, The Dance of Familiar Ghosts) (Tbilisi: Intelekti, 2016).

42 The process was only complete by 2006, when the last Russian bases in Adjara and Samtskhe-Javakheti left Georgia's territory. (The one in Abkhazia did not, for obvious reasons.)

43 Russia considered the situation in Pankisi a security threat to itself and pressured Georgia to allow its military forces to enter the Gorge and 'establish order' there; Georgia, however, refused and opted for US help through the Georgia Train and Equip Program. After this, the situation in Pankisi started to normalize, but Russia was angered by the precedent of the appearance of the US military on its southern borders. See J. Devdariani and B. Hancilova, *Georgia's Pankisi Gorge: Russian, US and European Connections*, Centre for European Policy Studies (CEPS), Brussels, Policy Brief No. 23, June 2002.

44 S. Lambroschini, 'Georgia: Russia Watches Warily as Saakashvili Comes to Power', *RFE/RL*, 6 January 2004, www.rferl.org/a/1051076.html (accessed 18 December 2018).

45 *Civil Georgia*, 'Saakashvili Warns over "Wahhabism Threat" in Georgia', 19 February 2004, www.civil.ge/eng/article.php?id=6258 (accessed 18 December 2018).

46 *The Economist*, 'The President of Georgia Wins His Standoff in Adjaria', 6 May 2004, www.economist.com/node/2652962 (accessed 18 December 2018).

47 K. Kakachia, 'End of Russian Military Bases in Georgia: Social, Political and Security Implications of Withdrawal', *Central Asia and the Caucasus*, 50:2 (2008).

48 J-C. Peuch, 'Russia Weighs in as Fighting Continues in South Ossetia', *RFE/RL*, 19 August 2004, www.rferl.org/a/1054397.html (accessed 18 December 2018).

49 Asmus, *A Little War*, pp. 137–40.

50 Saakashvili served as president one more year, until October 2013, but following the defeat of his UNM party in October 2012 parliamentary elections he gave up all effective levers to influence Georgia's policies.

51 I. Haindrava (ed) *Georgian–Russian Relations: Old Difficulties and New Possibilities* (Tbilisi: Caucasian House, 2013), p. 38.

52 'PM Appoints Special Envoy for Relations with Russia', 1 November 2012, www.civil. ge/eng/article.php?id=25407 (accessed 18 December 2018).

53 T. Romanova, 'Economic Links of Russia and Georgia and their Potential for Improving Bilateral Relations', in *Georgia and Russia: In Search of Ways for Normalization* (Tbilisi: Georgian Foundation for Strategic and International Studies, 2017), pp. 31–8.

54 S.N. MacFarlane, 'Two Years of the Dream: Georgian Foreign Policy during the Transition', Chatham House Russia and Eurasia Program, May 2015.

55 JAM News, 'Georgian Parliament Passes "Otkhozoria-Tatunashvili list" Sanction Bill', 22 March 2018, https://jam-news.net/?p=90162 (accessed 18 December 2018).

56 After bilateral diplomatic relations were severed, Switzerland served as facilitator of relations between the two countries by opening sections in its Moscow and Tbilisi embassies where a limited number of, respectively, Georgian and Russian diplomats serve. JAM News, 'Georgia Expels Russian Diplomat', 29 March 2018, https://jam-news.net/?p=93969 (accessed 18 December 2018).

57 I have elaborated on this point in 'Rhetoric for substance? GD's Abkhazia, S. Ossetia Policy Five Years On', *Civil Georgia*, 11 September 2017, www.civil.ge/eng/article. php?id=30429 (accessed 18 December 2018).

58 L. Tughushi (ed.) *Threats of Russian Hard and Soft Power in Georgia* (Tbilisi: European Initiative – Liberal Academy, 2016), www.ei-lat.ge/images/doc/threats%20 of%20russian%20soft%20and%20hard%20power.pdf (accessed 18 December 2018); N. Dzvelishvili and T. Kupreishvili, *Russian Influence on Georgian NGOs and Media*, 2015, Tbilisi, https://idfi.ge/public/upload/russanimpactongeorgianmediadaNGO.pdf (accessed 18 December 2018).

59 L. Thornton and K. Turmanidze, *Public Attitudes in Georgia: Results of an April 2017 Survey Carried out for NDI by CRRC Georgia*, www.ndi.org/sites/default/files/NDI%20 poll_june%202017_ISSUES_ENG_VF.pdf (accessed 18 December 2018).

60 'Pence Conveys US Support for Georgia in Visit to Tbilisi', *RFE/RL*, 1 August 2017, www.rferl.org/a/pence-us-baltic-nations-georgia/28651230.html (accessed 18 December 2018); J. LaPorta, 'State Dept. Approves Potential Javelin Missile Sale to Georgia', UPI, 21 November 2017, www.upi.com/State-Dept-approves-potential-Javelin-missile-sale-to-Georgia/8371511279229/ (accessed 18 December 2018).

Chapter 11

US–GEORGIAN RELATIONS: EXPANDING THE CAPACITY OF A SMALL STATE

Mamuka Tsereteli

The US–Georgian relationship since the independence of Georgia in 1991 presents an interesting case of partnership between large and small states driven by, but not limited to, common interests, historic geopolitical context, strategic priorities, domestic political agendas and strong personalities. Due to these multiple factors, Georgia managed to garner more focus and attention from Washington than many other, larger, and perhaps strategically more important countries. While there was no history of state-to-state relationships in the past, there was significant interaction of Georgians and Americans prior to Georgia regaining its independence. The first publicly known introduction of Georgians into the United States goes back to the late nineteenth century, when horse riders from the Western Georgian province of Guria joined Buffalo Bill's *Wild West Show* and travelled around the United States. They were presented to the US public as Cossacks or Russians, but they were, in fact, the first unofficial ambassadors of Georgia.

There were very limited political interactions between Georgia and the United States during the first Georgian republic of 1918–21, and the United States, unlike its allies (France, the United Kingdom and Italy), did not recognize the independence of Georgia. At the same time the American Relief Mission, led by Colonel Haskell, was present in Tbilisi, but the Mission was mainly focused on providing humanitarian assistance to the Armenian Republic. US congressman Walter M. Chandler, who was hired by the Georgian government to lobby in the United States on Georgia's behalf, travelled to the former Russian Empire in 1919 and urged the House Ways and Means Committee to support Estonian, Lithuanian, Latvian, Azerbaijani and Georgian sovereignty. He requested the Secretary of the Treasury Carter Glass, and the head of the American Relief Administration, Herbert Hoover, to send financial support to countries which served as potential barriers against Bolshevism.[1] But the Democratic Republic of Georgia, despite intense activity at the Paris Peace Conference in 1919, did not manage to insert itself even into the peripheral vision of the Americans. In the end the United States, like other Western powers, did very little to prevent the Bolshevik invasion and annexation of Georgia in 1921. The Allies supplied no arms, and the mandate that Georgia was pursuing was never granted. While the context is very different today, three decades of independent statehood since 1991 have shown Georgians that many of the geopolitical patterns that determined Georgia's fate in 1918–21 are still present and require significant attention.[2]

The Soviet period (1921–91) brought some economic and cultural interactions between Georgians and Americans. American businessman and diplomat Avril Harriman invested in Chiatura's manganese production in Western Georgia. The Soviet government, lacking resources in the 1920s, was keen to revive the manganese mines and production with Harriman's help. It was thought he might assist with US diplomatic recognition of the USSR. The policy of 'concessions' to Western investors was also important to the success of Lenin's New Economic Policy introduced in 1921. Harriman capitalized the Georgian Manganese Company with 4 million USD of his own money, agreeing to pay significant fixed royalties per ton to both the Soviet government and to the previous Georgian owners of the mines. In its first year of operations in 1925, Harriman's company increased the mine's production from 436,000 tons to 772,000 tons. But soon after, global prices declined and production became unprofitable. In 1928, Harriman negotiated a buyout agreement with the Soviet government.[3]

One of the most significant cultural interactions in the US–Soviet relationship was the travel of John Steinbeck with photographer Robert Capa to the Soviet Union, including Georgia, in 1948. After the trip, Steinbeck published *A Russian Journal*, detailing his experiences with a significant focus on Georgia. The text remains one of the best introductions to Georgia for Americans.[4] The US government started to pay some attention to the non-Russian ethnic groups of the Soviet Union in the early 1950s, and the first Georgian service broadcasting of the Voice of America from New York commenced on 26 May 1951. Radio Liberty started its own Georgian service from Munich in 1953. Some employees of Radio Free Europe and Radio Liberty joined Zbigniew Brzezinski's National Security Council under President Carter in 1977, and formed a Soviet Nationalities section, led by Paul Henze. A very experienced and knowledgeable group of experts collaborating with the group included Bill Griffiths, Richard Pipes and Alexander Bennigsen. In parallel, the Net Assessment unit at the Pentagon, in collaboration with the Rand Corporation experts S. Enders Wimbush and Alex Alexiev, began to research the different nationalities in the Soviet Union, including Georgians – which soon opened up a challenge to the Soviet Russian concept of a united Soviet people.[5]

Early years of independence

The Soviet Union began to fragment in the 1980s. The national independence movement in Georgia became a mass movement after Soviet troops killed twenty-one demonstrators in Tbilisi on 9 April 1989. Georgian nationalist leaders viewed the United States as a potential ally in their quest for separation from the USSR and international recognition. The parliamentary elections in Soviet Georgia on 28 October 1990, was the beginning of the end of Soviet rule in Georgia and brought Zviad Gamsakhurdia to power, first as the chairman of the Supreme Council of Georgia, and after the 26 May 1991 presidential elections, as president. Gamsakhurdia, the leader of the Round Table Free Georgia electoral bloc, made it his priority to establish relations with the United States. A parliamentary delegation and then a Georgian government delegation visited the United States in 1991 and held multiple meetings on Capitol Hill. On 31 March 1991, Georgia held a referendum on independence from the Soviet Union. Former US President Richard Nixon was in Georgia at the time, on a factfinding visit to the Soviet Union. He met Zviad Gamsakhurdia and visited several Georgian regions, before departing for Moscow.[6]

Diplomatic relations between Georgia and the United States were established on 4 March 1992. President George H.W. Bush announced the decision in a press statement.[7] On 23 April 1992, the first American Embassy in Tbilisi opened, with Carey Cavanaugh as Chargé d'Affaires *ad interim*. Kent Brown was appointed the first US ambassador in September 1992. The first official visit of a senior US official to Georgia was by the US Secretary of State, James Baker III, in May 1992, arriving in Tbilisi on the eve of Independence Day on May 26. Georgia opened its diplomatic office in Washington in 1993, with Georgia's ambassador to the UN, Petre Chkheidze, assuming the responsibilities of the Ambassador to the United States as well. In March 1994, Eduard Shevardnadze, the newly elected head of state, paid his first official visit to the United States. Due to his past career as the Soviet Minister of Foreign Affairs and his personal friendship with James Baker, Shevardnadze enjoyed strong personal support and respect in official Washington circles.

The first visit of a Georgian leader to Washington was significant for many reasons: it helped Shevardnadze establish personal relationships with President Clinton, his senior cabinet members and leading members of Congress. Shevardnadze also met the chairman of the Joint Chiefs of Staff, General John Shalikashvili, the highest-ranking Georgian American serving in the US government. The visit facilitated the beginning of Georgia's relationships with international financial institutions like the World Bank and IMF, both of which became vital to Georgia's economic recovery in the 1990s. Georgia opened its first fully staffed embassy in the United States in November 1994, under Ambassador Tedo Japaridze. The embassy was tasked to establish contacts with the different parts of the US government, and to solicit growing US political support and economic aid for Georgia.

By the beginning of the 1990s, after the fall of the USSR, the United States had developed several interests in the broader Black Sea-Caspian region. The United States, first and foremost, wished to maintain stability in the region to prevent the proliferation of nuclear materials and avoid ethnic conflicts. Potentially, the flow of refugees could destabilize US allies in Europe. It was important to support the sovereignty of the newly established states and provide both humanitarian and economic aid. American and Western companies were particularly interested in exporting the rich energy resources of the Caspian Sea basin to global markets. The American company Chevron was the leader of the exploration and development of the Tengiz oil field in Kazakhstan, while the multinational British Petroleum led the consortium with American companies Amoco, Exxon, Arco, Norwegian Statoil and others, in exploration and development of the Azerbaijani oil fields in the offshore area east of Baku in the Caspian Sea. All the commercial actors involved in these projects were looking at Georgia as a potential transit country, initially mostly for oil, but later also for natural gas. The success of these projects drastically transformed Georgia's global role from a small and unstable former Soviet state into an energy transit country with global significance. Georgia, led by President Shevardnadze, who understood the potential benefits of the oil development in the Caspian basin to Georgia, was a proactive participant in this process from the early years of Georgian independence.[8]

Domestically, 1991–94 was a very challenging period for Georgia, marked with dramatic civil and ethno-political conflicts, as well as political instability following the military coup against the first President Zviad Gamsakhurdia in December 1991–January 1992. But by the end of 1994, US support, and cooperation with the International Monetary Fund and World Bank, played a considerable role in stabilizing Georgia's economy. The parliament elected in 1995 under a new constitution, created with the help of US constitutional experts, supported Georgia's pro-Western course, and the first wave of legislative reforms was initiated, creating basic laws for entrepreneurial activities and the protection of investments. From 1995 Georgia became a good example for various international financial institutions, and most importantly at that time for the World Bank and the IMF, which provided Georgia with loans for budgetary support and the stabilization of the monetary system. This allowed Georgia to move forward from its temporary stopgap currency of Georgian 'coupons' to the introduction of the Georgian Lari.

US humanitarian assistance was a critical element in the survival of the Georgian state in those early years of independence, particularly during and after the conflicts in Tskhinvali region (South Ossetia) and in Abkhazia in the first half of the 1990s. US aid evolved from humanitarian to technical assistance, supporting reforms in a wide range of areas that included the economy, education, governance reforms and border security. In the 1990s, the US government provided over 860 million USD in total aid to Georgia, or 96 USD million a year on average.[9] In parallel with the humanitarian and technical assistance, the United States took a proactive stand in the promotion of energy infrastructure projects in the Caspian region. The Clinton administration established a special diplomatic position of Assistant to the President and the Secretary of State on Caspian affairs, with responsibilities for facilitating energy exploration projects in the Caspian region, and for the development of the special infrastructure for delivery of energy resources to world markets. The oil discoveries in the Caspian Sea necessitated a new transportation network and created opportunities for the South Caucasus to serve as an important link in a new transit route from Central Asia to Europe and the Mediterranean, via Georgia, Azerbaijan and Turkey.

The development of energy infrastructure became the primary focus and policy instrument of Western (and US) engagement with the South Caucasus. There was a desire in the United States and Europe to help newly independent states of the former Soviet Union build their own sovereign economies. The United States and regional countries like Turkey, supported a multiple pipeline strategy that envisioned the development of multiple new commercial pipelines crossing several countries, including Russia. The only regional country which did not gain any benefit from the regional energy strategy was Armenia. In the absence of a comprehensive peace plan, the territorial gains that Armenia obtained after its conflict with Azerbaijan in the first Karabagh war by 1994 seemed more valuable than participation in regional energy projects.

The close collaboration of the United States, Turkey, Azerbaijan, Georgia, as well as Kazakhstan in the implementation of the South Caucasian transit strategy, played a crucial role in building strong economic and trade links between the Caspian and Black Sea/Mediterranean Sea ports. The construction of the early oil pipeline between Azerbaijan and the Georgian port of Supsa was completed in 1999. This was followed by the commission of major oil and natural gas pipelines between Azerbaijan, Georgia and Turkey in 2005 and 2006 respectively. This solidified the region's dramatic break from the political and energy dominance of Russia. Despite serious conflicts in Nagorno-Karabagh, Abkhazia and Tskhinvali region (South Ossetia), political intimidation from Russia failed to prevent the construction of world-class infrastructure projects which changed the strategic configuration of the South Caucasus.[10]

Energy engagement with the region was accompanied by Western political support for the independence of the young states, including Georgia. This support grew into substantial Western geopolitical gains, reflected at the Istanbul Summit of the OSCE in 1999, where the Conventional Forces in Europe treaty (CFE) and the agreement with Russia to remove its military bases from Georgia were signed. The negotiations aimed to amend the CFE treaty concluded in 1990, which had imposed arms limits on NATO and Warsaw Pact countries. During the process of treaty amendments, Georgia developed closer relations with Moldova, Ukraine and Azerbaijan. With active intervention and support from the United States at the Istanbul summit in 1999, the final document reflected Russia's commitment to withdraw its military bases from Georgia. This process was completed in 2005, with the full withdrawal[11] of three Russian bases from Georgian territories. It was a great success for Georgian diplomacy and Georgian–American cooperation. The agreement on a major oil pipeline, or the Baku–Tbilisi–Ceyhan (BTC) pipeline, was signed at the sidelines of the summit. This created a foundation for stronger political and economic independence for the Black Sea-Caspian countries, and greater integration of the region with the oil and gas markets in the rest of the world.

The role of the United States was crucial to decisions about the pipeline projects. High-level communications between the US and Azerbaijan governments, facilitated by diplomats from Azerbaijan and Georgia in Washington DC, had a positive impact on the final decision. Former National Security Adviser Zbigniew Brzezinski, upon a request from the White House, travelled to Baku in September of 1995 to deliver a letter from President Clinton to President Aliev requesting his support for multiple pipeline options for the Azerbaijani International Operating Company (AIOC). A direct conversation between President Clinton and President Aliev took place in early October, and on 9 October 1995 the AIOC, with Aliev's blessing, announced its plans to use both the Baku–Novorossiisk (the pipeline route across Russian territory) and the Baku–Supsa routes (across Georgia and Turkey) to export initial oil volumes from the three main Azerbaijani oil fields.[12] This Baku–Supsa route put Georgia on the global pipeline map, and helped Georgia accumulate experience in the negotiations and then the implementation of complex economic infrastructure projects. It also led to improved state revenues after the pipelines were built. The decision of the AIOC became the first in the series of decisions on pipeline projects that made the US Multiple Pipeline policy successful. As a result, Georgia's territory is currently transited by the Baku–Supsa oil pipeline, the Baku–Tbilisi–Ceyhan oil pipeline, and the South Caucasus Gas Pipeline, also known as the Baku–Tbilisi–Erzerum natural gas pipeline, which sends Azerbaijani gas to Europe. The strategic benefits to Georgia are hard to overestimate. In addition to strengthening the energy security of Georgia and eliminating dependency on Russia, these projects increased monetary flows to the Georgian treasury, and facilitated closer political and economic collaboration between Azerbaijan, Georgia and Turkey, under the leadership of the United States.

From 9/11 to the Russia–Georgia War

The year 2002 was important in Georgia's history, as well as for bilateral US–Georgian relationships in particular. Russian pressure on Georgia accelerated after the Russian government accused Georgia of harbouring Chechen terrorists, and demanded military access to the Pankisi Gorge of Georgia, the northeastern part of country with a predominantly ethnic Chechen population. Russian military helicopters violated Georgian air space several times during the year, bombing Georgian territories. These developments added to the worsening of Russo-Georgian relations, particularly following Russia's second Chechen War in 1999, and President Putin's ascent to power, which complicated an already precarious Georgian–Russian bilateral relationship. In response to Russian accusations, and in light of the 'Global War on Terrorism' by the Bush administration after 9/11, Georgia requested American training of their armed forces in order to deal with potential terrorist threats from the North Caucasus. It was in Russia's interests at that time to support the US-led anti-terrorism effort: the 'War on Terror' helped justify Russia's own brutal military operations in Chechnya. The US Train and Equip Program was officially launched in May 2002 with the goal of training Georgian troops for antiterrorist military operations, and was specifically tailored to the needs of Georgia.[13] The programme was extended with the training and deployment of Georgian troops first in Iraq, and then in Afghanistan. The military cooperation launched in 2002 was a very important first step in US–Georgian military collaboration, which continues to play a significant role in bilateral US–Georgian relationships two decades later.

The year 2002 was also significant for another reason: on 22 November, President Shevardnadze formally requested Georgian membership of NATO. After the announcement, President George W. Bush officially pledged his support for Georgia's membership bid.[14] The commitment of Georgia to NATO values of democracy, the rule of law and free markets, strengthened its positive image among American political and diplomatic leaders, despite Georgia's internal problems with corruption, and weak and inefficient governance. These internal problems and weaknesses led to growing discontent among the Georgian population and to the 'Rose Revolution' of 2003, another milestone in the history of Georgian–American relations.

The roots of the Rose Revolution lay in part with a new Westernized elite of young Georgian reformers. Zurab Zhvania, the speaker of the Georgian parliament, led a small group of reformers who distanced themselves from President Shevardnadze and his policies after the presidential election of 2000. One member of this group, and leader of the majority fraction of Shevardnadze's Citizens Union in the parliament, Mikheil Saakashvili, took the most radical stance. He left the presidential party – the Citizens' Union – and formed his new National Movement of Georgia (UNM). In this new capacity as party leader, Saakashvili visited Washington several times and started to build his own network of contacts, cultivating his image as a reformer, criticizing President Shevardnadze for his policy failures, weak governance and growing corruption. He became a welcome guest at many Washington offices and was increasingly seen in Washington as the strongest political leader among the group of politicians who surrounded President Shevardnadze. When he emerged as a driving force behind the Rose Revolution, which swept him into the presidency in January 2004, many in Washington welcomed him as a relatively well-known entity. In particular, they supported his anti-corruption and reform-oriented programme. The United States considered the first peaceful, democratic and non-revolutionary change of power in Georgia important for Georgian statehood. Shevardnadze's resignation in 2003 released the United States from the embarrassing position of support for a tired old leader. Saakashvili's accession to power renewed the United States' democracy agenda in Georgia.[15]

In February 2004, Mikheil Saakashvili paid a state visit to Washington and in May 2005, President Bush paid a historic visit to Georgia. The US president's visit had tremendous diplomatic and political importance for relations between the two countries. As a result, bilateral relationships intensified: the US military expanded the training of Georgian troops for antiterrorist operations, and the number of Georgian troops involved in Iraq grew – reaching 2,000 by the summer of 2008. US economic assistance to Georgia also expanded. In the 2000s, Georgia became the largest per capita recipient of US aid in Europe and Eurasia. From 2001 to 2007, total aid to Georgia amounted to over 945 million USD – 135 million USD a year, on average.[16] Georgia became one of the first recipients of funds from the newly created foreign assistance agency Millennium Challenge

Corporation (MCC). Recognizing the progress of reform policies, MCC awarded Georgia 295 million USD for several significant infrastructure and developmental projects.[17] The initial Train and Equip Program was followed up by a Sustainment and Stability Operations Program through 2007 that supported Georgian troop deployments during Operation Iraqi Freedom.

One of the catalysts of the bilateral US–Georgian relationships during the Saakashvili and Bush administrations was the shared ideological views of influential members of Saakashvili's political team and leading neo-conservative members of the Bush Administration and Congress. Close personal ties between Saakashvili, President Bush, Senator McCain and others were highly publicized in Georgia. It made for extremely good public relations for the UNM. However, after 2007, Saakashvili's government and the UNM started to lose support as a result of repressive internal policies related to human rights, property rights and the treatment of private businesses. The decline of Saakashvili and his government's popularity accelerated due to the tragic consequences of the Russo-Georgian War in 2008. Saakashvili's close ties with the United States were beginning to hurt the public image of the US in Georgia.

Despite the close US–Georgian partnership, each side had different interests and motives. Washington saw Georgia as a country which had successfully reformed – a potentially useful model for other countries of the region. The Georgian case fitted well with its pro-democracy foreign policy agenda and the public relations campaign of the George W. Bush administration. Georgia, together with Turkey and Azerbaijan, was also part of the important global and European energy security network in the region. Georgia turned into part of the strategy for European economic and political enlargement.

By mid-decade, Washington was moving away from its broad regional policy in the South Caucasus to more of a focus on bilateralism. The US pro-democracy and pro-reform agenda was leading to complications with Turkey. Not all the countries in the region were as open as Georgia to President Bush's foreign policy agenda. Tbilisi looked at the United States as an advocate for Georgia in its difficult relationship with Russia, as a promoter of Georgia's integration into European security and economic institutions, and as a potential military ally and strategic partner. Saakashvili continued to move away from the policy of status quo with regard to the conflict areas in the Tskhinvali region and Abkhazia. The Georgian leadership was counting on increased US support in dealings with Russia. Saakashvili widely advertised his personal ties with President Bush and other political leaders in Washington, frequently exaggerating and overusing these connections for domestic political purposes, creating unrealistic expectations of potential American support. The Georgian government itself overestimated US support, and underestimated Russia's commitment to maintain the conflict areas in Abkhazia and Tskhinvali region as leverage on Georgia. The United States was increasingly preoccupied with wars in Iraq and Afghanistan and looking for greater cooperation with Russia in its counter-terrorist policies. NATO was refusing to accept Georgia, and the EU had no plans to go beyond the Black Sea in any enlargement plans.

August 2008

Several factors played a role in Russia's decision to invade Georgia in August 2008. For the Russian Federation, it was critical to prevent Georgia's movement towards greater Euro-Atlantic integration, and to make sure Georgia did not serve as a model for other former Soviet republics wishing for greater integration in the West's security structures. The war was critical for signalling to other nations in the region that Russia had limited tolerance. The Russian Federation also wanted to send a signal to the West that threats made by Russian leaders in response to recognition of Kosovo's independence in 2008 by the United States and other leading European powers, had real meaning. Most importantly, by invading Georgia and changing the de facto borders, the Russian Federation wanted to prove that the post-Cold War European security architecture was vulnerable and had to be renegotiated. Russian suspension of its participation in the Conventional Forces in Europe Treaty in 2007 was a step in that direction. The CFE treaty, one of the important legacies of the original Helsinki process on security and cooperation in Europe, established comprehensive limits on key categories of conventional military equipment in Europe and mandated the destruction of excess weaponry.[18]

Russia was searching for a formal pretext and a legal justification for its invasion of Georgia. Military provocations against the Georgian population in South Ossetia in 2008 triggered a Georgian military response. Multiple internal factors in Georgia played a role in determining that response. One was the large investment in defence spending and the political rhetoric of Georgian leaders emphasizing the country's readiness to resist aggression. There was also considerable political instability during the autumn of 2007 in Georgia, caused by large-scale anti-government demonstrations across the country. The government responded with a brutal crackdown, including a shutdown of an opposition TV station on 7 November 2007. As a result, President Saakashvili resigned and announced a snap presidential election. During the re-election campaign one of the major promises of Saakashvili was to resolve the issue of the territorial integrity of Georgia. After a very narrow and questionable victory in presidential elections in January 2008, Saakashvili's legitimacy as president was seriously damaged. To survive domestically, Saakashvili felt it necessary to respond strongly to the bombing of Georgia villages during the summer of 2008. Russians understood these internal dynamics better than policymakers in Washington. While Washington warned both Tbilisi and Saakashvili personally on multiple occasions not to fall into a Russian trap,[19] the potential scale of planned Russian military intervention was completely underestimated by Tbilisi and Washington.[20]

In addition to these internal dynamics, there were forces within Russia pushing for a war. Russia first suspended its participation in the CFE treaty in 2007. After modification of the treaty at the OSCE Istanbul Summit in 1999, it became an important international framework which restricted Russian military deployments on the borders of neighbouring states in the South Caucasus.[21] The US-led Western decision to recognize the independence of Kosovo against the will of Serbia was resented by Russia and became intertwined with a Russian strategy supporting the independence of Abkhazia and South Ossetia in 2008, as well as the annexation of Crimea in 2014.[22] In January 2006, at an annual press conference in the Kremlin, Putin declared that a 'universal principle' should be applied when dealing with 'frozen conflicts' and that Kosovo had become a model for resolving conflicts in the post-Soviet space: 'If someone thinks that Kosovo can be granted full independence, then why should we refuse this to Abkhazians or South Ossetians? We know, for example, that Turkey has recognized the Republic of North Cyprus.'[23]

Russia previously used 'frozen conflicts' in Moldova, Georgia and Azerbaijan to justify its own strategy of a military presence and control over these countries for almost two decades, but it never recognized any separatist territories' independence before the recognition of Kosovo. It was naive to expect that Russia would accept the Western narrative on the uniqueness of the Kosovo case and continue to stay within the legal framework of respect for the territorial integrity of neighbouring countries. The Russian response to the recognition of Kosovo's independence was neither understood nor properly evaluated by the United States and Georgia. In addition, in early April 2008, NATO at its Bucharest Summit declared support for Georgia's future membership, but did not push the matter through by providing Georgia a Membership Action Plan (MAP), required for the membership process to begin. This was a signal to Russia of a lack of commitment from the West to Georgia's national security. Russia realized there was a limited window of opportunity for action that would send a strong and lasting warning to the West, as well as to Russia's neighbourhood about the cost of permitting Western expansion in the former Soviet space. The intervention in Georgia was a positive public relations event for Russia and a popularity boost for Putin at home.

After the August 2008 war, the United States deepened its political and economic support for Georgia. The United States led a major campaign to prevent any support for the recognition of Abkhazia and South Ossetia as independent states. The Bush administration initiated crucial economic assistance after the war, helping Georgia deal with the consequences of both the war and the global economic crisis. Humanitarian assistance flowed to Georgia immediately after the war ended. Total US assistance to Georgia during the 2008–09 period amounted to 1.04 billion USD, which included 250 million USD in direct budgetary support and an additional 100 million USD from the Millennium Challenge Corporation (MCC) funds, taking the total amount of Georgia's initial MCC funding to 395 million USD.[24]

On 9 January 2009, the United States and Georgia signed a Charter on Strategic Partnership, an important document that created a new framework for strong bilateral relations. The first meeting of the US–Georgian Strategic Partnership Commission, held on 22 June 2009, launched four bilateral working groups on priority areas identified in the Charter, including democracy; defence and security; economics, trade and energy issues; and cultural exchange. According to the Charter's framework, senior-level American and Georgian policymakers would lead annual meetings on the topic of each work group, to review commitments, update activities, and establish future objectives.[25] The charter solidified the

American commitment to Georgia's territorial integrity, and the independent development of the Georgian state. The signing of the Charter was one of the last foreign policy actions taken by the Bush administration before transferring power to President Obama.

There are interesting differences between the administrations of President Clinton (1993–2000) and President Bush (2001–08) toward Georgia. The end of the Clinton era was marked by the strengthening of Georgian sovereignty. The United States brokered the withdrawal of Russian bases and insisted on limits on the Russian military presence in breakaway regions and the border regions of Georgia. The Clinton era was also marked by significant decisions on regional energy development, which made Georgia an integral part of the complex infrastructure of global energy. The Bush era ushered in deeper and broader bilateral mechanisms for diplomatic and military-security cooperation between Georgia and the United States. Georgia's economic sovereignty was strengthened significantly during this period, ending the country's economic and energy dependence on Russia. At the same time, the United States emerged as a key strategic ally of Georgia after the war. US politicians and diplomats became key arbiters of the quality of Georgian democracy. Being pro-American and pro-Western became the norm for Georgian politicians.

Evolution of the US–Georgian partnership: 2009–20

The Obama Administration brought another set of changes to the US–Georgian relationship. The new administration maintained general support for Georgia, but President Obama was personally less engaged with Georgia.[26] Georgia nevertheless remained important in US foreign policy in Eurasia. Vice President Biden visited Georgia during the summer of 2009 and delivered a major speech to the parliament of Georgia, demanding Russia pull back from the occupied territories, but he did not call the presence of Russian troops in Abkhazia and South Ossetia an occupation: 'I come here on behalf of the United States with a simple straightforward message: we, the United States stand by you on your journey to a secure free democratic and once again united Georgia.' The speech reflected a shift from an unconditional and uncritical approach to Georgia under Bush, to a critique of Saakashvili's record on democracy and media freedoms:

> Our partnership rests on a foundation of shared democratic ideals. That's what we are about. We will continue to support your work to fulfil the democratic promise of six years ago. President Saakashvili told parliament earlier this week – and we expect that he will keep that commitment – that there is much more to be done … Your Rose Revolution will only be complete when government is transparent, accountable and fully participatory.[27]

A new US policy on Russia was introduced by Secretary of State Clinton on 6 March 2009, in Geneva, at a meeting with the Russian Minister of Foreign

Affairs, Sergei Lavrov. In follow-up meetings, both sides expressed disagreements on important security issues. But the rapid return of the United States to the negotiation table with Russia after the 2008 invasion and Russia's occupation of Georgian territories was a significant US concession to Russian claims for political and economic hegemony in the region. The international condemnation of Russian actions was limited to a cold shoulder at international forums and suspension of the NATO–Russia Commission. In exchange for the US concession on Georgia, the Russian Federation allowed US military supply planes to fly over Russian territory to Afghanistan.[28] The rupture in the post-Cold War order in Europe, which was a consequence of the Russian invasion of Georgia, was put aside. The United States 'reset' policy, even with some tactical benefits for the US in Afghanistan, made the West look weak. The half-hearted Western response to Russia's violation of Georgian sovereignty and territorial integrity after 2008 led the Kremlin to conclude that it could get away with further acts which challenged international law. The invasion of Ukraine and occupation of Crimea in 2014 and the support of separatists in eastern Ukraine was one consequence of the 2008 war. The decision by the United States and the European allies to prevent the sale of defensive weapons to Georgia after the war in 2008 was interpreted by Moscow as a sign of the West's deference to Putin. In 2014, Western states responded to Russia's mounting military pressure against Ukraine by applying the same faulty policy of refusing the sale of defensive weapons on the grounds that it would lead to 'escalation'.[29]

The Obama administration exercised a more cautious approach to Georgia, but continued diplomatic support for territorial integrity and a non-recognition policy of the breakaway regions. Georgia remained a major recipient of US foreign aid, receiving non-military aid totalling 60 million USD a year on average from 2010 to 2017. In addition, Georgia was awarded a second five-year (2014–19) MCC grant of 140 million USD to support educational infrastructure and training, and to improve the study of science and technology. Georgia also received non-lethal US military assistance, including around 144 million USD in post-war security and stabilization assistance between 2008 and 2009. Since 2010, Georgia has received military assistance, primarily through Foreign Military Financing (FMF) aid, Coalition Support Funds, and Train and Equip and other capacity-building programmes. These funds have been used to support Georgia's deployments to Afghanistan in the International Security Assistance Force (ISAF) and in the follow-on Resolute Support Mission. Such funds strengthened Georgian border security, counterterrorism, and defence readiness. US military assistance to Georgia between 2010 and 2017 is estimated to have been around 74 million USD a year on average.[30]

Georgia's peaceful transition of power from the UNM to the Georgian Dream Coalition on 1 October 2012 was viewed as a positive signal by the United States. It was seen as a step forward in Georgia's democracy development, justifying continued US support. Both executive and legislative branches of the US government expressed support for Georgia, emphasizing the bipartisan character of the US commitment.[31] After the elections, monitored by democratic senator

Jeanne Shaheen and Republican Senator James Risch, Senator Shaheen issued a statement. She wrote: 'The fact is that democracy is a long-term effort, and it cannot be accomplished over the course of a single election. The democratic movement in Georgia is not yet complete, and there is much more hard work to be done, but the people of Georgia took an important step yesterday.'[32]

Bipartisan Congressional support to Georgia is a clear demonstration of commitment of the political class in Washington to Georgia. Over the course of the previous decade, there have been multiple legislative acts and resolutions with strong supporting language for Georgian territorial integrity and democratic development. Congress has persistently expressed firm support for Georgia's sovereignty and territorial integrity. The Countering Russian Influence in Europe and Eurasia Act of 2017 (P.L. 115-44, Title II, §253) states that the United States 'does not recognize territorial changes effected by force, including the illegal invasions and occupations' of Abkhazia, South Ossetia and other territories occupied by Russia. In September 2016, the House of Representatives passed H.Res. 660, which condemns Russia's military intervention and occupation of Abkhazia and South Ossetia. In the 115th Congress, the House passed the Georgia Support Act (H.R. 6219) by unanimous consent. In the 116th Congress, a similar bill (H.R. 598) was reported by the House Foreign Affairs Committee on 22 May 2019 and passed again by unanimous consent on 22 October 2019. In the 117th Congress, two co-chairs of the Georgia Caucus, Representatives Gerry Connolly (D-VA) and Adam Kinzinger again reintroduced the Georgia Support Act on 8 February 2021. The legislation affirms the continued support of the United States for the independence and sovereignty of Georgia, recognizes Georgia's commitment to democratic values including free and fair elections, and restates US opposition to Russian aggression in the region.[33]

This trend of bipartisan political and economic support for Georgia continued under the Trump administration. During a visit to Tbilisi in August 2017, Vice President Michael Pence stated that 'America stands with Georgia ... Today, Russia continues to occupy one-fifth of Georgian territory ... So, to be clear – the United States of America strongly condemns Russia's occupation on Georgia's soil.'[34] Aid for Georgia reached 70.8 million USD in 2018, increasing to 89.8 million USD in non-military aid in 2019. Following up on previous military assistance programmes, in December 2016, the two countries concluded a three-year framework agreement on security cooperation, which led to the launching in February 2017 of a three-year, 35 million USD training initiative, the Georgia Defence Readiness Program. This initiative is helping Georgia develop territorial defensive capabilities, providing some degree of deterrence against potential aggressive moves, most likely from the north.

In perhaps the most significant expression of US trust in Georgia, in November 2017, the US Department of State approved a Foreign Military Sale of over 400 Javelin portable anti-tank missiles, as well as launchers, associated equipment, and training, at an estimated total cost of 75 million USD. This decision ended the Obama-era restriction on arms sales, significantly improving the deterrence capabilities of Georgia. In addition, there have been joint military exercises with

NATO and the United States in Georgia since 2011. Initial exercises, such as Agile Spirit, were focused on counterinsurgency and peacekeeping operations. Starting in 2015, Agile Spirit included other NATO partners, and focused on conventional warfare. An important bilateral exercise, Noble Partner, was launched in 2015 and supports Georgia's integration into the NATO Response Force. More military exercises followed in 2019 and included fourteen nations and more than 3,000 servicemen, led by Georgian Defence Forces and the US Army in Europe.[35] While Georgia is a recipient of security assistance from the United States, the country has been itself a major contributor to international security. A Georgian unit of 850 officers and soldiers was the largest non-NATO national force in Afghanistan, and the fifth largest force overall including NATO forces. Georgian soldiers helped maintain the security and training of the Afghan military. Unlike some NATO member countries, Georgia had no so-called national caveats, meaning the Georgian military participated in combat and security operations with no limitations. Georgian troops left Afghanistan by the end of June 2021, following the decision of the United States to withdraw forces who served under NATO's Resolute Support peacekeeping mission. Both Georgian and US experts expect military cooperation to grow going forward, allowing Georgia to develop stronger capabilities as well as enhancing Georgia's compatibility with the United States, NATO and other allied forces. At the end of July 2021, Georgian and American troops, together with militaries from thirteen other nations, conducted a military exercise Agile Spirit under NATO auspices in Vaziani base, near Tbilisi.

The US–Georgian economic partnership is one area where potential for growth is very significant and still lies mainly untapped. The United States is a welcome investor and trade partner for Georgia, with moderate, but expanding trade. In 2018, the United States was Georgia's seventh-largest source of merchandise imports and eighth-largest destination for exports. The value of Georgia's export of goods to the United States was 190 million USD in 2018. The US export to Georgia was about 477 million USD, giving the United States a positive trade balance of 287 million USD.[36] The US government-owned Overseas Private Investment Corporation (OPIC) facilitates multiple investment projects by supporting American companies with more than a 500 million USD portfolio in important areas of the Georgian economy, such as tourism and the hospitality business, agribusiness, infrastructure development and education. Among OPIC sponsored projects are the iconic Marriott Tbilisi hotel and Funicular Restaurant with GMT Group. The Pace Terminals in Poti with Pace Group, the Georgian American University, Sante Products and others were all sponsored by OPIC (in 2020, OPIC renamed itself the Development Finance Corporation, or DFC).

Since the beginning of the US–Georgian bilateral relationship, the United States and Georgia have periodically discussed the possibility of a free trade agreement. Georgia has free trade agreements with the EU, Turkey, China, CIS countries and is currently working on a free trade agreement with India. It is a major political priority of Georgia to have a free trade agreement with its most important strategic partner. The United States and Georgia have established a High-Level Dialogue on Trade and Investment to begin this process. During Vice President Mike Pence's

August 2017 visit to Georgia, he expressed the United States' 'keen interest in expanding our trade and investment relationship with Georgia'. These bilateral engagements are positive and encouraging. At the same time, foreign policy priorities of the United States in the Caspian and Black Sea region have shrunk. Russia continues to militarily dominate these regions. American disengagement from different parts of the world is creating a geopolitical vacuum, quickly filled by Russia, China and other adversaries.

The Russian Federation is particularly assertive in this process. After the occupation of Georgia and the annexation of Crimea, Russian leaders claim that Europe is a different map now. Russia does not consider itself bound by international agreements which attempt to limit Russia's military presence anywhere in the world. Russia is in violation of the Conventional Forces in Europe treaty, which was an integral part of OSCE process, and which set limits on troops and equipment, including on Russia's border with Georgia, Ukraine and Moldova. Without significant challenge and push back from the United States, Russia will continue its assertive and aggressive advance in the Black Sea Region, where neither the United States nor NATO seem to have any coherent strategy. At the 2019 and 2020 NATO summits, the organization took more proactive steps in the Black Sea,[37] but a long-term strategy is essential to ensure defensibility of the NATO members in the region, and the security of other allies.

Conclusion

The US–Georgian partnership has been exceptionally positive since the independence of Georgia in 1991. Both countries consider each other strategic partners, and the relationship is continuing on multiple levels. Every Georgian administration since independence claims to be the most successful in advancing bilateral ties. Georgia demonstrates its loyalty to the United States in all international forums, providing both political, as well as military support when needed. By the time of the Russian invasion in 2008, Georgia was the second largest contributor of troops to Iraq. Later, Georgia became the largest non-NATO troop contributor to the operation in Afghanistan, participating in combat missions – unlike some NATO members – without restriction. Georgia is the largest per capita troop contributor in Afghanistan.

It is likely that the United States, under the Biden administration (elected in November 2020) will continue its strong political support of Georgia's independence, sovereignty and territorial integrity on the international stage. Many top officials in the administration and the president himself are well aware of Georgia's security challenges. But Georgia's commitment to democracy and the rule of law is an essential element of the bilateral relationship. While mutually beneficial, the US–Georgian relationship cannot be taken for granted. Both sides will need to continue their efforts to elevate this partnership at an even higher level. Georgia's internal reforms and pro-Western foreign policy, and further US support for Georgia's territorial integrity and Euro-Atlantic integration will be key factors contributing to the deepening of the strategic partnership between the two countries. It will be easier for Georgia to face local, regional or global challenges with the help of the United States. And it will be easier for the United States to advance its strategic interests in the wider region from Eastern Europe and the Mediterranean to Central Asia with the help of Georgia.

Notes

1 Five Struggling Republics, *New York Times*, 25 January 1920.
2 For more details on this period in Georgian history, see Stephen F. Jones (ed.), *The Making of Modern Georgia, 1918–2012: The First Georgian Republic and its Successors* (London and New York: Routledge, 2014). On the Georgian Democratic Republic (1918–21), see also Stephen Jones, 'Georgian Social Democracy', in Zurab Karumidze et al. (eds), *Georgia's European Ways: Political and Cultural Perspectives* ed. Zurab Karumidze et al. (Tbilisi: 2015), pp. 28–42.
3 Rudy Abramson, *Spanning the Century: The Life of W. Averell Harriman, 1891–1986*, Chapter: 'Mines' (New York: William Morrow and Company, Inc. 1992).
4 John Steinbeck wrote: 'Wherever we had been in Russia, in Moscow, in the Ukraine, in Stalingrad, the magical name of Georgia came up constantly. People who had never been there, and who possibly never could go there, spoke of Georgia with a kind of longing and a great admiration. They spoke of Georgians as supermen, as great drinkers, great dancers, great musicians, great workers and lovers. And they spoke of the country in the Caucasus and around the Black Sea as a kind of second heaven … ' 'In these terrific Georgians we had met more than our match. They could out-eat us, out-drink us, out-dance us, out-sing us. They had the fierce gaiety of the Italians, and the physical energy of the Burgundians. Everything they did was done with flair. They were quite different from the Russians we had met, and it is easy to see why they are so admired by the citizens of the other Soviet republics'. John Steinbeck, *A Russian Journal* (London: Penguin Publishing Group, 1999).
5 The members of these groups, including Brzezinski, had a significant intellectual impact on the formulation of the US policy towards Central and Eastern Europe, the Caucasus and Central Asia during the next several decades. Some of them became closely engaged with Georgia and played a significant role in deepening the US–Georgian partnership. Hon. S. Enders Wimbush, a former Fulbright scholar who first visited Georgia in 1976, and later served as the director for Radio Free Europe/Radio Liberty in 1986–93, led a group of international experts which tried to mediate the conflict in Abkhazia in 1992. In 1998, Wimbush founded the America–Georgia Business Council, where Paul Henze served as a founding vice-president.
6 Dimitri Simes, 'Behind the Kremlin Doors: What Nixon Discovered', *The Washington Post*, 14 April 1991 (accessed 22 December 2019), www.washingtonpost.com/archive/opinions/1991/04/14/behind-kremlin-doors-what-nixon-discovered/f4471902-d216-4fcc-9a84-2944ab3f8058/
7 US Embassy in Georgia, (accessed 22 December 2019), https://ge.usembassy.gov/our-relationship/policy-history/
8 Shevardnadze had experience of working with the American oil company Chevron in late Soviet times when Chevron became part of the oil consortium to operate Tengiz field in Kazakhstan. He talks about the project in an interview with *Moscow News* in

August 1991, after his resignation as a Minister of Foreign Affairs of the Soviet Union. The interview was covered by the *LA Times* on 6 August 1991, www.latimes.com/archives/la-xpm-1991-08-06-me-401-story.html

9   Cory Welt, 'Georgia: Background and US Policy', *Congressional Research Service*, 17 October 2019, https://fas.org/sgp/crs/row/R45307.pdf

10   Mamuka Tsereteli, 'Georgia as a Geographical Pivot', in *The Making of Modern Georgia, 1918–2012: The First Georgian Republic and its Successors*, ed. Stephen F. Jones (London and New York: Routledge, 2014), pp. 81–92.

11   Russia formally closed down and transformed another military base in Gudauta into a training base for peacekeepers, In reality, the training base remained a Russian military base.

12   Jofi Joseph, 'Pipeline Diplomacy: Clinton Administration's Fight for Baku-Ceyhan', WWS Case Study 1/99, p. 17, www.princeton.edu/cases/papers/pipeline.pdf (accessed 2 March 2013).

13   The official website of the US Marine Corps gives details of the training programme in Georgia. (accessed 1 May 2020), www.marforeur.marines.mil/News/News-Article-Display/Article/520719/gtep-a-unique-mission-for-the-corps/

14   'Georgia: Shevardnadze Officially Requests Invitation to Join NATO', *RFE/RL*, 22 November 2002, www.rferl.org/a/1101463.html

15   The US Commission on Security and Cooperation in Europe, frequently called the Helsinki Commission, produced a report in 2004 entitled 'Georgia's Rose Revolution'. The report provides brief but interesting analysis of the policies and events that led to the Rose Revolution. It also describes developments that followed it, which define both positive and negative legacies of the Rose Revolution. *Georgia's Rose Revolution, 2004* (accessed 3 May 2020), www.csce.gov/sites/helsinkicommission.house.gov/files/Report%20on%20Georgia%27s%20Rose%20Revolution.pdf

16   Welt, 2019.

17   Millennium Challenge Corporation, www.mcc.gov/where-we-work/program/georgia-compact

18   Treaty on Conventional Armed Forces in Europe, OSCE, www.osce.org/library/14087

19   The ADST Foreign Affairs Oral History Project, Ambassador Richard M. Miles, p. 290 at www.adst.org/wp-content/uploads/2013/12/Miles-Richard-M1.pdf

20   This is an impression of the author based on multiple conversations with policymakers in Washington and Tbilisi, as well as experts of the region.

21   The Conventional Armed Forces in Europe (CFE) Treaty and the Adapted CFE Treaty at a Glance www.armscontrol.org/factsheet/cfe

22   Mamuka Tsereteli, 'Can Russia's Quest for the New International Order Succeed?' *ORBIS*, May 2018.

23   'Tbilisi Fears Russia's Policy of "Universality"', *Civil.ge*, 2 February 2006, www.civil.ge/eng/_print.php?id=11688

24   Welt, 2019.

25   US–Georgia Strategic Partnership Commission (accessed 23 December 2019), www.state.gov/u-s-georgia-strategic-partnership-commission/

26   Archil Gegeshidze, 'Contemporary Georgian–American Relations: Key Features of the Evolution', GFSIS, 2017, www.researchgate.net/publication/319442833_Contemporary_Georgian-American_Relations_Key_Features_of_the_Evolution

27   'Main Points of Biden Speech in Georgia', www.reuters.com/article/us-georgia-biden-quotes-sb/main-points-of-bidens-speech-in-georgia-idUSTRE56M42320090723

28 Peter Baker, 'Russia to Open Airspace to US for Afghan War', *New York Times*, 3 July 2009, www.nytimes.com/2009/07/04/world/europe/04russia.html.

29 Svante Cornell, S. Frederick Starr and Mamuka Tsereteli, 'A Western Strategy for the South Caucasus', *Silk Road Paper*, February 2015, pp. 24–25.

30 Welt, 2019.

31 The author had an opportunity to participate in the conference call on the election of October 2, 2012, organized by the Atlantic Council. The reporters included monitors of the elections, Senator Shaheen and Senator Risch, as well as US Embassy staff in Tbilisi.

32 'SENS. Shaheen and Risch Monitor Successful Georgian Elections', 2 October 2012, www.shaheen.senate.gov/news/press/sens-shaheen-and-risch-monitor-successful-georgian-elections

33 H.R.598 – 116th Congress (2019–20), www.congress.gov/bill/116th-congress/house-bill/598

34 'Pence Reaffirms US Solidarity with Georgia, Denounces Russian "Aggression"', 1 August 2017, *RFE/RL*, www.rferl.org/a/pence-georgia-montenegro-nato-russia-baltics-visit/28652154.html

35 Laurie Ellen Schubert, 'Agile Spirit 2019 Kicks Off in Georgia', 29 July 2019, www.army.mil/article/225077/agile_spirit_19_kicks_off_in_georgia

36 United States Census Bureau, 'US Trade with Georgia' www.census.gov/foreign-trade/balance/c4633.html#2018

37 'NATO Foreign Ministers Agree to Enhance Security in the Black Sea Region', www.nato.int/cps/en/natohq/news_165253.htm?selectedLocale=en; Press Conference by NATO Secretary General Jens Stoltenberg following the meeting of NATO Ministers of Foreign Affairs www.nato.int/cps/en/natohq/opinions_174772.htm?selectedLocale=en

AFTERWORD

Tracey German, Stephen F. Jones and Kornely Kakachia

The third decade of the twenty-first century got off to a turbulent start, with the COVID-19 pandemic closing down economies and borders, undermining the perceived inevitability of further rapid globalization and integration. The common understanding that globalization made geographical and territorial boundaries less significant, making states less important, was turned on its head as countries around the world restricted a fundamental aspect of globalization, namely the movement of people and goods. Stephen Jones in his introduction to this book suggested that Georgia's foreign policy has been an instrument of defence and survival; this has never been clearer than today. Georgia faces a range of external threats that are outside its control, from the coronavirus pandemic to economic coercion and military occupation, and foreign relations have become even more crucial in defining the state's future.

The coronavirus crisis has seen entire countries put under lockdown, devastated countless businesses, killed hundreds of thousands of people and upended the lives of millions; it has also created unique challenges for small states. The pandemic intensified existing structural issues in Georgia, exacerbating socio-economic burdens, whilst undermining the country's ability to control external threats. It has had a major impact on trade linkages and relations with neighbouring states as Levan Kakhishvili and Alexander Kupatadze point out in the conclusion to their chapter. Small countries like Georgia have less resilience to global downturns in trade and production: tourism in Georgia makes up 6 per cent of its GDP; FDI makes up around 7 per cent, and remittances (in 2019), 9.8 per cent. Twenty-nine per cent of all remittances in 2019 came from Russia. COVID-19 will inevitably transform Georgia's economic relations with trading partners. This will also impact Georgia's foreign relations as trade patterns shift. Georgia's trade with Russia, for example, has been significantly affected by the pandemic. According to a report by Transparency International (Georgia) 'in March (2020), Georgian exports to Russia fell by 43 per cent, while total exports in January–March 2020 fell by 33 per cent (44 million USD).'[1] Russia has always emphasized the link between trade and politics in its relations with Georgia, imposing an embargo on Georgian goods in 2006, and once more after the 2008 Russo-Georgian War. One of the possible positive outcomes from the pandemic to date is the reduction in Georgia's economic dependence on Russia, which ultimately will strengthen Georgian security, and force greater diversity in trade relations.

While the governments of a number of great powers have struggled to control the pandemic, some smaller states like Georgia with scarce resources and a fragile healthcare system have shown inherent vulnerabilities. At the beginning of the crisis in 2020, despite a surge in cases in both the South Caucasus and wider post-Soviet neighbourhoods, Georgia kept confirmed cases below expectations, earning praise from the World Health Organization.[2] A sign of its success was the country's inclusion on the EU's first list of 'safe countries' agreed at the end of June 2020.[3] However, things began to change drastically later in the pandemic. Once a global success story, by the end of 2020 Georgia was recording around 4,000 new infections and nearly forty deaths per day. Measured per capita, these rates were the worst in the world.[4] A collapse in tourism, falling commodity prices, diminished remittances and disrupted supply chains have sharply increased poverty and unemployment in the country. Against this background, Georgia, with COVID-induced GDP losses and higher financial needs, faces the prospect of an acute economic crisis and unsustainable debt.[5]

All three South Caucasus states (Armenia, Azerbaijan and Georgia) appear to have been struggling with their response to the pandemic. Despite the fact that state authorities are already taking measures to mitigate the impacts, including policy measures and protocols to revive tourism and travel, all three states have remained largely isolated from one another. This will impact, in the short term at least, efforts to strengthen regional cooperation, underlining the case made by David Aprasidze in his chapter on the weak regional impulses in the South Caucasus. Jones noted in his introductory chapter that the endurance of a small state like Georgia depends on the art of diplomacy. Georgia has continued to actively pursue its foreign policy objectives. There have been diplomatic successes in Georgia's search for Western support and patronage. As this volume shows, this extends to relations with the 'other' Europe to the East. Lebanidze and Skardžiūtė-Kereselidze outlined the evolution of relations between Georgia and Poland; in May 2020 that relationship took another step forward with an unambiguous statement of Polish support for Georgia's sovereignty and territorial integrity. Poland's updated National Security Strategy noted that Russian aggression against Georgia 'violated the basic principles of international law and undermined the pillars of the European security system'. It stated that Poland would:

> take actions aimed at strengthening the independence, sovereignty and territorial integrity of Ukraine, Georgia and the Republic of Moldova, including support for their efforts to fulfil the European and Euro-Atlantic aspirations and engage in stabilisation activities in Poland's eastern neighbourhood, including within the framework of the Eastern Partnership.[6]

Such internal EU support – and it extends to the Baltic States – will be vital as Georgia continues to seek Euro-Atlantic integration. Located on Europe's periphery,

Georgia has been attempting for over two decades to redefine its relationship with Europe and break away from the post-Soviet geopolitical space. It is now entering a new chapter of internal development strongly driven by public opinion – one of 'irreversible Europeanization'.[7] After signing an Association Agreement with the EU in 2014, Georgia has reiterated its commitment to follow the European path, pushing forward with the reforms necessary for closer integration with the EU and expanding functional cooperation. In an era when anti-EU populism is becoming mainstream across Europe and Western leaders welcome strategic realignment under the banner of economic nationalism, this is a rare endeavour driven by both ideational and pragmatic calculations. However, while Georgia's Euro-Atlantic integration continues at the political level, popular resistance to certain European values, such as a society open to religious and sexual minorities, has become increasingly visible at the societal level, reinforced by the effects of Russia's propaganda.

One of the major weaknesses of Georgia's current Europeanization process is the gap between Georgian social values (though they are changing) and those in the rest of Europe. Such a gap exists because of Georgia's long isolation in the Soviet period, which continued through the internal wars of the 1990s. There has been a lack of common experience and participation in the public debates which surround the social and political changes that have taken place in Europe over the last twenty years. While Georgia's policymakers are convinced Europeans and depict the country as a part of 'Europe' in their rhetoric, there is limited understanding about the realities of closer integration with the EU, about European perceptions of Georgia, and the implications of European meta-policies, such as anti-discrimination reform and human rights issues. The EU is perceived as a foreign policy goal and addressed from the perspective of accession, with no recognition that Georgian society should begin to integrate into the EU public space without formal membership, by expanding its participation in common political and strategic discussions about the future of the EU. The breakthrough in Georgia's Europeanization plans may come more from societal participation and engagement, than from the formal process of institutional engagement.

The ruling Georgian Dream party, re-elected on 31 October 2020, announced that it plans a formal application for EU membership by 2024. The decision was announced a few weeks before the 2020 parliamentary election, and was later confirmed by a parliamentary resolution.[8] The resolution names EU membership as a priority, with no alternative available. Setting the deadline for an EU application is an ambitious move, especially considering the EU's current problems over the pandemic, immigration and other issues. No reaction to the announcement came from Brussels. On the other hand, a formal application for EU membership with a timetable may give a further push for internal reforms and bring Georgia closer to EU integration. One European commentator noted that 'Georgia's bold move is likely to end in initial disappointment, but it is obvious that Tbilisi needs to move forward in its relationship with the EU and that the Eastern Partnership has become something of a straitjacket for the country'.[9] The reciprocity deficit, identified by Cecire and Sabanadze, remains an obstacle for

Georgia's policymakers: European Member States continue to question Georgia's 'Europeanness'. They are discouraged by the country's distance from 'geographic' Europe, as well as by the persistent Russian threat. Enlargement fatigue amongst Western allies, concern about Moscow, and the contentiousness of candidate countries seeking membership, continues to undermine consensus regarding the future of NATO and the EU.

Georgia faces a number of persistent challenges that will impact its foreign policy in the future. While the pursuit of NATO membership and a closer relationship with the EU remain a central pillar of Georgia's foreign policy, Tbilisi will continue to court other external powers, such as the United States and China, in an attempt to counterbalance Russia. China, along with Azerbaijan and Turkey, has become increasingly important for Georgia as Tbilisi seeks to diversify its trade partners and markets, as well as diplomatic relations. The Georgian government has positioned the country as the South Caucasian hub of the southern Eurasian corridor, central to the development of China's Belt and Road Initiative (BRI), and specifically the China–Central Asia–Western Asia Corridor. China has become increasingly important to Georgia, demonstrated by the signing of a free-trade agreement in 2018. China is now the second largest exporter to Georgia, surpassing Russia. The free–trade agreement with Beijing complements the Deep and Comprehensive Free Trade Area (DCFTA) set up with the EU in 2014, which increases market access between Georgia and Europe. Infrastructure projects, such as the deep-water port at Anaklia, suggests that Tbilisi is looking eastwards, as well as to the West. Hopes that Anaklia would become a strategic trading hub between China and Europe have been damaged by scandal and Russian pressure to thwart the development, which would compete with Russia's Black Sea port of Novorossisk. However, speaking in June 2019, US Secretary of State Mike Pompeo signalled strong US support for the project. He declared that Anaklia would 'enhance Georgia's relationship with free economies and prevent Georgia from falling prey to Russian or Chinese economic influence'.[10]

China is a major factor in Georgia's economic and political future. However, Georgia's foreign policy diversification is not without risk and questions remain as to whether it can establish itself as a competitive transport corridor for goods moving from East to West. Deep-water port projects, like Anaklia, are crucial to Georgia's success as a transit centre. The geostrategic location of the South Caucasus, between Russia, Turkey and Iran, together with the role of external actors, including Western security organizations and, increasingly, China, will have a significant influence on Georgia's foreign policy orientation. Maintaining its attractiveness as a major transit corridor is a means for Georgia of not only improving its economy but protecting its sovereignty.

The rise in the influence of powers such as China has, to a large extent, been demand-driven, pushing Georgia towards greater diversification in its diplomatic and economic ties. But at the same time, Georgia will need to protect its domestic reform efforts from potential pressure from illiberal neighbours and partners. Western democracies and European organizations such as the EU and NATO cannot be complacent about their influence in the South Caucasus. Russia and

China are able to provide substantial economic support to Georgia, and could undermine Western influence and conditionality.[11] However, as polls of ordinary Georgian citizens suggest, China's authoritarianism is unlikely to influence Georgia's political course, which remains firmly westward. The new Biden administration in the United States will no doubt encourage Georgia's continuing engagement with its Western partners. China's growing influence may ultimately stimulate Europe and the United States to redouble their efforts to keep Georgia within the Western orbit.[12] If Tbilisi is able to successfully balance the interests of both regional and external powers, the country has the opportunity to benefit from the trade and communications connectivity across the South Caucasus, enabling it to capitalize on its geostrategic location.

Another key challenge for Georgia will be the importance of maintaining positive momentum in domestic politics. Jones points out that Georgia's mountains have never been sufficient to protect Georgian sovereignty, but 'Georgian democracy ... could, perhaps, protect its borders'. The approval of constitutional and electoral system changes in June 2020, prior to parliamentary elections to be held in the autumn of 2020, have been welcomed by the international community. The Parliamentary Assembly of the Council of Europe (PACE) concluded that the changes meant the 2020 parliamentary elections would now be 'far more proportional than was previously the case, which potentially could allow for a more plural and representative parliament'.[13] However, as a result of the conduct of these elections, the Georgian opposition decided to boycott the newly elected parliament. This has made dialogue, political stability and the creation of a 'loyal opposition' difficult to achieve. In an era where illiberalism is on the rise globally, it is more important than ever that Georgia protect its democratic gains and consolidate its credentials. This, more than increased military spending, will assist the country with its Euro-Atlantic aspirations and help it maintain its links to the EU, its values and its markets.

Notes

1   Transparency International, 'Georgia's Economic Dependence on Russia: Trends and Threats', 4 May 2020, https://transparency.ge/en/blog/georgias-economic-dependence-russia-trends-and-threats

2   'WHO Names Georgia as Country Performing Well in Fight against Coronavirus', 8 May 2020, https://agenda.ge/en/news/2020/1435

3   Council of the European Union, 'Council Agrees to Start Lifting Travel Restrictions for Residents of Some Third Countries', *Press Release,* 30 June 2020, www.consilium. europa.eu/en/press/press-releases/2020/06/30/council-agrees-to-start-lifting-travel-restrictions-for-residents-of-some-third-countries/

4   Giorgi Lomsadze, Georgia's COVID outbreak grows from molehill to 'Everest'. 7 December, 2020, https://eurasianet.org/georgias-covid-outbreak-grows-from-molehill-to-everest

5   Georgian Parliament Confirms 2021 State Budget. *Civil Georgia,* 30 December 2020, https://civil.ge/archives/389765

6   *National Security Strategy of the Republic of Poland*, approved on 12 May 2020 by the President of the Republic of Poland upon request of the President of the Council of Ministers, www.bbn.gov.pl/ftp/dokumenty/National_Security_Strategy_of_the_Republic_of_Poland_2020.pdf, pp. 6 and 25.

7   Kornely Kakachia, 'Europeanization and Georgian Foreign Policy', in *The South Caucasus between Integration and Fragmentation*, May 2015, European Policy Center report, p. 11.

8   For the Georgian government's 'Georgian Foreign Policy Strategy' for 2019–2022 (in Georgian), see https://nbg.gov.ge/en/page/money-transfers

9   'Should Georgia Apply for EU Membership in 2024?', Expert Comment #15, Georgian Institute of Politics, February 2021, http://gip.ge/should-georgia-apply-for-eu-membership-in-2024/

10 'Statements to the Press with Georgian Prime Minister Mamuka Bakhtadze as Part of the US–Georgia Strategic Partnership Commission', Remarks, Michael R. Pompeo, Secretary of State, Treaty Room, Washington, DC, 11 June 2019, www.state.gov/statements-to-the-press-with-georgian-prime-minister-mamuka-bakhtadze-as-part-of-the-u-s-georgia-strategic-partnership-commission/

11 Erica Frantz and Andrea Kendall-Taylor, 'The Evolution of Autocracy: Why Authoritarianism is Becoming More Formidable', *Survival*, 59:5 (2017), pp. 57–68.

12 See the Foreign Policy Research Institute's and Black Sea Strategy Papers' report *On the Fault Line: Georgian Relations with China and the West* (New York: Foreign Policy Research Institute, 2019), p. 12.

13 Parliamentary Assembly of the Council of Europe, 'Georgia Monitors Welcome Adoption of Constitutional Amendments by the Georgian Parliament', 29 June 2020, https://pace.coe.int/en/news/7942/les-rapporteurs-de-l-apce-pour-le-suivi-de-la-georgie-saluent-l-adoption-d-amendements-constitutionnels-par-le-parlement-georgien-?fbclid=IwAR1Qg70rbCiixDgrcer_V1q1cC8XphfKwp2zbtOJNyI9JJtdnCoYmm6wpiI

BIBLIOGRAPHY

Dmitry Adamsky, 'From Moscow with Coercion: Russian Deterrence Theory and Strategic Culture', *Journal of Strategic Studies*, 41:1–2 (2018), pp. 33–60.

Thomas Ambrosio, *Authoritarian Backlash: Russian Resistance to the Democratization in the Former Soviet Union* (Burlington, VT: Ashgate, 2009).

David Aprasidze, 'Consolidation in Georgia: Democracy or Power?', in *OSCE Yearbook 2015*, ed. IFSH (Baden-Baden: Nomos Verlagsgesellschaft mbH & Co. KG, 2016), pp. 108–15.

Bülent Aras and Pinar Akpinar, 'The Relations between Turkey and the Caucasus in the 2000s', *Perceptions*, 16:3 (Autumn 2011), pp. 53–68.

Clive Archer and Neill Nugent, 'Introduction: Small States and the European Union', in *Current Politics and Economics of Europe*, 11:1 (2002), pp. 1–10.

G.G. Arnakis, 'Turanism: An Aspect of Turkish Nationalism', *Balkan Studies*, 1 (1960), pp. 19–32.

Ronald Asmus, *A Little War that Shook the World: Georgia, Russia, and the Future of the West* (London: St. Martin's Press, 2010).

Pavel K. Baev, 'The Military Dimension of Russia's Connection with Europe', *European Security*, 27:1 (2018), pp. 82–97.

Bayram Balci, 'Strengths and Constraints of Turkish Policy in the South Caucasus', *Insight Turkey*, 16:2 (Spring 2014), pp. 43–52.

Michael Barnett, Clifford Bob, Nora F. Onar, Anne Jenichen, Michael Leigh and Lucian Leustean Faith (eds), *Freedom and Foreign Policy: Challenges for the Transatlantic Community* (Washington, DC: Transatlantic Academy, 2015).

R.P. Barston (ed.), *The Other Powers: Studies in the Foreign Policy of Small States* (London: George Allen & Unwin, 1973).

Burton Benedict (ed.), *Problems of Small Territories* (London: Athlone Press, 1967).

Tanja Börzel, 'The Transformative Power of Europe Reloaded: The Limits of External Europeanization', *KFG Working Paper Series*. KFG Working Paper Series 11, 2010.

Rogers Brubaker, 'Nationhood and the National Question in the Soviet Union and Post-Soviet Eurasia: An Institutionalist Account', *Theory and Society*, 23:1 (1994), pp. 47–78.

Michael Cecire, 'Georgia's 2012 Elections and Lessons for Democracy Promotion', *Orbis*, 57:2 (2013), pp. 232–50.

Stacy Closson, 'State Weakness in Perspective: Strong Politico-economic Networks in Georgia's Energy Sector', *Europe-Asia Studies*, 61:5 (2009), pp. 759–78.

Kristina M. Conroy, 'Semi-recognised States and Ambiguous Churches: The Orthodox Church in South Ossetia and Abkhazia', *Journal of State and Church*, 57:4 (2015), pp. 621–39.

Andrew F. Cooper and Timothy M. Shaw (eds), *The Diplomacies of Small States: Between Vulnerability and Resilience* (Basingstoke: Palgrave Macmillan, 2013).

Bruno Coppieters and Robert Legvold (eds), *Statehood and Security: Georgia after the Rose Revolution* (London: MIT Press, 2005).

Bruno Coppieters, Alexei Zverev and Dmitri Trenin (eds), *Commonwealth and Independence in Post-Soviet Eurasia* (London: Frank Cass, 1998).

Nathaniel Copsey and Karolina Pomorska, 'The Influence of Newer Member States in the European Union: The Case of Poland and the Eastern Partnership', *Europe-Asia Studies*, 66:3 (2014), pp. 421–43.

Svante Cornell, *Small Nations and Great Powers: A Study of Ethnopolitical Conflict in the Caucasus* (Abingdon: Routledge, 2005).

Svante Cornell and F. Starr (eds), *The Guns of August 2008: Russia's War in Georgia* (London: M.E. Sharpe, 2009).

Svante Cornell, S. Frederick Starr and Mamuka Tsereteli, 'A Western Strategy for the South Caucasus', *Silk Road Paper*, February 2015, pp. 24–5.

Benjamin de Carvalho and Iver B. Neumann (eds), *Small State Status Seeking: Norway's Quest for International Standing* (Abingdon: Routledge, 2015).

Laure Delcour and Kataryna Wolczuk, 'The EU's Unexpected "Ideal Neighbour"? The Perplexing Case of Armenia's Europeanisation', *Journal of European Integration*, 37:4 (2015), pp. 491–507.

Rick Fawn, 'Russia's Reluctant Retreat from the Caucasus: Abkhazia, Georgia and the US after 11 September 2001', *European Security*, 11:4 (2002), pp. 131–50.

H. Frazer, *A Case of Bandwagonning? Georgian Foreign Policy and Relations with Russia* (University of Oxford. MPhil in International Relations, 1997).

Andrea Gawrich, Inna Melnykovska and Rainer Schweickert, 'Neighbourhood Europeanization through ENP: The Case of Ukraine', JCMS: *Journal of Common Market Studies*, 48:5 (2010), pp. 1209–35.

Tracey German, 'Good Neighbours or Distant Relatives? Regional Identity and Cooperation in the South Caucasus', *Central Asian Survey*, 31:2 (2012), pp. 137–51.

Tracey German, 'Heading West? Georgia's Euro-Atlantic Path', *International Affairs*, 91:3 (2015), pp. 601–14.

Tracey German, 'Securing the South Caucasus: Military Aspects of Russian Policy towards the Region Since 2008', *Europe-Asia Studies*, 64:9 (2012), pp. 1650–66.

Diego Giannone, 'Political and Ideological Aspects in the Measurement of Democracy: The Freedom House Case', *Democratization*, 17:1 (2010), pp. 68–97.

Peter Gourevitch, 'The Second Image Reversed: The International Sources of Domestic Politics', *International Organization*, 32:4 (1978), pp. 881–912.

Heather Grabbe, *The EU's Transformative Power: Europeanization through Conditionality in Central and Eastern Europe* (New York: Palgrave Macmillan, 2006).

Bruce Grant, *The Captive and the Gift: Cultural Histories of Sovereignty in Russia and theCaucasus* (London: Cornell University Press, 2009).

Tamara Grdzelidze, 'The Orthodox Church of Georgia: Challenges under Democracy and Freedom (1990–2009)', *International Journal for the Study of the Christian Church*, 10:2 (2010), pp. 160–75.

Giorgi Gvalia, Bidzina Lebanidze and David Siroky, 'Neoclassical Realism and Small States: Systemic Constraints and Domestic Filters in Georgia's Foreign Policy', *East European Politics*, 35:1 (2019).

Giorgi Gvalia, David Siroky, Bidzina Lebanidze and Zurab Iashvili, 'Thinking outside the Bloc: Explaining the Foreign Policies of Small States', *Security Studies*, 22:1 (2013), pp. 98–131.

Michael Handel, *Weak States in the International System* (London: Frank Cass, 1990).

Björn Hettne and Fredrik Söderbaum, 'Theorising the Rise of Regionness', *New Political Economy*, 5:3 (2000), pp. 457–72.

Ted Hopf, 'The Promise of Constructivism in International Relations Theory', *International Security*, 23:1 (1998), pp. 171–200.

Adam Hug (ed.), *Traditional Religion and Political Power* (London: The Foreign Policy Centre, 2015).

Bal İdris (ed.), *Turkish Foreign Policy in Post-Cold War Era* (Irvine, CA: BrownWalker Press, 2004).

Robert Jervis, 'Cooperation under the Security Dilemma', *World Politics*, 30:2 (1978), pp. 172–73.

Ansgar Joedicke (ed.), *Religion and Soft Power in the South Caucasus* (London: Routledge, 2018).

Stephen F. Jones, *Georgia: A Political History of Independence* (London: I.B. Tauris, 2012) (Georgian version published by the Center for Social Sciences, Tbilisi, December 2013.)

Stephen F. Jones, 'Georgian Social Democracy', in Zurab Karumidze et al. (eds), *Georgia's European Ways* (Tbilisi: 2015), pp. 29–42.

Stephen F. Jones (ed.), *The Making of Modern Georgia, 1918–2012: The First Georgian Republic and its Successors* (London and New York: Routledge, 2014).

Stephen F. Jones, 'Soviet Religious Policy and the Georgian Orthodox Church: From Khrushchev to Gorbachev', *Religion, State and Society: The Keston Journal*, 17:4 (1989), pp. 292–312.

Stephen F. Jones, 'The Role of Cultural Paradigms in Georgian Foreign Policy', in *Ideology and National Identity in Post-Communist Foreign Policies*, ed. Rick Fawn (London: Frank Cass, 2004).

Stephen F. Jones and Neil MacFarlane (eds), *Georgia from Autocracy to Democracy* (Toronto and London: University of Toronto Press, 2020).

Kornely Kakachia, 'End of Russian Military Bases in Georgia: Social, Political and Security Implications of Withdrawal', *Central Asia and the Caucasus*, 50:2 (2008).

Kornely Kakachia and Michael Cecire (eds), *Georgian Foreign Policy: The Quest for Sustainable Security* (Tbilisi: Konrad Adenauer Stiftung, 2013).

Kornely Kakachia and Salome Minesashvili, 'Identity Politics: Exploring Georgian Foreign Policy Behaviour', *Journal of Eurasian Studies*, 6:2 (2015), pp. 171–80.

Kornely Kakachia, Bidzina Lebanidze and Volodymyr Dubovyk, 'Defying Marginality: Explaining Ukraine's and Georgia's Drive towards Europe', *Journal of Contemporary European Studies*, 27:4 (2019), pp. 451–62.

Kornely Kakachia, Salome Minesashvili and Levan Kakhishvili, 'Change and Continuity in the Foreign Policies of Small States: Elite Perceptions and Georgia's Foreign Policy towards Russia', *Europe-Asia Studies*, 70:5 (2018).

Levan Kakhishvili, 'Towards a Two-Dimensional Analytical Framework for Understanding Georgian Foreign Policy: How Party Competition Informs Foreign Policy Analysis', *Post-Soviet Affairs*, 37:2 (2021), pp. 174–97.

Faisal Karim, 'Middle Power, Status-seeking and Role Conceptions: The Cases of Indonesia and South Korea', *Australian Journal of International Affairs*, 72:4 (2018), pp. 343–63.

Zurab Karumidze et al. (eds), *Georgia's European Ways: Political and Cultural Perspectives* (Tbilisi: 2015).

Peter J. Katzenstein (ed.) *The Culture of National Security: Norms and Identity in World Politics: New Directions in World Politics* (New York: Columbia University Press, 1996).

Firuz Kazemzadeh, *The Struggle for Transcaucasia (1917–1921)* (London: Anglo Caspian Press, 2008).

Robert O. Keohane, 'Lilliputians' Dilemmas: Small States in International Politics', *International Organization*, 23:2 (1969), pp. 291–310.

Nicholas Kitchen, 'Systemic Pressures and Domestic Ideas: A Neoclassical Realist Model of Grand Strategy Formation', *Review of International Studies*, 36:1 (2010), pp. 117–43.

Jeffrey W. Knopf, 'Beyond Two-Level Games: Domestic–international Interaction in the Intermediate-Range Nuclear Forces Negotiations', *International Organization*, 47:4 (1993), pp. 599–628.

G.W. Lapidus, 'Insecurity: Russian Elite Attitudes and the Russia–Georgia Crisis', *Post-Soviet Affairs*, 23:2 (2007), pp. 138–55.

Steven Levitsky and Lucan A. Way, 'Linkage versus Leverage: Rethinking the International Dimension of Regime Change', *Comparative Politics*, 38:4 (2006), pp. 379–400.

Steven E. Lobell, Norrin M. Ripsman and Jeffrey W. Taliaferro (eds), *Neoclassical Realism, the State, and Foreign Policy* (Cambridge: Cambridge University Press, 2009).

Vahur Made, 'Shining in Brussels? The Eastern Partnership in Estonia's Foreign Policy', *Perspectives*, 19:2 (2011), pp. 67–79.

Neil McFarlane and Anand Menon, 'Of Wealth and Weakness', *Survival: Global Politics and Strategy*, 56 (2014), pp. 95–101.

John J. Mearsheimer, *The Tragedy of Great Power Politics* (London: W. W. Norton, 2001).

David Menashri (ed.), *Central Asia Meets the Middle East* (London: Frank Cass, 1998).

Natia Metsvirishvili and Maya Metsvirishvili, 'I am Georgian, therefore I am European: Re-searching the Europeanness of Georgia', *Central European Journal of International and Security Studies*, 14 (2020), pp. 52–64.

Lincoln Mitchell, *Uncertain Democracy: US Foreign Policy and Georgia's Rose Revolution* (Philadelphia: The University of Pennsylvania Press, 2008).

Andrew Moravcsik, 'Taking Preferences Seriously: A Liberal Theory of International Politics', *International Organization*, 51:4 (1997), pp. 513–53.

Hans Mouritzen, 'Small States and Finlandisation in the Age of Trump', *Survival*, 59: 2 (2017), pp. 67–84.

Marina Muskhelishvili and Gia Jorjoliani, 'Georgia's Ongoing Struggle for a Better Future Continued: Democracy Promotion through Civil Society Development', *Democratization*, 16:4 (2009), pp. 682–708.

Kalypso Nicolaidis and Robert Howse, 'This is My EUtopia": Narrative as Power', *Journal of Common Market Studies*, 4 (2002), pp. 767–92.

Ghia Nodia (ed.), *25 Years of Independent Georgia: Achievements and Unfinished Projects* (Tbilisi: Ilia State University, 2016).

Donnacha Ó Beacháin and Frederik Coene, 'Go West: Georgia's European Identity and its Role in Domestic Politics and Foreign Policy Objectives', *Nationalities Papers*, 42:6 (2014), pp. 923–41.

Kevork Oskanian, 'The Balance Strikes Back: Power, Perceptions, and Ideology in Georgian Foreign Policy, 1992-2014', *Foreign Policy Analysis*, 12:4 (2016), pp. 628–52.

Ken Parry (ed.), *The Blackwell Companion to Eastern Christianity* (Malden, MA: Wiley-Blackwell, 2010).

Robert D. Putnam, 'Diplomacy and Domestic Politics: The Logic of Two-Level Games', *International Organization*, 42:3 (1988), pp. 427–60.

Brian Rathbun, 'A Rose by Any Other Name: Neoclassical Realism as the Logical and Necessary Extension of Structural Realism', *Security Studies*, 17:2 (2008), pp. 294–321.

D. Rayfield, *Edge of Empires: A History of Georgia* (London: Reaktion Books, 2012).

B. Rezvani, 'The Islamization and Ethnogenesis of the Fereydani Georgians', *Nationalities Papers*, 2008, pp. 593–623.

Norrin M. Ripsman, Jeffrey W. Taliaferro and Steven E. Lobell, *Neoclassical Realist Theory of International Politics* (Oxford: Oxford University Press, 2016).

Thomas Risse, *Social Constructivism and European Integration* (Oxford: Oxford University Press, 2004).

Alexander Rondeli, 'Security Threats in the Caucasus: Georgia's View', *Perceptions*, 3:2 (1998), pp. 43–53.

Robert L. Rothstein, *Alliances and Small Powers* (New York: Columbia University Press, 1968).

Andriy Rukkas, 'Georgian Servicemen in the Polish Armed Forces (1922–39)', *The Journal of Slavic Military Studies*, 14:3 (2001), pp. 93–106.

Randall L. Schweller, 'Bandwagoning for Profit: Bringing the Revisionist State Back in', *International Security*, 19:1 (1994), pp. 72–107.

Anton Shekhovtsov, 'Aleksandr Dugin's Neo-Eurasianism: The New Right à la Russe', *Religion Compass*, 4 (2009), pp. 697–716.

David S. Siroky, Alan James Simmons and Giorgi Gvalia, 'Vodka or Bourbon? Foreign Policy Preferences toward Russia and the United States in Georgia', *Foreign Policy Analysis*, 13:2 (2017), pp. 500–18.

Karen Smith, 'Beyond the Civilian Power EU Debate', *Politique européenne*, 3 (2005), pp. 63–82.

Richard Swedberg, 'The Idea of "Europe" and the Origins of the European Union – A Sociological Approach', *Zeitschrift für Soziologie*, 23:5 (October 1994), pp. 378–87.

Baldur Thorhallsson and Anders Wivel, 'Small States in the European Union: What Do We Know and What Would We Like to Know?', *Cambridge Review of International Affairs*, 19:4 (2006), pp. 651–68.

A.P. Tsygankov and T. Marver-Wahlquist, 'Duelling Honors: Power, Identity and the Russia–Georgia Divide', *Foreign Policy Analysis*, 5:4 (October 2009).

Kevin Tuite, 'The Rise and Fall and Revival of the Ibero-Caucasian Hypothesis', *Historiographia Linguistica. International Journal for the History of the Language Sciences*, 35:1–2 (2008), pp. 23–82.

David Vital, *The Inequality of States* (Oxford: Oxford University Press, 1968).

Thomas de Waal, *The Caucasus: An Introduction* (Oxford: Oxford University Press, 2010).

Thomas de Waal, 'A Broken Region: The Persistent Failure of Integration Projects in the South Caucasus', *Europe-Asia Studies*, 64:9 (2012), pp. 1709–23.

Stephen M. Walt, 'Alliance Formation and the Balance of World Power', *International Security*, 9:4 (1985), pp. 3–43.

Stephen M. Walt, *The Origins of Alliances* (Ithaca, NY: Cornell University Press, 1990).

Stephen M. Walt, 'Testing Theories of Alliance Formation: The Case of Southwest Asia', *International Organization*, 42:2 (1988), pp. 275–316.

Stephen M. Walt, 'Why Alliances Endure or Collapse', *Survival*, 39:1 (1997), pp. 156–79.

Kenneth N. Waltz, *Man, the State, and War: A Theoretical Analysis* (New York: Columbia University Press, 2001).

Kenneth N. Waltz, *Theory of International Politics* (Long Grove, IL: Waveland Press, 2010).

Deborah Welch Larson and Alexei Shevchenko, 'Status Seekers: Chinese and Russian Responses to US Primacy', *International Security*, 34:4 (2010), pp. 63–95.

Alexander Wendt, 'Anarchy is What States Make of It: The Social Construction of Power Politics', *International Organization*, 46:2 (1992), pp. 391–425.

Anders Wivel, 'Living on the Edge: Georgian Foreign Policy between the West and the Rest', *Third World Thematics: A TWQ Journal*, 1:1 (2016), pp. 92–109.

Fareed Zakaria, *From Wealth to Power: The Unusual Origins of America's World Role* (Princeton, NJ: Princeton University Press, 1999).

Christoph Zürcher, Pavel Baev and Jan Koehler, 'Civil Wars in the Caucasus', *Understanding Civil War*, 2 (2005), pp. 259–98.

INDEX

www.ingramcontent.com/pod-product-compliance
Lightning Source LLC
Chambersburg PA
CBHW050410280326
41932CB00013BA/1802